FROM
ART TO THEATRE

FORM AND CONVENTION
IN THE RENAISSANCE

GEORGE R. KERNODLE

THE UNIVERSITY OF CHICAGO PRESS
CHICAGO & LONDON

The publication of this volume has been aided by a grant from the American Council of Learned Societies from a fund provided by the Carnegie Corporation of New York

INTERNATIONAL STANDARD BOOK NUMBER: 0-226-43188-6

THE UNIVERSITY OF CHICAGO PRESS, CHICAGO 60637

THE UNIVERSITY OF CHICAGO PRESS, LTD., LONDON

FOR PORTIA

ACKNOWLEDGMENTS

TO ALLARDYCE NICOLL I owe the first acknowledgment, not only for his continuing friendly help and patient advice, from seminar reports of nine years ago to published book, but also for his encouragement to cross the boundaries between nations and the boundaries between the arts in studying the sixteenth-century origins of the modern theatre. While my interest in the problems of the Renaissance stage began in the classes of two great teachers of Elizabethan drama—B. Iden Payne and George F. Reynolds—the immediate stimulus to look in new directions for stage origins came from the provocative questions of Karl Young, who was impatient that students of the Renaissance knew so little about how the modern theatre forms actually started.

The opportunity for research in France and Italy in the summer of 1935 I owe to the Yale-Rockefeller Theatre Collection, and for research in Europe in 1938–39 to a Sterling Fellowship from Yale, which was extended in the summer of 1939 by a Rockefeller Fellowship. The publication has been made possible by a generous grant from the American Council of Learned Societies.

For assistance in securing and preparing photographs for the illustrations I am grateful to Franz Schauwers of the Royal Library of Belgium, to Clark Mendum and Paul Kozelka of the Yale-Rockefeller Theatre Collection, to Miss Margaret Peters of the Cleveland Public Library, to Finley Foster and Ralph Wehner of Western Reserve University, and to Mrs. Blanche Godfrey of the Cleveland Museum of Art.

I wish to thank the English and American owners of copyrighted pictures for permission to reproduce them here. I regret that because of the war I could not request permission directly of the Continental owners.

In checking foreign titles I have had the help of Miss Kaethe Lepehne of Western Reserve University and Miss Charlotte Van der Veer of the Cleveland Museum of Art. I wish I could acknowledge the many friendly courtesies shown me in the many libraries and museums where I have hunted down the material.

In preparing the composite drawing of an Elizabethan façade, I had the technical aid of Mrs. Melanie D. Saunders. For the final sketch I must thank Orville K. Larson, who took time to draw it, out of the little time a soldier has.

Miss Virginia Shull has generously permitted me to consult in manuscript her valuable study of the influence of art on the English medieval religious drama.

For reading the manuscript and making valuable suggestions I am indebted to Gerald E. Bentley, George F. Reynolds, J. Holly Hanford, and Samuel C. Chew. Professor Ulrich Middeldorf has been especially helpful in getting the manuscript and the illustrations in final form for the press.

From first to last I have had the help of my wife, who has shared the labor, divided the worry, and multiplied the excitement in the long search for some of the origins of the modern theatre. It is to her that the book is dedicated.

GEORGE R. KERNODLE

ARLINGTON, VIRGINIA
March, 1944

TABLE OF CONTENTS

PART I. THE ROOTS OF THEATRE FORM AND CONVENTION: PAINTING, SCULPTURE, AND THE *TABLEAUX VIVANTS*

PART II. THE THEATRES OF ARCHITECTURAL SYMBOL: THE TERENCE ACADEMY FAÇADE; THE FLEMISH, ELIZABETHAN, AND SPANISH POPULAR THEATRES

PART III. THE THEATRES OF PICTORIAL ILLUSION: THE ITALIAN PERSPECTIVE SCENE; COMPROMISE IN FRANCE AND ENGLAND; THE BAROQUE SETTING OF WING AND BACKDROP, OF PROSCENIUM AND PAINTED PICTURE

LIST OF ILLUSTRATIONS

INTRODUCTION

THE PROBLEM OF THE RENAISSANCE THEATRE

THE modern theatre began in the Renaissance. Its characteristic form and many of its conventions are to be explained by its origin in the conflict of ideals in the sixteenth century—yet we have never fully examined the different experiments of that century to discover just what people wanted their new theatres to mean and to do.

We have argued about what the Shakespearean stage was like; but we have looked neither at the traditions of the visual arts which shaped that theatre nor at the other theatres of the time which showed different solutions of the same problem—different combinations of the basic patterns. We have argued about the Restoration theatre, about the compromise between illusion and formalism, between English and Continental elements; but we have never made a comparative study of the English and Italian beginnings of those elements. We have never asked what other combinations were made in Flanders, in Germany, in France, or in Spain that would throw light on the divergent principles of the English and Italian theatres. We have never asked how the contradictory principles of illusion and symbolism could both derive from a common heritage of European art.

The search for the answers to these problems has led me to a complete reinterpretation of all the theatres of the Renaissance. I am convinced that we must revise many of our ideas about the stage of Shakespeare, the stage of Corneille, the stage of Lope de Vega, and the stage of the Italian court spectacles. Not only can we throw new light on how each one functioned, but we can now explain how each one originated and why each one differed from the others.

Our efforts to explain the Renaissance theatres

as developments from the medieval religious stages have failed to illuminate more than a few details. Miss Lily Bess Campbell gave up the attempt and treated the perspective stage as a new invention inspired by the words of Vitruvius. Sir Edmund Chambers, after his long study of the medieval stage, found no continuity in form or convention from the medieval to the Elizabethan. He was so impressed with the differences that he has repeatedly dismissed the evidence other people have offered that the Elizabethan stage did preserve some conventions of simultaneous staging from the Middle Ages. But the real explanation is not in medieval drama; it is in medieval art.

If Miss Campbell and Sir Edmund had looked into the traditions of medieval and early Renaissance art, they would have found a full explanation of the new theatre forms. There in the paintings, sculpture, stained glass, tapestries, and *tableaux vivants* were the stage wings, proscenium arches, inner stages, curtains, side doors, upper galleries, heavens, and canopies they were looking for. There the principles of illusion and of symbolism were developed and associated with the types of background that were copied by Italian and by English architects. There the three types of organization of background—the realistic side wings of the Italian stage, the symbolic center accent of the Elizabethan stage, and the compromise flat arcade of the Teatro Olimpico— were all clearly differentiated long before the Renaissance theatre architects were born. There also was the germ of the compromises between illusion and symbolism which characterized the Restoration and other Baroque theatres. We can understand the problems of the Renaissance theatre architects only by studying how they

1

arranged and adapted the various patterns handed down to them by the artists.

It is time to recognize that the theatre is one of the visual arts. If it is an offspring of literature on one side of the family tree, it is no less a descendant of painting and sculpture on the other side. We know the plays of Shakespeare very well as literature. We can learn a great deal more about them as *drama* if we recognize that the Elizabethan stage was not an isolated invention but was, on the contrary, a logical result of the patterns and conventions of the visual arts of the Renaissance. Those patterns and conventions were merely varying adaptations of the art traditions of centuries, most of them dating, in fact, from the Hellenistic period, when painters and sculptors were imitating the Greek theatre.

But neither the theatre of Shakespeare nor any Continental theatre of the sixteenth century can be considered alone. Only by a comparative study of all the European theatres, as they derived from a common background in the visual arts, can we discover the basic principles, the determining characteristics, of each. To understand that background not only must we know the ways of the most advanced painters in oils, but we must know the patterns and conventions of the many anonymous designers of tapestries and stained-glass windows. We must know not only how religious subjects were visualized but also how the romantic stories of medieval legend and classical mythology, the popular characters of national history and allegorical fancy, were presented to the public. For the Renaissance theatres drew on the same subjects as secular art. They owe far more to painters, sculptors, and designers of *tableaux vivants* than they do to the medieval religious stages. The tremendous wave of creative energy which we call the Renaissance brought in new subjects, which had to be visualized in new ways. Not satisfied with canvas, plaster, tapestry, or marble, the artists created *tableaux vivants*. Not satisfied with living pictures, they called in the poets and created new theatres.

As a result of that creative energy, the sixteenth century saw more variant forms of the theatre than any other age has seen. The new types of theatres in Italy, Spain, France, the Low Countries, and England differed considerably from the earlier theatres and from one another. At first glance, the two most important ones—the Italian perspective stage and the Elizabethan stage—seem totally unrelated—indeed, at opposite extremes. One, disclosed by a front curtain, was illusionistic, with changeable painted scenery representing an actual place, perhaps a broad avenue with several side streets; the other was formal and nonillusionistic—a large, permanent architectural façade which remained throughout all performances. Quite different from either were the Hôtel de Bourgogne stage of Paris, with its reduced medieval mansions crowded into a small space; the Spanish curtain stage; and the Teatro Olimpico. Further, the English court theatre, the Flemish Rederyker façade, the Hans Sachs stage, the French *ballet de cour*, and several other new types show other important variations. We get the impression of unrestrained invention in all different directions.

Yet these theatres were not unrelated. A casual comparison indicates that they had much in common. Even the two opposite extremes—the perspective and the Elizabethan—are similar in many ways. In spite of its avowed principle of illusion, the perspective stage could open up its back wall to disclose a small inner stage, and occasionally an upper stage above that inner stage. There might even be built in front of the inner stage a projecting pavilion of columns supporting a roof. On all types of stages the main acting area projected forward in front of most of the background. On all there were formal entrance doors or ways, one or two on each side of the scene. These curious similarities among different types of theatres have challenged students for years, and many separate attempts have been made to trace the influence of one form upon another. But no one has gone behind the particular theatres to the basic traditions.

Especially for the Elizabethan stage, we have had study after study and theory after theory.

Students have attempted to trace it to nearly every form of dramatic presentation known in England, and to the most important stages of the Continent.[1] Most familiar is the innyard theory, advanced by Malone more than a century ago and developed in this century by G. P. Baker, who probably claimed too much for it. W. J. Lawrence, who accepted it, admitted that it did not explain the stage façade; and he pointed out the resemblance of the façade, especially in the side doors, to the screens of dining-halls in palaces, universities, and inns of court, where many performances took place. W. G. Durand suggested further similarities to performances in private houses. Lily Bess Campbell wrote her *Scenes and Machines on the English Stage during the Renaissance* to trace the introduction of perspective scenery in England. She not only showed the relationship of the English court stages to the Italian scenes but suggested that there was much that the English public stage borrowed from the Italian. T. S. Graves set out to prove that Burbage, when he devised the façade of his theatre in 1576, had in mind the English court stage, with its two side houses and formal entrances and occasional center structure. G. F. Reynolds called attention to the similarities in practice and conventions, especially in the use of movable scenic properties, between the Elizabethan public stage and the medieval religious pageants. Victor Albright said that the Elizabethan stage derived from the interlude platform. S. B. Marston based his reconstruction[2] on a possible relation to the Teatro Olimpico. Albert Feuillerat and Sir Edmund Chambers studied staging at court and in private theatres and private houses in both England and France, in an attempt to throw light on public theatre practice.

The Continental theatres, as well, have aroused the interest of students in search of theatre origins. Willi Flemming[3] has pointed out that the Jesuit theatre, which was formed by the 1570's, bears inexplicable relationships to the Teatro Olimpico, built in the next decade, as well as to the English and Dutch stages. He suggested the influence of the Terence woodcut illustrations on all formal stages. Creizenach[4]—one of the few to attempt an explanation of variant theatre forms with all of Europe in mind—suggested that the formal stage was devised in the Low Countries and taken over with changes by Spain and England. The Hôtel de Bourgogne scenery, as H. C. Lancaster[5] shows, is obviously closely related to the medieval religious mansions; but that cannot explain how it has so much in common with the ·perspective stage and with the Teatro Olimpico. Miss Campbell believed the court perspective stage to have been developed after the precepts of Vitruvius, who mentions perspective scenery; yet we find that the court architects built something quite different from what was achieved in the classical academies, where Vitruvius was also law.

All these studies have fallen short of the mark because they have been too limited. They have tried to prove the influence of form A on form B as if form A were the only possible source the creator of B had for his ideas. We could just as well prove that Botticelli's narrative paintings were the source of the Elizabethan stage. Some of them have the same formal side doors, the same use of interior scenes on a forestage in front of a formal nonillusionistic façade. It would not be too difficult to explain how Burbage knew the Botticelli paintings: Renaissance peoples had far more contact with one another than some students suppose. But still the theory would be unconvincing. A wider view would show that Botticelli merely preserved conventions that were available to the English in many of their own paintings, carvings, tapestries, and stained glass, not to mention their native *tableaux vivants*. Comparisons of two theatre forms have often been very useful and revealing; but, unless they go beyond the theatre and relate the stages to the whole tradition of Renaissance art, they are in-

[1] See the bibliography for chap. iv. The bibliography is arranged by chapters, and within the chapters by special subjects.

[2] Reproduced by Nicoll, *The Development of the Theatre*, p. 125.

[3] See the bibliography for chap. v.

[4] See the bibliography for chap. v.

[5] See the bibliography for chap. viii.

adequate. In the family tree we must not cry paternity where there is only cousinship. The earlier religious stages influenced many later painters,[6] but in the more complex forms of the Renaissance the line leads from art to theatre, rarely from theatre to theatre.

In studying each theatre separately we can go just so far. We soon meet problems that can be solved only by comparison with other theatres and with the whole tradition of art. We may think we have determined the basic principles, the working conventions, of one type of theatre. But immediately we meet inconsistencies. We discover that no form in the Renaissance developed without some stray reminders of other forms. We must determine what those other forms meant.

The Italian perspective scene, through engravings and drawings, through written descriptions, and through explanations of architectural theories, yields up to us its main principles. It appears to us as the first stage in world history completely devoted to the purpose of creating illusion, of counterfeiting the appearance of reality. We note how that purpose contrasts with the purpose of the English and Flemish stages, where the scene was a symbol of reality, not an imitation of it. We observe, in the working-out of the perspective scene, how two rows of wings led to a back shutter, how the floor was sloped up and the sky sloped down, how the floor was marked out in squares that seemed to vanish in the distance, how the houses were made thinner and set closer together toward the back of the stage, and how the back shutter was drawn so as to carry the vanishing lines of the side houses on to greater depth—all to achieve the ideal of the illusion of an actual street. Yet when we examine this perspective scene in detail, we find many inconsistencies. Among the houses, churches, and shops—structures we expect on a street scene—we find obelisks, altars, triumphal arches, tapestries, curtains, temples decorated with coats-of-arms, and pictures framed by columns and canopies like some elaborate modern billboard.

[6] Cf. the bibliography for chap. i, "I. Art and Theatre."

These do not belong on a Renaissance street. Further, the front house at each side may be a tower or a formal panel with columns and paintings. Although the rest of the scene is changed, that front house remains the same. Then, at the very back, many designs show a formal façade that could not be in any street. Sometimes a simple arcade, sometimes a two-story castle or temple, that façade can give painted glimpses of other streets or landscapes that have nothing to do with the main scene. Sometimes the stage plans call for opening up that back shutter and presenting on an inner stage such little distant scenes—all completely inconsistent with the ideal of illusion. Only when we find what these incongruous elements meant in the traditions of pictorial art can we understand how the audience would accept them in a show. Clearly, the basic principles of the perspective stage included other concepts besides illusion: this realistic setting included well-known art symbols of portraiture and tableaux.

That same perspective scene was to undergo a change in the type of side wings in the seventeenth century, when scene painting on flat surfaces was substituted for actual solid construction. Again we need to see the stage in relation to the whole art world, which in the Baroque period was turning from the solid forms of the Florentine Renaissance to aerial perspective and tones of light and shade. The Baroque stage designer followed the same tendency by devising flat wings and painting his shadows and depths rather than building them.

In France an adaptation of medieval theatre forms lasted into the 1630's, causing considerable confusion. A comparison of the conflicting medieval conventions with the concepts of the new perspective stage throws light on the critical controversy over unity of place which started with Corneille's Le Cid and kept the founders of Richelieu's Académie Française busy. The French stage was trying to serve two systems with conflicting conventions. Only when acceptable scenic compromises were worked out did the quarrel abate. Those compromises then became part of the perspective tradition that was handed on to later generations in England and other countries.

In England and Flanders, stages grew up which made no such attempt to create illusion as those of Paris and Italy did. In these northern countries the actors were not seen within a picture space surrounded on three sides by the scenery. Instead, they came onto a forestage from doors that never changed, and they acted in front of an architectural façade that had to serve for all kinds of scenes. Only within doorways or behind curtains could small changes be made. We have usually thought of the façade as completely neutral, a blank skeleton of doorways and inner and upper stages, which, like modern black drapes, could be supposed anything the author suggested. We have assumed that only by putting elaborate descriptions into the mouths of his characters or by bringing on movable trees, tents, thrones, or other properties could the playwright indicate a particular place. Yet in play after play the façade itself became a visual symbol—it became a castle, a city gate, or a backing for a throne, altar, or tomb. The upper stage and the under side of the penthouse became symbols of the heavens. Sometimes the façade was, at the same time, a symbol of a castle and a backing for a throne. It meant more to the audience than just a convenient arrangement of openings. To discover what meanings it had, we need more evidence than the plays themselves; we need to know how the public was accustomed to visualize its patriotic and romantic stories and its allegorical characters; we need to know the street theatres, to know how the many tableaux of coronation scenes, castle scenes, allegorical scenes, heaven scenes, were presented.

The method of studying one or two theatres apart from other arts has produced such monstrous results as the theory that the proscenium arch was derived from the Teatro Olimpico, built in 1580–84. Sheldon Cheney advanced the theory two decades ago and just recently Hendrik Van Loon repeated it as gospel. Yet Cheney himself in his volume *The Theatre* published earlier examples of theatrical prosceniums, and

many others are to be found. From early in the sixteenth century, stage architects used both partial and complete prosceniums. Related to each other the Teatro Olimpico façade and the proscenium certainly were, but as cousins. A formal frame had been used in art many centuries before, and for puppet stages and the *tableaux vivants* by the fourteenth century. With the help of the visual arts, we can now tell a more accurate story of the proscenium.

I first realized the close dependence of the theatre on the traditions of art when I undertook a study of the beginnings of Italian perspective scenery. I found that every single designer for the early perspective stage was trained in painting and was primarily a painter or architect who looked on stage designing merely as a special application of his skills. An examination of Italian painting of the fifteenth century revealed every characteristic or peculiarity of the new perspective scenery, worked out by the painter fifty to a hundred years before it was constructed on the stage. I began to find, also, forms and conventions which the perspective stage had made little use of but which I knew had been used in other Renaissance theatres. I had found at the back of some perspective settings a curious screen or arcade, with glimpses of little scenes beyond, rather similar to the background of the Teatro Olimpico. It appeared also in many fifteenth-century paintings. I wondered if the Teatro Olimpico, avowedly built to imitate the ancient theatres, might not derive as much from traditions of painting as from the remains of ancient Greece and Rome.

And what of the theatres of the Low Countries and England? I found that their characteristic features were just as definitely derived from the traditions of art as were those of Italy. The difference was that, while in Italy the perspective theatre followed the most progressive developments in painting, in the north the theatres followed traditions that were disdained by the more advanced painters. Therefore I examined the work of the many anonymous and obscure artists. In glass windows, in tapestries, in book miniatures, and in some oil paintings, but above all in the *tableaux vivants*, I found formal side doors, a central arch opened up for an interior, curtains back of a scene, and upper galleries for onlookers or musicians—the characteristic features of the new northern theatres.

The historians of fifteenth-century art, to my surprise, gave me little help. I wanted to know just what were the accepted conventions of space and background, the conventions familiar to everybody. The historians were most interested in how creative painters had broken away from convention in order to develop new forms. About the work of popular artists, which is always more conventional, more old-fashioned, than the work of advanced artists, they could tell me little. I found that the studies by Émile Mâle and Leo van Puyvelde of the relations of medieval art and theatre were concerned with the influence of the religious drama on the later realistic painters in matters of incident and character treatment. Nothing on the conventions of background! One short suggestive article by Oskar Fischel in the *Burlington Magazine* and incidental discussion in Miss Galante-Garrone's book on Italian medieval scenery gave me some help. Miss Bunim's book on space in medieval painting did not come out until 1940, and it does not treat the methods of organizing the scene.

With some good leads from Evelyn Sandberg Vavalà, I set about making my own account of the traditions of background in European painting. From students of Hellenistic and early Christian art I received far more help. Almost a dozen historians have traced the beginnings of the architectural backgrounds in art to the Greek stage as it took form in Athens in the fifth and fourth centuries B.C. and spread around the Mediterranean world in the following centuries. I realized that my story was the story of the influence of the Greek theatre on the modern theatre through the intermediary of some fifteen hundred years of painters' conventions. Yet the theatres of the sixteenth century owe their forms and conventions not only to what Hellenistic painters copied from the Greek stage but also to developments made as

concepts of space and reality changed in the passing centuries.

Before these forms and conventions were taken over for the mature theatres of the Renaissance, many of them had been used in street theatres and pageants, where they acquired new meanings and associations that they had not had in painting and sculpture. It seemed to me that the story of the Renaissance theatres could not be told until we knew what the public was accustomed to see in the street theatres and *tableaux vivants*. Historians have devoted much time to the religious stages of the Middle Ages, but few have paid any attention to the street-shows, where historical, romantic, and allegorical stories were made popular long before they were dramatized for the Renaissance stage. We have not realized that the fourteenth and fifteenth centuries had a secular theatre no less active than the religious. With the help of a Sterling Fellowship from Yale University, I spent most of 1938–39 in Europe hunting up the hundreds of accounts of these little secular stages, which art historians and theatre historians alike have dismissed as "pageants." I became convinced that the *tableaux vivants* furnish us with important links between art and theatre.

With a knowledge of the habits of mind established in art and pageantry, we can approach afresh the problems of the Renaissance theatre. We can describe with new understanding the different stages of different countries. We can, I believe, come much nearer to reconstructing in our minds what those stages meant to the audiences of the time.

The Rederyker stage of the Low Countries, for instance, is seen to be not a new formal architectural façade invented by some Flemish architect but a showpiece adapted from the *tableaux vivants*, to be used as a throne from which the Holy Trinity or Lady Rhetoric and the Liberal Arts may hear the poems and plays competing in their honor. Like other showpieces of the *tableaux vivants*, it was decorated with shields, torches, and statues and had several openings and inner stages, out of which the characters might come and in which arranged tableaux might be disclosed. With little adaptation, the forms and conventions of the street pageants were made to serve for the naïve allegorical plays of the Societies of Rhetoric.

The Elizabethan stage ceases to be a plain wall with doors, curtains, and a gallery which the audience had to clothe afresh with their imaginations as the dramatist suggested. It was a positive form already clothed with many associations. Both dramatist and audience had long been familiar with most of its conventions—in pageantry, in sculpture, in stained glass, in paintings, in tapestry—everywhere that the rich narrative lore of the sixteenth century was visualized. Whether the stage façade represented a castle, with banners hanging from its topmost turret and soldiers defying the enemy from an upper gallery, or the city gates, with an arch through which a welcome king came in and above which musicians played; whether it represented by one tree a grove or garden, or by its throne and tapestries a royal audience chamber—its forms and suggestions were already richly familiar. Even if it represented a ship, the audience was not completely at a loss. In pageants they had already seen ships combined with arches, columns, and canopies and hung with decorative curtains. In their minds the façade actually resembled in turn all these things. By comparing the Elizabethan stage with the Flemish stage and the Spanish stage, and by relating all the façade theatres to the traditions of the *tableaux vivants*, we can not only explain the origin of the Elizabethan stage—hitherto a mystery—but also throw light on many details of its construction and on many of its conventions and stage effects.

The Italian perspective stage becomes, through this new approach, not an invention devised to present in perspective the palaces that Vitruvius spoke of, but an adaptation in three dimensions of patterns and forms already worked out in fifteenth-century painting. Its side wings follow the pattern of the side houses of the painters and bring with them from painting to the theatre the ideal of realism—of the illusion of an actual place.

Like fifteenth-century paintings, it is an exterior street scene, with interiors presented only by opening up a curtain or an archway in one of the side wings. Its architecture, like the architecture in the Florentine paintings, is solid and exact, built out in three dimensions. Only in the seventeenth century, after the painters were affected by the Baroque interest in painted tones and shadows, do we find the stage settings less solid and more dependent on scene painting. The Italian perspective setting, the ancestor of all perspective stages from the sixteenth into the twentieth century, is seen in its place in the history of the visual arts.

When we know the common heritage of art and pageantry, we can understand how the proscenium frame resembled now the Elizabethan stage, now the Teatro Olimpico, and now the formal façade with side wings at the back of many perspective scenes. We can see how, with quite opposed ideals of scenery, both the Elizabethan and the Italian court stage could achieve at the back of the scene a formal façade decorated with columns, pierced by an arch to an inner stage, and finished at the top with a heavens from which gods might descend to the stage in front. We can understand better the quarrel about unity of place as the Italian perspective was imposed on other patterns in France and England.

Such a comparative study of all the Renaissance theatres yields to us the basic principles by which they differed from the medieval theatres of the fifteenth century, and also the principles by which they differed from one another. The greatest problem of the Renaissance stage was the organization of a number of divergent scenic elements into some principle of spatial unity. The medieval producer had scarcely known that problem. He kept a separate mansion as a center for each of his important incidents. Occasionally he might bring several mansions into the action at one time, or he might place several incidents in succession around one mansion. But he kept his mansions separated in time. He could spread his scenic elements down a long platform, around a public square, or around the streets of a whole city. But he had no need to stop the processional flow of time in order to produce a complex organization in space. The Renaissance producer, on the other hand, had to organize a number of mansions or scenic devices[7] in such a way as to attain both unity of design and unity of dramatic convention. He learned either to arrange them in rows according to the mathematical laws of perspective in order to gain the illusion of reality, or to develop a complex façade that with little or no change could take on the symbolic meaning of a number of different scenic devices. In each case he used one of the three principles of organization that had already been worked out in painting.

One of those principles emphasized the side houses of the design and left the center open for action or merely for the illusion of great depth. Already in fourteenth- and fifteenth-century painting the scenes with side accent were more realistic than those with a center accent; and the side house or side wing became the basis for the theatre of illusion. The opposite principle emphasized the center of the design and arranged a complex façade of archways, galleries, and side doorways about that center. From earliest times this center accent was a conventionalized architectural symbol. That is, the center structure was given a conventionalized pattern that did not attempt to copy nature yet could, by its resemblance in shape or in a few suggestive details, *mean* a castle, a city, a throne, or some other setting, just as carved figures on the chessboard can symbolize a castle or a bishop without closely resembling either. The *tableaux vivants* and Renaissance theatres that followed this principle of organization by a center accent also kept the dependence on symbolism. The third principle kept a flat scene by means of an arcade screen parallel to the front. It followed the multiple convention of the Middle Ages and kept side by side, without

resolving them into a unity, both formal architecture and illusionistic details.

The first principle was preferred by Italian painters of the fifteenth century, who developed their side houses into perspective street scenes with a remarkable illusion of the appearance of reality. The center accent was more favored by Flemish and English artists. First in their painting and sculpture, then more fully in the living show-pictures and show-architecture of the street theatres, the center pavilion was given both the architectural details and the conventions of all the traditional scenic emblems. While the side houses carried with them to the Italian perspective stage the principle of illusion, Elizabethan public theatres took over from earlier art and street-pageant forms the principle of architectural symbolism. These English and Flemish façades partly resembled the castles, thrones, pavilions, and other devices they represented; they partly symbolized those devices of locality by associations long established in art. The third type of organization, with a flat arcade screen, borrowed from both the other two and sometimes followed both principles at the same time. It might be given something of the appearance and the meaning of the northern façades, with a prominent arch or pavilion or throne at the center. Yet, behind the screen were often placed complete illusionistic little scenes, such as the perspective street scenes behind the flat arcade of the Teatro Olimpico or the small realistic interiors in the Terence revivals and the early Jesuit productions or the medieval scenic devices in the center niche or side doors of the curtain stages of Spain.

Analysis of these basic types of organization and of their basic principles of meaning provides the plan for this book. The Flemish and the English façade theatres, with their design based on a center accent and their convention of architectural symbolism, must be studied together. Both were derived in rather similar ways from the *tableaux vivants*. Then in a separate section we must examine the perspective stage of Italy, with its side accent and its convention of pictorial illusion. The stages of the flat arcade screen will be dis-

---

[7] I shall use the word "device" as it is used in contemporary accounts of both street pageants and court entertainments, to indicate a complete scenic element—a house, tree, tower, throne, mountain, etc. The word tells us that scenery was not used to indicate locale but as a "device" to present the characters who were visible in it or who stepped out from it.

cussed in two different places. Those in which the screen was treated as an organic façade back of the main acting area—the Terence stages, the Teatro Olimpico, the Jesuit stages, and the Spanish stages—will be related to the Flemish and Elizabethan façade theatres; while those in which the screen served as a proscenium frame will be related to the perspective settings which they helped to shape.

The first of the three parts of the book lays the groundwork by a study of form and convention of space and background in medieval art and in the *tableaux vivants*. The first chapter, on the traditions of painting and sculpture, may seem a long way from the theatre, but it is important. We must learn the shapes and conventions of the separate scenic elements before we can understand what happened when they were combined, and we must learn the patterns of organization long established in the minds of both artists and public before we can understand how these patterns were adapted in the theatres. As the link between art and the theatre, we must study the *tableaux vivants*, those amazing examples of show-pictures and show-architecture built as little street theatres for the welcome of a king. Since they have never received more than passing notice, I give in chapter ii a rather full account of their dramatic forms and a description of their meanings—as mountain, ship, castle, pavilion, arcade, triumphal arch, or emblematic façade. They are important both for the art historian and for the theatre historian: they were the most widely popular form of secular art for nearly three centuries, and they were the direct ancestors of the Flemish and Elizabethan stages.

In the second part of the book, I examine the theatres of architectural symbolism: the façade theatres of Flanders, England, and Spain and the related theatres of the schools, academies, and Jesuit colleges. As I could find nothing in English about the Flemish theatres, and very little in French or German, I spent six weeks in Belgium and Holland reading the plays and hunting up the documents. The Rederyker stage proved to

be even more important than I had suspected. I give here the first account in English of the stage of these Societies of Rhetoric and how it was used. Then, in chapter iv, I present a new explanation of the origin of the Elizabethan stage, which I believe throws a new light on many of the conventions and on some details of construction of the stage of Shakespeare. I include a drawing of a hypothetical Elizabethan façade (Fig. 47)—not to represent what I believe the stage actually looked like but to show what forms were available to the Elizabethan architect in the traditions of art and pageantry. The Spanish public theatre is a parallel case. While I do not make an extensive re-examination of the Spanish plays, I select enough illustrations to show that the Spanish stage, too, followed the patterns established in medieval art and in the *tableaux vivants*.

The third part of the book gives an account of the illusionistic theatres and how they finally came to drive out all the theatres of symbolism. First I describe the Italian perspective setting, which was copied directly from the patterns of fifteenth-century art, with only a few borrowings from the street theatres. Then I give an account of the proscenium arch and the front curtain as means of shaping the illusionistic scenes. Here is considerable new material to clear up the story of the beginnings of the picture-frame stage, which has been badly confused by the historians. In the last chapter I trace the introduction of perspective into France and England and the different compromises between illusion and convention that became part of the tradition of the repertory theatres into the twentieth century.

By a study of all the Renaissance theatres as part of the history of the visual arts, we can not only explain how these various forms were derived from old traditions but determine much more clearly the conventions of each. We can come much nearer to understanding just what the performance of a play meant to a man of the time—and that is the most important purpose of theatre history.

PART I

THE ROOTS OF THEATRE FORM AND CONVENTION

Painting, Sculpture, and the "Tableaux vivants"

THE knotted skeins of meaning of the Elizabethan, the Italian, and the Spanish, French, and Flemish theatres of the Renaissance can be untangled only by following each thread back to its origin in the art of the Middle Ages. For the principal meanings had already been established and the main problems of organization had already been solved by Gothic and early Renaissance artists. The new Renaissance theatres did not appear until well into the sixteenth century, when Italian painters had been experimenting with perspective drawing for nearly a century and northern architects had been presenting *tableaux vivants* in terms of emblematic devices for two centuries. Both the shape and the meanings of the wings, the backdrops, the heavens, the curtains, the proscenium frames, the side doors, the upper balconies, the inner stages—both the appearance of the stage and the function that each part would have in giving life to the play—had already been decided in the painting and sculpture of the Middle Ages. Hence we must seek our answers in the Middle Ages, first in the painting, stained glass, tapestries, and sculpture, then in the living art of the *tableaux vivants*.

For the Italian perspective stage, we want to know how the architect came upon the principle of the stage wing—the little houses at the sides that measured depth right into the picture space and carried the eye back by mathematical units to give the illusion of great depth. We want to know why the two rows of wings were exactly balanced. We want to know why the stage was higher at the back and sloped down to the front, so that we to this day speak of "upstage" and "downstage." We want to know how the Italian architects and audience could accept the opening of the backdrop to show an inner stage that might be a different place from the main stage—and on occasion three little inner stages. We want to know why the side wings, which were supposed to be part of a very realistic street scene, had often such unrealistic features as an archway which permitted the audience to see an entire inner scene. How did the various parts of the proscenium frame originate? Why was the proscenium so complex that to this day we have not only a proscenium as part of the architecture of the auditorium but also one or two formal wings—the "tormentors" and "returns" of the professional theatres? How can we explain the separation of forestage from main stage by a complex proscenium and curtain, and then the use of another formal proscenium at the back of the main stage that made a frame for the inner stage? How did this tendency to duplicate picture plane behind picture plane and stage behind stage originate, and how is it related to the principle of duplicating side wing behind side wing? The answers to all these questions we can find in medieval and early Renaissance art.

For the Shakespearean stage, we want to know just what the spectator saw in the mind's eye when he looked on the scenes presented on the forestage, under the "heavens," at the side doors, on the inner stage, or on the balcony. What preparation did an Elizabethan spectator have, from his experience with other ways of visualizing stories, for viewing a rapid series of scenes that

11

used the stage building as a castle, as a throne scene, as a house front, as a city gate, or in a dozen other ways? How did the Elizabethan visualize the dumb shows, the tableaux behind curtains, the prologues and induction scenes? What did the stage façade and its decorations mean to him? The answers to all these questions we can find in medieval and early Renaissance art.

For both the Elizabethan and the Flemish Rederyker stage we want to know how different symbols could be combined. How could a castle, an arcade screen, a throne-pavilion, and a triumphal arch all be combined into one structure? To what extent did each lose its pattern and its symbolic meaning when they were so combined? For the answer to this question we must look not only at medieval art but at the game of chess, at heraldry, and at the traditions of the *tableaux vivants*.

For all the façade theatres and for the proscenium arches of the illusionistic theatres, we want to know what were the different patterns of combination of illusionistic and formal elements. To what extent were columns and canopies and curtains blended into the symbols of reality, and to what extent were they separate formal framing devices thought of as outside the actual scenic background? The answer to this question we can find partly in medieval and Renaissance art and partly in the *tableaux vivants*.

For both the English and the Italian theatre—and, indeed, for all Renaissance theatres—we want to know the conventions of indicating interior and exterior. How could the Elizabethan see his forestage used as an exterior in one scene and in the very next see a bed brought out for an interior scene? What was the function of the inner stage in presenting interior scenes, and the meaning of a curtain in indicating an interior? These things we should know in order to understand many of the ways of the Elizabethan stage. Also, how did it happen that the center area in Italy was regularly thought of as exterior and hence that Italian stage settings were regularly exterior, with interior scenes shown only by

arches in the side wings, whereas on the Elizabethan stage the center section was the place for interiors while the side doors usually were thought of as exterior? The answers to these problems can be found in the traditions of artists evolving over the fifteen hundred years between the early Greek theatre and the Renaissance.

To understand the differences between the various Renaissance theatres, we want to know how the three types of organization—the side accent, the center accent, and the flat arcade screen—could all three derive from the Greek theatre. What variations were made by the painters of the Middle Ages as they handed the three types down to the Renaissance? How were the separate scenic devices—the age-old elements of trees, fountains, castles, doorways, mountains, and ships—reorganized and combined in the three types? How did it happen that the side accent was regularly associated with the ideal of illusion, while the center accent acquired a symbolic function and only in a conventionalized way resembled the things it represented? How could that center element take on the meaning and some details of the appearance of a number of different scenic devices at the same time? To what extent did the third type—the flat arcade screen—take on the symbolism of the center arch, and to what extent did it act as a formal framework to present or to disclose more illusionistic elements? How could it set a pattern, on the one hand, for the formal façades and curtains of the Spanish stage, the Terence stages, and the Teatro Olimpico and, on the other hand, for the proscenium arch to frame the perspective setting? How did it happen that the side accent, with its ideal of pictorial illusion, was established in Italy at the very beginning of the sixteenth century, while the Flemish and English public theatres followed the center accent, and the principle of architectural symbolism, well into the seventeenth century? The answers to these questions are to be found in medieval and early Renaissance art.

What were the meanings of the separate scenic devices—tree, fountain, mountain, tower, and ship—that entered into the more complex scenes of the Renaissance? We can find part of the answer in the *tableaux vivants* of the fifteenth and sixteenth centuries, when many of them were visualized on platforms and street corners for the reception of the king. But part of the answer must take us back long before there was any organized architectural background, to the earliest narrative friezes and to the ritualistic processions whose origins are lost in the early dawn of civilization.

We have too long ignored the continuity between art and the theatre. Because medieval drama had no organized stage settings, because it was never developed beyond a half-processional form that could depend on the use of single, unorganized scenic units, we have supposed that Renaissance architects invented the new complex stage patterns or borrowed them from one another. The scenic units themselves—the thrones, castles, trees, mountains, caves, ships, towers, and arcade screens—were present both in medieval art and in medieval drama. But the principles by which these units were organized into a complex unity had been developed in painting, sculpture, and the *tableaux vivants*. Hence we must trace the different methods of organiza-

tion of scenic background, from the simplest narrative friezes and dramatic processions to the most complex paintings and dramatized pictures of the Renaissance. We must ask how such elements as trees, towers, and mountains, without any architectural background, could serve to organize the picture space by giving a center or a boundary to a scene of people. Then we must watch the introduction of the architectural screen, in imitation of the Greek theatre, and the beginnings of complex organization of architectural background in space. We must trace the conventions of interior and exterior, and the other meanings of the separate elements as they became part of the three types of organization— the backgrounds with a flat arcade screen, with a center accent, and with a side accent. After we have analyzed the types of organization in painting and sculpture, we can examine the living pictures and living sculptures of the street show-pieces; and that will lead us directly to the Renaissance theatres. For the difference between fifteenth-century painting and sculpture and sixteenth-century theatres is a difference in degree of animation. The basic patterns that were achieved by the earlier artists were those followed by the later dramatists.

CHAPTER I

THE BEGINNINGS OF SCENIC BACKGROUND

Primitive Ceremonial, the Greek Theatre, and Medieval Art

I. TIME, SPACE, AND THE ORGANIZATION OF THE BACKGROUND: THE PRIMITIVE SOLUTION THE FRIEZE AND THE PROCESSION

WHY was there so little continuity between the medieval religious theatre and the new theatres of the Renaissance? What new desires, new needs, appeared in the sixteenth century which could not be satisfied by the miracles and mysteries? How did it happen that stage architects found in the traditions of painting and sculpture the means for satisfying those needs —means they could not find in the medieval performances?

We shall find our answer by tracing the growing maturity of man's aesthetic needs in the new age: in art and literature and, indeed, in politics as well, the Renaissance was dominated by the search for principles of unity. Where the Middle Ages had been content with many disparate units or details which were only loosely bound together, the new age felt that these units or details must be organized into some kind of unity. The men of the Renaissance wanted ever more splendid rulers, but they were learning to subordinate their feudal barons to an absolute king. The new producers and new audiences of the Renaissance wanted an even more splendid background than that of the religious pageants; they wanted to keep, or even increase, the diversity and complexity; but above all they wanted unity. In every aspect of art and literature men of the sixteenth century were ready for a more mature, more complex unity than was usually to be found in the Middle Ages. They were done with narrative and ready for drama. They were done

with the sprawling sequence of little religious plays that might last for days, and they were ready for a single play that had size and proportion. They still opened Chaucer's bundle of separate Canterbury stories, but they were ready for the more unified epics of Tasso, Spenser, and Milton. They still printed collections of short tragic narratives such as the *Mirror for Magistrates*, but they were ready for *King Lear*. In their new theatres they were done with the time art of the medieval narratives and processions and ready for the space art of the Elizabethan stage or the perspective setting. While a time art had to present each point of reference, each scenic element, separately, a space art could achieve unity by organizing all the separate elements into one picture or one architectural structure.

The Renaissance architects turned to painting and sculpture rather than to the medieval drama because the artists had already solved this problem of unity in a complex background. They had already learned how to stop the narrative flow of time and develop a dramatic scene in space. The artists had started with the same primitive narrative form that the medieval dramatists used; for the frieze corresponds exactly to the procession. They had tried those same primitive patterns of relating characters to scenic properties that the dramatists could use in a procession. But they had gone further than the dramatists and had used the architectural screen inherited from the Greeks to achieve a unity and an organization of space that was not possible in the frieze. The problem of organization is the same in art and the theatre, and the two must

14

be studied together if we would understand the achievements of the Renaissance.

The medieval processional form, whether an actual procession in a religious or civic festival or a pictured procession in the frieze form of art, used its scenic elements in a way very different from the way of the modern theatre. Its scenic units are not really background at all: they are conventionalized emblems, miniature symbols of reality, used in the telling of the story. They are more like the emblems of heraldry—sometimes simplified imitations of actual objects, sometimes so conventionalized that little resemblance to actuality is left. From earliest times, before the beginning of history, these emblems were carried in processions along with the characters related to them.

Their use in a ritual explains several characteristics which these emblems kept on into the Renaissance. For one thing, the same ones were used with little change from the time of the ancient Egyptians to the Renaissance. While in decorative detail the emblems might follow the fashions from Egyptian and Greek to Gothic and Renaissance, yet such is the conventionality of processional ritual, and of the ancient and medieval art which followed it, that the same few emblems appeared over and over again. In the friezes and in the dramatic processions the principal emblematic devices were these: the castle (or tower), the throne, the pavilion-temple, the arch or doorway, the ship, the mountain (or cave), and the various symbols of a garden (bower, tree, fountain, or a wall or hedge with a gate). Add to these the chariot and the monster (whale or dragon), and you have the repertory of the medieval pageant and of the Renaissance ballet and masque.

The second remarkable characteristic of these emblematic devices is that they could be interchanged or combined. The ship was not only an illustration of a sea voyage, it was often a ritualistic emblem or simply a decorative device. It could be a setting for a throne. For many centuries the *carrus navalis* was carried in joyful celebrations (hence *carnevale*); or a pageant ship might serve

for a spectacular entry of a knight on the tournament field.[1] A tree or fountain might symbolize a garden or might be only a decorative device to separate one scene in a narrative frieze from the next. Furthermore, on many occasions these emblems could be combined. The oriental combination of an elephant and a castle was familiar throughout the Middle Ages and remains to this day on the chessboard and in heraldic emblems and tavern signs. Hence we are not surprised to find a number of combinations in the later Middle Ages—such as a fountain or a tree on a mountain, or even a ship on a mountain—and to find the nonarchitectural devices combined with the architectural. We are not surprised at a castle or pavilion on top of a small mountain, an arch over a mountain, a throne on a tower or on a tree, or a sea and ship on top of a triumphal arch. We are not surprised, either, when some complex architectural structure represents one of the emblematic devices, as when a triumphal arch is used to symbolize a garden or the Elizabethan stage façade to represent now a castle, now a throne, now a triumphal arch, now a garden, and now a ship. In the next chapter, when we discuss the *tableaux vivants*, we shall examine in greater detail the meaning of each emblematic device. Here we are concerned with the use these devices were put to in the time arts of the procession and the frieze.

We may further distinguish these emblematic devices used in processions from a setting that is a complete pictorial or architectural background for action by examining two quite different uses of scenic elements in the Renaissance theatres. The dramatists in Italy, France, Spain, and England, long after they had a fully developed background, continued to stage some of their scenes in a processional manner. Onto the forestage they brought chariots, ships, towers, mountains, trees, and fountains, set them down long enough to play or dance a scene, then carried them off to make way for the next—all with

[1] Cf. George R. and Portia Kernodle, "The Dramatic Aspects of the Medieval Tournament," *Speech Monographs*, IX, 163 f.

little or no reference to the elaborate background the architect had provided. These portable elements could in no sense serve as background, they were but small picturesque centers for action. In Italy the main play might make use of a beautiful perspective setting representing a large square or street, but between the acts of the play the dancers and singers of the *intermedii* brought onto the forestage the same chariots, fountains, whales, or ships that they would have used in a street procession or on the ballroom floor. The spectacular pageant which passed over the stage had little or no relation to the beautiful painted setting back of it. Or in England many scenes were brought onto the forestage of the Elizabethan theatre and performed with the help of such movable properties as trees, thrones, arbors, wells or fountains, tents, shop fronts, and moss banks, as completely separate from the background as if they had been played in the market place of a medieval city. The processional method of performance continued to be important, and scenic elements or "properties" of the emblematic type continued to be used long after the more complex backgrounds were developed. Yet it was the background that marked the real achievement of the Renaissance, that set patterns of form and convention for all later theatres, and that established an organization in pictorial space as a substitute for the narrative time art of the medieval processions.

The medieval religious drama could not serve as a basis for the organization of that background because it remained essentially a processional drama. Its scenic elements were mostly of the emblematic kind and permitted only a very rudimentary kind of organization of several mansions together. It began and remained a time art, and its treatment of space and background was the same as we find in the frieze: in Egyptian wall paintings, on Trajan's Column in Rome, and on the Bayeux Tapestry. The earliest church plays grew out of a processional ritual centered, first, about the altar or the Easter sepulcher, then about various other stations, seats, or other emblematic structures set up around the church.

The performers, and sometimes the audience as well, followed the story from one station to another. The scenic elements gave no more organization to a scene than did the small ships, trees, or other emblems carried in a procession or sprinkled along a primitive carved or painted frieze. The great medieval cycles of plays developed, for the most part, from the popular outdoor religious processions of the summer season. In England the Corpus Christi or Whitsuntide processions were developed into a series of plays by stopping the actors long enough for dialogue. How simple a transition that was I realized from seeing the Procession of the Holy Blood in Bruges in 1939. A procession of many groups, with animals and pageant wagons, must of necessity go so slowly that pauses are frequent. Many of the groups in Bruges used a few lines of dialogue. Even when the actors and scenic devices did not stop, there was plenty of time for the miniature drama. And in the Middle Ages, even when each play was fully developed, the drama remained a time art: there was no more organization of background than we find in the frieze. Sometimes two mansions were related to each other on adjacent wagons or on the same platform, but they usually figured separately in the story. In France, especially in the sixteenth century, there were productions in which a number of mansions were placed in a line on one long platform; but, even if the scenic elements did not move, they were still of the same emblematic type, and the movement of the action from one mansion to the next was still on the pattern of the processional. The medieval religious drama never developed far beyond the type of narrative of the processional ritual and the painted or carved frieze. It continued to follow the type of background that the dramatists and public saw constantly in church painting, carving, and stained glass.[2]

[2] In Part I of the bibliography for chap. i, I give a bibliography (the first ever attempted) of works which discuss the relationship between theatre and art. They are nearly all concerned with the medieval period. A number of the authors, like Mâle and Cohen, were interested in those innovations in incident and characterization in the dramatic performances which

How did it happen that medieval painting was so far in advance of medieval drama in the use of background? How did it happen that in the later Middle Ages the problems of organization of space by means of architectural background were solved in painting and sculpture long before they were solved in the theatre? To answer these questions we must make a survey of the history of space and background in art, something the art historians have neglected to do.[3] For the artist had exactly the same problem of organization that the theatre architect had. He found in the traditional frieze an art of narrative time, an art that carried the eye of the spectator swiftly along with the story, without stopping long enough to organize the space into a unity. He found in his tradition exactly the same emblematic castles, towers, arches, *tempietti*, trees, thrones, ships, and monsters that were used in the dramatic processions. In fact, most of ancient art and a large part of medieval art were interested in the processional narrative time of the frieze and not in the organization of space. But the difference between art and the theatre before the Renaissance lay in this: artists preserved some of the gains made by the Greeks, while the theatre lost all effective continuity with the ancient world and had to begin all over again with the primitive organization of the procession.

In only two periods—the Hellenistic and the Renaissance—have artists had enough interest in space to stop the narrative flow of time and develop a more complex unified architectural background. In both those periods that interest in space soon carried them beyond the limits of painting and sculpture to work out their spatial concepts in the theatre. The Greek people did achieve in their theatre façade the organization of a number of separate scenic elements into a unified structure. In the Hellenistic age that followed, the artists used the same type of architectural background, as we can see in the Pompeian wall paintings. For several centuries, from the fifth century B.C. until the early Christian era, art and theatre developed side by side. In the Middle Ages, however, most of these gains in the organization of space were lost. The interest in narrative time was kept, but the interest in space almost disappeared. After Rome fell and the Christians drove the drama out of the old theatre buildings, the people saw only the most primitive type of dramatic procession. The artists did, however, keep some of the elements of background developed in the Greek theatre and handed them down to later artists and finally to later theatres. There was unbroken continuity in painting and sculpture, however poorly the transmitting artist understood the traditions he was copying. Sometimes he copied all of the architectural screen, sometimes only parts of it; but he did pass on several complex ways of defining the scene by the setting. Hence it happened that, all through the later Middle Ages and the Renaissance, painting and sculpture were almost always the more advanced arts and the drama was borrowing from them. When new interest in space, new needs for the exploitation of the picture in space, appeared in the fifteenth century, the painters and sculptors and devisers of *tableaux vivants* were ready. They developed the new Renaissance patterns of background for the new romantic and political subjects and offered models for the new theatre designers before the producers of the old religious plays had tried more than the simplest organization of the emblematic devices. Hence we trace the origins of the Renaissance theatres to painting, sculpture, and the *tableaux vivants* rather than to the processional form of medieval religious drama.

were followed by later painters. They have left the impression that most of the influence was from theatre to art. Van Puyvelde has made valuable corrections of Mâle, and both he and Miss Galante-Garrone have emphasized how much the Continental drama depended for its settings on the traditions of art. Miss Shull has recently shown that in England no less than on the Continent the dramatists followed the conventional patterns of art.

[3] Hinks in *Carolingian Art* gives a good summary of the problems of time and space in art and refers to more extended discussions. Miss Bunim's recent *Space in Medieval Painting* examines space only in the sense of depth into the picture plane. She has a good summary of the development of perspective at the end of the Middle Ages, but she is not concerned with the other conventions of using the architectural background.

There were, however, two primitive patterns in the frieze form of art and the processional drama, two rudimentary ways of organizing a

The first—the simplest way of relating characters to a scenic emblem—was to use that emblem as a nucleus, a center, and to group the

FIG. 1.—Scenes from the story of Medea. Central canopy-pavilion of a type derived from the Greek theatre and handed down to medieval painters as a means of presenting interior scenes. Characters partly within the structure and partly outside. From a Greek vase in Munich.

scene in terms of the background, which were retained even into the later theatres. In fact, the main difference between the Elizabethan theatre and the Italian perspective setting can be traced to these two primitive patterns of organization that are practically as old as narrative art itself.

characters around it, leaving the space between one scene and the next indeterminate. In very flat painting this nucleus might be merely a strong accent in the background—a throne, a tower, a mountain, a tree behind the figures to give emphasis to the center and unity to the scene purely by design.[4] The more complex method of organization was to use a device at the outside of the scene, where it would have an inclosing function in defining the limits of the scene. With two inclosing elements, space was unified and made exact. The eye grasped immediately the space between a tower or a tree at one side of the scene and a similar device at the other side. Even if another scene followed as part of the frieze, the eye paused to consider the scene as a space unit (Figs. 1, 5). As we should expect, those people who have been most interested in solving the problems of space are the ones who have made most use of the inclosing function—the ancient Greeks with an architectural screen and the Renaissance Italians with perspective. The inclosing pattern, with the accent at the sides, furnished the basis for the Italian perspective setting, with the action in an open center area inclosed by the wings at the sides. The center accent led to the conventional cluster of elements at the center—the pattern of the Elizabethan and the Flemish stages. Like the primitive nucleus scenes, these conventional façades of Flanders and England made some important concessions to time, both in the processional use of the separate parts of the façade as different places (multiple staging) and in the persistence of a single symbolic meaning through several scenes.

Both methods, actually, were used in the later medieval religious theatres. On the longer platform stages, such as that at Valenciennes in 1547, the different emblematic mansions served now as a nucleus, now to define a scene from the outside. But it was not really from these belated primitive solutions that the more complex developments came; it was from complex patterns established in art hundreds of years before these sixteenth-century religious productions. The more complex patterns required more than just the emblematic devices; they required an architectural screen as a background, as a basic

structure into which and against which the separate traditional devices could be set. By uniting the separate devices with a background screen, the artist could develop a very definite control of space. The way he made the combination determined which of the three main types of organization he would use. He could put a prominent doorway at the center of the screen and organize his whole dramatic scene around his center accent. Or by prominent features at the ends of the screen he could inclose and define it from the outside. Or when he opened the screen at several places—and the screen almost always bore the features (arches or panels) of an arcade—he created the effect of a number of separate nuclei equally distant from the front but united in the continuous structure of the arcade screen. On the Greek stage such doorways were usually united in time, but not always; and in painting and sculpture the arcade might replace the timeless row of portrait statues in niches. Hence later designers were more likely to use the flat arcade for a multiple setting and the center or side accent for a single time and place.

From the Greek stage, painters and sculptors derived not only a synthesis of architectural screen and individual nucleus but also important patterns copied separately from the arcade, the side house or wing, and the center arch. Each century through the Middle Ages gave its own interpretation to those traditions; but, in spite of varying concepts of space and convention, there were handed down to the Renaissance theatre, either separately or in combination, all three organizations—the flat arcade screen, the center pavilion, and the side house. The arcade and the center pavilion of painting were usually conventional structures, not resembling too closely any actual building. The side house was more realistic. Hence we find the Italian perspective scene making use of the side accent to achieve an illusion of reality, while the Elizabethan stage, basically more conventional, was a combination of the single devices, the center pavilion, and the

[4] Cf. the methods of organizing a flat design from the border inward and from a nucleus outward, as discussed by Adama van Scheltema in *Die altnordische Kunst*, and by Hinks, *op. cit.*, pp. 127–29.

side arches of the arcade screen. In all Renaissance theatre forms, as all through medieval art,
the influence of that arcade screen as a means of
organizing the narrative scene was great.

number of other cities in the eastern Mediterranean world. Although there had been rows of
niches in Asia Minor[5] and some vague attempts in
Egyptian art to organize several groups within a

Fig. 2.—Comedy relief. Section of stage front with architrave converted into a house with doorway, gable, and roof-line. Curtain against architectural structure for a dramatic performance, probably as symbol of an interior. Naples Museum. Anderson, Rome.

II. THE HELLENISTIC CONTRIBUTION: THE UNIFIED ARCADE SCREEN OF THE GREEK THEATRE AND OF HELLENISTIC ART

1. THE BEGINNINGS OF THE ARCADE SCREEN

The first arcade screen used to organize a group
of narrative characters was the scene structure of
the Greek theatre. Developed in Athens toward
the middle of the fifth century B.C., it was elaborated in the following centuries and imitated in a

single building, yet this is the first scenic structure which, complete in itself, served to organize
a number of separate elements and give them
unity. At first, perhaps, the stage façade did little
more than unite the three doors for the three
actors into a single design which could symbolize
a palace or temple. Soon, however, there were
ornamentation and elaboration. Columns and

[5] Strzygowski, "A Sarcophagus of the Sidamara Type,"
Journal of Hellenic Studies, XXVII, 113 ff.

pediments framed the entrance doors and divided the façade into panels. Portrait statues were added, as well as a second story and projecting wings at the sides called *parascenia*. Both the wings and the main façade at times had colonnades. On some level (we do not know which) panels of painted scenery were set into grooves between columns.

This scene painting on panels seems to go back to the time of Aeschylus, that is, practically to the beginning of a real architectural background behind actors. Whatever the position or the exact nature of the painted scene panels, the ones for tragedy and comedy, by the testimony of Vitruvius, were painted with architectural details. From a fairly early time, statues were placed in the panels of the scene front and between the columns.[6] Therefore, we know that, before there had been more than a very conventional incidental use of architecture in nontheatrical painting, the stage showed the artist and the public single portrait statues and actors in narrative scenes set in front of a solid architectural background, and probably sometimes in front of a painted architectural background.

Some Hellenistic artists followed very closely the model of the theatre. We know that the vase painters directly portrayed a large number of scenes from plays with their stage background.[7] Vitruvius tells in Book vii that the "ancients" painted in their rooms stage scenes of the Tragic, Comic, or Satyric type—exactly the types he tells us were painted on the stage. The wall paintings from the Roman villa at Boscoreale, especially two in the Metropolitan Museum of New York, seem direct imitations of the painted panels of stage scenery. These show us not only the three panels, with the balconies and houses of citizens of a Comic Scene, but even the red columns that seem to project forward in front of the panels. We know from the remains of the theatre at Priene and elsewhere that just such red columns or half-columns were used to hold and separate the painted stage panels.[8]

The indirect influence of the Greek theatre was very strong. Sculptors were borrowing from the stage screen when they used a row of niches, columns, and pediments to unite carved figures. A number of early Christian sarcophagi take the form of the stage façade.[9] In all of them human

Fig. 3.—Allegorical scene of Intelligence and Painting in front of a screen copied from the Hellenistic theatre. Niche-pavilion at center of arcade screen. Sixth-century manuscript of Dioscorides, No. Med. Gr. 1, National Library, Vienna.

figures are placed in niches with columns supporting arches and pediments. Usually one figure is in a niche and the next is in the interspace in front of a flat section of the back screen. Another early Christian form of sculpture with similar niches, openings, and columns is the altar screen of the Greek church. Karl Holl is convinced that this, too, derives from the façade of the Hellenistic theatre.[10] Many are the carved sarcophagi,

[6] Friend, "The Portraits of the Evangelists," *Art Studies*, V 143–46, and VII, 16.

[7] Séchan, *Études sur la tragédie grecque, passim.*

[8] Friend, *op. cit.*, VII, 20.

[9] Strzygowski, *loc. cit.*; and Morey, *The Sarcophagus of Claudia Antonia Sabina.*

[10] "Die Entstehung der Bilderwand in der griechischen Kirche," *Archiv für Religionswissenschaft*, IX, 365–84.

chests, panels, screens, rood screens, and reredos of the next thousand years which followed closely this sculptural tradition. Many are the paintings which blindly followed the arcade-screen pattern of the long-forgotten ancient theatre.

one of the *parascenia*. When the three types are placed together, it is apparent that they are separate parts of a single design, as Vitruvius says the three separate panels of stage scenery should be. Friend is convinced that they derive

FIG. 4.—Arcade screen as symbol of castle-city and backing for a throne. Side doors. From tenth- or eleventh-century manuscript of Prudentius' *Psychomachia* in St. Gall. From Merton.

Not only was the whole arcade pattern taken over by artists, but each separate part of the stage arcade furnished a model for relating a character or group of characters to an architectural background. For instance, the Evangelist portraits of the seated type in early Greek and Latin Gospel manuscripts have in the background three types of structure—one corresponding to the central section of the stage façade and each of the others to

directly from the stage.[11] The side panels show how closely the typical Byzantine and Carolingian side house was dependent on the form of the *parascenium* of the Hellenistic stage. The open colonnade of this stage gave the pattern to an open-baldacchino type of building (Figs. 1, 4, 18). The two columns and gable pediment became a house front with a gable above, and the

[11] *Op. cit.*, VII, 14 ff.

architrave over the other columns was interpreted as the roof of the house. We shall find that the two-sided house became quite important in the Romanesque and Gothic periods, when vanishing lines were carefully rearranged to give depth by perspective.

2. CONVENTIONS OF THE ARCADE SCREEN: EXTERIOR FORM AND INTERIOR SUBTERFUGE

Painters took over from the theatre not only the main pattern and the separate parts of the arcade screen but also a whole series of conventions of telling the story in terms of those architectural forms. The most important of those conventions had to do with methods of presenting interior scenes by means of architectural forms which were all regularly exteriors.

A student of early painting is struck immediately by the fact that, no matter what type of scene was represented, the architectural backgrounds were composed entirely of exterior forms, a very important fact for both painting and the theatre. For more than two thousand years the artist thought of both himself and his characters as in the open air. As late as the Renaissance this tradition was so strong in art that stage settings in most countries were regularly exteriors, while in painting the interior had to make its way very gradually, either as a separate tradition or by concessions and compromises in the treatment of the separate parts of the exterior background itself.[12] Although architects in the sixteenth century began to build theatres inside palace walls and underneath roofs, yet until yesterday they persisted in treating the whole auditorium as an exterior: they built little roofs above the boxes and painted the ceiling with clouds and stars.[13]

The audience of the ancient theatre, of course, was in the open air, and, no matter what the nature of the scene, the characters came in front of an outdoor scene structure, or at least into an open colonnade, to act. When an object or a body or a group of people had to be shown as

inside a building, a special machine or movable inclosure or a curtain had to be employed. Painting took over not only the outdoor type of background but the tradition of showing all kinds of scenes in front of a screen or within an open pavilion or side house.

The simplest way for an artist to treat an interior scene was frankly to bring it out in front of the flat architectural screen or one of the central doorways or side houses he derived from the theatre, just as the Greek dramatists must have done. Hence we find, from early Christian and Byzantine art right down to the Renaissance, interior scenes placed in the open in front of exterior architectural forms (Figs. 1, 3, 4, 5, 6). The seated type of Evangelist portrait we have already noticed[14] presents the figure at his desk as though at work in his private study, set before an architectural screen and sometimes before side houses. In Carolingian ivory carving, the Nativity often appeared in front of a stone archway with ass and ox looking out of upper windows, or against the exterior walls and towers of a conventionalized Bethlehem. The Last Supper, throughout the Middle Ages, was pictured in front of an architectural screen, often with side houses which bring the background partly around the scene.[15] The "Last Supper" from the twelfth-century mosaic in the cathedral of Monreale is a good example.[16] The side houses with roofs are clearly exteriors. While Da Vinci omitted the sky and roofs and added a slight interior quality, he used the basic form of architectural screen and side wings, and the copy of his painting in a tapestry in the Vatican reintroduced the sky above. Even the Healing of the Paralytic is shown in front of exterior forms. The screen and side houses have roofs, and the bed is let down in front, *outdoors*. The painting tradition was followed in the production of the *mystères* at Valenciennes in 1547; the Cailleau miniature shows the bed of the paralytic being let

---

[12] Hinks, *op. cit.*, p. 169.

[13] Kernodle, "The Outdoor Setting," *Theatre Arts Monthly*, XXI, 558–61.

[14] Friend, *op. cit.*

[15] Loomis, "The Table of the Last Supper," *Art Studies*, V, 71–88.

[16] Panofsky, "Die Perspektive als 'symbolische Form,'" *Vorträge der Bibliothek Warburg, 1924–25*, Fig. 18.

FIG. 5.—Two scenes from an eleventh-century Byzantine Gospel. Frieze forms. Scenes organized around a throne-tower as nucleus or by side towers as inclosing element. Beds and table in front of the outdoor screen inherited from the Greek theatre. MS grec 74, Bibliothèque Nationale, Paris.

down in front of a roofed pavilion.[17] The two Giotto pictures I reproduce here (Fig. 11) show the same outdoor screens with side wings or side houses.

FIG. 6.—St. Matthew on castle-throne. Symbol of heavens above. From an ivory book-cover of the second half of the eleventh century. Victoria and Albert Museum, London.

Not all interior scenes, however, were so frankly brought out in front of an exterior structure. A number of subterfuges were resorted to, many of them apparently derived from the methods of the ancient theatre. The most important device was to place the characters under the roof of an open type of center pavilion or side house. Sometimes

[17] Cf. the twelfth-century Monreale mosaic (*ibid.*, Fig. 20) with the same scene at Valenciennes in 1547 (Cohen, *Le Théâtre en France au moyen âge*, Vol. I: *Le Théâtre religieux*, Pl. XLVI).

the house was opened up by arches almost as large as the whole walls; but more frequently in earlier art it was no more than a baldacchino of roof and columns.

One model for the open baldacchino was the colonnade of the ancient theatre façade, which led to pediments and architraves above. Another possible origin is suggested by the well-known Greek

FIG. 7.—Noah's Ark in the Caedmon Manuscript, about 1000 A.D. Castle on a boat. Side towers framing center panel. Glimpses of interior in center archways. MS Junius 11, Bodleian Library, Oxford.

vase in Munich with scenes from the Medea story (Fig. 1). The dead body of the bride is on a platform under a six-column baldacchino. We are intrigued by the suggestion that this may represent the stage *eccyclema*, that curious device of the ancient theatre for rolling interior scenes, especially fresh victims of violence, out into the open.[18]

Here, then, we have one very important convention of painting: that the group of characters of an interior scene are shown partly inside the

[18] Flickinger, *The Greek Theater and Its Drama*, pp. 237 ff. Miss Bieber thinks it rather an imitation of one of the temporary structures used as a part of the setting in the theatre of classical times (*The History of the Greek and Roman Theater*, p. 60).

house and partly outside. The convention continued throughout the Middle Ages to the Renaissance. In many Annunciation scenes, the Virgin is placed under a baldacchino or within an arch, while the angel, part of the same scene, is placed in the open. In the fourteenth century, Duccio painted his scene of the "Apostles' Farewell to the Virgin" partly inside and partly outside a side house. Part of the bed and most of the characters are brought forward where they can be more clearly seen.[19] In the Renaissance theatres (we are not surprised to observe) characters and even beds might be brought forward onto the exterior forestage after an interior scene had been begun inside a side house or on an inner stage.

Another way the early artist had of treating an interior scene was to put it behind an arch, either a lone arch or part of a larger structure. A doorway in ancient art is essentially an exterior form. In Egyptian art, ritual, and drama it is often a symbol of the resurrection from the tomb. In Greek art the artist and audience are outside, viewing the outside of the doorway. But behind the opening may be an interior. This seems to follow the practice in the Greek theatre of showing interior scenes within the central doorway. Bulle believes, from a study of Pompeian painting and other evidence, that the Hellenistic stage must have had rather extensive means of showing interiors in small rooms back of the façade and that the pattern was taken over by art.[20] Although many medieval painters felt free to put exterior views of landscape or houses behind an archway, yet from Hellenistic times to the Renaissance the arch was a frequent device for marking an interior. We shall find it important in the story of the proscenium arch in the Renaissance.

Two other framing elements—the floor and the ceiling—served the artist at times as conventions of interiors. In northern miniature and altar painting of the Romanesque and Gothic periods a tile floor pattern (usually in perspective) was an unmistakable symbol of an interior. Many painters clearly marked where the interior started by such a pattern. In Italy, where open courtyards and sometimes the streets had patterns of brick and tile, the convention had no meaning. Both painters and stage designers put most ingenious perspective designs on the open street, yet it is interesting to note that early stage designers, such as Serlio, began the perspective floor pattern only on the rear stage, leaving the flat forestage with square patterns without perspective. Perhaps the outdoor example of the Italians was responsible for the death of the convention in the north before it left any visible traces on the newer forms of the theatre. That the medieval religious stage may have followed it on occasion is suggested by a line in the English Chester play of *Christ Betrayed*:

> Lo! here a parlour already dight
> With paved floors and windows bright.[21]

Likewise, the coffered or beamed ceiling, which throughout the Middle Ages indicated an interior, disappeared in the Renaissance. Bulle relates it also to the alcove inner stage of the theatre. And, of course, the roof above the Roman stage offered another pattern. We see it projecting above the arcade screen in the scene from the ninth-century London Alcuin Bible[22] and above a number of Giotto's interior scenes. In places it was transmuted into a painted or cloth canopy. A painted canopy distinguished the interiors from the exteriors in the scenes sculptured in the fourteenth century on the north screen around the choir in Notre Dame de Paris. Especially in northern countries, a cloth canopy or valance, usually in combination with a hanging cloth, indicated an interior. Several of Cailleau's miniatures for the Valenciennes *mystères*, as notably that of the Last Supper, indicate that cloth valances, as well as cloth backings, decorated interior scenes on the French medieval stage even when baldacchino structures were used. The artists more often combined several symbols of the interior.

[19] Van Marle, *The Development of the Italian Schools of Painting*, II, 58.

[20] *Untersuchungen an griechischen Theatern*, pp. 230 ff. and 280 ff.

[21] Deimling and Matthews, *The Chester Plays*, II, 267. Here, as throughout the book, I have modernized the spelling.

[22] Panofsky, *op. cit.*, Fig. 15.

In art one of the most intriguing, and for the theatre one of the most important, conventional means of indicating an interior is the curtain. Not only a curtain which could be pulled over an archway in front of a scene, but also a hanging was very closely following the theatre. About curtains on the earlier Greek stage we know nothing. That they appeared in the Hellenistic theatre would seem to be indicated by two curious references in the *Onomasticon*, or word list, of

Fig. 8.—The death of Edward, from the Bayeux Tapestry. Late eleventh century. Side towers framing an interior scene of two stories. Curtain for upper level. From a copy in the Victoria and Albert Museum, London.

over a door, a looped drape over a screen, a cloth hung against a wall, a woven backing for throne or bed, and even a cover draped over a table or chair recurred through the centuries to tell that here was an interior.

Woven or matted hangings, as used over doors or elsewhere in houses, appear fairly early in Egyptian art,[23] but their use as a convention of an interior dates from Hellenistic times, when art

Pollux. In the first section of chapter xix he writes: "The *cortina* must be named and also the curtain, according to what Hyperides says in the Patroclus: Nine princes were feasting in a colonnade, shut off on one side by a curtain." In the next section he writes: "In comedy a shed is added to the house, represented on woven hangings, and is a stable for beasts of burden."[24] The

[23] Smith, *Egyptian Architecture*, Pl. XIV, No. 4.

[24] See, further, the testimony of Pliny that the theatres of Roman times were ornamented with carpets and paintings (Bieber, *op. cit.*, p. 342).

"woven hangings" added to the house may have been like the cloth hanging against an exterior wall behind a banquet of Dionysus and behind a comedy scene (Fig. 2) in two reliefs in the Naples Museum. Those and several other quite theatrical sculptures would suggest a stage origin. As late as the fifteenth century, Fra Angelico and many other painters, both north and south, felt free to indicate an interior scene by a decorative

neatly tied to posts beside the deathbed scene of Edward in the Bayeux Tapestry (Fig. 8).

A curtain over the side doors is frequent from the fourth and fifth centuries. The Terence manuscripts, in particular, pass it on from one artist to another, sometimes as full curtains, sometimes as no more than a towel thrown over a door frame.[25] Some artists tell you that the Evangelist is indoors in his study by putting a cloth over his

a   *b*

FIG. 9.—Two late fourteenth-century miniatures. Side towers and center arch made into compact façade framing an interior scene. Exterior door and window in side towers. MS fr. 2203, Bibliothèque Nationale, Paris.

cloth hanging against an exterior screen or even against trees (Figs. 11, 13). Or, if neither house, screen, nor tree was available, true believers, like Jan van Eyck, could persuade angels to hold up a curtain that Our Lady might be indoors even in an open landscape.

The other curtain of Pollux—a curtain in a colonnade for an interior scene—was copied many times in the succeeding centuries. Sometimes it was a stray veil of cloth wandering in festoons across the columns of manuscript pages. Sometimes it spread out and threatened to cover the entire scene until it was tied securely in a loop to a column on each side. We see it thus

reading stand or over the back or arm of his chair.

The actual walls of many medieval palaces and even churches were painted to imitate curtain hangings. The association was so complete between cloth curtains and interiors that in fifteenth- and sixteenth-century painting any arch, niche, screen, house, or even mountain or cave could be made into a proper habitation by the magic of a piece, large or small, of woven fabric. It is no wonder that the many French, Flemish, and English *tableaux vivants* and the

[25] Jones and Morey, *The Miniatures of the Manuscripts of Terence.*

Hans Sachs, the Flemish, English, and Spanish theatres made extensive use, with old or new conventions, of curtains.[26]

It was an important contribution that the Greek theatre made to the history of art. This arcade screen not only enabled the Hellenistic age to unify a complex scene, but it served the same purpose during some fifteen hundred years for artists who had long forgotten the Greek theatre. Different generations made their own variations in the traditional forms, interpreting them according to changing concepts of space. They could not have explained why their background structures were all exteriors, and often they confused the conventions of interiors. They knew only that an architectural screen, whether with arches or with solid panels, made a pleasing background for figures, that a center pavilion was an emphatic setting for throne or temple scene, that an upper niche or throne would distinguish the figure of honor from the characters below, and that a side house, whether separate or in combination with the screen, finished off the scene well at the side. We must watch how they developed these three types of setting, for they added many new variations in form as well as in meaning as they handed down the Greek screen to the Renaissance theatres.

III. THE MEDIEVAL DEVELOPMENT: THE THREE TYPES OF BACKGROUND IN MEDIEVAL AND EARLY RENAISSANCE PAINTING AND SCULPTURE

Not only was the complex organization of the Greek theatre copied by painters and sculptors, but each separate part was taken over and handed down as a separate tradition. The arcade screen as a flat background, the center pavilion as a center nucleus, and the side house as a side accent became part of the heritage of later painters. Thus we may explain the fact that, whereas the Greek stage combined all three types of background, each Renaissance theatre was dominated by one type and showed the influence of the others only in subordinate parts—the

Elizabethan stage, for instance, in its side doors and the perspective stage in its back shutter. Hence we can study each type separately and watch how the arcade screen, the central façade, and the side house were elaborated in the Middle Ages and early Renaissance before they left their impress on the Renaissance theatres.

1. THE FLAT PLANE: THE ARCADE SCREEN

The arcade screen, as an imitation of the entire theatre background, was used by artists in two ways: first, as a conventionalized backing for an earthly or heavenly throne and, second, as a means of controlling space. The conventionalized use was already developed in the theatres of the time of the Roman Empire. The remains of the theatres at Ostia, Palmyra, Ephesus, and Aspendos indicate that immediately above the central doorway of the stage was a niche for paying special honor to a statue.[27] Hence we find recurring throughout the Middle Ages a conventionalized arcade screen used as a background for a throne (Figs. 4, 11, 17), as a background for allegorical characters (Fig. 3), or for the support of a heavenly throne (Fig. 19) or of such heavenly groups as the Resurrection scene and the heavenly choir over the rood screen in the medieval church. The widespread use of such a throne-of-honor in the ancient theatres and in medieval art and its reappearance in the church structures and pageants of the Gothic period and in the tournaments and the Flemish theatres of the Renaissance, suggest that it may have been based on a pattern of the King of the Festival, who in primitive festivals presided over contests and ceremonies in his honor.[28]

The other use of the back screen in painting was as a means of controlling space. From the Hellenistic theatre it derived several space conventions which were developed during the Middle Ages and became important for the later theatre. It was common, for instance, to show openings

---

[26] Cf. chaps. ii, iii, iv, v, and vii.

[27] Bieber, *op. cit.*, pp. 358, 368, 371, and 378 ff.

[28] The arcade-of-honor as built in the street theatres is discussed below, in chap. ii, pp. 86–89; and as it influenced the Flemish and Elizabethan theatres in chaps. iii and iv.

and niches in the screen, disclosing some space behind it, and to show columned structures projecting and defining a narrow space in front of it. Indeed, the screen had become the plane to which space was related. While primitive art established the surface of the painting as the plane of reference and manipulated figures either on the surface or set back from it, Hellenistic art established this screen as the plane of reference and portrayed space as extending a short distance both behind and before it. It remained the characteristic plane of reference, to the limited extent that depth was defined at all, throughout medieval painting. Vitruvius states that this was exactly the method of the ancient scene painters, who from Agatharchus had sought to relate lines to the point of sight, "so that [Vitruvius writes] though all is drawn on a vertical flat façade, some parts may seem to be withdrawing into the background, and others to be standing out in front."[29] Thus we find the characteristic treatment of space and background in Hellenistic art, as in the scene painting, to be by one architectural screen and two shallow planes of depth, one before and one behind that screen.

In many works of imperial Rome and in most of early Byzantine and Carolingian art, depth almost disappeared, as figures and objects were organized on the surface according to a conceptual rather than a realistic relationship. The two planes of depth were lost or barely indicated. Yet the architectural screen was not lost. Its column-and-arch structure was retained in a characteristic frieze with a row of columns and arches inclosing individual portrait figures. Both the figures and the arches were flat on the surface.

After the period of Byzantine flatness, when artists again sought depth, the space in front of the screen was once more used for the figures or the characters in the narrative event. Then the screen became a closed solid background with its arcade form merely indicated by columns or panels or sometimes lost altogether (Fig. 4). A second type of scene was developed when the

screen was kept at the surface and the space back of it was regained by pushing figures and small scenes back of the arches. Then the row of arches became a row of frames for separate scenes. The many complex groups of frames, such as triptychs, polyptychs, etc., in Romanesque and Gothic churches are developments of the Hellenistic arcade screen, as well as of other framed forms in art. The two types, that with front arcade screen and that with back solid screen, were next combined to give one solid wall behind the separate arches. In this way, besides using the Hellenistic single arcade screen, with two planes of depth for figures in front of and behind it, the late medieval artist frequently dealt with a single plane of depth between two screens, a front and a back. Then, when the back screen was opened up, in turn, to show a second plane of depth behind it, the new space was bounded by a third solid screen at its back; and that, in turn, might be opened up to show a third plane of depth and a fourth screen, and so on.[30] This doubling of the architectural screen, a frequent practice by the beginning of Gothic art, may be considered as the beginning of the principle of duplication of outline forms, one behind the other, which became the most effective device of Renaissance perspective painting for representing great depth, and hence the model for the wings of the stage.[31] Also in this front screen, as controlled by the principles of perspective, we see the modern concept of a frame in front of all the space of the picture, and hence of the proscenium frame of

[29] *Vitruvius*, p. 198.

[30] The fourteenth-century paintings in St. Stephen's Chapel of Westminster Palace (Borenius and Tristram, *English Medieval Painting*, Pls. 57, 58, and 61); Simon Marmion's "Youth of Saint Bertin," in Berlin (Winkler, *Die altniederländische Malerei*, p. 118, Fig. 69); Alesso Baldovinetti's "Annunciation" at the Uffizi (Venturi, *Storia dell'arte italiana*, VII, Part I, 549, Fig. 307; van Marle, *op. cit.*, XI, 77). This last shows ten arches behind the central arch. Cf., further, the paintings of Filippo Lippi, Bartolo di Fredi, and Sassetta.

[31] Cf. the discussion of the perspective wing in painting in Sec. III of this chapter (pp. 44 ff.) and also the stage wing (chap. vi) and the duplication of picture plane and proscenium (chap. vii). The use of this sequence of planes in Baroque architecture was discussed by Professor Brieger in his lecture, "The Baroque Equation: Illusion and Reality," at the Metropolitan Museum of Art on January 27, 1943.

the theatre, which finally stood in front of all the space represented on the stage.

A number of further developments were possible in the treatment of the open arches of the back screen. The simplest method of doubling put a plain screen or closed arcade behind the open arcade to produce a kind of loggia, as in Giotto's "Apparition at Arles," in the Bardi Chapel of Santa Croce in Florence, and in Duccio's "Jesus in the Temple," in the Museum of the Duomo at Siena. In the late fourteenth and the fifteenth centuries two, three, or a dozen planes of depth were added by placing rows of arches behind the first row to produce elaborate loggias and even temple and church structures in a skeleton form of archways and columns. The scene of Joachim driven from the temple, painted by Giovanni da Milano in fresco in Santa Croce in Florence in 1365, presents the main characters in front of a large church structure of many rows of open Gothic arches. Sometimes separate interior rooms were placed behind the arches, as in Sassetta's "Birth of the Blessed Virgin," at Asciano, and in several of the paintings done about the middle of the fifteenth century in Spain by Dello Delli (Nicholas the Florentine).

Or, if a small distant exterior scene were put in an arch, a striking effect was achieved. Before the end of the fourteenth century, this distant scene showed artists how effectively the impression of distance was created by a framing arch. Well before a front arch had been used to inclose a deep scene, these back arches with distant views brought into painting a new concept of space—as a "seeing-through"—a concept which, put on a mathematical basis, became the principle of perspective. In both painting and the theatre the architectural screen remained important as the plane through which perspective space was to be viewed.

These small distant scenes also introduced a problem which Renaissance painters never could settle with any agreement—the relation of the several small scenes to the eyepoint and to the perspective of the front scene. Was each small scene independent, with its own vanishing-point? Or were all inner scenes parts of one unified scene, with one vanishing-point? Even in the seventeenth century the artist, if he used the small extensions, felt free to treat the little scenes either as vanishing to the main point of the main scene or as separate scenes with different vanishing-points, so that the eye had to turn from one direction to another to see them. Thus the back screen often had an ambiguous function—as a backing for a unified front scene and as a multiple frame for independent inner scenes. In the theatre one thinks immediately of the five openings in the architectural screen of the Teatro Olimpico, with inner scenes leading to seven different vanishing-points, so placed that at least one would be visible from any seat in the house. But that belongs to a later story. Let us return to painting.

As perspective painting was developed, the back architectural screen became much less important and tended to disappear. The multiplication of the side houses pushed it farther and farther back. Sometimes only a small triumphal arch in the distance, or the illogical columns and arch in Ghirlandaio's "Adoration," in S. Trinità in Florence, remained as a vestige of the once space-limiting screen. Often more realistic structures, such as temples or buildings with several arched entrances, were substituted. In the north, when it survived the realism of the Flemish, it was compacted with the center pavilion into a conventionalized façade. As a backing for the Madonna portraits it remained for a long time, at least in part, in both southern and northern painting. But by the end of the fifteenth century, when the landscape views at one or both sides of the portrait were developed, it disintegrated, leaving now only a row of terrace columns beside the central seat, now only the platform at the bottom. By the time of Titian, all architecture, even the formal seat, had dissolved; and only a pattern of a portrait face against a cloth with a distant landscape at the side remained. Yet the theatre, as usual more formal and more conventional than other arts, kept the screen and the rows of arches long after painters had plunged into the spaceless, featureless atmosphere of the Baroque.

2. THE CENTER ACCENT: THE CENTER PAVILION

A central scenic element as a nucleus is one of the oldest means of organizing a scene. I have pointed out the use in early art of the emblematic scenic devices around which characters might be grouped. The drama of the medieval church depended almost entirely on the use of a central nucleus. Yet, from the time architectural background began in ancient art, there has been visible the tendency to use a more complex structure at the center of the scene. Because that central structure was elaborated in the late Middle Ages and became the model of the Dutch and Elizabethan stages, we must study some of its early forms and watch how it was developed and conventionalized in the later centuries.

The basic central form handed down from ancient art was the center pavilion, a structure often combined with the architectural screen, the tower, and other devices. Like the screen, it preserved its conventional and nonillusionistic character even in scenes which the artist was trying to make very realistic. Whereas the side house was made more and more realistic in the late Middle Ages, the center pavilion was not. If the artist had to make it resemble something in nature, he used it as a projecting portico in front of a tower or a regular façade, but he kept its open form.

One may note five or more different types of center pavilions, types which at times are distinct but again borrow from one another. The individual arch, used to mark a single figure or compact group of figures, is the simplest form and perhaps the oldest. It is quite frequent in Byzantine and Italo-Byzantine mosaics and was used for centuries in manuscript miniatures. Also very old is the tower. I have pointed out that it was used to separate scenes in a frieze (Fig. 5). Or, as the nucleus of a scene, it could frame a single figure or throne or surround a single arch con-

taining a person or scene. The third form—the open ciborium—was usually a round dome supported by columns. When the dome was elongated, the artist had a tower. The tomb, whether a simple ciborium or a tower with an arch and door, was so important throughout the Middle Ages that we may speak of it as a separate tradition. The fifth form—the temple—in early Christian art was often similar to the tomb. In the later Middle Ages it consisted most frequently of a hexagonal base and roof with four front columns defining three open arches (Fig. 12). The Renaissance borrowed both the hexagonal and the rectangular four-column ciborium type.

The ciborium over the altar, because of the importance of the tomb of Christ, was prominent in church ritual and in religious art. As the scenic element associated with the earliest religious drama, that of the Easter sepulcher, the ciborium may have been the model for later religious scenes. Hence it is important to know what it looked like. Two very good studies have been made of the traditions of the sepulcher in relation to medieval drama. Bonnell concluded that the Easter sepulcher was a separate structure in the church, related in form to the ciborium type of altar and to such canopied monuments as tombs and catafalques. It was, he believed, "characteristically a little structure comprising a canopy supported by pillars (usually four), and capable of being enclosed with curtains or rich hangings, within which was to be found a low altar-like table to hold the coffer or sarcophagus."[32] With naïve enthusiasm at having defined one type of pavilion, which undoubtedly was important in later art and drama, he jumped to the untenable conclusion that all religious stage structures followed this single pattern. N. C. Brooks followed him with a more thorough study, tracing the round dome and tower-like upper story of earlier centuries to the tradition of the sepulcher of Christ at Jerusalem as it was built

---

[32] Bonnell, "The Easter *Sepulchrum* in Its Relation to the Architecture of the High Altar," *PMLA*, XXXI, 712. The ciborium as central building in later Italian painting is studied by Jane Morrison, "The Central Building in Italian Painting."

and rebuilt by different emperors and copied by generations of artists.[33]

Since the center pavilion remained somewhat conventionalized and nonillusionistic even into the Renaissance, it is important to note some of the conventions it acquired in the earlier centuries. As a tower it might have a round dome like the sepulcher, or an open top with castellated walls. The open top was so similar to the conventionalized tilted walled city that a little city with many tiny roofs might be shown inside the top of the tower, and guards or defenders might look over the edge. Further, the arch or niche below might be made to resemble the gate of the city. Thus by the Carolingian period the center pavilion could represent a city with a large gate and walls and towers above—a very important convention for both later art and theatre.

The second story was also important. Sometimes the roof or the arch was simply decorated with the "town canopy" of little houses and towers so frequent from early Byzantine times to the fourteenth century.[34] Sometimes the side posts of the arch would project upward as little turrets, and the pavilion would resemble another form about which we shall have more to say— the door or inclosed space between two towers. The conventional painter of the early Byzantine and Carolingian periods often put secondary characters, such as the soldiers sleeping outside the tomb of Christ or the watching angels, into the upper corners of the picture. Later copyists frankly placed them on the roof, or on a gallery around the roof, or inside the upper windows. The

angels of the Nativity in Carolingian art sang from the walls or upper windows of the conventionalized walled city of Bethlehem. Hence the painters of the Romanesque and Gothic periods felt free to put onlookers, trumpeters, singing angels, or any other musicians or heavenly persons on a gallery at the top of any pavilion or tower- or city-like structure. When the pavilion was conventionalized into a façade, as of a castle front or of a garden close or other form, the upper gallery was kept for musicians, for city guards, for onlookers, or for allegorical or heavenly beings. Or, as we have seen, an upper niche or throne was used for a figure of honor.

The pavilion could be used for almost any scene. Thus for the Nativity, instead of the earlier rock cave or wooden hut, many fifteenth-century artists, both in Italy and in Flanders, used a conventionalized center pavilion of broken or ruined arches, with a gallery above for the heavenly choir or the star.

While the pavilion could serve as a complete background, it was often combined with the screen and with side houses to produce a complex design. The throne-pavilion of the Sultan is set against a screen in Giotto's painting of St. Francis (Fig. 11). The elaborate center pavilion in Gentile da Fabriano's "Presentation in the Temple" (Fig. 12) is combined with a back screen, which is developed on one side as a loggia, and with side houses. The open arches of the pavilion are doubled, just as arches in an arcade screen were, and some of the characters are shown inside the structure and some outside. The gallery above is clearly indicated, though no onlookers or musicians appear there.

3. THE COMPLEX FAÇADE AT THE CENTER: THE CASTLE AND OTHER FAÇADES

Much more important than the simple pavilion was the development of a complex structure at the center of the scene. In the Romanesque and Gothic periods that structure took the form of a conventionalized castle and acquired conventions which were very important for the theatre façades of Flanders and England.

---

[33] *The Sepulchre of Christ in Art and Liturgy*, pp. 84 ff. D'Ancona believed that most of the *luoghi deputati* used in Italian medieval drama to represent a region, a city, a palace, or a room had this open-baldacchino form (*Origini del teatro italiano*, I, 192). Miss Galante-Garrone sees no necessity for imagining structures above the actors (*L'Apparato scenico*, p. 31). It is perhaps significant that practically every one of the pageant wagons in the Louvain procession of 1594 had either a baldacchino or at least an architrave supported by columns (van Even, *L'Omgang de Louvain;* Kernodle, "The Medieval Pageant Wagons of Louvain," *Theatre Annual*, 1943).

[34] Cf. the towers and gables in the ciborium of the tomb of Boniface VIII in old St. Peter's (Venturi, *op. cit.*, IV, 161).

Fig. 10.—"Christ and St. Thomas." Fourteenth-century sculpture around the choir in Notre Dame de Paris. Side towers framing center space. Basic pattern for both Italian scenes, which made the center an exterior, and northern façades, which made the center an interior niche or inner stage. Alinari.

a

b

FIG. 11.—Two scenes from Giotto: "Death of St. Francis" and "St. Francis Walking through Fire." Fourteenth century. Outdoor screen with side accents, center pavilion as throne, curtain against screen as symbol of interior and as backing for a throne scene. S. Croce, Florence.

Among a number of variations can be traced one basic pattern for the center façade: a center archway or pavilion, flanked by side arches, porticos, or side towers. The central section was nearly always an interior, and the side panels were usually exteriors. Either the central panel or the side towers or both might be more than one story high, and a gallery above was quite frequent.

There were several patterns in the Hellenistic theatre for such a tradition. The central door of the theatre, the "Royal door," was larger and more important than the others and was flanked by two smaller doors. Further, each doorway was flanked by columns—often a pair on each side, forming a panel leading up to a pediment above. Between the columns were statues. Just such pairs of columns are frequent in Gothic art, not only beside arches but decorating the front standards of seats and thrones.

Whatever complex patterns were derived from the ancient theatre, they were combined in the Romanesque and Gothic periods with the pattern of the castle, which for several hundred years was the most important background device in art. This castle became the most frequent scene in the *tableaux vivants* and had a great influence on the Renaissance theatres. While it might be varied in several ways, it kept its basic pattern— a center panel, where an interior arch might be opened or at least a niche indicated, flanked by one or two side towers. The scene of the death of Edward, which I reproduce here from the Bayeux Tapestry (Fig. 8), indicates one of the simplest forms. Two castle towers with exterior doorways flank and frame an interior. Here the center panel has two stories and the upper story has that ancient symbol of an interior, the curtain.

The castle appeared very early in art. In reliefs from many different periods in Egypt, a castle is the scene of battle or serves as a framing motif beside a group of characters. Some castles in Egyptian art show three tiers or even five; some are combined with mountains or other scenic elements; and some serve as galleries for musicians.

Many times a castle is a symbol of a city. Indeed, in Egyptian writing the name of a city is regularly surrounded by a castellated circle. In representations of a sovereign visiting a city, the speech of welcome or submission is usually given from a miniature castle, much as it actually was in the fifteenth century in western Europe. This conventional tower or castle remained important in art even after the fortified castle ceased to be important in civic and court life.

Conventionalized castles were used as background by many ivory-carvers in the ninth and tenth centuries.[35] The Adoration scene might be in front of a castle, with separate towers backing the cloth-draped thrones of Herod and Mary. An Evangelist or a Saint would sit or write in a niche framed by one or two towers (Fig. 6). A curtain over the niche or draped anywhere in the composition tells us he is indoors. In a lunette above or in an upper story of the tower, his symbol or a heavenly being would be placed. Even the Nativity became a castle scene when the walls of the city of Bethlehem were so flattened that the city towers at the sides filled the height of the scene and the distant walls became a framing arch between the towers. Noah's Ark in the Caedmon manuscript of about A.D. 1000 was but a castle with two towers framing a three-story structure (Fig. 7).

Throughout the Gothic period the arch or screen or center pavilion, flanked by one or two castle towers, remained one of the most frequent types of background for any narrative scene. Often—perhaps by analogy with the side house, which had a portico or other doorway on only one side—the two towers were not the same size, and it might be that only one would have a doorway. Of course, the courtly romances and the literature of wars and fighting, whether representing Jerusalem, Troy, or Roncevalles, would call for scenes in and around castles and fortified city gates. But even for portraits and for allegorical scenes, where there was no particular appropriateness, the castle was a popular façade in art.

---

[35] Goldschmidt, *Die Elfenbeinskulpturen aus der Zeit der karolingischen und sächsischen Kaiser.*

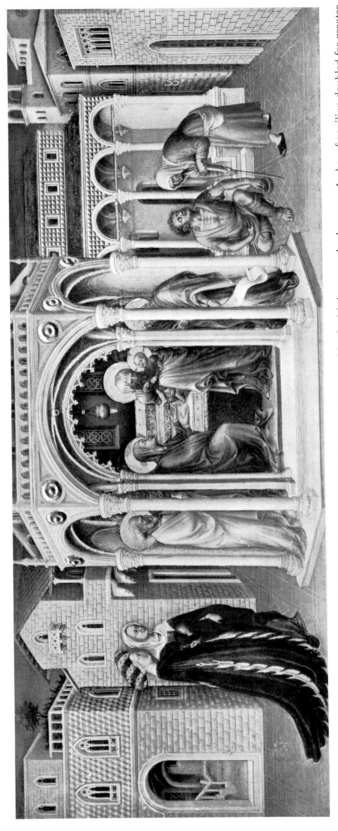

FIG. 12.—Gentile da Fabriano's "Presentation in the Temple" (1423). Center pavilion combined with houses as back screen. Arches of pavilion doubled for greater effect of depth. Gallery. Characters partly inside, partly outside. Louvre. Archives Photographiques.

Outside the flat arts it was no less common. Tombs were shaped like castles. Dishes for food, lanterns, thrones, chimney pots, and mantelpieces and a dozen different ornaments in earth, wood, or ironwork were made in the semblance of castles.

other scenic device, yet throughout the Middle Ages several other forms kept a similar pattern and brought down to the Renaissance a convention of a complex façade. Probably many of the free-standing thrones in early medieval drama

Fig. 13.—Konrad von Soest's "Coronation of the Virgin." Early fifteenth century. Tower-throne scene. Side wings, curtain backing, gallery for heavenly musicians. Cleveland Museum of Art.

The name "forecastle" for a structure on a ship reminds us of the wide use of the term, and the popularity of a castle in heraldry attests the acceptance of a conventionalized design of two towers flanking an arch.

Although the castle influenced nearly every

were of this type. In later Gothic art the throne was nearly always backed by either a castle or an arcade (Figs. 4, 5, 6, 11, 13, 17, 25, 31).

When side houses or doorways were added at the sides of the center panel, the pattern was established of an arch or gable joining two side elements. An interesting example is the four-teenth-century carved scene of Christ and St. Thomas in Notre Dame de Paris (Fig. 10). Here we can see how closely this tripartite pattern is related to both the Italian and the northern developments in the Renaissance. If the center is considered as an interior, then the design becomes a single structure with a complex façade of the type frequent in Flemish art and on the Flemish and English stages. If the center becomes an exterior, as it more often became in Italy, then the two side houses frame an open street scene which can be extended into depth by repeating the two side houses in rows.

In English art, several of the thirteenth-century bed scenes and other interiors in the glass of St. Thomas' Chapel in Canterbury Cathedral relate the characters to a three-arch screen. In several the center arch is developed as a special pavilion, and in a few cases it has a projecting pavilion of two columns and a canopy.[36] In the work of the popular artists in Italy in the fourteenth, fifteenth, and sixteenth centuries we find far more examples of a complex center façade than in the major works of the great artists. We have only to turn over the pages of Schubring's *Cassoni* to be impressed with the lack of originality of the painters of narrative scenes on marriage chests. For Dido's temple or Solomon's temple or Solomon's royal seat or the palace of King Ahasuerus, each artist played slight variations on the design of a center pavilion or center arched niche, regularly interior, with interior paintings or curtains or furniture, joined to side arches or arcades or buildings clearly exterior. In their different ways, Fra Angelico's perspective niche behind "St. Lawrence Giving Alms" and Antonello da Messina's curious interior of "St. Jerome's Study" are variations of the old convention of relating a center interior to flanking exterior elements. Many sixteenth-century windows by Flemish artists in the Cathedral at Brussels, in Westminster Abbey, and in King's College, Cambridge, show this same pattern.

The complex façade served especially well for bringing into one design a number of characters related to one another. The "Poor Man's Bible" made popular the interest in presenting next to a single scene the archetypes of that scene. At the sides of each incident of the life of Christ were grouped archetypes from the Old Testament.[37]

The façade with a heavenly throne likewise served to unite a number of characters into one design. From the Hellenistic period to the Renaissance the heavenly throne served to give unity to a complex structure. The Hellenistic theatre façade was dominated by the statue of Dionysus set high above the central door. Later Dionysus had to share the heavenly throne with Nero, and the façade became a pantheon of statues. Throughout the Middle Ages the Last Judgment was one of the most frequent and most impressive subjects in art. On the walls of the church or on the large altarpieces it made familiar a pattern of many characters set into an architectural structure of several stories dominated by the heavenly throne. The Doomsday plays carried it into the public streets. For several centuries the monumental tombs presented the Judgment Seat of Christ at the top of a structure that contained, on different levels, the sarcophagus with its effigy, the Mother and Child, and attendant Saints and Virtues. The pre-enactment of the resurrection of the effigy was made so dramatic that we must return in the next chapter to consider the tombs as dramas in stone (Figs. 20, 21, 22).

Less frequent than the castle but very similar in structure was the façade as church. The fronts of actual churches, such as, notably, in England, the west front of Wells Cathedral, gave the artist a model of several stories of figures leading up to a gable of the Divine, flanked by two towers—as, of course, that façade was following older models in art and architecture.

With the development of civic and royal processions on the Roman model—that is, from fairly early in the fifteenth century in Italy— the artist had another structure to use as a model for his façade: the triumphal arch. From the

---

[36] Especially the center medallion of the third row from the top of the second window of the north choir aisle, reproduced by Nelson, *Ancient Painted Glass in England*, Pl. LV; note also several in the east window of Becket's Crown (*ibid.*, Pl. VI).

[37] Kristeller, *Biblia pauperum*.

FIG. 14.—Mosaic of "Death of the Virgin" in St. Mark's, Venice. Begun by Giambono in early fifteenth century, finished by Castagno or Mantegna. Scene in front of arch; gallery; God sitting in a heavenly throne above the arch. Perspective street scene of several arches and houses back of the main arch. Anderson, Rome.

traditions of both medieval art and pageantry, the Renaissance triumphal arch, as we shall see, acquired the power of representing castle, city gate, city, nation, or even garden. But some

throne-of-honor at the keystone of the arch sits God the Father in a "Glory" (Fig. 14).

With the arrival of Renaissance architecture in the first third of the fifteenth century in Italy and

FIG. 15.—"St. Clare Repelling the Saracens." Late fifteenth-century Milanese. Conventional façade as symbol of a city. Façade decorated with columns, statues, and festoons. The Virgin and Saints in the gable. Miniature from the Sforza Book of Hours. Add. MS 34294, fol. 210b, British Museum.

artists used it frankly as an ornamental conventional background. The scene of the death of the Virgin in the mosaic of St. Mark's in Venice is placed in front of a beautiful triumphal arch with a castle gallery around the top. In the

nearly a century later in the north, the façade entered a new phase. While it was made on occasion to resemble some of the new church fronts, or doorways, or palace façades, it was not assimilated to any one architectural model but

Fig. 16.—Jan van Scorel's "The Last Supper." Conventional façade as framework for a scene. Museum, Brussels

42

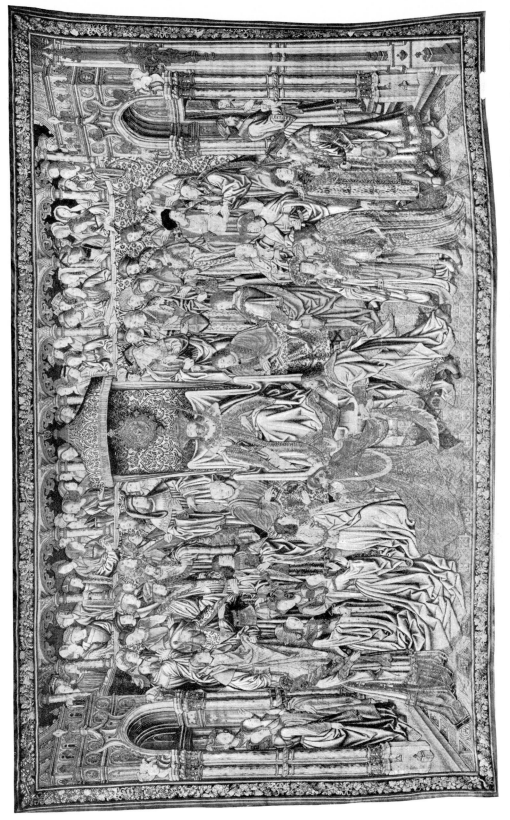

FIG. 17.—"David Receiving Bathsheba." Fifteenth-century Flemish tapestry. Arcade screen as backing for a throne scene. Gallery at top of screen. Curtains hung against screen and perspective floor pattern as symbols of interior, although side wings are exterior. Cluny Museum, Paris. Archives Photographiques.

became an independent form, a form especially adapted to frame or present narrative scenes or portraits. Painters and designers for tapestries still used it in the sixteenth century. Scorel, Barend van Orley, Blondeel, Coninxlo, and Gossaert, of the Flemish painters, made use of it. Scorel's "Last Supper," in the Brussels Musée d'Art Ancien, shows the supper scene as a small round plaque held up by two cherubs in front of an elaborate architectural façade with side columns and a pediment canopy (Fig. 16). Jan Mostaert's "Christ before Pilate," formerly in the collection of Sir John Ramsden,[38] shows how useful the composite façade could be in presenting successive scenes from a single story. Pilate sits on a slightly raised platform under a canopy supported by square, figured columns. Christ and his guard stand in front of one of the columns. Inside the canopy is a stage with two smaller scenes. At the side of the façade behind a rail is the "Ecce homo," and on a gallery above that, the scourging.

Far more frequently than in painting, the conventionalized façade appears on the engraved frontispieces of books. For centuries title-pages followed closely this art tradition, with side columns supporting an elaborate architrave and perhaps a second story. The columns outline one central open space for the title, and often also side panels where portrait statues or allegorical or illustrative figures may be placed. It is no accident that the framing arch on the sixteenth- and seventeenth-century stages was called a "frontispiece." Both book and stage design derive from a single tradition. Indeed, from the end of the fifteenth century the pageant and stage architects took the lead, and painters, engravers, and sculptors merely followed. The pleasing threefold pattern of a prominent central panel with a canopied gallery or upper panel and side arches or niches was used throughout Europe. When the flanking arches were prominent, it approached

the form of the arcade screen. But, in contrast to the open street at the center of the perspective scene, this formalized façade kept the basic pattern of the center accent.

Even in Italy, in the face of new opposite tendencies, the center accent remained of some importance. The painters of composite narrative scenes, especially, liked the conventional façade, though they often added side arches and even side wings. The painters of the *cassoni*, or marriage chests, and some prominent painters like the Botticelli were fond of such nonillusionistic backgrounds. We wonder if they may have been influenced by stage productions. We are sure the processions and street theatres had a strong influence on the charming and fanciful engravings for Francesco Colonna's *Hypnerotomachia Poliphili*, published in Venice in 1499 and copied with local variations in a Paris edition a few decades later.

But in Italy the center accent was soon reduced to a very subordinate position at the back of a deep street scene. A new force had appeared in art. A new science had been discovered which was so alluring that the conventionalized forms were quickly abandoned—abandoned before they could leave much impress on the budding theatre. A new technique enabled the artist to draw great space straight into his picture and paint a large number of realistic houses on a small canvas. The new courtly theatre adopted the new science, and in the course of a century it spread to northern countries to transform conventionalized architectural stages. The ideal of illusion gradually crowded out all more naïve conventions. That new technique, that new science of mathematics and illusion, was "perspective." And it is to that story we must now turn.

4. THE SIDE ACCENT: FROM SIDE HOUSE TO THE ITALIAN ILLUSIONISTIC PERSPECTIVE SCENE

If the center pavilion and the castle façade enabled the artist to emphasize the center of the scene, he used the side houses when he wanted a wider sweep with a large open space in the center. Even when he used a center structure, he

[38] Reproduced by Friedländer, *Die altniederländische Malerei*, Vol. X, Pl. VII; cf. further the "Ecce homo" of Strigel in the Germanisches Museum in Nuremberg, reproduced by Gregor, *Weltgeschichte des Theaters*, p. 163, and Borcherdt, *Das europäische Theater*, p. 8, Fig. 1.

often also used side accents to define his space and inclose the scene from the sides. In the later Middle Ages northern art was more fond of the center accent and a complex structure of buildings in the center. Italian art, on the other hand, preferred the open center.

To the realistically inclined medieval painter, the side house was the most useful form. Even if he opened it as a baldacchino to show what was happening within, it still resembled an actual building. For the Italian Renaissance painter it was the most important form: out of it he built his perspective street scene. While the open form of the house could easily be interpreted as a courtyard, the closed form definitely called for a street.

In ancient art the side house normally had a front parallel to the picture surface, and a side face which receded by oblique or converging lines toward the center of the picture, that is, as those lines would be seen at an eyepoint located opposite that center. It was the receding face which finally enabled the fifteenth-century Florentine painters to break away from the frieze forms, establish a single location for the eye, and develop the perspective scene.

In Byzantine and Carolingian art, when there was least interest in depth, this receding face, with its implication of a location for the eye, almost disappeared; or it was brought up to the same plane, parallel to the front, and in this case it did not matter on which side of the front face the side face was placed. Often it was mistakenly put on the outer side of the front face, away from the characters at the center of the scene. The eyepoint moved from setting to character, as along a frieze.

Perspective in any age has depended on the fixing of the eyepoint at one place and on the organization of the whole scene as one space unit. While the concept of a single picture as a unit has existed since earliest times, in many ages it has had to give way to the time demands of the frieze. In proportion as artists have given prominence to the single unit and have been able to organize architectural backgrounds, they have

developed perspective or some other convention of unity and reality.

Greek painters from a very early date were interested in methods of gaining depth and reality—methods which led them away from the level frieze form. Polygnotus tried a high view and put his figures on several rows of landscape. Apollodorus is said to have made important innovations in the development of perspective. But, it is interesting to note, the first real attack on the third dimension was made in the middle of the fifth century by the first stage painter, Agatharchus, that is, by the first person to deal with paintings that were primarily architectural. He employed perspective to gain the illusion of depth and is said by Vitruvius to have written a treatise on perspective which led Democritus and Anaxagoras to study the problem.[39]

By the Hellenistic period the laws of linear perspective were well understood; and, though not all vanishing lines were drawn to one point, yet the concept had become established that there should be a single eyepoint, opposite the center of the scene. The orientation of the lines of the scene to a single eyepoint was applied not only to small single scenes but also to such complex scenes as the three-panel form, already noticed, and to the elaborate framing architectural structures in the Pompeian and Boscoreale wall paintings. The central and side panels of the wall paintings might be flat scenes of human figures, or even flat decorative designs, but they were framed in a complex architectural screen of many columns, arches, and little roof projections. All the receding lines of this screen were carefully related to one eyepoint—an eyepoint determined by the height of a person standing on the floor and opposite the center of the central panel.[40] Only in the upper panels is there sometimes an inconsistency. In some paintings, although the upper lines come down steeply toward the main vanishing-point, yet upper floors have been drawn—floors which would not be

[39] Swindler, *Ancient Painting*, pp. 201 and 225; *Vitruvius*, p. 198; Friend, *op. cit.*, VII, 16; Bunim, *op. cit.*, pp. 22 ff.

[40] Swindler, *op. cit.*, pp. 327–29 and 367 f.

visible from the main eyepoint. This again may be an imitation of the appearance of the upper levels of the stage as seen from the higher seats in the auditorium.[41] There is little depth within the panels themselves. Perspective is the particular characteristic of the inclosing architectural background—the element most closely related to the theatre.

The perspective of Hellenistic art, following the flat form of the classic stage, is concerned with a single plane of depth. The architectural structures represented in most of the pictures could be built in a depth of ten or at most twenty feet. We find a complete confirmation of Spengler's interpretation of the difference between the classic mind and the Western mind: classic perspective is quite finite, while that of the Renaissance could be extended indefinitely by duplicating the diminishing motifs.

In imperial Rome, however, the sure perspective control of space established by Hellenistic artists began to wane, and in Byzantine and Carolingian art it almost disappeared. Realistic mathematical representation to give the illusion of actual people and actual space was replaced by a conventional presentation of conceptual relationships of people to one another and to the background. A large emperor would be encircled by small figures of his subjects, all on the surface of the painting or carving. The artist turned from the outer architecture of reality to the inner architecture of the mind. The exploration of space was given up, and the flat frieze form again dominated narrative art. Only the most conventional, ill-understood indications of depth were retained.

The flat centuries, however, did preserve several vestiges of the concept of a central location of the eye. The new perspective scene, first achieved in Florence in the fourteenth and fifteenth centuries, was not a free invention of the human mind. It was an organization on mathematical principles of just those vestiges handed down through the centuries. The motifs of the side accent—ceiling, floor, and receding face of

the side house—all separate elements in earlier painting, were combined in the Gothic period, especially in Italy, to form a unified scene shaped from four sides, with an open center space going to great depth straight into the picture.

The element that first showed perspective lines was the ceiling. A shallow coffered ceiling in front of the architectural screen or in an alcove dates from the fourth century B.C. and may be related to the stage. Often its beams had more than one vanishing-point, but for over two thousand years it preserved the concept of a central location of the eye. In the Gothic period, as we have noticed, it served as one convention of an interior. In the Italian perspective scene, which dealt primarily with exterior forms, it disappeared.

While a tiled floor with foreshortening had been used in early drawing in Asia Minor and Italy, it was not developed, curiously enough, in Hellenistic art. The small platform and the little group of steps at the sides were the only elements to receive perspective lines at the base of the scene. Only in the mosaics and paintings of the later Middle Ages did the foreshortened floor reappear. In the twelfth and thirteenth centuries it was quite frequent, though the vanishing-point or points might be quite low in the picture. In the north, as we have seen, it served as a convention of an interior. For the Italian perspective scene it was quite important. There remained but to organize all the floor lines to one point and bring that point up to the center of the picture—feats first accomplished, apparently, by Ambrogio Lorenzetti in his "Presentation of Christ in the Temple" of 1342, in the Uffizi, and his "Annunciation" of 1344, in the Accademia, Siena.[42] Both painters and scene designers of the Renaissance exercised their ingenuity in devising interesting and complex perspective floor patterns, patterns which derived far more from the imagination than from reality.

The most important element for later perspective was the receding face of the side house. Sometimes it was flat or was made to recede off

[41] Curtius, *Die Wandmalerei Pompejis*, p. 53.

[42] Panofsky, *op. cit.*, p. 279 and Pl. XIV; Bunim, *op. cit.* pp. 145 f.

the picture rather than toward the center. Yet through the ages the side house with a correctly receding face was never completely lost. Whether as a single house at the side of the scene or as two houses framing a scene, it carried on the convention that the eye was fixed at one place opposite the open exterior space.

Here, by the beginning of the fifteenth century, when the study of scientific perspective began, are all the elements of the perspective scene ready for synthesis and development. Here are architectural elements at top, bottom, and sides so designed as to leave the center open for the characters. The top is brought down toward a distant center, and a floor pattern with converging lines goes straight away from the eye into the distance, with lines parallel to the front measuring the distance unit by unit as it recedes. Here are two side houses with receding faces related to a central location of the eye. All are exterior forms, all put the architectural emphasis at the border of the picture, to define an open space at the center for the characters. Only two steps remained before the achievement of the full perspective scene. The first was to establish, by practice and by mathematical theory, the placement of the eye at one fixed central point for the entire picture. The other was to apply to the side house the principle of indefinite duplication of diminishing forms already worked out in the little extension scenes behind the arches of the back architectural screen.

The idea of a single vanishing point was more a conception of theorists in mathematics and optics than of the early painters themselves. Early comments on painting, such as those by Cennino Cennini, are not concerned with theoretical perspective. Much more discussion is to be found in the works on optics. Euclid furnished the foundations, but it was largely from the Arabian *Handbook* of Alhazen that the West received its theory. In the thirteenth century the theories were enlarged by Peckham and Vitellio.[43] There was considerable discussion of whether parallel lines should be carried to a single point; and Vitellio in the twenty-first theorem of the Fourth Book of his *Optics* argued against the one-point theory. Renaissance conceptions of mathematics, apparent in changing definitions of space, had to be established before there could be a basis for scientific perspective. Nicolaus Cusanus and Giordano Bruno, as Panofsky has pointed out,[44] came to define space as endless and geometric. Cusanus' statement that any point could be considered as a central point from which the rest might be considered marks the turn from a theological view to a more realistic view of the world and of space. This concept provides the foundation for the straight-line geometric perspective that underlay Renaissance art.

The Greeks, as may be seen in the well-known compensatory curves in columns and temples, recognized that the perception of space by the eye is actually in terms of curves, thus anticipating the views of such modern psychological investigators as Hauck, Jaensch, Peter, and Helmholtz. On the other hand, Renaissance perspective was based on a straight-line geometric system, with front faces parallel to the picture plane and receding faces aligned by a few straight perspective ground lines. Panofsky insists that only after space was conceived of as continuous, endless, and geometric was it possible for the artist to draw his space as entirely projecting into the depth of the picture.[45] It must be remembered that Hellenistic perspective, as shown in the Pompeian and other paintings and as described by Vitruvius, represented parts of the structure projecting out in front of, as well as behind, the plane of the screen. Modern perspective places the scenic structure all well behind the picture plane.

Once that central point was achieved, third-dimensional space for the picture became limitless. The architectural screen could be pushed back into the picture until it disappeared, leaving an open limitless street or landscape seen *through* space, as indicated at the sides of the picture by repeated similar forms. Once the

[43] Toesca, "Prospettiva," *Enciclopedia italiana*, XXVIII, 359 f.; Doehlemann, "Die Entwicklung der Perspektive in der altniederländischen Kunst," *Repertorium für Kunstwissenschaft*, XXXIV, 392–422 and 500–535.

[44] *Op. cit.*, pp. 304 ff.   [45] *Ibid.*, pp. 278 ff.

scientific method of directing lines was achieved, then as never before an illusion of the actual appearance of things was possible. Linear perspective was the structural, as aerial perspective was the impressionistic, means for attaining the two most important goals of Italian Renaissance art—depth and illusion.

While the four sides of the scene were occasionally brought to one center point by artists in the fourteenth century, it is in the second quarter of the fifteenth that the first examples occur of an application to the front scene of the indefinite

Vasari attributed the discovery of the use of a ground plan and intersecting lines to Brunelleschi. He considered perspective one of the prime achievements of the age and tells of the interest shown by Masolino, Uccello, Donatello, Andrea del Castagno, Piero della Francesca, Bramante, Raphael, and Lucas of Holland. His famous story of Paolo Uccello's obsession with the solution of problems of perspective might have been applied to almost any fifteenth-century Italian painter.

"He left [Vasari wrote] a wife who used to say that Paolo would remain in the night long in his

FIG. 18.—Neroccio's "Episode from the Legend of St. Benedict." Fifteenth century. Side houses doubled, with cornices of upstage house carrying perspective lines toward central vanishing-point. Open type of side house at right, more realistic type at left. Center pavilion. Uffizi, Florence.

duplication of diminishing forms. Masaccio in his "Resurrection of Tabitha and St. Peter Curing the Cripple" in the Carmine Church at Florence had dared draw three successive arches in the perspective face of a side house. A decade later, in 1435, Masolino da Panicale, in painting the "Banquet of Herod" in the Baptistery at Castiglion d'Olona, put so many arches into the side house that he achieved the effect of indefinite duplication into the distance.[46] After the middle of the century, arches, columns, and whole houses were multiplied.

The pages of Vasari's *Lives of the Painters* are filled with the excitement of the new technique.

[46] Reymond, "L'Architecture des peintres aux premières années de la renaissance," *Revue de l'art ancien et moderne*, XVII, 42.

study to work out the lines of his perspective and that when she called him to come to rest, he replied, 'Oh, what a sweet thing this perspective is.'"

What a sweet thing indeed! Luca Pacioli wanted to put it in the Quadrivium for all university students to study.

The first theorist to write on the new art was Leone Battista Alberti, whose *Della pittura libri tre* was finished in Latin in 1435 and in Italian in 1436. His account grew out of the discussions of the group of artists, led by Brunelleschi, who were interested in architectural forms and the handling of space. In that group were Donatello, Lorenzo Ghiberti, Luca della Robbia, and Masaccio. Alberti, who had been a student of mathematics, emphasized the importance of geometry for the painter. Realism was the main object of all method, and a fixed eyepoint was absolutely essential. He first stated the important Renaissance concept of the picture plane as a section cutting the pyramid of lines from eye to object.

His treatise was followed, about 1482, by the *De prospectiva pingendi* of Piero della Francesca. The first work to be published was brought out in French in 1505 by Jean Pélerin, who called himself Viator. But it is in the *Notebooks* of Leonardo da Vinci, which circulated widely in manuscript, that we find the fullest expression of the early Renaissance concepts of perspective. He based his conclusions on the geometrical concept of the pyramid of lines and stated clearly the law that the more distant objects will appear smaller. Also clearly developed in the *Notebooks* is the idea of control of space by the repetition of diminishing objects placed one behind the other at regular intervals in depth—the theoretical basis of the stage wing.[47]

Even more distinctly new in the Renaissance was the development of aerial perspective, the painter's own method of giving the illusion of distance by the use of color and intensity. The ancients had learned to show a more distant plane of depth by the paleness of the color. In several Pompeian paintings a more distant, paler structure is seen inside the main screen. But there is little gradation of tone.[48] The gradual fading of a tone through many degrees is the achievement of an art that seeks great limitless distance carried straight into the picture depth by many separate architectural elements— the perspective art of the Renaissance.

Aerial perspective was well understood by fifteenth-century painters and theorists. Alberti spoke of it, and Masaccio was praised by Vasari for his mastery of it. But an age as fond of architectural structure and geometrical exactness as fifteenth-century Florence would not find extensive use for it. It remained for the Baroque painters to dissolve Florentine clarity into studio brown and the blue haze of the atmosphere.

In the Leonardo *Notebooks* we do find great interest in aerial perspective. What is important for the wing structure of the perspective stage, we find the principle that more distant objects lose their effect of thickness, while those nearer must be represented in three dimensions.[49]

Here, then, in the latter part of the fifteenth century, well before the perspective stage took it over, was developed in both theory and practice a type of scene with a background of rows of architectural forms organized by the art of perspective to give the illusion of limitless depth. The scene was an open street with very strong perspective lines vanishing to one point near the center of the picture. That meant that, although the front faces were placed parallel to the picture plane, every side of a structure going into the distance was drawn as it would appear from one eyepoint opposite the vanishing-point, at a manageable finite distance in front of the picture plane.

To give that effect of great distance we have seen how the space was shaped by the four sides of the picture from the picture plane (or near it) to great distance in the center. The top, the bottom, and the sides were given separate characteristic treatment. At the top was the sky, where, of course, the only straight lines that could be drawn were roof lines. When the tops of the first side houses were shown, there might be a narrow strip of sky above them; then over the smaller, more distant structures toward the center the sky would be seen down near the vanishing-point.

At each side was a row of houses diminishing sharply toward the vanishing-point. Two faces of each house were drawn: a front face parallel to the picture plane and a receding face toward the center of the scene. The roof line of the receding face slanted down toward the vanishing-point, and the base line slanted upward; the rows of houses, following the perspective lines of the floor, seemed to come closer together at the back.

There were two kinds of side houses: a realistic solid type and an open type, either with large arches or sometimes with no walls at all but only

[47] *Notebooks*, pp. 211 f.   [48] Curtius, *op. cit.*, p. 179.   [49] *Notebooks*, pp. 213 and 218 f.

columns that outlined the structure and supported a roof or a solid miniature upper story.
By means of the loggia-like open form, interior
scenes could be presented within the structure of
a building.

Although each house had sharply converging
lines which made it appear quite deep, the most
effective device for depth was the multiplication
of diminishing forms.[50] Back of one side house
was placed a second, smaller than the first, its
receding face carrying further into the depth the
perspective lines of the first. Often the receding
face of the second was set on the same floor lines
as the first. Usually a space, as for a side street,
was left between one house and the next.

The essential character of the inclosing perspective scene called for the center to remain
open, even into great depth. At the back of the
scene, however, often appeared one of the other
two architectural forms. A temple or triumphal
arch or other variation of the center pavilion was
popular. Or a complex façade, made somewhat
realistic with arches or niches or perhaps a
portico, might be used. In many perspective
scenes the back architectural screen was preserved. Behind its arches, as in earlier Gothic
painting, little landscapes, or even complete
miniature street scenes, might carry the eye on
to further depths, "fit," in the words of the stage
architect, Sabbatini, "for a battle of flies."

The concept of the picture plane usually implied some framing element at the front. The
scenic background might begin almost at the
picture plane, or the frame might represent a
"window onto space" with everything placed
some little distance back. The floor element
usually began near the picture plane, sometimes
with the effect that it came forward beyond the
plane of the other elements. That is, artists were
not sure just where to place the abstract picture
plane in relation to the space they represented.

The characters of the event were usually placed
rather near the front, in the open street. If there
was a space in front of the front houses, some of

the characters might be there. For more specifically interior scenes, characters would be put in open
side houses or in the loggias or colonnades; but
there was no sharp separation of interior and exterior—the painter was dealing primarily with
exterior forms.

As we have seen, not only was the technique
of linear perspective carefully worked out, but
the effects of aerial perspective were studied and
applied to give the impression of distance to
those parts of the setting at the back; in particular,
colors and outlines were softened and objects were
drawn without thickness—a side house, for instance, without a receding face.

The fifteenth-century painter was very eager
to give the impression of reality—to create the
illusion of great space. His side houses were made
more real than those of earlier painters; his
doors and windows were given realistic proportions and details; his columns, balconies, roofs,
and decorative details were drawn in the style of
architecture of the day. The impression of an
actual street of Italy was created in his picture.
Yet, when we speak of the close approach to
reality made by the painters, we must remember
that there is no question of photographic reproduction of complete actual houses as they
were lived in. A façade with one or two windows
was made to give the impression of an actual
house, and many of those painted were conventionalized structures not actually possible. The
artist was dealing with conventional, formal
architectural elements: columns, arches, baldacchinos, miniature side houses, temples, and open
pavilions. His ideal of reality called for a correct
impression of actual thickness and space in
elements which were often highly conventional
in form. Again, many street scenes were painted
with little thought of particular appropriateness
to the story enacted. The same type of stately
formal architectural background might be placed
behind the characters of any episode from the
Bible or from popular romance, if the event did
not specifically require a meadow or forest. The
illusion was one of depth and the accurate painting of three-dimensional architectural structures

[50] Cf. the duplication of outlines of arches discussed above,
pp. 30 f., and in chaps. vi and vii.

rather than one of appropriate locale. Even when recognizable places were painted, the details were highly conventionalized, if judged by the standards of later centuries. Yet realism and illusion were prime objectives of the Renaissance painters, and the convention of an open street scene organized by perspective enabled them to represent space and depth with an illusion of reality that had not been possible before.

That brings us to the sixteenth century, the century that saw the birth in every country of western Europe of new architectural forms of the theatre. We have analyzed the organization of space in painting by three different elements of architectural background. We have watched in the Middle Ages the disintegration of the flat form of arcade screen that had been the form of the classic theatre. We have seen how two other complex conventions were developed, differing from each other as they emphasized the center structure or the side accents. We have finished our story of painting in the flat. Now we must see, first, how these traditional forms were developed in three dimensions in sculpture and in the *tableaux vivants*, then what happened when the different theatre forms emerged.

CHAPTER II

SHOW-PICTURE AND SHOW-ARCHITECTURE

The "Tableaux vivants"

OF THE many new theatres of the sixteenth century, one only—the Italian perspective stage—stemmed directly from painting; and one only—the Paris Hôtel de Bourgogne—was derived directly from the medieval religious stages. All the rest owe their forms and conventions to the traditions of the visual arts by way of the street theatres. The Flemish and Elizabethan stage façades can be traced directly to the street *tableaux vivants* built for royal entries. Many of the effects on the Spanish stage follow the patterns of the *tableaux vivants*, and even the perspective stage in many details shows their influence.

That the *tableaux vivants* have been so grossly neglected by historians is probably due to the fact that they are halfway between painting and drama. Art historians have neglected them because for the most part they followed outmoded conventions of painting. Drama historians mention a few as examples of the love of spectacle, but they have not found the addresses and dialogues of much literary interest. Withington gives a sampling of quaint items from the English pageants but, like the others, has failed to realize that the stationary pageants established patterns and conventions which were important for the public theatres. In them the rich lore of romantic examples and allegorical concepts was dramatized for a wide public long before the new theatres appeared.

The *tableaux vivants* were born of the desire to make visual art more active—to make it breathe and speak with living actors. Not satisfied with the contemplative narrative art of painting,

stained glass, tapestry, or carved panel, artists created showpieces—show-pictures and show-architecture—for a more positive ritualistic or festival purpose. They gave dramatic form to tombs, altars, and shrines—stone showpieces built to last forever. They placed lay figures or living actors in the street tableaux, which would be taken down after the festival. Some of the street theatres, filled with living actors, were visible only a few minutes as the entering king paused on his triumphal way. For that moment a historical picture or an allegorical group impressed him with the ancient glory of the city, with its genuine loyalty, and with its hopes for the future clemency, as well as the future glory, of the ruler.

Although music and speeches were often added to the showpieces, they remained closely bound to the traditions of medieval and early Renaissance art which we have been tracing. Hence they must be examined with constant reference to painting and sculpture. We find in the street theatres not only the same patterns of organizing characters and background that we found in painting but, in even more splendid form, the same emblematic scenic devices that were traditional in all narrative arts. Showpieces, built by the hundreds in the fourteenth, fifteenth, and sixteenth centuries, can tell us, even better than painting and tapestry, what meanings were associated with these units of background—the mountains, thrones, pavilions, castles, arcades, triumphal arches, and façades. To understand the Renaissance theatres we must know the meanings of each unit, as well as the principles of organization. And to understand the changing patterns of the living tableaux, we must first examine the most purely architectural examples of the show-piece—the altar and the tomb. In altar and tomb the sculptor took one step beyond the painter by presenting in three-dimensional figures a dramatic ritual, a ritual that is held unfinished until Judgment Day.

I. ALTAR AND TOMB AS SHOWPIECES

In their form, as in the subject matter of their figures, both medieval altars and tombs must be regarded as "show-architecture"; that is, they are forms devised to present, organized in a structural unit, the figures of a single event. As the altar was a symbol of sacrifice, its reredos must present the scenes and figures associated either with some martyrdom or with the Crucifixion. The medieval tomb was a confident invocation of the Last Judgment, a little drama in eternity— a ritual in stone of the call of the angel on the day of glory, when the dead man will arise and look into the welcoming faces of the Madonna and Child under the eyes of the Father sitting as judge. In the Renaissance, classical and allegorical characters joined the structure, to bear witness through eternity to the good qualities of the dead man.

By the sixteenth century, sculptors had solved well the problem of organizing those characters into a compact architectural structure. Their final solution was a rather flat façade of columns framing one or three panels on a first level and supporting one or two superior levels for heavenly figures under some kind of canopy. In simple architectural form this kind of tomb established a pattern which was followed by the more complex street stages and by several of the Renaissance theatres. We can learn much about the tendencies of the street tableaux if we examine the steps by which sculptors achieved the Renaissance façade.

The early ciborium over altar and tomb has already been discussed as a model for the center pavilion in painting. It was derived principally from imitation of the sepulcher of Christ at Jerusalem. It was applied to altars as well as to tombs, because, of course, an altar is an image of a tomb and was usually built over the tomb or some relic of a martyr. The altar at St. Peter's in Rome is built over the tomb of St. Peter, and we see the early type of ciborium, a canopy supported by four columns, over that altar to this day. As I have already pointed out, this pavilion or open-ciborium form was quite important in later medieval painting and in the religious drama.

More important for later theatres, however, were the altar reredos and the corresponding backing that was developed for tombs. This backing first appeared in the eighth and ninth centuries with the spread of the cult of relics. When relics were placed in reliquaries on the altar or in the sarcophagus underneath, the altar became also a shrine and was given a backing to support carved or painted scenes related to the martyr. Sometimes the altar was then moved to the wall, and a flatter canopy without supporting columns was suspended against the wall; but more often a space was left at the back for pilgrims to pray at the shrine. Then the reredos became a free-standing structure that seemed to rest on the back edge of the altar.[1]

In the Gothic period this reredos was ornamented with a number of small scenes of religious incidents. Sometimes small paintings were divided between a central panel and two side panels that folded over to close the shrine. Sometimes all three panels were organized into a compact façade, crowned at the top by a panel of the Virgin, the Father on his throne, or the Trinity in Glory (Figs. 19, 23).

In some few places the reredos borrowed from the form of the arcade screen for the main altar; and, as we shall see, the rood screen was often a backing for a secondary altar for parish Masses. At Tarragona Cathedral in Spain an arcade screen supported the Gothic reredos, with side doors leading to the chapel of the Blessed Sacrament behind. At Saragossa the pattern was kept, but niches with statues were substituted for the

[1] Bishop, *On the History of the Christian Altar*, pp 12 ff.

FIG. 19.—French stone altar of the Resurrection. Early sixteenth century. Three panels. Combination of medieval scenic details with the formal architecture of the façade. Heaven at the top. God on the heavenly throne surrounded by a choir of angels. Louvre. Archives Photographiques.

54

FIG. 20.—Tomb of Roberto il Savio. Fourteenth century (1343–45). Four levels above the sarcophagus. Resurrection of the effigy. The king on a throne in a curtained pavilion. Madonna and Saints. God the Judge in the gable. S. Chiara, Naples. Alinari.

55

side doors. A similar reredos was built for the Mayor's Chapel at Bristol, England. Three panels of the screen were divided by towers with a niche and canopy. In the center was a painting, and in

levels, with heavenly characters on an upper stage. In fact, the tomb backing was, so to speak, a sculptural pre-enactment of Judgment Day. It had as one model the Easter sepulcher, which

FIG. 21.—Tomb of Cardinal Rinaldo Brancaccio. Fifteenth century. Angel of the Resurrection waking the effigy. Madonna and Saints. God leaning out of the gable. Trumpeting angels on the roof. S. Angelo a Nilo, Naples. Alinari.

the side panels were doorways.[2] Gothic tombs were developed on similar lines. They, too, were moved against the wall, and the superstructure was flattened into a backing. Like the altar and like so many pavilions and towers in painting, the tomb backing often had several different

figured prominently in Easter ceremonies. Quite dramatic must have seemed the new gilt sepulcher delivered to the Church of St. Mary Redcliffe in 1470, which had a "heaven made of timber and stained cloth . . . . the holy Ghost coming out of heaven into the sepulcher."[3]

[2] Bond, *The Chancel of English Churches*, p. 61.

[3] Park, *Nugae antiquae*, I, 12 f.

Sepulchers and tombs, like practically all medieval structures that figured in religious ceremonies, were decorated with flags, pennons, shields, and, on occasion, lighted tapers.

tomb of Roberto il Savio in S. Chiara in Naples (Fig. 20) is a Gothic structure dating from 1343. The outer framework is a somewhat flattened form of the four-column gabled ciborium. Within the

FIG. 22.—Tomb of Cardinal Ascanio Sforza. Sixteenth century. Flattened façade. Three panels. Allegorical figures. Emblematic decorations. The figure of God free-standing on the top. S. Maria del Popolo, Rome. Alinari.

The principal change from Gothic tomb to Renaissance façade was in the flattening and simplifying of the architectural backing—the same change that practically all the showpieces underwent. We can watch that change by comparing three Italian tombs of the fourteenth, fifteenth, and sixteenth centuries (Figs. 20, 21, 22). The

inclosing shell is a separate four-story structure built against the wall. The lowest story is the actual tomb. Next above is the effigy, represented as in an interior, angels pulling a curtain aside and mourners standing behind against a tapestried wall. Above that, within a columned ciborium, sits a regal figure on a throne. Cur-

than those of Bruges and were first to receive the themes and other influences of the Italian Renaissance. But so close was the resemblance from one city to another that we are able to treat the *tableaux vivants* as one subject.

This unity of the street theatres is not surprising when we consider that the courts were in close contact with one another and that the street shows were the prize exhibits when a court group went from one country to another. From the Norman Conquest on, the English court kept close touch with Paris. Most English kings before Edward IV married French princesses; in fact, Edward III and Richard II in the fourteenth century were the first kings whose wives were not French. Richard II's second wife was French, and in the fifteenth century Henry IV, Henry V, and Henry VI all went to France for queens. Both Henry V and Henry VI had triumphal entries into Paris, Henry V as the son-in-law of the French king, young Henry VI as King of France himself. Then in 1514 Louis XII married the sister of the English king, and many Englishmen were in Paris for the triumphal entry.

Between Flanders and France there were the very closest of ties. A French prince, the Duke of Burgundy, in the fourteenth century married the heiress of Flanders, and his house soon acquired the other provinces of the Low Countries. When the French crown regained rebellious Burgundy in 1477, the Low Countries came under the Emperors Maximilian and Charles V, and were then in close touch with Austria, Italy, and Spain.

The trade relations between England and Flanders had been extensive for centuries and, with the development of the wool trade under the Plantagenets, became of even greater importance. Edward III married Philippa of Hainault and was frequently in the Low Countries with armies or diplomats. In the fifteenth century the English joined with the Burgundian dukes in many intrigues against France, and the combined English and Burgundian forces were able to put Henry VI on the French throne. In 1468 Charles the Bold married Margaret of York, sister of Edward IV, and many English saw the street-shows put

on in Bruges for her arrival. The Emperor Charles V was entertained with tableaux in London in both 1520 and 1522. Many English and Scottish nobles commissioned works of art from Flemish artists, and in the sixteenth century so many Flemish workers in stained glass had crossed to England under the employ of Henry VII, Wolsey, and others that there were bitter disputes with English workers.[8]

Froissart tells us that the entertainments for Richard II in 1390 were copied after the Paris shows of the year before for the entry of Isabel of Bavaria. The Paris and the London tableaux for the entries of Henry VI are scarcely to be distinguished. When Philip II entered London in 1554 as the husband of Mary, he found fewer Renaissance architectural structures than were built for him in Antwerp in 1549, but many of the same stories and allegorical devices. The principal motifs and forms were common property in all countries; hence, while I shall point out some of the local divergences from one town to another, I shall treat the whole subject as one.

The shows for the royal entry were an expression of the wealth and generosity of the city. Except for those built by special guilds and the corporations of foreign merchants, they were planned and paid for by the city. Preparations were often begun six to ten months before the arrival was expected. First, the city officials had to decide on the histories and allegorical devices to be presented. Often the members of the Chambers of Rhetoric were called in for ideas, and prizes were offered for the best shows. In Paris some tableaux were devised by the Basoche, the festive club of parliament law clerks, which usually devoted itself to farces. The city of Mons in 1515, when it learned that Charles V would visit it after visiting most of the other cities of the Provinces, sent a commission to watch what was done in Brussels, Malines, Louvain, Antwerp, and Bruges. The commission consulted with historians and brought back *histoires par escript* for

---

[8] Borenius and Tristram, *English Medieval Painting*, pp. 42 f.; Knowles, "Disputes between English and Foreign Glass-Painters in the Sixteenth Century," *Antiquaries' Journal*, V, 148–57.

their own spectacles. For some of the devices they ordered sketches in Brussels, and they hired members of the Chamber of Rhetoric to write all the speeches.[9]

For the elaborate shows at Bruges in 1515, those in charge gathered months beforehand at the Blind Ass Tavern to make their plans and charged their drinks to the city. They paid a goodly sum to Willem d'Hollande for his sketches for the stages and hired one person to take charge of each show and two persons to act as daily superintendents to see that all the building and painting was progressing according to schedule. Again, just before the great day, the Blind Ass was the scene of last-minute planning and the writing of mottoes and inscriptions.

At Lyons in 1548 some work began about six months before Henry II and Catherine were expected. One man, Sève, was responsible for planning all the tableaux and triumphs, and another, Bernard Salomon, made the designs and superintended the painting. Then each tableau was put in charge of one man, who was given all the carpenters and painters he needed. The stages were to be ready fifteen days before the event so that a different group might arrange the characters, the silk costumes, the hangings, properties, and so on.

Many kinds of artisans were required to prepare for an entry. Most structures were built of wood, which was covered with cloth and painted. Wood-carvers were often hired for the sculptural and decorative detail. Sometimes leadworkers and glassworkers were needed as well. The Antwerp reception of Philip II in 1549 required 895 carpenters, 234 painters, 16 wood-carvers, and about 500 other workers over a period of several months.

For that same occasion, 137 actors were used in the shows the city built, without counting those of the foreign merchants. Far fewer actors had sufficed in Bruges in 1515, for the prince's party had moved so slowly that some of the actors were able to be in more than one tableau. In fact, three actors appeared in as many as three shows each, and several actors were in both of the last two. Throughout the period women took women's roles, in sharp contrast to the use of boy actors in the religious drama. Actors were clothed in fine taffeta and other silk cloths.

Just as nearly every artist in Italy was hired at some time for the church dramas and *sacre rappresentazioni*, so in France, the Low Countries, and England many of the best writers and artists—Lydgate, Ben Jonson, Middleton, Gringoire, Fouquet, Holbein, van der Goes, van Mander, and Rubens among them—were hired to prepare street theatres.[10]

The peculiar character of the royal procession determined the distinct form of these street-shows. They differed sharply, on the one hand, from the regular religious plays that were performed on platforms and, on the other hand, from the pageant wagons that were moved in procession from street to street in many cities of the Low Countries and England. From those forms, however, they borrowed some elements.

The early street-shows inevitably had some contact with the regular religious plays, since they dealt with the same subjects. We read that actual religious drama was performed on the street for royal entries in Paris in 1422 and in Coventry in 1456 and 1461. But these were exceptions. Already in 1313, when the king of England, Edward II, and his French wife, Isabel, were entertained in Paris, the religious scenes were performed in silent pantomime. A different audience occasion required a different kind of show. Although the Confrérie de la Passion built a number of street theatres in front of their hall in Paris, they did not use their regular plays or scenery. Their shows were planned by the same authors who were in charge of all the other spectacles.

Especially in Italy, the royal procession took on some of the features of the religious processions. Officials and musicians, dressed in festive regalia,

[9] Accounts quoted by Gachard, *op. cit.* References to the individual royal entries will be found in the chapter bibliography, arranged by country and date.

[10] Kernodle, "Renaissance Artists in the Service of the People," *Art Bulletin*, XXV, 59–64.

marched out to meet the royal party. A triumphal procession was formed which included groups dressed as people of various countries, ancient and modern, or as allegorical characters. Along the streets moved great triumphal chariots, or pageant floats, built as castle, temple, or mountain. The populace was the audience, just as it was for the religious processions. The king was only the climax of the show, a show designed to impress the people with the grandeur of their ruler and to celebrate their joy in their good fortune. The themes and pageants of the Roman triumphs were rifled for the new Caesars—the Medici, Sforza, and Este princes.[11]

In northern Europe the royal procession kept some aspects of the triumphal parade. City officials and musicians met the prince and marched back with him. Often a special group, perhaps maidens with flowers or with torches, led the march. As the Italian influence increased in the sixteenth century, the marching pageant might be made more important.[12] The entry of Henry II and Catherine de Medici into Rouen in 1550 was a combination of Italian triumph and French entry. Outside the city the king stopped and reviewed a great procession of pageant wagons, chariots, and marching characters. That procession, with the king following, then marched into the city and passed by the various *tableaux vivants* erected in the streets. Some tableaux were not opened until their special audience, the king, arrived before them. While the street theatres were designed for the royal audience, the procession, including the king, provided a show for the whole people. Most of the early pageants for Lord Mayor's Day in London were devices carried in the procession, but from the middle of the sixteenth century the one or more stationary theatres built to welcome the mayor were given the greatest prominence.

Normally, in northern countries, the processional element was incidental. The one audience was the noble visitor—a moving audience that advanced from outer gate to city hall or palace. Often a stranger or rare visitor, he must be taken along streets decorated with cloths, tapestries, and special paintings to see the most important fountains, buildings, and squares. As he approached each new place, music from a special gallery or scenic device, or perhaps hidden, must welcome him. Addresses and allegorical shows must impress on him the loyalty of the subjects, their special compliments, and at times their needs. Hence both the dramatic conventions and the scenic forms of the *tableaux vivants* were determined by their origin as street decoration; they were never drama. They were showpieces, looking like picture or architectural structure or heraldic device—showpieces that by means of living actors were able to move, to speak, or to sing; showpieces that took their places beside the tapestries, the painted "histories," and the ornamented gates and fountains as part of the decorations for a festival.

The relation between art and festival is very old and in some places persists to the present day. Paintings, statues, and monuments were important in ceremonies and celebrations long before living characters were added. In the earlier centuries of the Christianization of western Europe, the church authorities took over and gave a Christian interpretation to the old pagan ceremonies at fountains, wells, and tombs and also to the old customs of carrying sacred objects around the villages and fields at particular seasons. Within the church ritual itself, at the different seasons of the church calendar, those objects, carvings, and paintings associated with the event to be commemorated were put in important positions, given special decoration and lighting, and made the center of ritual, music, adoration, and prayer. From such use of art in ritual, the *tableaux vivants* derived the pattern of disclosing a picture or statue with music, ceremony, and the removal of a cover. From ritual and art, also, was taken over the custom of using torches and other lights around a picture and some of the conventions of adding information not in the picture by means of title-boards, in-

[11] Burckhardt, *The Civilisation of the Renaissance in Italy*, pp. 418 ff.

[12] Chartrou, *Les Entrées solennelles*, pp. 53 ff.

scriptions, mottoes, and a prologue-presenter who spoke to the audience and explained the show.

In the development from picture to spoken drama a number of steps can be outlined logically and to a certain extent historically. The simpler conventions, however, did not disappear when more dramatic methods were introduced; and in the sixteenth century all forms, from the simplest to the most complex, might be found side by side on the same occasion.

The simplest elements of speech already existed in painting before anyone thought of using living actors. In Egyptian and many other primitive types of writing the picture and the word are inextricably mixed. Although alphabets were in time developed far beyond the pictograph, until they contained no element of the picture, the picture never completely lost the printed word. In the border, or in any blank space, might be a short title or a long inscription explaining the contents of the picture or the circumstances of its creation. In imitation of actual buildings, where column or cornice might bear words, the architectural background in a picture was a place where the artist might add, by language, information he could not give through his characters alone. Names of characters and even bits of dialogue were written above and around the heads on a number of Greek vases. In Byzantine art such inscriptions were usually inclosed in little compartments in the background or border, and speeches and mottoes were placed in banderoles next to the characters or in their hands. The Byzantine *Guide to Painting*,[13] which summarized centuries of traditional practice, gave appropriate mottoes and speeches for every character and scene a painter was supposed to use. Many medieval sculptors followed the convention and carved a roll on which an inscription was written for each character to hold in his hand. The street theatres could imitate such practices directly, and inscriptions on the architectural structure (Figs. 26, 29, 31, 32, 38) or silent, motionless figures with banderoles in their hands persisted into the seventeenth century.

[13] Didron, *Christian Iconography*, Vol. II, Appen.

Lay figures, life-sized, painted and dressed in regular costumes, served for some of the tableaux, while others had living actors. In many of the accounts it is difficult to decide which are living actors and which colored figures: the two might even be mixed in the same show. There was apparently no difference in treatment, except where sculptural figures might adorn a canopy or proscenium next to the living actors of the main scene. There was an added attraction in seeing living actors, even if they did not move or speak. Such observers as Calvete de Estrella were impressed both by the lifelike quality of the lay figures and by the ability of actors to hold positions without moving an eyelash.

It was a simple step to add movement. Silent pantomime was used in hundreds of the *tableaux vivants* and made, as we shall see, important contributions to the regular Renaissance theatres, especially to the "dumb shows" of Flanders and England. As a picture which moved in pantomime, the tableau could present narrative incidents and yet remain within the silent convention of art. This was one way of breaking the time limitations of a space art. Even dialogue and explanation could be added by means of the traditional rolls and inscriptions, either within the picture or on the frontispiece. To fit into the moving time scheme of narrative, such a roll, which is permanent and timeless, must be kept hidden and revealed at the right moment. Some odd results might follow if the narrative moved fast. In 1458, when Peter tried to walk on the water of a Ghent river to his Lord, who was secure on an artificial island, he sank into the water to his neck and seemed likely to sink deeper. At that moment he thrust out of the water a paper roll reading, in Latin, "Lord, save me!" The Lord replied by opening his roll with the answer, printed likewise in Latin. An angel suspended from a bridge closed the incident by letting down a tent-canopy over the Master, leaving Peter, we suppose, to scramble out as best he could.

The simplest form of speech in the *tableaux vivants* was the direct address to the prince by a character in front of a picture or a scenic device.

The address of welcome in early times would be made at the city gate, which would serve as a symbol of the city. Later, other elaborate symbols were built: a triumphal arch, a coat-of-arms, or some other striking device. Emblems or allegorical characters might adorn the device, and the "expositor," dressed as the city or the founder or special hero, would point out and explain the device and decorations as a part of the ritual of welcome. Usually, of course, the device contained living figures, either still or moving in pantomine; and here we see the beginning of the convention that a "prologue-expositor" might reveal and explain the tableau or play while making a direct address.

The convention of pantomime action behind an expositor may have been reinforced at times, as Herrmann thinks, by medieval interpretations of the ancient theatre.[14] It seems to me we do not have to go further than the *tableaux vivants* themselves for an explanation. The main purpose of using living characters was to catch the attention and interest of the prince. The "expositor" was already known in the church drama. In the early play of the Prophets, he called forth each Prophet, described him, and presented him to the audience to give his prediction of Christ.[15]

The "presenter" or expositor was often dressed as a particular character and sometimes had a separate stage. The elaborate allegory of the Virtues sitting on different branches of a fleur-de-lis in 1498 in Paris was explained to Louis XII by a doctor dressed in scarlet and holding a roll of paper as a symbol of his learning. At Bruges in 1515 the first structure, representing a forest, was appropriately opened by a savage man and a savage woman—two figures from the same type of folklore as the legend of Lyderic pictured within the forest. King Ptolemy explained an elaborate horoscope of King James when the boy-king entered Edinburgh in 1579.

The platforms for the presenter were, as we shall see, important prototypes of main stages and upper stages for English and Flemish theatres. By the end of the sixteenth century, a separate stage for the presenter made occasion at times for little musical shows. The elaborate triumphal arches erected at Avignon for the queen in 1600 and at Montpellier for Mme de Montmorency in 1617 were accompanied by small stages of the baldacchino-pavilion type, in which musicians played and speakers pointed out and explained the scenic wonders of the arch.

Dialogue was the next step, and a very easy one. Either the purely narrative pictures could be given the necessary dialogue, often already indicated on rolls or inscriptions, or the address to the prince could be brought inside the picture by dressing an actor as a direct or indirect representative of the visitor. Then the prince (or his prototype David, or Gideon, or Charlemagne, or Edward the Confessor) could receive, inside the show, the crown, the praise, or the exhortation intended for the real person outside.

That step, which completed the progress from picture to little drama, was taken in the second quarter of the fifteenth century in England, France, and Flanders alike. In England the poet Lydgate was quite important in developing the speeches and dialogue of traditional shows in which there had been little speech before.[16]

For themes for the street theatres, designers drew on the entire range of literary, artistic, and popular lore and developed a number of special subjects besides. As in painting and literature, most of the characters and stories represented in the fourteenth and fifteenth centuries were drawn from the Bible. Historical figures and scenes from the romances of chivalry became increasingly popular, and the sixteenth century saw the whole world of classical mythology and history picturized. There was no such violent break between medieval period and Renaissance as we find in

---

[14] *Forschungen zur deutschen Theatergeschichte*, pp. 279 ff. From the earliest centuries after the fall of Rome to the end of the fifteenth century, the theory was current that Roman comedy had been read by the poet in a pulpit and acted out in pantomime by actors behind him.

[15] Chambers, *The Mediaeval Stage*, II, 52 ff.

[16] Withington, *op. cit.* I, 106 and 141 ff. and notes; Welsford, *The Court Masque*, pp. 52 ff.; Chambers, *op. cit.*, I, 397; Worp, *Geschiedenis van het Drama en van het Tooneel in Nederland*, I, 45 f. and 50 f.

the regular drama. Earthly kings were placed in the same scenic thrones that the King of Heaven used, and nymphs and goddesses found their places among the religious virtues without causing any special change in dramatic forms.

The designer of the biblical *tableaux vivants* used the same subjects that he did when planning the carving, the painting, and the stained glass of the church. Sometimes he followed figure-sculpture in the use of single figures and figures in series. By means of living actors he could make the Prophets, Apostles, Nine Worthies, and patron saints of the guilds more vivid than any the public ever saw in stone. Such single figures he could use dramatically. Each Prophet at Ghent in 1458 sang a song, opened a paper roll with an edifying inscription, and pointed the duke the way to the next show.

At Bruges and Ghent, Philip of Burgundy saw just the scenes that artists were painting on canvas and board. Those at Bruges in 1440 included the Sacrifice of Isaac, Queen Esther, Mary Magdalene washing the feet of Christ, the Nativity, the Tidings brought to the Shepherds, St. Dominius, Joachim and Anna, St. Peter, and the Transfiguration. At Ghent in 1458 the selection was expanded to include such popular semi-romantic scenes as David and Abigail and Solomon and the Queen of Sheba. The crowning achievement was a reproduction with living figures of the prize painting of the Cathedral of St. Bavon. On a stage fifty feet long and thirty-eight feet high, built in three stories and covered by a white curtain, was a reproduction as a living tableau of the "Adoration of the Lamb," painted a few decades before by the brothers van Eyck.[17]

Contemporary figures sometimes appeared among the Bible characters, just as a donor might be painted as a part of an Adoration group. Especially in Flanders, the mysticism of the fifteenth century taught that divine personages could be brought very close to the daily lives of the devout. In some instances, as in Amsterdam in

1594, figures representing known painters were put in tableaux. In order that the crowds at the reception of William of Orange in Brussels in 1577 might realize more fully that the shows of the liberation of biblical peoples from tyranny applied to contemporary affairs, the Rhetoricians who devised them placed in each an actor representing a contemporary merchant or working-man.

FIG. 23.—*Tableau vivant* at Brussels in 1496. Three tableaux in one structure with a tableau of the Trinity and torches above. Front curtains for both levels. Miniature in manuscript, Print Cabinet, Berlin. From Herrmann.

Biblical scenes had a special use as prefigurations of modern events, even where the interest of the show as a whole was primarily secular. Just as artists of the later Middle Ages grouped around each event in the life of Christ the events of the Old Testament which symbolized it—the sacrifice of Isaac for the Crucifixion, Jonah's story for the Resurrection, etc.—so the devisers of tableaux in many places reinforced a modern scene by coupling it with a similar scene from Bible history. A scene of Louis de Nevers, Count of Flanders, granting privileges to the city of

[17] Bergmans, "Note sur la représentation du retable de l'agneau mystique des van Eyck," *Annales de la Fédération Archéologique et Historique de Belgique*, XX, 530.

Bruges was more likely to impress Charles V because it was accompanied by a scene of Moses bringing the Tables of the Law down from the mountain (Fig. 26).

One subject from religious art—the descent of a heavenly messenger—received special development in the street theatres because of its spectacular effect. The Annunciation was already popular in church drama, and Vasari tells us what splendid effects some fifteenth-century artists were able to get in Italian churches. It was easy to adapt the messenger to the occasion of the royal entry: the angel would bring a crown either to a king on the stage or to the actual sovereign as he rode up before the show. An important variation made the angel a representative of the city, let down either from the city gates or from a scenic device symbolizing the city, to present the keys to the king. Sometimes she brought a special gift, perhaps an abstract quality, Justice or Clemency, which the inhabitants did not wish their ruler to lack. The machine for descent was usually a seat in a circle of cloud, a Glory copied after the *mandorla* of painting. In the street theatres, as later in the Elizabethan and perspective stages, this heavenly shuttle proved an ever pleasing device.

Gradually, secular stories from the romances, from popular history, and from classical literature increased in number. Several characters from classical mythology had been known throughout the Middle Ages. Venus had appeared along with Pluto among the heathen devils in hell and as an underground siren in the Tannhäuser legend. She now became more respectable. Charles the Bold was quite startled at Rijssel in 1468 when he was confronted with three nude ladies as Venus, Juno, and Athena. A similar Judgment of Paris show was produced as a matter of course in Brussels in 1496. For Charles VIII at Rheims in 1484, Venus took the quite unobjectionable form of a mermaid in a fountain. Soon Pan, Ceres, Saturn, Flora, and many other classical characters appeared and joined the abstract allegories to enforce a moral or theme. By the middle of the sixteenth century, while traditional religious scenes were still occasionally produced, the most popular narrative *tableaux vivants* told the romantic stories of Pyramis and Thisbe, Lucrece, Apollo and Daphne, Diana and her nymphs, Samson and Delilah, Esther and Ahasuerus, the heroes of the Trojan War, or the knights of Arthur and Charlemagne and the victors over Turk and Moor.

Likewise, religious shepherd scenes were transformed into Renaissance pastorals. Tidings brought to the shepherds were sung at Paris in 1437, at Bruges in 1440, and at Ghent in 1458. Singing shepherds and shepherd songs appeared in most of the French entries. By 1530, when Queen Eleanor entered Paris, a little allegorical pastoral in the Renaissance secular style was dramatized and played.

By a tradition whose origin is lost in antiquity, birds, flowers, perfume, and music must accompany the festivities of a joyous entry, and these were provided in dramatic ways typical of the changing decades. For Henry VI in 1431, from the reproduction of the coat-of-arms of the city of Paris allegorical characters representing the Clergy, the University, and the Bourgeoisie released birds from red hearts and threw violets and other flowers on the passing lords. In 1486 in Troyes, in front of a graceful bower of rocks and verdure young maidens plucked flowers, made bouquets, and sang for the king. Perfumes were provided on many occasions. In the fifteenth century, angels with censers appeared. In 1595 at Lyons, the agreeable odors came from two classic altars dedicated to Piety and Clemency.

Musicians sometimes surprised the entering party by playing from a hidden spot; but, more often, they also were built into a show. In the fifteenth century David with his choir of musicians furnished the sweet concord of sound. He became Apollo in the following century, and his choir the Nine Muses. As humanistic learning became important, the Seven Liberal Arts forgot their quarrels, took up their theorbos and viols, and made harmony in the public streets. Sometimes minstrels, sometimes angels, sometimes classic nymphs, played and sang. In Edinburgh in 1579 it was Dame Music and her scholars.

Themes for the street-shows were often chosen for their special appropriateness to certain places. This, too, followed an old tendency of medieval art. In church or castle the artist planned many scenes because of a real or fancied appropriateness to the location: the baptismal font would be decorated with scenes of the Baptism of Christ and of the Last Supper, which was the next and associated sacrament; the Adoration of Christ was especially appropriate for the altar: its characters became adorers of the altar. The lavatories in Wenlock Abbey, in Shropshire, and in the cloisters at Gloucester are decorated with scenes of Christ walking on the water.

Bridges, which were effective places for defense of the medieval city, suggested to the city fathers that castle gates and towers be erected there, with speeches or shows of welcome. Later a triumphal arch, likewise a symbol of a city gate, might take the place of a warlike structure. Or some designers thought of boats; and Noah's Ark appeared on London Bridge when Queen Margaret entered for her coronation in 1445.

Public fountains, where the people came for water, suggested a number of themes and structures. Here the populace and visitors could expect free wine as an expression of the generosity of the city. The wine-drinking was more than the merriment of a festival occasion: it was a kind of civic communion in honor of the new sovereign. The Ponceau fountain in Paris, on the route to the royal palace, was dramatized in several different ways. As a fountain was one symbol of a garden (a frequent fixture in illustrations of the Garden of Eden), gardens and bowers often appeared here. Many times a *lis*, with water and wine flowing from its branches, established the fountain as a national emblem. Or the fountain might be made a spiritual emblem. Once a pelican, a symbol of Christ's life-giving blood, was represented; and several times the Lamb of God, the fountain of sacrificial blood, was placed here. In London the two great conduits, because of their tower-like structure, were developed as castles rather than as fountains.

The city itself, or the province, might be repre-

sented by a character or a structure. In Antwerp and Ghent and in a number of English cities, the legendary founder, often a giant, might give the greetings to the entering prince. Following the example of the ancient Romans, many medieval cities traced their foundation to a Trojan hero. "Troyes" was explained by its citizens as "New Troy." At Rheims, where all French kings came for coronation, the figures of Remus and the she-wolf celebrated the supposed founding and naming of the city. Ghent put forward both Gideon and the Emperor Gaius, sometimes vaguely merged, as the patronymic founder.[18]

Associated cities and corporations within the city could have their symbolic figures or scenes. Other cities of Flanders might appear among the shows of any one Flemish entry, and various Norman cities in a Norman. The trade-guilds, especially, vied with one another in shows. The simplest kind would be a painting or a *tableau vivant* of the coat-of-arms; the more ambitious guilds would show the life of their patron saint or of a famous mayor or other person who had been a member. When they arranged pictures of general civic interest, as at Bruges in 1515, they usually added in the framing device emblems, statues, and even whole scenes representing the mysteries of their own trade. At Paris the university either had its own show or was represented by allegorical characters in the shows of other groups. At Caen in 1532, Francis I saw a show of Minerva distributing the fruits of study and the waters of science to the five faculties of the university. Local legends and famous citizens entertained or impressed the visitor. Rotterdam in 1549 proudly displayed to Philip II a tableau of her native son, Erasmus, at his work.

It was especially incumbent on groups of foreign residents to arrange spectacles. They nearly always put into *tableaux vivants* or paintings the characters and stories related to their own country. Sometimes those stories were as far fetched as the legend of Constantine and St. Helena, chosen by the English merchants in Antwerp in 1549 because St. Helena was sup-

[18] Worp, *op. cit.*, I, 42.

posed to have been English.[19] On other occasions the foreigners' decorations and shows served a real educational purpose in acquainting the city with the history and taste of other nations. The entry of Charles V into Bruges in 1515 was probably as important in architectural education as a modern "world's fair." The arches and other structures built by the Italian merchants gave many people their first opportunity to see the Renaissance architecture of Italy.[20]

The most frequent kind of subject, and often the most interesting, had a direct relation to the entering prince and the occasion of his journey. Whether to honor him or cajole him, the whole range of literary and popular lore was searched for examples which could be made to resemble him or the deeds he had done, or the deeds the citizens wanted him to do. The principle of prefiguration so elaborately developed in late medieval theology and art, by which each religious incident became a symbol of many other events, was applied to the entry as a whole. Not only were tableaux in pairs frequent, matching an event in recent history by an event in biblical or classical history, but the entering prince or his coronation must have prototypes. At Rheims the earlier coronations—that of Pharamond, the first king of France, and of Clovis, the first Christian king, and of St. Louis—were shown on stages as prototypes of the contemporary event. When Margaret of York entered Bruges in 1468 to marry Charles the Bold, the *tableaux vivants* showed scenes of famous pairs or of events related to marriage. On stages appeared Adam and Eve, Cleopatra given in marriage to King Alexander, the marriage at Cana, the marriage of Esther, and a dramatization of the Song of Solomon. The arrival of the Queen of Sheba bringing gifts to Solomon was a favorite theme, symbolizing the entry of a new queen and the new territories she usually brought.

The voyage of Philip to Italy and the Low Countries in 1548–49 to be installed as ruler was the occasion of a long series of spectacles elaborately described in the account of Calvete de

Estrella. Over and over again history was combed to find examples of a father or a ruler who in his lifetime turned over the power to the young hero. In painting, in bas-relief, in lay figures, and in live figures, Charles and Philip saw the stories of Solomon and David, Philip and Alexander, Vespasian and Titus, Charlemagne and Lodovico, Count Theodoric of Alsace and his son Philip, Abraham and Isaac, Pharaoh and Joseph, Constancio and Constantine, and Frederick and Maximilian.

Famous people of the same name appeared as personages to honor the latest prince. St. Catherine welcomed to London both Queen Catherine in 1421 and Catherine of Aragon in 1501; and St. Margaret welcomed Queen Margaret to London in 1445 and to Coventry in 1456. Anne of Brittany found a row of the five Annes of the Old Testament waiting for her in Paris in 1504. All over the Netherlands, and in England as well, the famous Philips gathered to honor Philip II, king of Spain, count of Flanders, and husband of Queen Mary. Genealogical trees, the civic equivalent of the Tree of Jesse, were frequent, often with living actors on all or the more important branches. In France the tree was often a *lis*. In London in 1554, two elaborate trees springing from Edward III united at the top with Mary and Philip of Spain. Two rose trees, a white and a red, united when Henry VIII came to the throne and reappeared in 1558/59 with an added branch holding Elizabeth.

Sometimes a ruler was equated with a particular hero of the past. The boy-kings, Henry VI of England and Charles VIII, were honored by shows of David when they were received in France as king. Gideon was the special hero to honor Philip, Duke of Burgundy.

Not all shows were for general ornament and flattery. The street theatres could serve to bring the particular needs and hopes of the people to the mind of the ruler. To gain forgiveness for a recent revolt against the duke, the citizens of Bruges in 1440 not only sent their city fathers out to meet him with bared heads and feet but reinforced their appeal with *tableaux vivants* of ancient

[19] Calvete de Estrella, *El felicissimo viaje*, pp. 220 ff.

[20] Körte, *Die Wiederaufnahme romanischer Bauformen.*

rulers who showed clemency to their erring subjects. Again in 1515 Bruges citizens needed special consideration from their count. For several decades the river to the sea had been silting up, and Bruges, once the richest city in the world, saw its business firms move, one by one, to Antwerp. When the young prince Charles V, grandson of the emperor and heir of both the Netherlands and Spain, came to be installed in his provinces, Bruges outdid herself. First she showed him in tableaux the glorious history of Bruges and the special honors and privileges granted her by the earlier counts of Flanders. One allegorical group represented Riches standing behind the Graces and the Arts, with an inscription explaining that though the arts stood first they must be supported by wealth. Then the prince was led before two scenes which went to the heart of the situation. The first showed a despairing lady named Bruges being deserted by Business and Merchandise. The next one did more than present the problem: it suggested the solution. In it Law and Religion were forcibly preventing Business and Merchandise from deserting the lady.

The religious conflicts in the sixteenth century, especially in the Low Countries and Britain, made it extremely important that the ruler have the right opinions. The chronicler gives us a quite touching description of Elizabeth receiving from a *tableau vivant* a book marked "Truth." Edinburgh gave Mary a sincere welcome on her return from France in 1561 but wanted to make it quite clear that the Catholicism of France was hated. As a warning of the vengeance of God on idolaters, a tableau was presented of Korah, Dathan, and Abiram destroyed while offering strange fire upon an altar. A still more significant interlude had been prepared—a priest burned at the altar while elevating the Host—but the Earl of Huntly persuaded the authorities, with some difficulty, to content themselves with the one. In 1579 the young boy James was first given a serious sermon, then regaled by typical Renaissance entertainment more pleasing to the

appetites. Dame Religion invited him into a church, where a preacher made a

notable exhortation unto him, for the embracing of Religion, and all her Cardinall Vertewis, and of all Morall Vertewis. Thereafter he came furth, and maid progres to the Mercat Croce whare he beheld Bacchus with his magnifits liberalitie and plentie, distributing of his liquor to all passingers and beholders, in sic apperance as was pleasant to see.

In Flanders the shows presented now Heresy stamped out, now Inquisition with a bloody face, according to which of the shifting factions was dominant. The Rhetoricians at Ghent in 1539 made such strong attacks on churchmen that their printed plays were proscribed.[21] Yet, when Philip was received at Amsterdam in 1549, the tableau of the Rhetoricians showed Faith binding Heresy and Error with hook and chain. Brussels in 1577 welcomed William of Orange, the Protestant, with scenes of David, Moses, and Joseph saving the people. The following year Archduke Matthias of Austria was brought in as governor by the Catholic nobles and saw himself presented even more gorgeously as Scipio Africanus and as Quintus Curtius plunging into the yawning abyss in order to save his people from pestilence.

The *tableaux vivants* could ornament the city with pleasing scenes from religious, courtly, or popular literature, just as a rich man might ornament his walls with tapestries or a father his daughter's hope chest with paintings. They could also follow as vigorously as the most daring playwrights the political and religious controversies of the day.

The *tableaux vivants* brought to a wide audience practically the entire range of subjects available to either artist or dramatist. At a time when secular art and literature were appealing to a small aristocratic audience, the street theatres were on view for the entire population. They give us a far better index of popular taste and interest than either Renaissance drama or painting can give.

Hundreds and hundreds of street theatres were built. A glance at the bibliographical lists will show that Paris, Rouen, Lyons, Bruges, Ghent,

[21] Cf. below, chap. iii.

and Antwerp averaged several important occasions every decade in the sixteenth century. London had spectacular street theatres built for royal entries in 1501, 1520, 1522, 1533, 1546, 1553, 1554, and 1558. While there was no royal entry in London between 1558 and the magnificent reception given James in 1603, yet the same or similar devices were built in the provincial cities for the Progresses of Elizabeth and in London for the annual Lord Mayor's Pageant. From the 1540's the lord mayor met at least one stationary show to give him welcome, and sometimes more than one. In the latter part of the century those shows became as elaborate as any for the royal entries, and in the hands of George Peele they became short plays.

The English dramatists knew the street-shows well. Not only Peele but Jonson, Middleton, Dekker, and Heywood wrote for them. A comparison will make clear, I believe, not only that many particular scenes of Elizabethan drama were derived from the *tableaux vivants* but that they provided the basic pattern of the English stage façade.

III. STREET THEATRES: THE STAGE FORMS OF THE *tableaux vivants*

1. FESTIVAL DECORATIONS

The arrival of the sovereign—duke, king, or cardinal—was a great festive occasion. In a sense the whole city, especially the streets along the procession, became a show. While some attention was paid to the officials and musicians who would meet the sovereign and march with him back into the city, the principal thing was for the city itself to make a good impression.

The gates, the houses, the windows, the fountains, the palaces, and even the citizens themselves, were decorated with festive garments of tapestries, painted cloths, boughs, and flowers. French accounts from the ninth and tenth centuries mention the splendid decorations, the hanging of cloths and tapestries on the houses, when the king made a royal entry. English accounts begin with the coronation of Richard I in 1189; but the decoration of London houses

with costly tapestries on this occasion is mentioned as though the custom had been established long before. When Henry III in 1236 brought his new queen, Eleanor of Provence, through London on the way to Westminster, he was met by a procession of the mayor and aldermen and three hundred and sixty citizens mounted and richly dressed, each man carrying a gold or silver cup to denote the privilege claimed by the city of being chief butler to the kingdom at a coronation. The city was hung with flags, banners, chaplets, tapestries, and rich silks, and at night countless lamps and cressets lit up the streets. When Edward I brought his second wife, Margaret of France, to London in 1300, six hundred citizens put on livery of red and white, with symbols of the guilds embroidered on the sleeves. The rich cities of the Low Countries vied with one another in the splendor of the street decorations. Often trumpeters and other musicians awaited the duke, not only at the gates but at every square, and at regular distances beautiful maidens on special stands or seats might hold torches to light his party. In all countries special hospitality was offered by the city to all. Everywhere the fountains would run with free wine, and the whole city would devote itself to providing a festive show.

Before actual street theatres were built, and also long after, the buildings and monuments themselves were turned into shows. Not only were they decorated with cloth, greenery, and torches, but they were called into positive dramatic service. Since many of the temporary street theatres followed the patterns of actual buildings and monuments, we must notice how real architecture was adapted for show-architecture.

The church façade was especially useful. Almost as frequently as the city gate, it was the structure from which an angel descended to address or crown the king. From the roof of old St. Paul's in London, an angel came down to cense with the great censer the entering Henry VII in 1487; in Bruges in 1440, when a *tableau vivant* of the Adoration of the Shepherds was shown to Philip the Good, angels sang the "Gloria in excelsis" far above, from the façade of the church of the Jacobins. Without the use of any figures the church of St. Géry at Valenciennes was made into a show for Charles V in 1540—it was adorned with green boughs and torches, and musicians played as the emperor approached.

The convention that the upper part of a façade was appropriate for heavenly and virtuous personages—a convention already well established, as we have seen, in painting and monumental sculpture—served also when live or temporary statuary was added to the building. When Charles V entered Messina in 1536, he saw a heaven of clouds and golden stars built above the door of a church; from it a chariot bearing twenty-four angels descended to greet him and present him with tokens of triumph. The throne of the Heavenly King, frequently used at the top of church façades, church doorways, tombs, and other sculptured structures and at the top of a mansion in the religious plays, gave the pattern for a similar throne of an earthly ruler. In Troyes in 1486, for the entry of Charles VIII, there was constructed above the door of the church a *ciel* in the form of a military tent, called the "Tent of Peace," in which sat a king surrounded by giant figures of virtues, here probably artificial. Real actors represented a beautiful lady in a chariot untying a Gordian knot of quarrels on a stage erected over the door of the church of St. John at Lyons when Queen Eleanor, the second wife of Francis I, made her entrance in 1533.

Other city buildings, as well, were decorated with greenery or cloth and lighted with torches. A number of buildings already had features which lent themselves well to special festival use: the gallery around the edge of the roof of most churches and of such buildings as the town hall of Brussels and the Bruges market building was already available for trumpeters and holders of torches and banners; and the Bruges belfry, among other buildings, has a small gallery from which one could address the crowd in the street. As we shall see, the speaking stage and the upper gallery in front of a show-device carried the same pattern into the sixteenth-century theatre.

More significant for us than the conversion of ecclesiastical or civic buildings to show uses was the decoration of city gates. From the city gate was derived the shape of the triumphal arches of western Europe and of a number of tableau structures—part castle, part gate, part triumphal arch—which, in turn, were patterns for the regular theatres of the sixteenth century. But, before we anticipate too much, let us examine just what was done at city gates to make them into such important showpieces.

At the very simplest, the gate would be decorated with cloth, banners, and coats-of-arms, and musicians would play from the battlements. Here was another example of a gallery for musicians or for speeches of welcome high above the other performers. For the entry of Philip the Good into Bruges in 1440, the notches of the battlements of one of the city gates were filled with musicians. When the same sovereign came to Ghent in 1458, the first gate was hung from top to bottom with black and gray woolen cloth and decorated not only with his arms but with the arms of all the knights of the Order of the Golden Fleece, which he had founded, and trumpeters played from the top at his approach. Inside the arch of the gate, against a blue cloth of heaven, were placed the sun, the moon, and the stars, with twenty torches to make them shine. The second gate, inside the city, had a canopied heaven on top and was also covered from roof to ground with arms of the knights of the Order. Likewise, when Philip's great-great-great-grandson, Philip of Spain, entered Bruges in 1549, over the city gate were the arms of the prince, a canopy with a picture, many lighted torches, and six trumpeters. When Queen Elizabeth entered Kenilworth in 1575, the trumpeters on the gate were built up to represent giants of Arthur's day, and a little drama was enacted below: a menacing Hercules was overcome by the queen's beauty and yielded the keys. When she entered the city of Norwich three years later, she found the gates newly repaired and adorned and the city waits ready to play music as the inside of the city was uncovered to her view.

The ceremony of welcome to the city was sometimes even more elaborate, and the gates then became little theatres. When Henry V returned to England after Agincourt, the towers of London Bridge, which formed his gate of entrance, were the scene of a pageant of the Giant Porter and his wife who held the keys to the city. The towers were adorned with banners of royal arms, and on their front was inscribed "Civitas regis justicie." Trumpets and other wind instruments were played from the top.

The angel or maiden of the city, bringing keys, crown, or special gift, was sometimes let down from a real gate, even long after special structures were built for her. Often a cloud or some emblematic device, such as a ship or a tent built high on the gate, served as a starting-point for the lady.

On a number of occasions the gate itself, like the triumphal arch, served as a façade structure for *tableaux vivants*, either built against it or arranged on top. The elaborate spectacle of the Heart of Paris, which opened up to disclose Loyalty and Honor to Anne of Brittany in 1504, was built over a real gate. When Philip II arrived in Ghent in 1549, he found set against the gate of St. George two elaborate allegorical *tableaux vivants*, one above the other. They were covered by curtains which were drawn aside as trumpets sounded.

Fountains, as I have pointed out, were frequently the scene of shows and spectacles. The two London fountains—the conduit in Cornhill and the Little Conduit in Cheapside—were made into special show-places, and their castle-like towers served as structures for characters and music. When Henry V returned from Agincourt, the tower of the Cornhill conduit was ornamented with many arms, and on top under a tent-pavilion a company of hoary prophets, dressed in gold and crimson, let loose many small birds and sang psalms. The tower of the Cheapside conduit was decked with green and with escutcheons, and on it was a similar group of the Twelve Apostles. When Henry VI returned from his Paris coronation, the Cornhill conduit, which was circular and

castellated, had a circular pageant of two levels. A boy-king stood surrounded by Virtues; above them stood Dame Clemency, who spoke. The Little Conduit was decked with a heavenly throne, on which sat the Trinity surrounded by a choir of angel-musicians. The verses addressed to Henry by God the Father were inscribed on the throne.

Actually, by the sixteenth century, there was so little difference in treatment between the real gates, façades, and towers and the more or less conventionalized façades and arches erected as theatrical scenery that no separate story can be told.

2. EMBLEMATIC SCENIC DEVICES

Now to the street theatres themselves. Not satisfied with street decorations, special paintings put up as ornament, or permanent architectural features, the city fathers wanted special stages built—special scenic ornaments. Not silent monuments or tapestries, but living pictures—hearts that would open and speak, fountains that would run and speak, arbors from which trumpets, viols, and singers could be heard, or castles that would open up for little plays. They ransacked art, heraldry, pageantry, folklore, and romance for scenic devices and structures.

The first type of stage structure we must consider was that which reproduced the traditional emblematic scenic devices handed down in art, as we have found, from the time of the ancient Egyptians. The most important of these were the garden (with its several symbols), the mountain, cave, or rock, and the boat. The castle, equally ancient, is so frequent and so important that I shall describe it separately later.

The garden could be represented in several different ways. In medieval art it could be a patch of grass and flowers, a tree, a fountain, or a plot of space with a hedge, a fence, or a wall around it. Or it could be a walled-in place with flowers, tree, and fountain all combined into one. The street theatres used any one or several of these symbols, and sometimes combined them with others. Occasionally in a *tableau vivant*, as in art from the time of the Egyptian reliefs and of the Greek vases, a single tree could represent a garden. Eden, for instance, where the tree was important in the story, could be represented by a single tree, though it usually had a fountain also. Late in the Middle Ages, the expulsion scene was popular, and the gate might suffice. In the Dutch religious play *De eerste Bliscap van Maria*, the Tree of Knowledge was the scene of Paradise. In Louvain, leatherworkers were paid for making a leather tree for a garden.[22] One of the Vasi engravings, reproduced by Ferrari, of the scene for the festival of the Chinea in Rome would indicate that as late as 1774 a single tree, in front of a formal architectural façade, could represent the Garden of the Hesperides.

The fountain is perhaps the most protean of the scenic devices. On one occasion a symbol of a garden, on others it was an independent monumental and scenic form; at still other times it became an open pavilion, a castle, a temple, a grotto, a cross, a fleur-de-lis, an Agnus Dei, a tree, a triumphal arch, or a structure to support an upper stage or an orchestra of musicians. As a symbol of a garden the fountain furnished a picturesque background for Paris and the three goddesses, both in the early woodcuts for *La Destruction de Troye*[23] and in the *tableau vivant* at Brussels in 1496. A grove of three fountains served as a device for the Grocers to compliment Henry VI and present him with foreign fruits when he returned to London from his coronation in Paris in 1432.

City fountains, as we have noticed, served as scenes, the monumental structure determining what form the show should take. While the tower-like shape of the London fountains suggested castle scenes, the Cross fountain at Coventry suggested putting angels or Children of Israel high on the arms of the cross to sing and cast down cakes and flowers. As the city fountain was a symbol of the generosity of the city, so the tableau fountain— now as fleur-de-lis, now as the garden of the city or of the country—was a symbol of the flourishing realm of the prince. Whether as part of a grotto or as part of a triumphal arch, the fountain retained something of the same symbolism it had as part of a garden.

The garden with a hedge or fence was perhaps the most popular type in painting. It appeared especially in such illustrations as those of the *Roman de la rose*. A pair of lovers or a noble lady with her maidens might appear in such a garden. The Madonna, following the theological concept of the *hortus inclusus*, or "inclosed garden," would appear in a formal seat surrounded by the grass and walls or fence of a garden.

On the stage there were a number of examples of the hedge or fence. Professor Cohen quotes from mid-fifteenth-century religious plays the directions for trees, fruit, and flowers for Paradise, to be seen over the palings.[24] In the *tableaux vivants* the fenced garden was usually given an allegorical significance: it represented the city, the nation, or the blessed state of prosperity. Ghent was fond of a garden for a maiden representing the city. When the duke arrived in 1458, from a seat in the midst of a garden hung round with green woolen cloth, a girl of about ten, dressed as a bride, with emblems of the city, walked down the steps of the platform to greet him. A very similar maiden, a lion in her lap, sat within a woven-reed fence about eighteen inches high to greet Alexander Farnese in Ghent in 1585. The water-color sketch shows a canopy above and the hangings of a royal seat—all within a proscenium frame and curtains.

We have a woodcut of a garden built as a street theatre in Bruges for Charles V.[25] The lower scaffold was covered with cloth painted with flowers; around the garden was a lattice fence with posts of verdure and green garlands. In the center, amid trees, flowers, and birds, sat Orpheus, and outside the fence two wild men stood guard. The garden signified, as a Latin inscription indicated, the reign and the realms of the young prince, flourishing in goods, in honors,

[22] Van Puyvelde, *Schilderkunst en Tooneelvertooningen*, p. 215.

[23] Reproduced by Dubech, *Histoire générale illustrée du théâtre*, II, 72.

[24] *Histoire de la mise en scène*, p. 91.

[25] Reproduced by Dubech, *op. cit.*, I, 175, and by Bapst, *Essai sur l'histoire du théâtre*, p. 97.

and in virtuous delights. This platform would seem to be tilted forward to show the interior—as all such gardens should be. They were not well adapted to stage scenery and soon gave way to more theatrical symbols—a bower or an arched gateway.

The bower (an arbor, woodland cave, or grotto) would serve as a background for actors who could be seen from one side more easily than in an inclosed garden. The *preaul*, or trellised summerhouse, was used for several of the miniature scenes at the Lille banquet of 1453. Maidens in front of a rocky scene of grass and flowers gathered bouquets to offer to Charles VIII when he entered Troyes in 1486. Similarly, maidens danced and threw flowers from a pleasure garden for Louis XII in Rouen in 1508.

Some arbors may have had the shape of an architectural screen, like the woody bower behind the Madonna and Saints in the painting by Jan Gossaert in Hamburg. Other arbors were given other architectural forms. It was especially easy to adapt an arbor to the form of a pavilion, with columns, canopy, and either cloth or greenery on one or three sides. An elaborate arbor built for revels after the jousts at Whitehall in 1511 took the form of a pavilion with purple columns and an elaborate carved and painted canopy.[26] The court revels for Epiphany in 1516 called for an even more elaborate "Gardyn de Esperans," with columns, canopy, and rock of gold and imitation marble,[27] and the same English tradition continued into the seventeenth century. The bower for a pastoral scene for the entertainment of the King of Denmark at the English court in 1606 had cloth of crimson taffeta and a canopy on top.[28]

Many structures were imitated in greenery and flowers. A castle of greenery or a triumphal arch of flowers occurs a number of times. As a show for Louis XII in Genoa in 1507, the shield of France

was hung against a little chapel of pomegranates and oranges.

The architectural façade, by a curious metamorphosis which may be observed in several French *tableaux vivants* early in the sixteenth century, acquired the power to represent a garden. The development came through the use of the gate of the garden, previously small, to represent the whole garden, and thereby a country or city. This was perhaps made easy by the acceptance, already general, of an arch as a symbol of a city or realm. The Garden of Eden, the background for the marriage of Adam and Eve among the shows in Bruges in 1468, was "made by subtle craft after the form of a castle gate." The Garden of Gethsemane was represented in the twentieth play of the Towneley cycle by a gate. At Paris in 1502, for the visit of Philip the Fair, a shepherd representing Paris stood at the gate of a close to show that peace reigned in Paris. Three garden tableaux with elaborate gateways appeared at Lyons in 1515 for the entry of Francis I. One garden with medieval walls was here tilted as on a mountain. At the small gate in front were an armed man and a terrible bear, and on the wall at the back sat a beautiful lady named Peace. In the second example only a conventional arched gate was shown for the garden. The third represented the conquest of Milan by Francis. Across the large gateway of the close or garden were the arms of Milan and the words "Le Jardin de Milan." Within were people, flowers, and trees with golden apples. Hercules (Francis) was delivering the garden from its keepers and getting the apples of gold. The miniature shows the whole scene inclosed by a columned pavilion and canopy.[29] At Lyons in 1548 a triumphal arch, a *portail antique*, was painted as the Park of France. Within the portal were two goddesses embracing. This is another example of the substitution (here logical enough) of architectural forms for emblematic devices. The garden gate is as good a symbol as a hedge or

[26] Brewer and Gairdner, *Letters and Papers of Henry VIII*, II, 1495.

[27] *Ibid.*, p. 1509.

[28] Nichols, *The Progresses of James I*, IV, 1074 f.

[29] Reproduced by Guigue, *L'Entrée de François Premier Roy de France en la cité de Lyon* and by Mourey, *Le Livre des fêtes françaises*, p. 27, Fig. 16.

a patch of grass and is a much more practical and more stately scenic background.[30]

Less varied and picturesque than the garden was the mountain. A miniature mountain or a mountain with a cave continued from primitive art through the Middle Ages with little change. The Nativity, among other Bible scenes, was long pictured as taking place in or in front of a cave, for here again the device could establish the locale symbolically, without representing a complete cave or mountain in scale or actually inclosing the characters. On some occasions it was identified with a garden—the Mount of Olives, for instance, with the Garden of Gethsemane.

Like the garden and the triumphal arch, a mountain could be a symbol of a country. At the entertainment in 1501 for Prince Arthur and his bride, Catherine of Aragon, the masquers entered on two mountains bound together, one representing England, one Spain. At the English revels at Epiphany in 1513, six lords and six ladies entered in a "Rich Mount," a rock of gold set with precious stones and planted with broom to signify Plantagenet and with red and white roses and fleurs-de-lis. For an entertainment at the English court in 1518 a rocky cave was decked with the arms of the Church, the Empire, Spain, France, and England—a symbol that these were leagued together against the Turk. From it came knights who fought a tourney and masquers who danced. In Bruges in 1515 two mountains were built on top of a double boxlike *tableau vivant*. One, the symbol of the Butchers, was adorned with cattle and sheep, some built in the round, some painted flat. The other mountain, for the Fishmongers, was adorned with fish, sirens, and a merman in armor.

As in the case of the garden, the mountain, cave, or rock could be combined with other devices and with formal arches and screens. Renaissance courtyards and parks were filled with fountains in the form of rocky grottoes—grottoes which took the shape and often the columns and adornment of the arcade screen. Such grottoes were popular in the Baroque theatre and usually stood in the position of the back screen or wall.

Less compatible structures were also combined with the mountain. It was simple to put a tree, a tower, a castle, or a pavilion on top of it. Paradise was built on a mountain for the French play of the Resurrection which was formerly attributed to Jean Michel. As Professor Cohen points out, the mountain served not only for the Mount of Olives but also for the meeting of the Virgin and the Apostles.[31] Even a ship could be shown on a mountain, as it could also be shown above arches and gateways. A note in the manuscript of the *Ludus Coventriae* indicates that the Flood and Noah's Ark were built on top of a mountain.[32] A mountain was used as a base for a throne for allegorical figures at the entry of Philip II to Lille in 1549.

Hence we are not surprised at the free combination of mountains and arches and columns in various arrangements. In a fifteenth-century carved scene of the crowning of St. Eligius, in the museum of the cathedral at Bruges, a sleeping figure in the background rests on a miniature mountain with two small trees. He and the mountain are framed by a stone arch supporting a castle-canopy. In Bruges in 1515, above the mountain and the sea on top of a *tableau vivant* was a gallery with painted pennons, lights, and musicians. The pattern was already acceptable that a mountain scene could be part of an architectural structure. In the sixteenth century many rocks, waves, and patches of seaweed indicating either mountain or sea were built in panels of triumphal arches, or even at the top of arches. Even when the old device was not lost in the architectural structures of the Renaissance, it was often relegated to a minor part as a detail of the structure or in front of it.

Very similar is the story of the ship in *tableaux vivants* and pageantry. A popular emblem as long as there has been either pageantry or narrative

[30] Cf. the several symbols of a garden—wall, gate-throne, and the upper-stage canopy called the "Garden of France"—all in the tableau for Princess Mary at Paris in 1514 (see below, Fig. 37).

[31] *Op. cit.*, pp. 81 f.

[32] Fol. 24 (*Ludus Coventriae*, ed. Block, p. 41).

art, the ship has served as a device for carrying an important personage or important insignia in processions. In the *tableaux vivants* and in Renaissance pageantry it became a picturesque mount for torches, tapestries, or pennons or for the entry of dancers to the hall or of a knight to the tournament field. In 1515 and again in 1582 the ship was the city of Bruges, happy under the sunbeams of the new ruler; in 1514 it served as a symbol of the city of Paris to welcome Mary Tudor as queen. This last example is of particular interest: it, too, was built into a Renaissance façade of columns, tapestries, and canopy, while in front on the apron stage stood an expositor who explained the show to the queen (Fig. 35).

There were several other devices which can be briefly mentioned before we turn to the castle. The genealogical tree—the civic counterpart of the Tree of Jesse in religious art and pageantry—served not only for the family tree of the sovereign but also at times as a framework for allegorical characters. The dresser or sideboard, used at banquets to display fine metal vessels, served as a scenic device to display characters at Ghent in 1458 and at Louvain in 1515. A heart, built either to sustain characters or to open up and reveal them, was popular in France, and a number of variations were played on the fleur-de-lis—it was used as a fountain, as a genealogical tree, or as a tree full of royal Virtues.

Italian pageantry had stressed for years the ornamental architectural decoration rather than the emblematic device. Triumphal arches, columns, obelisks, pyramids, and temples were used in Italy long before they appeared in the north. When in the middle of the sixteenth century they began to be copied in the north, they were treated much as the old devices had been: combined with other devices; hung with tapestries and paintings, arms, and banners; and used as bases for allegorical characters and addresses of welcome and admonition.

One new device appeared in Lyons in 1533. On a platform was Polthystor fighting the Hydra —in an amphitheatre. Renaissance theatre architects were just becoming interested in Roman theatre forms, and it is interesting to find a medieval device—the *tableau vivant*—copying the new-old Roman structure. In Antwerp, in both 1594 and 1600, elaborate spectacles were prepared in the form of an amphitheatre, not for a combat but to display rows of beautiful women holding emblems of the guilds—a new device of show-architecture. The example of 1600 used a cylinder built, like tableaux at Rouen since 1485, on a turntable, so that the archduke and archduchess might see whole circles of beauties turning before their eyes. Inigo Jones put an amphitheatre on the stage for the masque, *Albion's Triumph*, in 1632.

The main thing we observe in the use of these various emblematic scenic devices is that for the street theatres there was no idea of a stage on which one built scenery—no conception of a background locating the action of a play. The designer wanted to build spectacular ornaments copied from the illustrations he knew in stained glass, tapestries, painting, sculpture, and illuminated manuscripts. He built them on walls, on gates, on fountains, on the fronts of buildings, or, lacking such bases, on platforms in squares, along the streets, or into the streets that branched off the way of the procession. He wanted these boats, these gardens, these rocky caves to come alive by the appearance of a character to address the duke, or by the sudden disclosure of hidden characters, or by a striking arrangement of historical or allegorical personages. Hence the device would be built either with a stand inside for the characters or with a projecting platform somewhere in front. There was no stage in the usual sense. The structure of the device was complete. It was a showpiece and either served to display characters or provided a picturesque housing from which characters could make a sudden appearance. Something of that meaning was kept by Renaissance theatres, especially the Elizabethan.

3. THE CASTLE

Much the most interesting and picturesque of medieval scenic devices was the castle,[33] and it

[33] Cf. pp. 36–38, for a discussion of the castle as a means of securing a center accent in painting, and chaps. iii, iv, and v, for discussions of the influence of the castle on the Flemish, the Elizabethan, and the Spanish theatres. Cf. chap. vii for the

was much the most important for the Renaissance theatres. So ubiquitous were its towers and walls and so varied its forms and conventions that it would be difficult to find a type of artistic illustration, social ritual, pageantry, or allegorical fancy in which it did not take a prominent place. Of course, for the aristocracy the whole of daily life and thought centered in the castle; and to the lower classes the castle was a symbol of their sovereign and hence of the whole realm, and its walls were their protection in time of war. It is no wonder that it was the central scenic device in secular narrative art and in pageantry and that it was important in religious and allegorical art and literature.

While the castle was of minor importance in the religious theatre, it was of first importance in the pageants and the *tableaux vivants*. It contributed considerably to the Italian perspective stage, and it had a very close relationship to the Dutch and the Elizabethan stage façades. Hence we must examine carefully the forms, conventions, and meanings of this colorful device.

On many occasions the castle was just another device to bring masquers or dancers or musicians into the hall or a knight onto the tournament field. Indeed, one manuscript book of "all manner of Orders concerning an Earles House," gives these directions for the masquers and morris dancers: "When they have finished, they disappear into a tower or anything devised for them."[34] The castle or tower was the most popular of such structures. How a series of devices could be used for spectacle appears from the accounts of the Disguisings at Westminster in 1501 for the entertainment of Catherine of Aragon. At the jousts on the previous day several different pageant devices had been used. One nobleman had been brought onto the field in a ship. Another had arrived in a pavilion of white and green silk, four-square, with turrets and pinnacles above. The Earl of Essex had entered in a great mountain of green, with trees, rocks, and beasts on it, and at the very top a beautiful young lady. At the banquet the following night, a similar castle, ship, and mountain, all apparently built on wheels, were brought into the hall for more appropriate use in a spectacular ritual to introduce the dancing. First came the castle, drawn by two lions, a hart, and an elk, two men inside each beast in the fashion of a circus-clown act. Children sang from the four towers as eight beautiful ladies looked out. Next entered the ship, and from it descended Hope and Desire, who presented themselves as ambassadors to the ladies from the Knights of the Mount of Love. Then the mountain was drawn in; the knights descended and besieged the castle. It was an old court game, represented in art from the ninth century and probably played many times in medieval entertainments, when the ladies would usually defend themselves by throwing flowers or candy or perfumed water. But love must prevail, and they were finally persuaded to leave the castle. They and all the other guests danced long into the night.[35]

On other occasions the castle served a similar decorative purpose for morris dancers to make their entry or for a band of musicians. At the side of the hall or on the street the castle (it might as easily be a cave or a grove) was an effective box for a band of musicians. On into the Baroque period, in tournaments, operas, and ballets, the castle as an entry device remained popular. If not medieval knights or virtuous ladies, then Scythians, Moors, Furies, dragons, monsters, serpents, and fauns came forth from towers and castles.

One interesting relic of the castle as spectacular entry remained long as a device for fireworks: a stationary or movable castle would be burned, and dragons and other monsters would be driven out amid flying flames and firecrackers. Sometimes this custom was given special symbolic meaning. At Bruges in 1582 the burning of a large castle of wood painted in mixed colors signified the razing of the castles which had been nests of Spanish tyranny.[36]

The castle, more than the ship or garden, was

castle as proscenium frame and chap. viii for the influence of the castle on French settings.

[34] Collier, *The History of English Dramatic Poetry*, I, 24 f.

[35] Leland, *Collectanea*, V, 359–61; George R. and Portia Kernodle, "Dramatic Aspects of the Medieval Tournament," *Speech Monographs*, IX, 161–72.

[36] Kernodle, "The Magic of Light," *Theatre Arts Monthly*, XXVI, 717–22.

likely to be given a meaning. Even when used as a device for dance entry, as in the English royal entertainment just described, its form was too suggestive, too reminiscent of the long associations with castles, both real and painted, for it to be purely decorative. Obviously, it would most often signify a city or realm. A castle was usually the last stronghold, the mightiest and most impregnable fortification, within the city. Some cities had grown up around a castle and bore the name that it had originally borne. Not only was there a castle at the highest part of the city, but each gate in the city walls was a small castle, with towers, drawbridge, and arched gateway. Any story or painting dealing with an entrance or a siege of a city would give prominence to the little castle of the gate.

There were other traditions in art itself which reinforced this meaning. The Carolingian tilted walled city, frequent in ivory carving, was assimilated into the castle. How easy such assimilation would be appears from the conventionalized representation on many carvings. Usually the walled city had a small gate between two towers at the center of the panel at the bottom, a corresponding panel between two towers at the top, and two or three towers carrying the wall around the sides. In many carvings and in some of the manuscript miniatures the small towers at the sides of the city are enlarged to fill the vertical height, and the distant wall becomes merely an arch between two towers.

Jerusalem was perhaps the city most often represented in medieval art and pageantry, serving both in biblical scenes and in romances of the Crusades. Nearly always a single gate or a conventional castle sufficed. In a number of miniatures and woodcuts, the Temptation of Jesus takes place with both Christ and Satan on top of a castle. The woodcut in the edition of 1511 of the *Passion* of Jean Michel, which was played in 1486, represents Jerusalem as a castle with Jesus and Satan on top.[37] In the large scene by Cailleau of the Valenciennes stage, Jerusalem is a gateway in the back screen and a tower be-

yond. The small illustration of the Temptation shows the two characters on top of the tower.[38] Likewise, the Entry into Jerusalem was regularly a castle gate. We see a good example in the glass of the Malvern Priory,[39] and we find the characters in this scene of the *Ludus Coventriae* mentioning the castle. For *Tobias*, given in Lincoln in 1564, were built "the city of Jerusalem with towers and pinnacles, the city of Raignes with towers and pinnacles."[40] No less, in visualizations of medieval romances of the Crusades against the Saracens, Jerusalem was a castle.

Of course any other city or realm could be represented by a castle. In 1453 two castles were erected in the Cathedral Square in Milan, one of the Romans and one of the Valsesi, for presenting the story of Coriolanus.[41] Emmaus was a castle in the Coventry, Chester, and *Ludus Coventriae* cycles. One structure, apparently, in the French *Mystère de la Passion d'Arras* was referred to in the course of the play as Nazareth, Rome, Tarsus, Sheba, Arabia, and Arimathaea. One castle gate in the York cycle represented, first, a distant place, then Jerusalem for Christ's entry.[42] A castle represented Troy in a number of pageant and tourney scenes of Greeks and Trojans. All three of the early romantic Netherland plays, *Gloriant*, *Lanceloet*, and *Esmoreit*, required one or two castles, for such scenes as the dukedom of Brunswick, Damascus, Sicily, and the Castle of the Red Lion. The English court plays of the sixteenth century usually called for two structures, of which one or both were most frequently a castle or a city. On the Elizabethan public stage the architectural façade was given the meaning of a city-castle in play after play—but more about that hereafter.

---

[37] Reproduced by Dubech, *op. cit.*, II, 54.

[38] Cohen, *Le Théâtre en France au moyen âge*, Vol. I: *Le Théâtre religieux*, Pl. XLV.

[39] Rushforth, *Medieval Christian Imagery*, Fig. 12.

[40] Quoted from *Historical Manuscripts Commission Reports*, *XIV*, VIII, 57 f., by Reynolds in "Some Principles of Elizabethan Staging," *Modern Philology*, III, 72.

[41] Ghinzoni, "Trionfi e rappresentazione in Milano," *Archivio storico lombardo*, XIV, 820.

[42] Shull, "The Stagecraft of the Mediaeval English Drama," pp. 131 f.

FIG. 24.—Castle as triumphal arch, Bruges, 1515. Center section and side towers. Gallery for musicians. Decorated with shields and portraits.

FIG. 25.—*Tableau vivant* over an arch, Bruges, 1515. Throne scene inside the center arch of a castle. Side towers. Gallery for musicians. Decorated with banners and shields.

FIG. 26.—Double *tableau vivant*, Bruges, 1515. Biblical tableau as prefiguration of the modern scene: Moses delivering the Tables of the Law and Louis de Nevers, Count of Flanders, granting special privileges to the city of Bruges. Outer structure an imitation of the Cloth Hall. Gallery for musicians. Folding door-shutters. A Prophet on inside of door, with a short speech printed on a banderole.

FIG. 27.—*Tableau vivant* above triumphal arch, Bruges, 1515. Charles V before Jerusalem. Angels promising him victory in delivering the city. Complete formal proscenium with symbols of heaven.

When we come to the discussion of the triumphal arch, we shall find that it, likewise a symbol of a city or realm, took on many of the characteristics of the castle. Indeed, many arches took the form of city gates, while in others the towers, the castellated walls, the galleries, the banners, musicians, and torches were those of the castle. Most of the arches for James's entry into London in 1603 were elaborate castle structures. Even when Queen Victoria and the Prince and Princess of Wales were received in English cities in the nineteenth century, the arches took the form of castles.[43]

An interesting variation of the theme of a besieged fortress was the castle of hell and limbo. In medieval painting the hell-mouth is often the entrance to a fortress tower. In the Towneley *Harrowing of Hell*, Satan sits on a throne within a castle which is assaulted by Christ.[44] Professor Cohen points out a number of examples in French performances. At Bourges the hell-castle was drawn in procession through the town before the performance. In the four towers were shown souls in torment, and on top was an enormous serpent breathing fire.[45] The Christ who could storm that flaming castle was a champion indeed. Surely, nobody in Bourges stayed away from that performance.

The allegorical castle, following the courtly romances, served frequently as a symbol for the conflict of good and evil. *The Castle of Perseverance* is a good example. Often, however, the castle was used in allegory only as a picturesque setting. For instance, the castle in Giotto's "Triumph of Chastity" in the lower church of St. Francis at Assisi has no suggestion of conflict. The central tower with its large window is a frame for the portrait of the face of Chastity. The gallery below is merely an exhibition rack for the attendant characters.

What did the castle look like—this castle which could serve equally well as a heraldic emblem, as

a dish for a roasted hog's head, as a standard for the arms of jousting knights, as a tomb for a bishop, as a tabernacle for the Eucharist, or as a box for noble ladies at the tournament? While sometimes it was a single tower, its most typical form was four-sided, with four towers in the corners—like a miniature version of the central building of the Tower of London. When painted in the flat or built as a façade, only the two front towers would be shown, with a gable or a gallery above and a large niche, gateway, or arched view of an interior in the center of the front. Of course, realism would suggest that it be the color of stone, but stone is very dull for a vivid decorative device; so, often enough, it was gay with bright paint and silver and gilt. In Bruges, in 1515, the tower built by the Aragonese was covered with red and silver, which in the light of the hundreds of torches shone like real gold and silver. All over it were set sparkling stones like jewels. From its doors a company came out in bright colors and set off artillery and played instruments. When Elizabeth was entertained by Sir Thomas Pope in 1556, six knights in rich colorful harness entered from a device of a castle of cloth of gold set with pomegranates about the battlements and decorated on the front with the shields of the knights. Some castles were painted to imitate the finest bright-colored marble; sometimes a castle was painted completely green or covered with painted or real boughs and flowers.

Even if the castle itself were dull, the decorations put on it could convert it into a festive showpiece. Like the houses themselves at festival time, the scenic castle could be hung with tapestries, curtains, and painted cloths. When Henry VI returned to London in 1432 after being crowned king of France, he was greeted by Virtues in a tower which was hung about with silk and arras. A castle built on the tournament field at Greenwich in 1524 was adorned with a cloth painting of Antioch in four pieces. The Temple Bar—the ancient gateway between London and Westminster—when redecorated for the entry of Edward VI, was painted and fashioned with castle battlements and buttresses, then hung with

[43] Kelly, *Royal Progresses and Visits to Leicester*, pp. 556 ff. and 618 ff.

[44] Shull, *op. cit.*, pp. 197 f.

[45] Cohen, *Histoire de la mise en scène*, pp. 92 ff.

arras and fourteen standards of flags. The conduits, already shaped like towers, were hung round with arras and made into little street theatres with musicians above and actors on a platform. The boat-castles—the famous Bucentaurus of Venice and its imitations at Lyons and elsewhere—were highly decorated with costly hangings. The Italian *castello d'amore*, which in Venetian festivals was covered with tapestries, green boughs, and flowers, was decorated at Treviso in 1304 with fur and purple and scarlet cloth.[46]

Shields, arms, and other heraldic adornment sometimes almost covered the castle, not only when it was used as a shield-standard on the tournament field, but also when it served as a device for a knight or as the symbol of a city or kingdom. At the gateway to the close of Canterbury Cathedral we can see today how heraldic devices can make even dark-colored stone bright and sparkling. If we think also of the many banners, pennons, and flags, the candles and torches by night, and the trumpeters and musicians, we can understand why the scenic castle was greatly admired.

As with all other devices, a regular location for musicians had to be provided. The castellated top, either of the walls or of the towers, served the purpose well. Some castles had, besides, a gallery at a lower level. The castle but follows a tradition, handed down by artists for centuries, that heavenly angels and other musicians should have a gallery at or near the top of any scenic device.

But how were these scenic castles used? How were characters related to them, and what were their theatrical conventions? The simplest use of a scenic castle was to put characters on top of it. When Alfonso entered Naples in 1443, he was met by a procession in which moved a large tower. Its gate was guarded by an angel, and from its top four Virtues sang to the king. This is

placing Virtues in a castle container just as one might today put celery stalks or dahlias in a bowl or vase. From such a castle in one of the *tableaux vivants* in Brussels in 1496 a woman leaned over to drop the fatal stone on Abimelech. The ingenious designer, however, could make more interesting use of a castle by opening it up or making it a background for a scene.

I have described the art tradition of a castle with a large archway at the center, in which a scene, perhaps an interior, could be placed, flanked by two towers. Many of the street theatres followed just that form, as, for instance, several of the castles constructed along the street or on the gates for the entry of Isabel of Bavaria into Paris in 1389. At the gate of the Châtelet a wooden castle opened to show a large complex scene. At one side, in a seat arrayed like a king's "bed of justice," was the figure of St. Anne. At the other side was a group of trees from which came first a hart, then a lion and eagle who threatened the hart and the bed, then twelve maidens with swords to defend the hart and the bed. All the action took place within the castle. Both a lower and an upper stage, such as we saw in the Bayeux Tapestry (Fig. 8), appeared in a castle theatre built in Grace Street, London, for the entry of Catherine of Aragon in 1501. From the lower floor, apparently in a gateway, a man arrayed like a senator, called Policy, addressed the princess. From an upper floor, perhaps from an arched doorway or a small projecting gallery, Nobleness gave her his advice.

The convention that the top gallery of a device could represent heaven, which we found frequent in painting and sculpture (Figs. 6, 13, 14, 19, 20, 21, 22), was carried over into the scenic castles. From the top of a castle in 1377 a figure of a golden angel bowed and offered a crown to the young Richard II. In Paris in 1389 for Isabel of Bavaria, one of the arches, built like a castle, had on its top a cloudy heaven full of stars (apparently a Glory) containing the figures of the Trinity. In London the conduit in Cornhill, a permanent castellated tower, had on several occasions a heaven built on its summit; in 1415, after

[46] Canestrari, *Il Castello d'amore;* Brotanek, *Die englischen Maskenspiele,* pp. 325 f. On the widespread popularity of the social game of the castle of love see Coulton, *Life in the Middle Ages,* I, 90 f.

Agincourt, a canopy on four posts supported by angels was built above it. The canopy was painted to resemble a sky and clouds, and an image of the sun was placed in a throne beneath, surrounded by a choir of angels singing and playing all kinds of instruments. Again in 1501, when Catherine arrived to marry Arthur, the top of the conduit was decorated with an ingenious revolving astrological device as symbol of the heavens, with Raphael sitting on a pinnacle above and three famous astronomers on a canopied bench below. When Mary and Philip made a triumphal entry into London in 1554, an elaborate castle was built at the Fountain of St. Brigit. On top of it was a sky sustained by four columns, whence a crown was let down to be presented to Philip. Often the castles on city gates or triumphal arches also had a heaven above or in front, from which an angel, or a maiden representing the city, could be let down with gift or speech of welcome. It is significant that a canopy supported by columns with ceiling painted like the sky is frequent in these representations of heaven; sometimes the ceiling inside a triumphal arch might be painted as sky. The Elizabethan stage offers another example of this same heaven-canopy above a theatrical structure.

The most theatrical development of the castle occurred where it was made into a façade, with the characters either incorporated into it or placed on a stage in front. The placing of figures in the gateway and the upper-story openings, some instances of which we have already noticed, was a step in the direction of the façade. There were three ways in which the castle could be developed further as a façade. One was to make the main gateway, and sometimes the upper-story openings, into niches (or a little gallery would serve for higher figures); the second was to build out from the castle or tower a pavilion consisting of canopy and columns, on the model long established both in art and in pageantry; and the third way was to build in front of the castle a complete little platform, such as was often seen in front of cave, fleur-de-lis, arcade screen, or any other device.

The fronts of churches and other Gothic buildings furnished many models for building single figures and whole scenes into niches or galleries in the wall. Figures of the French king and twelve peers with their blazons and arms adorned the upper part of the castle front built for the "Passe of Kynge Salhadyn," when Queen Isabel entered Paris in 1389. The drawing I reproduce of an English tournament façade of about 1500 shows a center niche built into the castle wall (Fig. 33). A similar or larger niche must have been built into the castle of the Fountain of St. Brigit for a scene of a virgin surrounded by maidens—a show-piece built for the entry of Mary and Philip. The virgin received the crown from the heaven-canopy above and presented it to Philip with a Latin address. A number of the street theatres in Bruges in 1515 had, besides the *tableaux vivants*, niches for arms, emblems, or statues, either between the stages or above or in the towers of the castles.

The castle with a pavilion built in front of it reminds us constantly of the Flemish and Elizabethan stages and is a form which is fairly frequent in Flemish manuscript illuminations and woodcuts; it can be traced to the combination of the throne-pavilion with other devices in Hellenistic art. We have noticed a pavilion built out in front of another structure in the Canterbury windows. The most fully described early example in the street theatres was built in London for Henry V in 1415 on his victorious return from Agincourt. At the end of the bridge a beautiful painted tower was built. At its front was a splendid pavilion, almost as high as the tower. Under the pavilion was an image of St. George, armed, his head crowned with laurel, gems, and precious stones. Behind him was a crimson tapestry with his arms. A triumphal helmet hung at his right and a shield at his left. In his right hand he held the hilt of a sword, and in his left a scroll which extended along the turrets of the tower with the words "Soli Deo honor et gloria." A choir of boys as angels sang, this time from another structure near by. When Charles V was received in London in 1520 on a visit to Henry VIII, the *tableaux vivants* had projecting canopies in front of both castle walls and single towers. Over one archway were built three great towers, into the front of each of which was set a canopy and throne, for figures of Charlemagne, the emperor, and the king—an arrangement which carried on an art tradition of combined throne and tower that was older than Charlemagne (Figs. 4, 5, 6, 13). An even more splendid street theatre was built in Cornhill. At the two sides of a façade were two towers filled with musicians and decorated with escutcheons and vanes. Between these towers, under a rich cloth of estate, was an elaborate throne scene of King Arthur surrounded by attendant kings, dukes, and earls. In front of the whole façade a poet appeared and recited to the imperial and royal audience.

More and more frequently the castle was used simply as a background with an apron stage in front, its towers, gallery, archway, and windows serving, of course, as occasion required. The St. George scene, for instance, so popular in England, was several times shown in pantomime or still tableau before a tower or castle. The tower was used dramatically at Coventry in 1474 as a station from which actors representing the father and mother watched St. George save their daughter from the dragon on the stage below. When Edward VI entered London in 1546/47, the pageant of St. George was again on a stage against the tower of the Little Conduit, which was elaborately hung with arras, streamers, banners, and targets. On the tower, among the city waits who were making the music, were two other symbols of England: Edward the Confessor on a throne and a golden lion.

How the castle became a conventional background for quite varied scenes is illustrated by the entertainments given before the English court for the Christmas revels of 1516. A castle of timber was built in one end of the hall, which served first as an appropriate background for a play about Troilus and Cressida given by the Children of the Chapel. After the comedy, there appeared a herald, who announced three strange knights to do battle with the knights of the castle. The audience was thereupon transported from Troy to the romantic pageant land of the medieval tournament. Not only knights but a queen and six ladies came out of the castle and made speeches, and seven minstrels played music on the walls and towers.[47] Two different scenes were played before the same castle in Portugal in 1525 for the marriage of King John. The play, *Fragoa d'amor* by Gil Vicente, set its first scene on the road to an allegorical castle. By the second scene the characters had come up before the castle.[48] We remember the castle that served both for the beginning and for the end of Jesus' journey in the York *Entry into Jerusalem*. A similar space convention existed in several of the Dutch romantic plays, for which one or two castles were built at the back of a platform stage.[49]

Two of the Flemish *tableaux vivants* used castles as backgrounds of stages which were inclosed by a pavilion or a proscenium frame. The scene I reproduce from the Bruges *tableau vivant* of 1515, showing Charles V being promised victory before Jerusalem (Fig. 27), has a castle façade for the city at the back of the scene; and the whole space is framed by a curious proscenium arch, the inside of which, like a triumphal arch, is painted with stars and moon. A similar street theatre was built in Tournai when Philip entered in 1549. Before a city gate Esther pleaded with Ahasuerus for the Jews. Over the whole scene was a canopy supported by four columns and adorned with a painting of Glory, Peace, and Justice.

In Italy as well, in the fifteenth century, before the introduction of perspective scenery, the castle served as a background for performances. In Ferrara, the *Cefalo* of Correggio, one of the first plays to use classical material, was put on in 1487 before a castle façade built from one wall to the other in the palace hall. Here also the medieval space convention was preserved. Cephalus went some distance away to hunt, and Procris from a window watched his return. Again, at the same court in 1491, the *Menaechmi* was put on before a façade which was a "prospect of four

[47] Brewer and Gairdner, *op. cit.*, II, 1505.

[48] Williams, *The Staging of Plays in the Spanish Peninsula*, p. 34.

[49] Kalff, *Geschiedenis der Nederlandsche Letterkunde*, II, 48 f.

castles."[50] The description—"the place for those to come out who give the performance"—indicates that in Italy scenery was no more illusionistic than in northern Europe. Even some decades after the perspective stage was developed, the setting served mainly as an interesting device from which actors could make an appearance.

The many later examples of the castle in ballets, masques, pageants, and operas need not concern us here. The greatest importance of the castle in the Renaissance was the patterns it gave to the theatres—the proscenium arch to the theatres of pictorial illusion and the symbolic façade to the Flemish and Elizabethan theatres. But those patterns we must leave to later chapters.

4. THE PAVILION

The story of the pavilion as a scenic device is more quickly told than that of the castle. In fact, part of it has already been told, for in a number of instances, as for *The Castle of Perseverance*, the pavilion was assimilated by the more picturesque castle; on other occasions it was made into a tent. Yet throughout the period it remained a separate tradition, and we see its mark on the Renaissance theatres. It was characteristically a three-dimensional canopy supported by columns, designed to ornament and frame such an object as a tomb or altar and permit it to be seen and approached from three or four sides. When it was combined with flatter forms, it would be a canopy projecting out from the other structure with only two columns; and, of course, there were many canopies, both actual and in art, that projected without any supporting columns. In painting and sculpture and for the religious plays, it could have a curtain hung at one or three sides or on all four sides, to be drawn to disclose the object or scene within. Except as it sometimes was made to resemble a tent or a throne- or bed-canopy, it remained a nonillusionistic structure of columns and roof-canopy with or without curtains.

I have already pointed out how it originated in art and how it preserved the convention of an interior. Of course, when the curtain was used, it

added another symbol of the interior. The accounts of the Flemish processions, especially the sketches of the Louvain pageant wagons of 1594,[51] prove that, with very slight indications, if any, of actual places or buildings, the baldacchino canopy was widely used as a setting for wagon *tableaux vivants*. For the stationary platforms, we know from the Lucerne and the Valenciennes sketches that many medieval mansions were formal architectural pavilions, even if the Mons producer's manuscript published by Cohen called for much realism of detail. However real some houses may have looked, we cannot escape the conclusion reached by Miss Galante-Garrone that the formal pavilion remained one normal type of mansion in religious drama to the end of the medieval period. On the other hand, to conclude, as Bonnell did, that it was the only type of structure, is to forget not only the hell-mouth and the circular Glory of Paradise, but the gardens, ships, castles, towers, chapels, and arched gateways that were built wherever there was any attempt to use more than the simplest scenic devices.

In the *tableaux vivants* of the street theatres, the pavilion was important. One of the simplest uses was to frame a single figure. At Ghent in 1458, at each turn of the way was a Prophet on a platform under a pavilion, with an identifying quotation on a scroll, to point out the way or direct attention to the next show. Likewise, a statue or actor representing the Virgin or a king or noble person would most likely be placed under a pavilion. Of course, by the sixteenth century the architectural decoration of column and canopy followed the newer Renaissance styles.

The presence of the curtain already made the pavilion resemble a tent, and "tent" and "pavilion" were almost synonymous terms on the

---

[50] Creizenach, *Geschichte des neueren Dramas*, II, 207 ff.

[51] The manuscript with its sketches was burned with the Library of Louvain in 1914, but fortunately the sketches had been copied in lithographs for van Even's *L'Omgang de Louvain*, published in 1863. The pageant wagons, nearly all of which have a baldacchino canopy supported on corner columns, are very helpful in visualizing the English wagons (Kernodle, "The Medieval Pageant Wagons of Louvain," *Theatre Annual*, 1943, pp. 58–76).

battlefield and on the field of a tournament. In painting, a tent was substituted for an architectural pavilion by a number of artists, especially to give a soft rich background for a formal portrait of the Virgin, whether seated or standing. The tent would partly inclose and frame the figure and might be carried at the top to a jeweled crown. In both the English *Pride of Life* and the plays of the Cornish rounds the main characters were revealed seated in tents that could be closed.[52] A number of the *tableaux vivants* used a tent for a scene. Sometimes a tent gave a curtained background even when there was a box or castle or pavilion inclosing the whole scene, tent and all. Two of the political *tableaux vivants* at Bruges in 1515 were housed in tents painted in yellow, red, and white. At the inauguration of the mayor of Norwich in 1556, Time addressed him from underneath a round pavilion, richly adorned with targets, with a naked Moor standing on the top, a target and a great dart in his hand.

One of the most interesting pavilions was that built in the garden at Richmond when Queen Mary received the Princess Elizabeth in 1557. It had the form of a castle and was hung with cloth of gold and velvet. The walls were painted in checkered compartments, in each of which was alternately a lily in silver and a pomegranate in gold.[53] This structure shows the most typical purpose of a pavilion (to frame a royal seat), the adornment of the interior with some symbol of an interior (cloth and painted design), and the shaping of the canopy after an elaborate architectural pattern.

5. THE ARCADE

The arcade screen did not end its theatrical career with the Greek and Roman stages. Nor was its Renaissance influence confined to such deliberate imitations of the classic stage as the Teatro Olimpico, built for a small rich club of scholars and connoisseurs. Through the traditions of art it gave the basic pattern to numbers of *tableaux vivants* and left many traces on the new theatres from London to Rome.

The simplest form of arcade as street theatre was a row of niches for portrait figures. This derives from an old tradition of religious art. The rows of saints painted or set in mosaic on so many Byzantine church walls were developed into rows of carved stone figures on both interior and exterior walls of Gothic churches. The Disciples were in demand in every church. Rows of Prophets became more popular from the eleventh century—probably, as Weber contends,[54] because of the development of the theme in church drama. In the later Middle Ages, as allegory became an all-pervading interest, the Virtues were painted or carved in rows of niches or arches.

The street theatres followed the fashion and built, in a free-standing arcade structure, rows of niches for figures of the virtues and royal qualities. Such an arcade screen served also for the portrait figures of the ancestors or predecessors of the prince. Nearly everywhere Philip II was received, an arcade row of famous Philips flanked a figure of the present Philip set in the center niche.

As a backing for a throne, the arcade was almost as popular as the castle. I reproduce one example from the eleventh century (Fig. 4) and two examples from late medieval art: Giotto's throne of the Sultan (Fig. 11) and a Flemish tapestry of David receiving Bathsheba (Fig. 17). In both later examples the curtain backing (symbol of an interior) covers the arches that appear in other paintings. This screen was constructed in three dimensions many times, both for actual kings (as an audience or reviewing seat) and for actor-kings in the tableaux. The large painting in the museum at Ghent of the inauguration of Charles II of Spain as Count of Flanders in 1666 and the many engravings of Hapsburg ceremonies in the eighteenth century show the persistence of the arcade in actual royal ceremonies. The throne-arcade built as a street

---

[52] Shull, *op. cit.*, pp. 252 and 284 f.

[53] Nichols, *The Progresses of Queen Elizabeth*, I, 18.

[54] *Geistliches Schauspiel und kirchliche Kunst.*

theatre for the entry of Archduke Ernest to Brussels in 1594 (Fig. 31) shows us a throne-pavilion in the center of a two-story arcade as a background for a scene of allegorical figures on a platform at the front. Similar is the throne-arcade back of the scene of the "Judgment of Solomon" shown on the public square at the end of the procession at Louvain in the same year (Fig. 51).

a pattern taken over, as we shall find, in many Renaissance façades. For another pattern of an important figure set at the top of an arcade we must go into the church to examine the rood loft, which regularly supported, high above the congregation, a figure of Christ on the cross. From the time Constantine erected a row of six columns in front of the altar of St. Peter's, the screen

FIG. 28.—Arcade-of-honor, Paris, 1549. Columns, gallery, and spectators painted on a back cloth. On the forestage, a living figure as a nymph offering gifts to Henry II.

This combination of throne-pavilion with an arcade screen and a forestage provided an important pattern for the Elizabethan stage.

An even more elaborate type of arcade had a heavenly pavilion or a heavenly throne set on the top. We have observed a heavenly throne above the doorway of the Roman theatre and on top of castles and other devices in medieval art. Especially did such scenes as the Judgment Day require a heavenly throne set above other scenes—

was used to combine formal architectural elements with sculptured figures, especially one sacred figure above. In the Eastern churches of Jerusalem and Byzantium, twelve columns, symbols of the Twelve Apostles, were united into a solid screen to hide the Mass from the laity.[55] Holl, as we have already noted,[56] is convinced that this form was derived from the façade of the

[55] Hassett, "Altar," *Catholic Encyclopedia*, I, 362–67.
[56] See chap. i, p. 21.

Hellenistic stage. Western screens, which were never completely closed, often had only three or five panels.

On a gallery at the top of the rood screen the accompanying figures of the Crucifixion—John, Mary, and others—could be added. This gallery sometimes served for the reading of the Epistle and the Gospel and sometimes for absolutions and benedictions. In the later Middle Ages the organ and a choir of singers were added to the rood loft—another pattern of musicians on a gallery at the top of an architectural device. The same pattern, without the religious figures, appeared in arcades supporting minstrel galleries in the great halls of palaces and colleges, like those to be seen until recently in Magdalen College, Oxford, in Charterhouse, in the Middle Temple, and elsewhere in England.

As a simple arcade the rood screen must often have been the background of dramatic representations.[57] If it had an open central arch, the side niches might be made into shrines or decorated with paintings—another example of the central arch with side panels. Sometimes the center was a closed niche for a rood altar where parish Masses could be held, the open side arches serving as entrances for the ministrants. Just how this type of screen would have been serviceable for a drama performed within the church is shown in a painting of Goertgen tot St. Jans in the Rijksmuseum in Amsterdam. The scene takes place before the altar, and the entering characters come from the two side arches of the screen.

The principal dramatic importance of the rood screen was its pattern of placing a figure at the top to be honored. In exactly the same form it had in the church, the rood screen was sometimes reproduced as a street theatre. At the Paris fountain called the Ponceau there was erected in 1437 an arcade for the procession of Charles VII. On a "terrace" above was the image of John the Bap-

[57] Fischel, "Art and the Theatre," *Burlington Magazine*, LXVI, 7 f.; Brooks, *The Sepulchre of Christ in Art and Liturgy*, p. 56. For the influence of the rood screen on the façades of Renaissance architecture see Horst, *op. cit.*, pp. 142 ff.

tist showing the Lamb of God (symbol of a fountain); a choir of angels, also on the gallery, sang while the procession passed underneath, just as the church choir would sing for a church procession. This rood screen built across a street

FIG. 29.—Façade as proscenium frame for a tableau, Antwerp, 1549. Philip II, with Clemency, receiving Antwerpia, who wears as crown an 8-foot model of the Cathedral tower. Framed paintings as background. Side niches flanking center pavilion with gable. Structure 100 feet high and 65 feet wide.

was soon absorbed, with its choir gallery and figure of honor, into the triumphal arch.

At the top of the arcade screen a royal pavilion or royal throne could easily be substituted for the figure. For an actual royal party to view such exhibitions as jousting and tournaments, the upper story was better than the one-story arcade throne. We find that this form was built in

Antwerp in 1549 when Philip II was to see jousting in a square, and in the same year in Paris at a
tournament for Henry II and Catherine de Medici.

Sometimes this arcade-of-honor was made even
more elaborate, with two- or three-story structures and statues, thrones, and paintings. A
by virgins in the center niche of the lower arcade
and St. Ursula in the niche of the second story;
on the top gallery were figures of the Trinity and
saints, and six angels casting incense. The side
arches were painted and covered with curtains of
cloth of tissue, blue and red. In front of the

FIG. 30.—Arcade-of-honor, Antwerp, 1549. Ten ladies presenting the ten Provinces to Philip II

double rood screen had occasionally been built in
the church, but on the streets this type of structure was made much more splendid than it could
ever be in a church. Arthur, Prince of Wales,
and his bride, Catherine of Aragon, saw in 1501
as they entered London, two especially handsome
specimens of the arcade-of-honor. Double arcades, thrones, hangings and paintings, and holy
figures on the top gallery were all combined. The
first arcade showpiece, built near London Bridge,
presented St. Catherine on a throne surrounded
pageant were two posts painted with roses and sur-
mounted by rampant lions. The second arcade-
of-honor was built at the entrance of St. Paul's
churchyard. A group of Virtues formed a tableau
on a platform in front of a two-story arcade.
On the first level a row of stately pillars framed
painted pictures. On the second level were three
seats: the center a heavenly throne in which sat
Honor, the two side seats empty but marked for
the prince and princess.[58] We shall find that this

[58] Nichols, *London Pageants*, pp. 26 ff.

throne-of-honor or arcade-of-honor was an important forerunner of both Flemish and Elizabethan stages.

Within the panels or arches of the arcades there were sometimes placed very interesting decorations. By means of an arcade frame a series

from which hung cloths with coats-of-arms of contemporary princes. How such a row of paintings could be made dramatic we see from the accounts of the reception of the Duke of Anjou and Alençon in Ghent in 1582. A maiden named History addressed him from before an arcade of

Fig. 31.—Arcade-of-honor, Brussels, 1594. Majesty enthroned. Piety, Prudence, Fortitude, Magnanimity, Justice, Clemency, Obedience, Envy, Adulation, two angels of Good Fame.

of flat paintings could be converted to a show-piece; and, especially in the Low Countries, long arcades of paintings were put along the sides of the street as elaborations of the traditional street hangings. When Charles V and Philip II entered Dordrecht in 1549, they passed between two rows of framed paintings of the contemporaneous rulers in northern Europe. For Alexander Farnese's entrance to Ghent in 1585, rows of columns supported racks for torches and an architrave

pillars and paintings of the Victory of Constantine; above, on the "frontispiece," were inscribed Flemish verses.

Not only cloth paintings but elements of the emblematic scenic devices might be placed in the separate arches of the arcade. In Lyons in 1548 two such arcades were built as backgrounds for allegorical figures. In one tableau a group of statues represented different rivers, and the arches behind them were filled in with a representation of rocks with brush and birds. The other tableau was a row of three nymphs—Faith, Religion, and Hope; in the screen of Ionic columns behind them were set three rocky caves, and above on the cornice were represented Justice, Prudence, and the royal arms. In Lille in 1600, for Albert and Isabella, a row of portrait statues was placed in the arches of a screen, each figure framed by a little tent open at the front.

It was but a step further to put a whole scene in each arch, to make a composite proscenium frame inclosing a row of separate scenes. On the occasion of royal visits the large hill of Bourgneuf at Lyons was usually the scene of a row of niches or of panels between columns. In 1548, for the arrival of Henry and Catherine, an arcade in the form of a triumphal arch was built against it. Between the columns of the arcade were several little houses, from one of which came Bellona to offer the king a helmet, while from a house on the other side came Victory to offer him a palm and a crown.

These individual scenes are similar to the scenes in the arches in the woodcut illustrations of Terence and Plautus which first appeared in 1493. When we come to examine the arcade theatres of schools, the Teatro Olimpico, and the Jesuit stages, we shall find that they derive from both the street-theatre arcade and the tradition of Terence illustration.

Whether at the back of the scene or as a frame for one or several inner stages, the arcade screen kept for the most part its formal, nonillusionistic character. It could give splendor and stateliness to a scene, but it could not indicate a definite locale. Hence we shall find that, while in the early Renaissance it was often mixed freely with other forms, later, more realistic generations either made it the front of a building or confined its use to such a purely formal element as the proscenium.

6. THE TRIUMPHAL ARCH

The Roman triumphal arch had a distinct form. A large central opening was usually flanked by two smaller side arches. Columns set into the solid structure usually marked out panels between the archways and one or three panels in the rectangular space above. The deeds of the hero, carved in bas-relief, filled the panels. It was thus a permanent showpiece in stone.

The newer, more temporary show-arches erected in the late Middle Ages, even in Italy, where many Roman archways remained, did not follow the ancient pattern exclusively but borrowed much from the castle and other scenic devices. In northern countries the Roman outline was introduced only after the other patterns were well developed, and the medieval types, especially the castle, have persisted to the present day.

The usual sixteenth-century triumphal arch, of which thousands were built, was a street theatre, an architectural showpiece, borrowing not only from both medieval and Roman architecture but from all other decorative and scenic forms of the time. It was a showpiece not only for sculptured scenes of history and allegory but also for torches, for banners, for inscriptions, for tapestries, for paintings, for arms and shields, for *tableaux vivants*, for speeches of welcome. While it usually signified a city or a realm or a guild in the city, it might take the form of a city gate or an arcade screen, or it might be transformed into a rock, a cave, a sea, a ship, a temple or be covered by boughs and flowers. Sometimes all or part of it was disclosed by the removal of a curtain. Usually musicians played or sang as the royal party approached. Knights waited under triumphal arches until their turn to enter the tournament field, or dancers until they came onto the floor of the hall. Curtained *tableaux vivants* might be played in the arch, in a panel above, in a pavilion or other device built out from its walls, or on the gallery above. It could take on something of the shape and any of the conventions of the other scenic devices, and it contributed to the other devices.

I have already noted the practice of transforming city gates into showpieces by adding music, hangings, characters, and even speeches and dialogue. The substitution of a temporary structure along the way of a procession was an

ERNESTO AVSTRIACO &c.

OPVS TRIVMPHALE LVCENSIVM.

FIG. 32.—Façade with flat perspective painting, Antwerp, 1594. Niches at sides for allegorical figures. Cressets and banners

innovation that was bound to be made. Whether for letting down a maiden to deliver the keys, or for trumpeters to play from the gallery, or for painted or living pictures, this decorative structure could be more colorful, more showy, and more flexible as a stage than the actual gates.

To indicate the meaning of the arch, an allegorical figure, or at least a symbol such as a coat-of-arms, would usually be added. At the entrance to the market of Bruges in 1440 was an arch made in the form of a castle to display the banners and arms not only of Bruges but of all the lands of the duke. As the party entered the square, a large band of musicians on the castle played. But the first gate arch the duke passed had, besides musicians, a pavilion above, with David, seated, displaying a motto written on a roll. Often a maiden representing the city was placed above. In Douai, in 1516, on a sumptuous gallery above the gate arch stood the maiden Douai surrounded by protecting Virtues. To enter Edinburgh in 1503, Queen Margaret went under a triumphal arch resembling a castle, built in the characteristic form of two towers with central opening between. From windows in the towers angels sang, and in the center niche or window an angel stood to present keys to the queen.

A most elaborate arch-pavilion made of columns and curtains represented the city of Messina, when Charles V visited it in 1536. On satin hangings in three colors it showed the devices of the city and of the emperor. The heaven was of the same satins, and at the corners nude children held the coat-of-arms of the city.

In England throughout the sixteenth century, arches in the form of castles represented the city for the visiting sovereign. The elaborate arches built for the entry of James into London in 1603, for which we have not only detailed descriptions but engravings, illustrate well the extent to which the arches had taken on the characteristics of other scenic devices and had become scenic theatres. All had living figures, and most had both a gallery for musicians and a speaker's gallery, from which speeches written by Middle-ton, Ben Jonson, and other prominent authors were delivered. All were complex façades, deriving chiefly from the castle but combining in one unified architectural structure the separate thrones, niches, galleries, pavilions, paintings, curtains, and *tableaux vivants* of the other street theatres.

The first one was built in Fenchurch Street. It is called "Tuscan," but the classic columns were merely incidental to the elaborate theatre façade, which had castle towers and battlements at the top. As the "forehead" or "battlement" of the edifice, there was a medieval town-canopy with recognizable models of the prominent houses, towers, and steeples of the city, on which were inscribed "Londinium" and "Camera regia." There were four levels for living characters: on the top level sat Monarchia Britannica with Divine Wisdom at her feet, surrounded by six Civic Virtues; beneath these was one of the speakers, Genius of the City, supported by warlike Force of the City; below that level, in a pavilion which projected forward beyond the rest of the façade, was the other speaker, Thamesis, leaning his arm upon a gourd; the lowest level, just above the actual archway, was a gallery for the musicians.

An interesting combination of scenic castle and classic architecture was the façade of the arch of the Dutch merchants on the same occasion. The girls in the tableau were all natives of the Low Countries, and painters and workmen had been imported. When James approached it, musicians on the topmost gallery played. There, instead of a figure of God, was a painting of an earthly king on a throne. When the trumpets played, a curtain in the center level opened to disclose a *tableau vivant* of seventeen maidens, all dressed in conventionalized Roman costumes, representing the seventeen provinces of the Low Countries. Behind them were tapestries, and at the sides of the inner stage were niches with painted figures of biblical and historical kings. The maidens rose and made reverence to the king, but "as we read that with the Romans no one spoke from triumphal arches, so here no one spoke." However, on the gallery a scholar stepped out and read a greeting in Latin verse. The very top was decorated with obelisks, coats-of-arms and other heraldic insignia, and banners.

Later arch façades were rarely quite so elaborate. For Charles II in 1661 a spectacular stage effect of Rebellion sinking into perdition was produced in the *tableau vivant* of an arch. But the peak had been passed. Most Baroque arches followed not the Roman form but the form of the flat façade, which had the power to absorb into itself all other scenic devices, even the picturesque medieval castle and the classic triumphal arch.

7. THE FAÇADE

The most important development of the street theatres in the sixteenth century was the pattern of the architectural façade. While it derived from several of the older devices, we must consider it as a new, separate form. Although it might continue to show some characteristic details of the medieval devices, it gave increasing prominence to its formal architectural structure—the columns that framed the panels and the decorative canopy above. The remarkable fact about the façade is that it could take on the symbolic meaning of any of the older structures and that increasingly they were assimilated to its forms: they were made flatter and given framing columns and a canopy. The façade is the transitional form between the stylized realism of the medieval devices and the purely architectural symbolism of the Flemish and Elizabethan stages. We must watch how it took to itself the power to represent every other scenic device.

In the street theatres the façade was rarely recognized as a separate, independent scenic device. It was a tendency, a disease to which all other scenic devices were subject. From the end of the fifteenth century on, and increasingly in the sixteenth, the castle and the pavilion were flattened into a wall, either as a complete device or set at the back of a platform, and the arcade was compacted into a cluster around one large doorway. The mountain, the cave, and even the tree, the fountain, and the ship were not left free-standing but were built against, and sometimes into, a scenic screen which would give them a backing and sometimes partly inclose them by side columns and a canopy above.

The main outlines of the façade we have watched in the development of the tomb and the altar. From complex medieval ciborium these monumental sculptural forms were compacted into an almost flat screen of columns, panels, cornices, and gabled pediments. In our study of medieval painting we saw how the façade acquired such conventional arrangements as the two or three stories, and the side panels which could be flat panels, niches, doorways, or even towers. The façade in the street theatres followed closely the tendencies in painting and monumental sculpture.

The upper story deserves special attention. The question of an upper story in the medieval religious mansions has aroused some controversy. Further, the appearance of an upper story in the Renaissance theatre in every country in western Europe gives the convention considerable importance for us. The principal conventional use of the upper stage was as heaven. The theory was advanced by the Parfaict brothers in the eighteenth century that the normal stage of the medieval religious drama in France was composed of a number of stories or galleries, one above the other, to a great height. Each level, they believed, might be a different city or country, or various interiors. In the nineteenth century the theory was repeated by many and fully developed by Morice, with the interpretation that a three-level stage was normal, to represent heaven at the top, earth or purgatory in the center, and hell in the cellar. This theory appealed to English students because certainly the Elizabethan façade placed heaven above and earthly scenes on the main level, and hell, while not actually shown, beyond an occasional hell-mouth, was indicated as the cellar. In our time, however, Professor Cohen has attacked the theory vigorously and with apparent success. He has shown that the normal performance of a French religious play was on a horizontal platform with all mansions on the same level. Heaven was never above hell or purgatory; in fact, it was regularly at the opposite end of the platform; and the principal earthly places were not underneath heaven but in a row beside it. While the mansion of heaven usually had two stories and the throne of God was on the higher level, the lower part was used either as a doorway or for such scenes as the Resurrection or the reappearances of Christ—scenes directly related to heaven.

For the street theatres, the *tableaux vivants*, we

The heaven in the upper story or in the gallery, canopy, or gable above an earthly scene dates in painting and sculpture, as we have seen, from Byzantine and Carolingian days. The pattern of the Last Judgment scene was preserved in sculptured tombs, the heavenly figures waiting above for the deceased to rise from his earthly bed. The vertical pattern was especially important in the many real gates and artificial street theatres in which an angel came from a heaven-device to the king below.

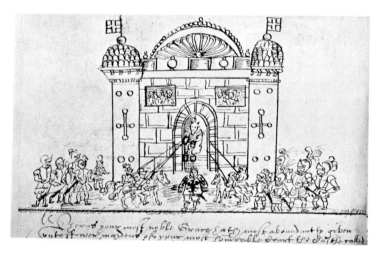

Fig. 33.—Castle façade for a tournament. English about 1500. Renaissance decoration at top. Paintings as decorations. Unicorn in the niche holding four shields of the courses to be chosen by participants. MS Harley 69, fol. 20ᵛ, British Museum.

must just as resolutely reinstate the old theory.[59] It was perhaps originally based on accounts of religious scenes in street theatres and mistakenly applied to all religious performances. Increasingly from the late fifteenth century, a single, somewhat flat, unified architectural structure prevailed for the *tableaux vivants*. It corresponded to the single mansion of the multiple stage. From traditions of art and sculpture this façade derived the convention of several stories, with heaven at the top. Hell in the cellar is not a part of the *tableaux vivants;* it was not a dainty dish to set before the king.

[59] Miss Shull (*op. cit.*) has recently pointed out that in a number of English medieval religious stages God or an angel descends from heaven to the earth (sometimes the Garden of Eden) below.

The heaven on top of a castle we have already observed, with examples from France, the Low Countries, and England. Any of the other devices as well might have heavenly figures above. The tournament façade which served as a background for a weeping maiden at a fountain at Chalon-sur-Saône in 1449–50 had an image of the Virgin and the Christ child at its top.[60] For Charles V's visit to London in 1520, an elaborate pavilion, a "quadrant stage," was built over a scene of roses, animals, and fish. On the canopy were painted the stars, and in the roof, "in a type in the top," was a heavenly scene of the Trinity surrounded by singing angels. In 1533 for Anne Boleyn, a canopy built against a façade "with a type and a heavenly

[60] La Marche, *Mémoires*, II, 142 ff.

roof" was a background for a stage with the figure of St. Anne. First a falcon came from the "type," or canopy, to the stage below, then an angel descended and set a crown on the falcon's head. At the coronation procession of Edward VI, a phoenix and angels descended from a heaven above to crown a young lion. At Rouen in 1508 a variation was played on the gift-from-heaven motif. A theatre called "The World" opened to permit Renown, holding a crown, to be raised by an engine and set in the heaven above. This was a secular counterpart of the Assumption of the Virgin, which was played on many religious stages.

Often in the sixteenth century, not the Heavenly King but the image of the earthly sovereign, or an important allegorical figure, was placed in the heavenly throne. When Arthur and Catherine entered London in 1501, beside the Temple of God, which had the heavenly group with singing angels, were a pavilion with a throne for Raphael, the angel of marriage, above the stars and spheres, and another with a throne for a figure of the royal bridegroom in the middle of a whirling Glory of clouds—the Glory which usually served for a divine personage. In 1554 a heavenly pageant was built in Fleet Street with a king on the throne, and around him were Justice, Truth, Mercy, and (instead of Peace) Equity. From the top of the pageant descended Sapientia with a crown in each hand to present to Philip and Mary. In another street was a pageant with Orpheus above and the Nine Muses below, all making music. When Queen Eleanor visited Lyons in 1533, she saw a *tableau vivant* of mariners in a boat without a rudder. They looked to the heaven above, where a figure of the queen sat on a rainbow with a Glory of the seven planets revolving behind.

Sometimes, as in the tombs we examined, there was more than one level of heavenly figures. A number of tombs had the Virgin and Child on a level below the Father or the Trinity. One street theatre, built in Paris in 1517, had Charity in a great sun on the topmost level, a group of goddesses with coats-of-arms below, then figures of the

pope and the king of France on the main stage. Similar façades of several levels, with a throne-pavilion at the top, were built on triumphal arches in Antwerp in 1594 and in London in 1603.

The further story of the façade is the story of the absorption of all the other devices—the architectural forms were flattened to conform with it, and the emblematic devices of gardens, rocks, and trees were combined with back wall, columns, and canopy. That story is already partly told. We have only to examine the form and conventions of the façade as it took over the meanings and some of the details of the other devices.

In the façade we can see, besides the scenic devices, a trace of the earliest decorative element—the cloth and the standard to hold it. When the fronts of houses did not seem suitable, some tapestries and cloths were hung on special frames built free-standing at the sides of the street. Some of these frames, as we have seen, were made into long arcades of hangings. Others were developed as single showpieces, somewhat like a modern billboard. When canopies and columns and perhaps torches were added, a theatrical façade was created. When Margaret of York arrived in Bruges in 1468 to marry the Duke of Burgundy, she found erected in front of the Hôtel de Ville a rich tableau structure showing the arms of Burgundy. Around the tableau were twelve blazons of the arms of the duke's provinces; at the two sides were painted two archers, with wine flowing from a structure at the foot of each. The top of the frame was finished by some kind of tabernacle, at the side of which stood figures of St. George and St. Andrew. When, on later occasions, an orator or actors in a scene were put in front of such a screen, in the fashion of the mountebank stages, then the show-cloth façade was made theatrical.

In the case of the show-picture, the formal framing elements at top and sides gave it its distinct character, as was the case with all the other devices when they were combined with the façade. Even the castle lost its peculiar medieval character and took on some degree of the formal, stately character of Renaissance architecture. The Renaissance façade of the street theatres was far

FIG. 34.—Tableau at banquet in Binche, 1549. Pavilion similar to penthouse of Elizabethan theatre. Symbol of heaven above the canopy. Part of a fountain, a separate tableau, at the right.

less illusionistic and far more conventional than the individual devices had been in the fifteenth century.

The one architectural form most visible in the canopy of the façade was the pavilion. We have seen how this device changed from Gothic to Renaissance by simplification of its structure and decorations. It remained a decorative roof supported by four columns. I have pointed out how the tomb pavilion was flattened into the pediment and framing columns of the Renaissance tomb. Not only in Italy, but also in the painted tombs built onto walls in many English churches in the sixteenth century, we can see the reduced form of the medieval pavilion.

The first important type of pavilion to be converted into a backing for a tableau was the canopy or "estate" of the king's throne. For official audiences, well before any street theatres had been built, this canopy was a roof with only the two front columns visible. We find such a pavilion with Gothic detail built as a background for a scene in Rouen for the entry of Charles VIII in 1485. Rich pillars supported a tabernacle, which was ornamented in its arches with royal insignia. Under the tabernacle sat a king surrounded by royal Virtues, who sang and made addresses. On a stage in front of this *tableau vivant* shepherds appeared and performed a little play. In 1483 in Paris, a three-level throne-façade was the backing for a stage from which Labor, Clergy, Merchant, and Nobility spoke greeting to young Marguerite of Flanders, fiancée of the dauphin. In the heavenly throne at the top was the king, below were a boy and girl as Marguerite and Charles, and on the lowest level were figures of M. and Mme Beaujeu, who escorted the dauphine.

The pavilion-canopy projecting from a façade, with or without two supporting columns, became more and more frequent, and might be built over any kind of scene and over any scenic device; it could even be built over a castle gateway. The street theatre at the square of the Holy Innocents in Paris in 1514 is a significant complex example. Like nearly all the street stages of 1514 and 1517 in Paris and 1515 in Lyons, it was built as a

façade with a canopy, in which was a throne-of-honor where several Virtues stood, surrounding a lily under an arch. On the lower level of the stage was a tilted, walled-in garden, in the center of which the body of a woman was emerging from a rose. The gate of the garden close was flanked by two castle towers, and in the gate sat the figure of Peace. Thus, both the garden and its castle gate were built against a façade with a canopy above (Fig. 37).

For Elizabeth in London in 1558/59, the street theatre built in front of the Little Conduit had a castle-canopy and a façade of hills beneath. Two hills representing a decayed and a flourishing commonwealth framed a cave between them, from which came Time and Truth. Here was expressed in terms of hills the castle-front pattern of two towers framing a gateway. A little stage or "standing" was built in front for a child to explain the show to the queen and to present to her the book which Truth brought.

Trees could also be used as show-façades, often with a canopy or archway above. The tree, *lis*, and fountain were frequent in tournaments as frames for shields and arms and were similarly used as street decorations. On the model of the Tree of Jesse of wall paintings and stained-glass windows, a flattened tree was built, usually against a supporting screen, to present the noble ancestry or a group of related allegorical characters. On a stage in Rouen in 1485, more than forty-four ancient notables who sang and played instruments were placed on several different levels on a tree which slowly turned on a pivot. At the top was a throne with an actor as the young King Charles VIII. Above the whole tree was an elaborate canopy with small mechanical figures of the four Evangelists, a lamb which bowed to the king, cherubim, and seven lamps with shields of the seven parts of Normandy. On the stage in front of the spectacle was John the Evangelist and also an angel, who stepped out of a cloud to explain the show by opening a long roll with verses in praise of the king. While that spectacle was built in three dimensions and only the stage in front gave it direction, most of the later tree-shows were flattened to be seen from one side only. When Louis XII entered Paris in 1498, he saw at the Châtelet a *lis* holding nine portraits of kings leading up to Louis at the top. On the yellow and violet pavilion built "at the front of the scaffold" was a king on his throne surrounded by Counsel, Justice, People, Church, etc.—the civic equivalent of the heavenly throne.

The miniatures for the street theatres of 1514 in Paris and 1515 in Lyons, published by Baskervill and by Guigue (Figs. 35, 36, 37), show us just how the neat, compact Renaissance pediment with two supporting columns could inclose, like a picture frame, the central scene of fleur-de-lis, garden, ship, arch, or what not. When the pavilion came forward beyond the whole scene, as in several shows at Rouen in 1485, the form approached the boxlike structure which in Brussels in 1496 and in Bruges in 1515 inclosed the tableaux like a proscenium. When it was built back of part of the stage, as in many cases in England, France, and the Low Countries, it set a pattern for the Flemish and Elizabethan theatres.

Sometimes the emblematic device would support the upper levels without the help of an inclosing pavilion. A tree or a *lis* often sustained a cloud with heavenly beings. A rock or mountain might be constructed like a façade to present characters at several levels; for instance, a show at Dieppe in 1531 was built as a rock supporting a scene of David and Bathsheba, with a row of caverns below, which opened to disclose Virtues. A similar show for Philip in Lille in 1549 presented an allegorical group of Cheerful Virtues on top, above a cavern for a dragon, a lion, a salamander, and a woman, Fear.[61] More frequently the rock or mountain served simply as a façade, tilted or vertical, with niches for characters. As a "Mountain of Fame" or "Temple of Fame," such a façade persisted in Baroque operas, ballets, and masques. Like other devices, the rock- or mountain-façade could have not only niches but galleries on the front or at the top. Thus a show at the Châtelet in Paris in 1437, for the entry of Charles VII after the English had been driven out, was a composite rock-façade with biblical and allegorical scenes. On top was a gallery with shepherds receiving the angel of the Nativity and singing "Gloria in excelsis"; an arch opened up to show a Seat of Justice with Divine, Written, and Natural Law; and below, apparently as a kind of sculptural bas-relief, were Paradise, Purgatory, and Hell, with Michael in the midst weighing souls.

A number of stages in different countries were backed by a façade consisting of an arch combined with other devices. We have noticed in sculptured groups an arch over a mountain or over trees. Many of the French designers put a garden archway over a lily. An interesting composite façade, comparable to the combinations we have noticed on triumphal arches, was built in Milan when Louis XII of France made his victorious entry in 1507. At the back of a stage an arch of green leaves had on its top an artificial mountain about the height of a man, encircled with rows of shields and supporting a figure of Our Lord, naked and flagellated. At the front of the stage were two seats covered with cloth of gold, in which were placed the personages of St. Ambrose (the patron of Milan) and the King of France.

The fountain, like the tree, the mountain, and the pavilion, could be built against a back wall or combined with castle, pavilion, arch, or arcade to serve as the backing of a scene. A most interesting example is the show of the Judgment of Paris among the *tableaux vivants* for Joanna of Castile, wife of Philip the Fair, in Brussels in 1496. Inside an inclosing box, Paris lies downstage at one side. The garden is symbolized by a fountain at the center built against an arcade screen with two side arches. Through these side arches, on a little circular runway, move the three goddesses, like figures of an astronomical clock.

What, then, was this façade? More and more it was a flattened architectural structure with columns set either against or close to the wall, supporting an architrave and often upper panels,

---

[61] This is the nearest I have found in the street theatres to a hell scene on the lower level. Similar was the lower stage in a show in Antwerp for the Duke of Anjou and Alençon in 1582, which showed Discord being put behind a prison door.

Fig. 35.—Ship as part of tableau façade, Paris, 1514. Cotton MS, Vespasian B II, British Museum

FIG. 36.—Allegorical *tableau vivant*, Paris, 1514. God in heaven holding a heart and a *lis*. A king and queen in triumph. Below, France and England, seated, with Amity, Peace, and Confederation. Minstrels sang from behind. A forestage for an expositor. (The text belongs to the manuscript and not to the tableau.) Cotton MS, Vespasian B II, British Museum.

FIG. 37.—Allegorical *tableau vivant*, Paris, 1514. At top a rich tabernacle (the upper stage) called a throne-of-honor, holding a crown with a *lis* in a garden called the Garden of France, and four maidens as Pity, Truth, Force, and Clemency. Below, a city with Peace seated on a throne in the gate, Discord at her feet. Back of her the Pope, the Unique Desire of Princes, and a rosebud rising to the height of the throne-of-honor. In the rosebud a girl who made the oration. Cotton MS, Vespasian B II, British Museum.

Fig. 38.—Triumphal arch, Antwerp, 1635. Designed by Rubens. Baroque façade. Crowned figure of Honor and speakers' gallery above the arch. *Tableau vivant* in the upper panel. Historical and allegorical figures in the side panels and on top. Painted marble columns.

incloses the stage picture. The picture within the *tableaux vivants* set a number of patterns for both the inner stages and the main scenes of Renaissance theatres.

Inside the tableaux the artist was far more conservative than painters in oil of the same period. A neutral or figured background was abandoned by progressive painters at the end of the fourteenth century, but figured backgrounds and cloths and tapestries were used inside the *tableaux vivants* throughout the Renaissance. Many descriptions of street-shows mention the rich tapestries, usually borrowed from palace, city hall, or church, to hang behind the characters. The show of David and Abigail at Ghent in 1458 was in "a stage richly hung within and without with costly tapestries." The curtain background, long a tradition of painting, was used in such stage forms as the German school drama, the theatre of the Meistersingers in Nuremberg, and, of course, the Spanish public theatres.[63] It had many uses on the Elizabethan stage, and it persisted in some places on the inner stage of the perspective scene. Especially as a background for thrones and as a symbol of an interior, it lasted into the seventeenth century.

While most of the tableaux at Bruges in 1515 were painted inside with formal patterns, that of the merchants from Franche-Comté followed the newer practices of painting. Inside the boxlike structure was a royal seat, and the background was painted as landscape. Renaissance painters in both Italy and Flanders were very fond of landscapes as background, putting them behind almost any kind of scene or a single or group portrait. How cloths painted as landscape could be hung back of *tableaux vivants* set in a shallow stage framed by a proscenium we can see in several of Rubens' paintings. His portrait of Elijah, in the Louvre, and his series of Triumphs, in the Louvre, the Prado, the Boymans Museum of Rotterdam, and elsewhere, all show a loose cloth spread under and back of the figures and looped over a cord or part of the proscenium above (Fig. 39). I suspect that Rubens was borrowing

[63] Cf. chap. v below.

directly from the street-shows that he saw and helped design.

Some *tableaux vivants* were not treated as pictures but as actual stages, and on them could be built the same kind of scenery used by the theatre of the time. One of the scenes at Ghent in 1458 had two mansions, a form frequent for the Dutch secular plays and in the English court theatre. On one side was a castle representing the realms of the duke, defended by the Three Estates and a Giant and a Lion. On the other side, in a wilderness of trees and hedges, were wild animals that threatened the castle. A castle or city gate with towers and walls was built or painted as background in one of the shows at Bruges in 1515. At Tournai in 1549, and for several shows at the entry of Archduke Matthias into Brussels in 1578, a conventional view of walls symbolized a city (Fig. 40): there was no concept of placing the characters within the setting. Indeed, for the tableau at Bruges in 1515 of Artaxerxes undertaking the rebuilding of Jerusalem, the ruined city was not shown on the stage at all but was painted on the back of the door which swung open to disclose the show. Most painted backgrounds were as conventional as the river scene which was often painted in the panel back of a statue or living figure personifying a river.

More complex groups of mansions did appear inside a few of the later living pictures. At Lille in 1600 several stages had small mansions somewhat like the Hôtel de Bourgogne scenery as sketched by Mahelot. For a show of the local legend of the death of Finart at the hands of Lyderic, five mansions were built—a door, a tower, a throne, a hovel, and a tree. This combination of a curtain background with separate mansions, as we shall see, was a pattern of the Spanish theatre of the time.

Perspective scenery never really played any part inside the stages of the street theatres. Sometimes in Italy perspective scenes were used to present allegorical groups in honor of a monarch, but only on large indoor or courtyard stages. The smaller street theatres remained shallow. Bapst

FIG. 39.—Rubens' "Triumph of Charity." Imitation of a *tableau vivant*. Painted cloth as a background hung against architectural façade. Prado, Madrid. Anderson, Rome.

was intrigued by his discovery that the authors of both the first two French treatises on perspective had engaged in preparing *tableaux vivants*.[64] Yet the sketches of buildings which Jean Pélerin (Viator) published in 1505 in his book on perspective show conventionalized façades and triumphal arches of a kind already familiar in the street-shows (Fig. 57) but no street scenes of great depth of the Italian type. Only as a flat painting is there any record of a perspective scene used as a street decoration. The first time was at Lyons in 1548, for the entry of Henry II and Catherine. These sovereigns, who on the same occasion at night saw the first perspective stage scenery in France, saw in the street at the Change a little drama of Neptune and Pallas on separate platforms, in front of a view of Troy painted in perspective on flat canvas. We notice that the Lyons designers kept separate the two traditions. Real perspective scenery, with wings and back shutter, was for the court entertainment at an evening function made brilliant with lights. The street theatre, where the royal party paused for but a moment, retained the flat symbolic background.

The most interesting scenic effect inside the boxes of the *tableaux vivants* was the device of suddenly changing a scene. This was achieved in the street theatres of France more than half a century before scene changes became general in the perspective stages of Italy. Of course, there was no idea of changing the locale in the modern sense; few tableaux attempted to indicate a locale. The change was a miraculous or spectacular transformation, by means of a pivot which turned a device around and showed the other side. The first examples I have found appeared in Rouen in 1485 for the welcome of Charles VIII. When the curtain, hanging between proscenium columns, was drawn aside, Charles saw an elaborate structure of a tree all sere, representing a country desolate. From a fountain representing the king, water was brought to the tree. Immediately the whole structure was turned around, to show the other side, which was green and flourishing.

[64] *Op. cit.*, pp. 61 ff.

Another revolving tree built for the same occasion served as a stand for raised degrees, on which sat more than forty-four actors dressed as people of the ancient world to sing and play instruments. It turned slowly to show the ancients sitting all around. A sphere built at Rouen in 1550 for Henry II was turned to disclose an elaborate scene of Francis I as a tree-fountain, bearing

FIG. 40.—*Tableau vivant*, Brussels, 1578. Scipio bringing Asia and Libya under subjection. The liberated peoples at the side. The freed city painted on the background.

several fruitful branches. The turning scaffold for seated figures became in Antwerp in 1600 a cylinder inside the shell of an amphitheatre, on which scores of beautiful ladies sat holding shields of the guilds and societies of the city. The turning spectacle—as tree, as sphere, as mountain, as temple—was to reappear many times in *ballet de cour*, masque, and opera and on the Spanish public stage. This revolving machine was developed in the north several decades before Italian architects experimented with the neo-Vitruvian *periak-*

toi—those three-sided wings used for a century to effect a spectacular change of scenery before the eyes of the audience.

The chief importance for later theatres of these inclosed boxes of the street-shows was in setting the pattern of an inner stage on which a tableau could be disclosed behind a curtain or shutter. Many inner stages, especially in the northern theatres, retained the rather conventional background of tapestries or symbolic properties that belonged to the tradition of the street tableaux and only later acquired the illusionistic painted setting that was copied directly from painting.

But it was not the interior, it was the complete structure of the *tableau vivant* that was of most importance for the Renaissance theatres. Nearly every theatre in the sixteenth century, both north and south, showed that influence. To the perspective stage the street tableaux contributed a pattern for a proscenium that was not merely a formal, neutral border but was itself a scene, a show-device, with the festival atmosphere and decorations of a castle, an arcade, or a show-façade. To the theatres of Flanders and England the street-shows contributed even more—they set the basic patterns for the stage and contributed many of the dramatic conventions as well.

PART II

THE THEATRES OF ARCHITECTURAL SYMBOL

*The Terence Academy Façade; the Flemish, Elizabethan,
and Spanish Popular Theatres*

WE COME now to the theatres themselves. We are ready to search for their basic principles by comparing them with one another and by comparing their forms and conventions with the traditions of the pictorial arts.

All the Renaissance theatres may be divided into two main groups: theatres of pictorial illusion and theatres of architectural symbolism. The principles of both are implied in the painting of the fifteenth century. The theatres of pictorial illusion, as we shall discover in Part III, merely carried out in three dimensions the dominating ideals of the new art—realism and illusion. Yet the other principle—the stylization and conventionalization of reality into a symbol—existed in painting alongside the principle of the suggestion of an actual place. The habit of dealing in symbols, a habit which dominated medieval art and ritual, did not disappear with the turn to humanism in the Renaissance. We have observed the increasing stylization of reality in the *tableaux vivants;* we have noticed that it tended to combine all scenic devices into a pure architectural symbol and that a façade with columns, archways, upper galleries, and a canopy took on the power to represent any other emblem of reality, whether city gate, throne, temple, mountain, or garden.

This process of stylization was carried even further in the actual theatre façades than in the *tableaux vivants.* While the castle of the street theatres might have Renaissance columns, a heaven above, and a throne-pavilion in front, it usually kept some suggestion of stonework and battlements. The façades of the Renaissance theatres, however, although they continued to represent castles and the other devices, apparently lost most of the actual painted detail of the medieval symbols. They carried a little further the tendency already present in the earlier visual arts to make a decorative architectural structure symbolize reality. We can understand that tendency if we remember the astrolabe and the pieces on the chessboard. The astrolabe served as a symbol of the heavens, though it had no more resemblance to what man saw in the sky than a telescope has, or the signs of the zodiac. Modern chessmen retain only the vaguest resemblance to the castles, bishops, knights, and kings and queens they continue to represent. Because some theatres carried this architectural symbolism to its full development and others carried the desire for illusion to full realization, there was possible the wide divergence we find between the Elizabethan stage and the Italian perspective setting—both of which derive from the traditions of the visual arts.

As we discovered in examining the habits of medieval painters and designers, there were three different ways by which a complex scene could be organized—the side accent, which inclosed the center space; the center accent, which provided a façade and perhaps inner stage for the action; and the flat scene, which provided several archways as more or less equally important centers of action. Of the three, the side accent was associated with the ideal of illusion and gave the basis for the Italian perspective scene. The center accent led to the development of the con-

109

ventionalized façade, the pattern for the Flemish and Elizabethan public theatres, and for some effects on the Spanish stage. It is easy to point out the differences between these two main types of theatres, the symbolic and the illusionistic. But the third method of organization—the design with a flat arcade screen—cuts across both types.

We find not only theatres in which the arcade screen was given a symbolic function—they can be classed with the other façade theatres—but also those in which it was a part of the perspective scene. In the illusionistic scene the screen was finally given a formal function either as a front proscenium or as a frame for the inner stage. Hence I must treat separately the two uses of the screen—the one as an independent façade and the other as a framing device for the perspective setting. We shall soon recognize how similar are the two, and we may then realize how closely akin are all the Renaissance theatres.

I describe in Part II the several theatres of architectural symbol—the theatres that used a more or less formal architectural façade at the back of the playing area. They did not pretend to resemble the places they represented, but they were not purely negative. They were more than mere doorways and upper stages by which the dramatist had to re-establish each new scene in the minds of the audience. They derived from the *tableaux vivants* (whose conventions they took over) the power to suggest, by decorations and re-membered associations, the places they symbolized. All the façade theatres show very clearly their dependence on the patterns and conventions of the *tableaux vivants*. Some of them, especially the Elizabethan, were developed much further than the street theatres had been, but they carried on many of the conventions used in the living tableaux.

The two most important theatres to use a façade as an architectural symbol at the back of the playing area were developed in Flanders and England. But other variants of the conventionalized façade appeared in the public *corrales* of Spain, in the school productions of Plautus and Terence all over Europe, in both the college and the public productions of the Jesuits, and in the magnificent theatre of the Olympian Academy of Vicenza, which has been preserved to our time. All the theatres of architectural symbolism must be studied together if we would understand any one of them, and we must begin with the Flemish theatres of the Rederykers—theatres which early in the sixteenth century, if not before, used one formal architectural façade as a background for all types of scene.

CHAPTER III

THE FIRST STAGE FAÇADE

The Rederyker Stage in the Netherlands

THE first of the nonillusionistic Renaissance stages was developed in Flanders in close relationship with the street theatres. In fact, this stage was often built in the public square, and its plays were little more than an elaboration of the dramatic patterns of the *tableaux vivants*. From the late fifteenth century into the beginning of the seventeenth century the drama of the Low Countries consisted of allegorical plays called *spelen van sinne*—"theme plays," or plays on a meaning or a text. They were presented by means of an architectural façade which was an adaptation of the façade we have studied in the *tableaux vivants*. For these plays its chief function was not to present an actual place but to serve as a throne-of-honor, as a means of disclosing didactic tableaux, and as a symbol of a type of show.

Flemish artists in the Renaissance produced some of the finest painting the world has ever known—it would be, perhaps, too much to expect an equally fine creative power in drama. While there was a great amount of dramatic activity, the plays were not comparable in quality with the Renaissance drama of France and England. The next age lost the taste for naïve allegorical drama, and the sixteenth-century plays were soon forgotten. The early editions have never been reprinted, and many of the plays are still in manuscript. A number of Dutch and Flemish scholars in recent years have been studying and editing the material, but as yet no satisfactory account has been written. Creizenach drew the attention of scholars outside the Netherlands to the very interesting engravings of the stages of 1539 and 1561, but he learned little of

how those stages were used. Endepols, without much discrimination, cited details of the performance of the Rederyker plays as incidental to his study of the earlier Netherlands theatre. Historians outside of Belgium and Holland have repeated the same few remarks that their predecessors made and have considered that they have disposed of the Rederyker stage. As that stage forms an important part of our story, we must examine the material from a fresh angle and describe it anew from the point of view of art and theatre. I present here the first account in English of the plays and stages of the Societies of Rhetoric and the first account in any language of how those stages were related to the tableau tradition and to the other theatres of the time.[1]

I. THE SOCIETIES OF RHETORIC

Toward the end of the Middle Ages, guilds or societies began to grow up in most cities of Europe for the encouragement of activities in

[1] I base my account of the history of the societies on the accounts in van Duyse, *De Rederijkkamers in Nederland*, and Kalff, *Geschiedenis der Nederlandsche Letterkunde*, and a few other sources which I indicate in the notes. For information on the plays and their stages I depend on the dialogue and stage directions of the plays themselves. Most of them are printed, without titles or authors, in the volumes devoted to a single contest or *landjuweel*. In the bibliography for chap. iii I give a list of these volumes, and I refer to each play by the name and location of the society that produced it. Most of the manuscripts are at the Royal Library in Brussels, but only a few of the volumes of printed plays are there. Most of them are so rare that I found only a single copy. The University Library at Ghent has the largest number. I found only two volumes outside the Netherlands—one at the British Museum and one at the National Library in Paris—but neither volume was duplicated elsewhere. It is no wonder there has been no thorough study of the plays. One shudders to think what the war may do to these unique copies.

111

learning and the arts. While in some countries, as in England, the old trade-guilds took over the production of religious plays and in France the law clerks, the "Basoche," devoted themselves to dramatic entertainment, in other places new societies were organized, cutting across old professional affiliations. In Paris the Confrérie de la Passion devoted itself entirely to the religious drama, and the clubs of "Fools," the "Enfans sans Souci," to the production of satiric farces. In Nuremberg, the Meistersingers in their earlier years were devoted mostly to music and lyric poetry, but later they developed their own actors and plays.

In northern France and the Low Countries, the Rederyker Kamers, or "Chambers of Rhetoric," were the chief centers for the creation of poetry, music, and plays. Starting in the fourteenth century for religious purposes, they soon devoted themselves chiefly to poetry and drama. Many societies were founded early in the fifteenth century, and by the sixteenth century scarcely a town was without a chamber or a branch of a chamber from a larger city. The city of Ghent had five, and there were seven in Audenarde and its suburbs.[2] A few societies, "Gezellen van den Ebattementen," were organized to put on popular secular comedies on feast days, but most of them gave both serious plays and comedies. As the interest in allegory developed in the fifteenth century—and nowhere was it more popular than in the Low Countries—their plays were almost altogether the *spelen van sinne*, theme plays which could include much comic material within a quite serious framework.

Each chamber chose its name, its blazon, and its emblems. The names were nearly all from fanciful religious images: the Fountain, the Rose, the Book, the Eyes of Christ, the Vineyard, the Violet, the Rose Wreath, Jesus with the Balsam Flower. The blazons and images were ingenious and illustrate the great love of intricate symbolism and involved allegory.

For each chamber there was elected a "Keizer" and princes, deacons, and elders. Most of the

writing of plays and poems for public occasions was the duty of the "Factor," or poet. Each society had its regular Fool, who played a principal part in the farces and amused the people at times of public processions and royal entries. There was a tabard with the insignia of the order, which the members wore at functions. They would go to church together wearing the tabard and march together at the funeral of a member. Whenever a member married or a priest member said his first Mass, the whole society celebrated with a banquet.

The regular meetings of the earlier societies were devoted to the reading of poetry written by the members. The oldest Ghent society, De Fontein, had a regular ritual of competition. The society met every three weeks on Sunday afternoon. To one member was given a garland. Within three days he had to produce, arbitrarily, a "refrain," a formal short poem. Before the next meeting every member had to produce another poem on the same model. The results were read, and the holder of the wreath gave a prize to the winner. With a celebration and the drinking of wine, the wreath was passed on to another.

So near were the different towns of Flanders to one another that conclaves and competitions among several societies were inevitable. The yearly contest, the *landjuweel* ("jewel [or 'prize'] of the land"), stimulated an enormous activity in the creation and public performance of music, poetry, and drama. Like the poetic exercises at Ghent, the contests were guided by rules and forms. All contestants had to create works according to a certain plan and often according to a subject agreed on beforehand. Ten to twenty societies would gather together, and the public interest was very high. Probably nowhere since the Athens of the fifth century B.C. has there been a wider participation in the arts than was achieved at these Flemish contests.

The first competitions in plays are said to have grown out of the medieval shooting contests, which brought together for a celebration and match the members of various clubs. Either at the same occasion or inspired by that example, the

[2] Van der Straeten, *Le Théâtre villageois en Flandre*, I, 20.

Chambers of Rhetoric started play competitions early in the fifteenth century. In 1413 six societies competed at Audenarde with plays in honor of the Holy Sacrament, and in 1426 Dunkirk gave a festival of farces. In Ghent in 1432 there was a great contest of plays held in celebration of the

Marie of Burgundy was heir to the archduke of Austria and the German emperor, and his wife was heir to Ferdinand and Isabella of Spain. Both his father and his father-in-law were long-lived, and he never came into the inheritance, which passed instead to his son Charles V. But in

FIG. 41.—Hans Sebald Beham's "The Feast of Herodias." Early sixteenth-century woodcut. Conventional façade; center tower between side arches; figure of Honor above.

birth of a son to Duke Philip the Good. The first contest in Holland took place in 1441 in Sluis.

The period of the flowering of the societies and of the splendid competitions began at the end of the fifteenth century and continued until the years of conflict with the Spaniards in the third quarter of the sixteenth century reduced the Flemish cities to a poverty that few societies survived. The wider development began under Philip the Fair in the 1490's. That young son of Maximilian and

Flanders he was count by inheritance from his mother, and there he spent most of his time, in the palace of his grandmother in Malines.

Philip was much interested in the activities of the Chambers of Rhetoric, and he organized many societies together under a head society. Through his influence they developed in a more secular direction and first became interested in political subjects. They were to play a prominent part in the political controversies of the next

century and to have their share in the bitter conflicts of the Reformation.

In 1493 Philip called the societies together at
Malines and instituted a yearly festival and competition. While the records are not complete,
there is some mention of contests nearly every
succeeding year until past the middle of the following century. Many of the contests involved
only ten or fifteen societies from near-by towns.
We hear of notable *landjuweels* in Brussels, 1493;
Antwerp, 1496; Louvain, 1505; Malines, 1515;
Louvain, 1529; Ghent, 1530; Brussels, 1532;
Malines, 1535; Ghent, 1539; and Diest, 1541. We
have complete editions of the plays performed at
Ghent in 1539, at Rotterdam in 1561, at the
magnificent *landjuweel* in Antwerp in 1561, and
at some later festivals. There were some of interest
into the seventeenth century; but by 1625 the
French drama and the professional theatre were
arriving, and the importance of the Chambers
was over.

Although the societies devised *tableaux vivants*
for royal entries,[3] their chief creative activity was
centered in the *landjuweel*. For it they wrote songs,
poems, orations, ballads, farces, and theme plays.
Each society devised a triumphal entry procession
and a procession to church, exhibited a special
emblematic blazon, and showed an ingenious
"poetical point," in which various objects and
emblems were arranged, like a charade, to illustrate a moral or quotation. There were separate
prizes for the best play, the best farcical entertainment, the most beautiful blazon, the best
acting, the best poem, the best reader of a poem,
the best orator, the best song, the best singing,
and the fool who entertained best "without
villainy." Sometimes tourneys were part of the
festivity. At Haarlem in 1607 there was a prize
for the best fireworks display. Some of the prizes
were plates or vessels of great value, but sometimes the highest prize was a rose hat.

The Ghent *landjuweel* of 1539 attracted a great

deal of attention because its plays brought the
societies into conflict with the Spanish and church
authorities. Of the three classes of plays, the farces
and the *amoreuse* aroused no opposition; but the
serious religious allegories contained a number
of satirical attacks on churchmen and abuses of
the church, and emphasized in their doctrines
trust in the Scriptures. Charles V and his sister
Marie, queen of Hungary, who was regent of the
Low Countries, were determined that the anti-
Catholic movement which was causing such
trouble in Germany and England should get no
foothold in the Provinces. The printed editions of
the plays were seized, and an edict was published
forbidding any performances by the societies
without the permission of the religious authorities.
After that there were far fewer *landjuweels*, and
the societies turned from religious questions to
purely secular subjects.[4]

In 1561 the officials of Antwerp persuaded the
new governors, Cardinal Granvill and Margaret
of Parma, to permit a *landjuweel* to be held. As
the plays were to be based on a theme of learning
and artistic creation, there seemed no offense.
There followed what was perhaps the most
magnificent drama festival ever held. The city of
Antwerp spent more than a hundred thousand
guilders, which would represent almost as many
pounds sterling today. Each of the nine chambers
which entered made elaborate preparations, for
which their cities contributed heavily. The
Wreath of Mary Society of Brussels spent between thirty and forty thousand guilders.

The festival lasted a month. The streets of
Antwerp were decorated as for a king. On August
3 the brothers of the Society of the Violet, who
were hosts, rode outside the city on splendid
horses to welcome the visitors. Each member
wore a colored mantle and bright plumes and
wreaths, and the Fool was dressed so fine he
could not recognize himself. Then the visiting
societies made their magnificent entries into the
city, each with an elaborate pageant procession.

---

[3] 1515 at Bruges (Gachard, *Voyages*, II, 531 ff.); 1549 at
Tournai (Calvete de Estrella, *El felicissimo viaje*, pp. 148 ff.);
1558 at Ghent (van Duyse, *op. cit.*, I, 48). See also bibliography
for chap. ii, "Entries: Low Countries."

[4] Letter of Richard Clough to Sir Thomas Gresham, August
4, 1561 (Burgon, *Life and Times of Sir Thomas Gresham*, I, 377 f.),
and Loosjes, *De Invloed der Rederijkers op de Hervorming.*

There were 23 triumphal chariots and 197 wagons. Each society had a Fool who had his curious device and a motto. On August 4 the city fathers gave a reception for the officers of the societies. On the next day took place the processions to the church, again with pageants and allegorical devices. On August 6 the Fools had their competitions, the main item of which was to see which could drink the longest draught. The officers had a banquet on August 7, and the plays themselves began on August 8. The opening was a play of welcome given by the Society of the Violet, of Antwerp, which, as host, did not compete for the prize. The regular theme plays lasted until August 23, when the prizes were given in a dramatized ceremony. Then followed as a postlude the minor competition, the *haagspel*, for other societies who could not afford the expense of entering the main contest. It lasted until September 2, when the hosts gave a play as a ceremony of farewell.[5]

The compiler of the edition of the plays was ecstatic. He wrote an introductory discourse on the Greek and Roman theatre and the glories that poetry had known. It seemed to him that never had poetry flourished as in his time. This *landjuweel* of 1561 seemed, indeed, the jewel of all. Parnassus was moving to the Netherlands. Just as Italy had Petrarch and Ariosto, and France had Marot and Ronsard, so now the Muses were choosing the Netherlands as a home.

Alas, how short-lived was this dream! In just over a decade the fair and wealthy city of Antwerp was a smoking ruin, never again to be the busiest port in the world or the favorite home of the Muses. In the course of the bloody persecutions carried on by the Spanish king in the name of religion, a runaway army sacked and burned the city and murdered thousands of its inhabitants. There were a few more *landjuweels*, mostly in the Holland provinces, which had gained their freedom, but never again a festival as splendid as that given by the Violet in 1561.

The *spelen van sinne*, or theme plays, for each contest were concerned with a single prede-

termined question. Each society chose the answer it would make and worked out an allegorical play to prove or enforce that answer. As we should expect, the earlier questions were religious. At Antwerp in 1496, where twenty-eight societies competed, the question set for all was "What was the greatest miracle which God wrought for the saving of mankind?" The prizewinners used the answer "The taking-on of human nature," and others gave "The shedding of Jesus' blood" and "The making of peace between Father and man."[6] At Ghent in 1539 we know the subjects for several activities. The poems were all written in answer to the question of which animal of the world has the greatest strength, and the Fools competed in answering which people of the world show the most foolishness. For the *spelen van sinne* the subject was a most serious religious question: "What should a dying man put his faith in?" The answers did not vary greatly, and the dramatized sermons on salvation were so earnest that it is hard to see why the authorities were aroused.

Although the Rotterdam meeting of 1561 again had a religious subject, not so the great Antwerp festival of the same summer. The members of the societies were then ready for a Renaissance subject. The officers laid twenty-four secular questions before Margaret of Parma, the new governor, and she approved three. The first two were "Which experience of learning brings the greatest wisdom?" and "Why does a rich miser desire more riches?" But they found most appealing the third, which concerned learning and creative activity: "What can best awaken man to the liberal arts?"[7] Several societies gave a religious answer, "The spirit of God"; but most gave typical Renaissance answers: "Truth," "Love," "Praise," "Reward," "The wisdom which works through love," "The joyful consideration of the excellence of the arts," "The natural love of knowledge." The first prize was given to the

---

[5] Van Even, *Het Landjuweel te Antwerpen in 1561*, pp. 32 ff.

[6] Visschers, "Een Woord over de oude Rhetorykkamers," *Belgisch Museum*, I, 149 ff.

[7] Or, as it was translated by Richard Clough in his letter to Sir Thomas Gresham, "Whatt thinge doth most cause the spirit of man to be desyrus of conyng" (Burgon, *op. cit.*, I, 379).

society whose play answered "Praise, honor, and reward," and the second for the play on "The hope of eternal worldly and heavenly glory."

The Prologues, which did not have to relate to the plays they preceded, were in this instance concerned with an entirely different question, "How rewarding to us are the upstanding merchants who deal righteously?" After the main *landjuweel* was over, the smaller societies who entered the *haagspel* competed on the question, "Which profession [or handwork] not now highly esteemed would bring the most reward and nobility?" The prize play was concerned with "The reclamation and cultivation of the land."[8]

Most of the later festivals gave their poets and playwrights problems of the time. At Rotterdam in 1598, one of the two themes plunged the playwrights into one of the most important questions in a time of doubt, confusion, and conflicting faiths, by asking "How can the student learn the right doctrine [or judgment] from his teachers?" The other was an important cultural question: "Wherein are we to be extolled above the Romans?"

The processional entries at Leyden in 1596 were all dramatizations of the recent tyrannies and persecutions. On one pageant wagon was the Paris Massacre of St. Bartholomew's Day; another covered the whole subject of tyranny from Cain and Pharaoh to Philip II. By 1624 religious differences no longer made men so bitter, and a humanistic, classical education was taken for granted. The poets gathered at Amsterdam in that year to answer the question, "In what does man enjoy his greatest rest and pleasure?"

II. THE REDERYKER PLAYS

So strong was the hold of allegory on the Netherlands that the sixteenth-century stage saw practically nothing else. Even the religious plays were moralities. Dramatizations of Bible narrative and saints' legends never had the importance in the Middle Ages in the Low Countries that they had in France and England. No extensive cycle was produced. The great re-

[8] Van Even, *op. cit.*, pp. 18 f.

ligious processions developed elaborate pageants and absorbed creative ability of actors and artists, but they remained visual in their appeal. Historical and romantic narrative, which was dramatized in France and England by the third quarter of the sixteenth century, inspired only secular tableaux in Flanders: it did not break the hold of allegory. The three early romantic plays—*Esmoreit*, *Lanceloet*, and *Gloriant*—had no successors until the seventeenth century. The street theatres, as we have seen, used historical material chiefly as a visual symbol of some theme or concept.

The sixteenth-century Flemish drama was dominated by these two tendencies: the desire to visualize—to present realistic pictures to the eye —and the tendency to symbolic, abstract thinking—to present type characters that illustrate a theme. Both the realism and the allegory we find in Flemish art. From the beginning of the fifteenth century Flemish painters had surpassed all others in the technique of painting realistic detail. Their heavenly beings were presented in local costume with the utmost realism of detail. When they painted human beings, they not only kept the same realism and vividness but showed an increasing interest in classifying man by some abstract scheme and painting him from some satiric or allegorical point of view. Louis Maeterlinck has brought together for study the large number of paintings and carved figures designed to illustrate some popular proverb. We see this same interest in texts and proverbs continued in the sixteenth century in the paintings of the Breughels.

The visualization of a theme remained a dominant purpose for the theatre in our whole period. We see it in the semidramatic form of small mechanical figures at the splendid Banquet of the Pheasant given at Lille in 1453. In miniature was shown one man beating a bush for birds, while a nobleman and his wife ate the birds in a little arbor—a visualization of an old proverb.

We must remember the close relationship of the Rederyker societies to the *tableaux vivants* of the triumphal entries. It was the duty of every important guild in the city to help with the street-shows; and from the Rederykers, whose special concern was with drama and poetry, more was expected than from the rest. In many cities they were closely associated with the Guild of St. Luke, the painters' organization, and were quite interested in relating painting, poetry, and drama. In Antwerp the St. Luke's Guild and the Violet Chamber had united in the fifteenth century.[9] Hence the Rederykers not only put on shows themselves for the entries but took part in supplying ideas, speeches, and actors and singers for the shows financed by the city or by other guilds. For the triumphal entries they were accustomed both to competition and to the use of tableaux to enforce a theme. Many cities gave prizes for the best shows and decorations prepared for the arrival of the duke. In the street theatres the societies had produced many tableaux which they had made dramatic by the addition of simple dialogue or a speaker to explain.

When they came to write plays for their own meetings, they followed not so much the few dramatizations of Bible stories, like those developed at Maastricht, as the patterns of the *tableaux vivants*. Just as the street theatres had a more positive educational purpose than the religious art of oil or glass, so the new morality plays brought religious doctrine to the audience more directly than the biblical plays could. The Rederykers wanted to point out the moral in words and drive it home in speech. The type of play which served this purpose was the *spel van sinne*—the "play of meaning."

Just as the street theatres had sometimes changed the direct address to the duke into an action with a character on the stage representing the duke, so, instead of directing a sermon to the audience, the dramatist brought the audience on the stage in the form of Youth, or Most Men, or Mankind. On the stage the author could control him and even put the right questions into his mouth. Like a good Fleming, he was picture-minded and demanded visual instruction. That gave his adviser, usually named Spiritual Under-

standing, just the opportunity he was waiting for. By means of a show-façade at the back of the stage, Spiritual Understanding disclosed, one after the other, a number of tableaux to prove his points. Only occasionally was there any real action or story; for the most part the *spelen van sinne* were illustrated lectures in dialogue.

The archetype of the *spel van sinne* is not hard to reconstruct. In fact, there was preserved, alongside the more elaborate forms, a simple type of visualized theme with a speaker in front of the picture. That simple form—nearer art than drama—was the "poetical point." At most of the *landjuweels* each society prepared one for competition. On a stage was disclosed a *tableau vivant* devised to illustrate a quotation, which was usually printed on part of the framing architecture of the picture. In front stood a character who spoke the *presentatie*, which was a rhymed discourse, sometimes in the verse form of the "refrain," to explain the picture.[10] For instance, the society from Hertogenbosch disclosed in 1561 at Antwerp a scene of a tree, a vine, birds, grapes, and two characters. The four stanzas which were read compared the growing of the tree to the life of man. The Bergen-op-Zoom chamber illustrated the creation of light and day by four characters representing Night, Sin, Aurora, and Apollo—a typical Renaissance mixture of biblical, classical, and allegorical fancies. To represent the Golden Age of primitive happiness the Diest society placed around a figure of the world Saturn with his child and scythe, Janus of the two faces, and Copiecornu with a horn of plenty (Fig. 45). For the more complex *spelen van sinne*, there was needed, not a setting for the dialogue (for the dialogue was as free of time and place as the *presentatie*), but a show-façade which would permit a number of different tableaux to be shown either at one time or successively.

III. THE REDERYKER STAGE

What kind of stage did the Rederykers use? In a large hall or more often in the public square itself they erected an open platform, which was

[9] Van Duyse, *op. cit.*, I, 82 ff.

[10] *Ibid.*, pp. 238 ff.

backed by an architectural façade serving as a background not only for the plays but also for songs, poems, and other entertainments and ceremonies. More than a stage setting, it was a decoration, a showpiece to celebrate the occasion. First of all, it had to provide a heavenly throne for the figure of the person in whose honor the contest was held. Here it follows the pattern of a heavenly throne at the top of an arcade-of-honor, which we described in chapter ii in connection with both castle-shows and arcade-shows. Most of the plays given at Ghent in 1539 used the façade as a throne-of-honor with a tableau of the Virgin or of the Holy Trinity placed above to preside in the position they had in many of the tombs and *tableaux vivants*. At other times Honor[11] or Wisdom[12] was enthroned, or, more frequently in later decades, Lady Rhetoric sat in the throne-of-honor (Figs. 43, 44, 46). Rhetoric or Victoria[13] would be let down to earth in a cloud machine to give the prizes. While the façade had to be able to reveal a number of tableaux, its most important effect was this high throne-of-honor. Further, like any street-show, it was adorned with several shields, usually those of the emperor or king, of the city, and of the society which was host.

Let us look, first, at the function the façade served in the reading of the poems. The welcome of the hosts was often dramatized in a ceremony, a little play similar to the *tableaux vivants*. At Schiedam in 1603 the play of welcome given by the brothers of the Red Rose was a little allegory of Rhetoric speaking to other characters. Then two comic Vices—Contempt-of-Reason and Scorn-of-the-Arts—speak of the decorations prepared for some approaching event. One of them

says: "Getting ready to adorn some noble art— Rhetoric by name, according to this sign." Such a play usually required a backing in which was not only the name Rhetoric but an allegorical representation of Lady Rhetoric sitting above the whole contest given in her name. All the plays, songs, and poems at the Leyden competition in 1596 were presented in front of a figure of Rhetoric on a high seat surrounded by three attendants and the Seven Liberal Arts. We cannot tell from the description whether a flat painting, sculptured figures, or live persons were used. At Vlaardingen in 1617 the play of welcome dramatized the disclosure of a heavenly throne of Wisdom and the entry of Rhetoric with a number of Virtues. She led to their small seats Love, Virtue, Joy, and Knowledge; then she herself climbed above into the great throne. When all were seated, Love read off the blazon of each visiting chamber, and the performances of plays and poems began. The last stanza of one of the poems was read by the character Love, apparently the same Love of the play of welcome, now described as "sitting on the triumphal arch with Vlaardingen." We know enough of the show-façade of the street theatres to be able to picture a structure with an arch below and a pavilion above for the heavenly throne. Likewise, the play of welcome at Flushing in 1641 concluded by Rhetoric's going above to sit by Love. Love says: "Come, maid Rhetoric, sit here by my side on this heaven's throne." Mercurius and the other characters tell her that the performers are ready to read the poems, and they ask permission to leave the stage. The *tableau vivant* façade gave a setting and dramatic framework for the poems and songs.

The poems and the plays were intimately related in a number of ways; indeed, one of the poems—the formal "refrain"—was already a dialogue. The last of its three or four stanzas was regularly read by a different person, often the prince of the society. In the Vlaardingen competition just mentioned, it was a character in the dialogue of welcome who read the last stanza. A large number of the plays themselves ended with

[11] At Antwerp in 1561 the society from South Louvain presented a "poetical point" with Honor on the high throne, surrounded by the Virtues and Vices.

[12] At Antwerp in 1561 the Olive Branch Society of Antwerp made the climax of its play a vision of Wisdom in a heavenly throne surrounded by the Liberal Arts. At Vlaardingen in 1617 Wisdom on a heavenly throne was a speaking figure in the plays of both societies from Amsterdam.

[13] In both the welcoming and the concluding plays at Antwerp in 1561 Victoria presided from the heavenly throne.

a formal refrain of the same pattern as the poems read. The last stanza was read by a different character, and it pointed and summarized the moral, just as the last stanza of the poem did. Most of the plays were of such a purely allegorical and didactic nature that they required no more definite suggestion of locale than did the reading of the poems.

Both poems and plays called for a formal façade at the back which could provide entrances for the main actors and frames for allegorical *tableaux vivants*. That is exactly what we find at the *landjuweel* of Ghent in 1539 and of Antwerp in 1561. From both we have engravings showing the façades, engravings which have interested Creizenach and all later students because in appearance they suggest the Elizabethan stage façade.

The stage setting at Ghent in 1539 (Fig. 42) was composed of three sections, resembling a center tower with two side towers. Each little tower had two stories—a lower doorway and an arched window above. At the very top of each was a round temple-pavilion with a figure on its roof holding a torch and an emblem. The lower side doors formed part of an arcade of five doorways, which cut straight through the center pavilion. The center tower had both a lower and an upper pavilion of columns coming forward onto the forestage and supporting circular architraves. They show no curtains, but we know from the stage directions that at least the upper stage, and possibly the lower pavilion also, had curtains for the disclosure of *tableaux vivants*. Above the upper stage were also small figures, eight in number, holding torches and three coats-of-arms. Above the figures the roof rose to a large center temple, which also held more figures with torches. Every individual feature here had already appeared in the *tableaux vivants*—side towers with doors; a center pavilion of two columns projecting forward and supporting an architrave and roof; a second story or gallery; a third story of torches, emblems, and allegorical figures; a formal arcade of five openings. We shall find that, within the pavilion, the gallery, the doors, and the windows, were disclosed dumb

shows, which relate the *spelen van sinne* even more closely to the street theatres of the royal entries.

The structure of the background at Antwerp in 1561 (Fig. 43) was in every way a more advanced Renaissance façade. Just as Renaissance sculptors had reduced the free-standing columns and the complex pavilion of the medieval tomb to a neat, compact, flat façade, so this stage was flatter and more compact than that of Ghent. At the very top were the expected coats-of-arms, and at the center in an encircled heaven was the figure of Rhetoric. Several times she was pointed out in the plays and described as holding a light in one hand and a golden book in the other. At the center openings of both the lower and the upper story were curtains; the side openings, which served as entrances, were apparently left uncurtained. This reminds us of the custom, very old in art and frequent in the street theatres, of placing interiors or other scenes that needed to be inclosed or covered, at the center of a façade with exterior doorways at the sides. The resemblance, likewise, to the formal arcade and to the throne-of-honor is obvious.

The Antwerp façade was designed for the Violet Society by Cornelis Floris (Cornelis de Vriendt), the most prominent architect of the city. He and his brother Franz, the painter, were members of the St. Luke's Guild, which for nearly a century had been united with the Violet Society. Franz, like many other Netherland artists in the sixteenth century, had studied in Italy.[14] By the middle of the century the interest in the new Renaissance art and architecture was very strong. Different books of Serlio's *Architecture* had been printed in Antwerp in Dutch in 1539 and 1549, before there had been a complete edition in Italy. It is not surprising that the façade of 1561 should have been more classical than the earlier one. As the main action of the theme plays called for only occasional use of the façade, there was no need for the realistic detail usual in the street theatres.

In one play (that produced by the society from Diest) this stage façade served as a castle, as a throne-of-honor, and as a background for portable

[14] Van Even, *op. cit.*, pp. 20 f.

properties of a medieval type. The Induction to the play was begun by the character Love, "coming out of the Castle of Trust, dressed in artful manner, on her head bearing a wreath of red roses." She prayed to God, then announced a living Rhetoric watched the other contests and as a statue of Rhetoric was watching, directly above her. In the actual play the façade was not used, but several properties and an arbor were brought onto the forestage. For several scenes the

FIG. 42.—Stage façade for the *landjuweel* at Ghent, 1539

that she would return into the Castle of Trust while men strove to win the rose wreath. The next two characters came in at opposite sides of the stage. Apparently, the classic architectural façade could serve as a castle front, perhaps with the addition of a name plate over the center door. Later in the play she appeared in a seat above and watched the play going on below, just as allegorical characters "lead Man before an arbor, made all open that what happens within may be seen from all sides." The arbor bears the name "Worldly Rest." They bring Man wine and a banquet and he sleeps. From that sleep, Self-satisfaction, Desire for Knowledge, and Industry try to awaken him, but he falls asleep again each time. Fear of Poverty uses a hammer and wakes him for a while. The arbor is taken out, and for one scene Man is seated and a counter and books are placed before him. The nature of the allegorical action is such that it is perfectly simple for the characters to decide what is to be done to Man were needed. In the same year at Rotterdam, in the play of the senior society of Haarlem, several characters entered out of "Moorish Land." At Schiedam in 1603, in the play by the society from Gouda, two different characters came

FIG. 43.—Stage façade for the *landjuweel* at Antwerp, 1561

and then call for scenes and properties to be brought in.

By the use of name-boards, such as "Castle of Trust" or "Worldly Rest," the various doorways of the façade and such portable scenery as arbors could be converted into the few specific places that out of entrances marked "Tent of Poverty" and "The Holy Spirit." In the Haarlem play of the same festival Riches sat in the house called "God's Blessings," while the orphans entered from the "House of Hardship." Between the two, apparently in front of the façade, were the chairs "Fleshly" and "Forgetfulness." Likewise the doorways, windows, and upper stages often seem to have been labeled when the *figueren*, or tableaux, were shown.

A number of interior scenes were played. While some were frankly brought out in the front, like the desk and books we have noted, and others were played inside a portable arbor-pavilion, yet many seem to indicate an inner stage where a room of fair size could be visible. Either an inner stage or a portable arbor with curtains is called for by the Louvain play given at Antwerp in 1561. Man first enters with five characters as his Five Senses; he says he will go and sit in "Contemplation," and a little later he and his companions are disclosed, apparently by the opening of a curtain. The same society made a similar use of an inner stage in their farce, a short witty scene about various kinds of beer, in which they disclosed "Bacchus sitting before his vineyard, with four animals by him, as Lion, Monkey, etc."

More extensive scenes on an inner stage appeared in the festival at Rotterdam in 1561. A gay tavern scene was included by the chamber from Schiedam. Mankind and his companions start looking for a tavern and find the sign "Dark Understanding"; they knock, and the landlord comes out and invites them in. Inside they find a table ready and a daughter named Strange Fancies serving. The noise of the festivities wakes up Gnawing Conscience, who was sleeping above. He reproves the merrymakers and draws the moral. A similar scene of riotous living, not in a tavern, was produced in the Amsterdam play. The marginal direction reads: "Here they play and sing within the curtains." Presently the Announcer opens the curtains to disclose the Jew sitting with General Badness and two clowns.

In a play given at Vlaardingen in 1617 by the White Lavender Society of Amsterdam, we learn that characters discovered on an inner stage might come forward on the forestage, just as in some of the street theatres and on the Elizabethan stage. A curtain was pulled aside to disclose three farmers sleeping. Two devils pranced around them derisively and departed. The farmers woke,

talked for a while, and with a "Let us go in" made their exit.

The curtain over the inner stage apparently suggested by convention an actual wall or door. In *The Gratitude of the Orphans*, given by the Schiedam society in 1604 as a means of thanking the city officials for helping with the *landjuweel* the summer before, one character, Bodily Sickness, "comes out, knocks on the curtain, and speaks." He is calling other characters out of a house to help him.

The function of the façade in the action of the plays, we must conclude, was not completely negative. The arched doorways might be negative entrances, but they could, with or without signboards, be imagined as definite houses or whole countries from which certain characters were to enter. The center curtained opening could be a doorway into an inner room, or, with the help of a tavern sign, a tavern. The curtain itself could be thought of as a door at which one knocks. The upper stage, while primarily for heavenly and allegorical characters, could contain others who could watch the happenings below and engage in dialogue. The old machine for descent appeared in practically every *landjuweel* I know of, to bring down, now the Holy Spirit, now Victoria, now Hope, to the characters on the forestage.

The whole façade could serve as the front of a building, with the interior of that building represented on the inner stage, or as a castle and also as a gate to a vineyard; and there is some indication that a façade could represent a ship. In *Charon the Skipper of Hell* there was at the back of the stage a structure that served both the general functions of the façade and also as a boat. In the *Play of Hero and Leander* the structure is mentioned several times as "above," then later we hear of "a guard on the ship singing." Not only was the façade a microcosm connecting heaven with earth, it could also represent a great many places on earth.

IV. THE *figueren*, OR TABLEAUX

The most significant use of the stage façade was not, however, for the actual needs of the plays themselves but for the *figueren*. In fact, many of the plays were little more than question and answer betweeen Mankind and a spiritual adviser, who taught him not only by word of mouth but by "shows" or tableaux, which were disclosed by means of the architectural façade. It is these shows, so closely related to those given in the royal entries, that we must examine more fully. As their significance has not been recognized by most students of the theatre, I shall describe them in some detail. They were so important on many occasions that we may consider the plays they adorned as illustrated dialogues or as dramatized visual art—another form of the Renaissance theatre which derived from the traditions of art.

It is somewhat difficult in particular instances to determine the exact nature of the *figueren*. Some were probably paintings disclosed by a curtain;[15] others undoubtedly consisted of real actors, who formed silent pictures, either singly or in groups. Some characters held banderoles, some moved in pantomime, and some were given speech and even acted little plays within the play. Sometimes a *figuere* was completely separate from the main play and was displayed and explained as a painted picture. Again a character might be introduced in a *figuere* and then play a leading part in the dialogue on the main stage. There was not nearly so much consistency in the Low Countries as there was in the handling of the dumb shows on the Elizabethan stage. The Flemish and their neighbors in the Holland provinces used nearly all the dramatic conventions and scenic forms which they found in the *tableaux vivants* of the royal entries.

First, let us examine the *figueren* shown in the Ghent plays in 1539, which were of a type much nearer painting and less elaborately developed than the later ones. Van Duyse, the only person who has written any extensive study of the Rederykers, has suggested that most, if not all, of the tableaux at Ghent may have been paintings

rather than living pictures.[16] At the beginning of each play is a list of the *personagen*, and never is any character in a *figuere* listed unless he has also a speaking part in the play. But, by comparison with the street theatres and with the *figueren* in later plays, we conclude that, while a few of the shows at Ghent may have been paintings or groups of lay figures, the larger number were played by living actors.

As we should expect from what we know of the façade in tombs and in *tableaux vivants*, the heavenly throne in the upper story is frequent. The Divinity was made a speaking part by the society from Arcele. A *figuere* of the Trinity above in a throne was disclosed. Then God the Father gave answer to questioning from the characters below. In other plays the climax was a revelation of a *figuere* of the day of glory, Christ with the Saints or with all the Virtues beside him, the figures of Sin, Death, and Hell under his feet. While some of these shows of Judgment Day may have been paintings, the stage structure indicated in the engraving had space for quite large heavenly gatherings; and we know from the popularity of the street theatres that few chances would be missed for making such show-art come alive with real flesh and blood.

One of the simplest shows was that of the four ages of man in the play from Lessines. To illustrate the sermon which the character Trust-in-the-Scripture was giving to Mankind, there was shown, first, a naked child, then a youth of twenty, a man of thirty, and an old gray man, each holding a banderole with a Latin inscription from the Bible. The adviser pointed out the significance of each age. These were most certainly living actors, probably walking across in view one after the other. It would have been easy to have such single characters come through one of the doors onto the main stage and go out another; but, considering the care with which the other shows were separated from the actors on the main stage, I would rather believe that they were on the upper stage or made their appearance at a door or window.

---

[15] In *Een Spel van sinnen opt derde tvierde ende twijfste Capittel van Twerck der apostolen*, printed in 1557, one *figuere*, of the Whore of Babylon seated on a dragon, is indicated as a painted cloth, while all the other *figueren* had live actors.

[16] *Op. cit.*, I, 233 ff.

Not only were banderoles carried by actors and revealed to indicate bits of dialogue, they were placed before or around characters, and even on the front of the stage structure, to supply names, places but, like the names in the architrave in the Terence illustrations, to identify characters. Sometimes on the front of the curtain of the upper stage was hung a roll with the words of Christ;

FIG. 44.—Tableau to illustrate a poem, Antwerp, 1561. Lady Rhetoric on a heavenly throne. Bibliothèque Royale, Brussels

mottoes, and speeches.[17] The speeches might either be appropriate to the character at that moment or serve only for general identification. The stage façade bore signs not only to identify and in several plays there was revealed on the front of the building, when Stephen gazed upward to the vision of the Resurrection, an inscription of the words which he was supposed to be speaking.

One complex show in the play given by the

[17] Cf. chaps. i and ii for a discussion of words and mottoes in ancient and medieval art and in the *tableaux vivants.*

society from Deynze was an interesting series of consecutive movements made while the adviser described and commented on them to Mankind. As these could scarcely have been successive still tableaux, shown by opening and closing a curtain, they must have been a tableau moving in pantomime with a lecturer in front. First was shown Christ dead on the cross, and Living Hope took him down. Then Christ came alive in her lap, proceeded to resurrect the dead, rose to heaven by a machine, and stood at the right hand of God, while Stephen looked on below. A vivid picturization of the Creed!

The play produced by the Brussels chamber at Ghent had little tableaux in which speech was used to enforce the sermon in dialogue. All the speaking characters were listed in the *personagen*, but their speeches were never directed to the main characters; what was heard was no more than the voicing of the short single speeches usually put on banderoles. When Adam in the Garden was shown, God spoke to the serpent. Christ on the cross was first disclosed; then after fifteen lines of the dialogue on the forestage he spoke his well-known prayer. The other shows—the breaking of the gates of hell, the Resurrection, the Shadow of Death, and Christ sitting at the right hand of God—all were played without speech and described by the characters below.

A large group of the *figueren* in these plays at Ghent in 1539 were the usual religious scenes of church teaching. Like so many altarpieces and windows and like the *tableaux vivants* at Bruges in 1515, a number of scenes were accompanied by their prototypes from the Old Testament. The Ypres play disclosed three scenes at one time, probably by means of the two windows above the side doors. The center pavilion in the upper story would have served well for the Presentation of Christ in the Temple. It resembled the open columns of the temple traditional in medieval art. At the two side windows could have been shown the blind Isaac blessing the young Jacob, and Jacob blessing his kneeling son—both prefigurations of the Presentation.

Three different scenes were shown at one time by the Bruges society, with some vague allegorical relationship. The two Old Testament scenes were of Adam and Eve breaking the commandment and of Cain slaying Abel. The main show was an allegory similar to the English *Castle of Perseverance*. Within a *schansmande*, or fortification, were three persons—Homo, a woman with her eyes bound, and a man sleeping on his back. The fortification was attacked from without by World, Flesh, and Devil. Unless this was all displayed in a painting, it must have been enacted in the large, tower-like center pavilion. We know that the façade structure of the festival at Antwerp in 1561, which resembled a fortification much less than this one, could serve as a castle. Considering the frequency of the castle façade in the *tableaux vivants*, there seems little doubt that this structure also could become a castle. Later in the same play three other scenes were displayed at one time: Susanna loved by Daniel, the three children in the furnace, and the Children of Israel crossing the Red Sea pursued by Pharaoh. We might say that surely the scene in the Red Sea was a flat painting—but not necessarily. Boards shaped and painted as waves and pivoted to rise for the Children of Israel were included among the machines Furttenbach told how to make in the following century. It was quite within the resources of the times to show either a still or a moving tableau with living actors.

Three other *figueren* shown in 1539 deserve special attention, two of them fountains. One fountain, in the play from Thienen (indicated only in the edition of 1564), was a magic crucifix out of which blood began to flow as the characters in front were speaking of the living fountain of Jesus. A more elaborate device was disclosed in the play from Courtrai: above the fountain there was an image of the Lamb, likewise running blood. The third noteworthy tableau, in the play from Lessines, had some kind of visualization of the city of Antioch before which the Maccabean mother and her seven sons were brought. This may again have been the whole stage façade imagined as a city gate, as in some of the *tableaux vivants* and on the Elizabethan stage; or it may have been the painted walls of a city on a painted cloth background, of the type we know the

Rederykers used in the "poetical points" a few decades later (Fig. 45).

As a very similar religious subject was used at the Rotterdam festival in 1561, the *figueren* were much the same as those at Ghent. The Old Testament prefigurations of various events in the life of Christ were shown—Adam and the serpent, Isaac, Job, Jonas, and even "King Manasses, defeated, sitting in despair." The Crucifixion and the Resurrection appeared in many plays as the last hope for a man who thought himself lost.

The Antwerp tableaux of the same year were quite different. With a Renaissance question— "What can best awaken man to the arts?"—the whole world of classical story and secular allegory was opened up. Goddesses and nymphs replaced biblical characters. Apollo and the orchestra of Nine Muses were brought in from the street theatres. Rhetoric or Wisdom sat above in God's throne, and either Rhetoric or Victoria descended to crown the efforts of man. Instead of a great climax of all the Powers gathered about the heavenly throne at the Resurrection of Christ, the *pièce de résistance* repeatedly used here was a disclosure of the Seven Liberal Arts grouped around Wisdom.

Like the earlier shows, some of the Antwerp *figueren* were tableaux without movement, some moved in pantomime, some were little dramas with speech or dialogue within the picture, and some had characters who spoke to the main characters, Mankind and his spiritual advisers. One was an elaborate painting, or possibly a model, of a ship marked "Spiritual Inspiration," with sail "Love," rudder "Righteousness," and anchor "Trust," sailing in waters marked "Worldly Unrest." In the pantomime scenes, such as that of the sleeping Hercules being awakened by Virtuous Desire, the characters are usually described to Mankind as in movement.

While the upper stage was used for goddesses, muses, and allegorical nymphs, the lower inner stage seems to have served for a number of interior scenes of sleeping figures; for Man's adviser usually pulled aside the curtain himself to show them. Thus were displayed not only the sleeping Hercules but a scene by the Malines Rederykers of Homer, Virgil, and Ovid sleeping before they were awakened to the arts. In the Brussels play, Reward, who herself had first been disclosed sitting on a mountain between her daughters Glory and Fame, later in the play showed Man a *figuere* of Plato sitting reading a book, with Aristotle and other philosophers around him.

While that mountain may have been in the inner stage below and have been removed before the scene of the philosophers was needed, we find two mountains shown in a scene that was probably on the upper stage, in the play of the Peony brothers of Malines. In fact, all six openings of the façade seem to have been used at once by these enterprising Rederykers. In a place named "Contemplation," which must have been the lower inner stage, were disclosed Art and three Graces. At the same time, doubtless at the side openings, were shown two other scenes, of Speculation and of Practice, each with two nymphs by her. In the upper stage center was revealed an elaborate scene of the Seven Liberal Arts between two mountains named "Glory" and "Riches." This indicates that the upper stage was much larger than a glance at the engraving might lead one to suppose. Then a few lines later is the direction: "Here are shown two more women as Painting and Sculpture." Unless these two pushed their way among the Liberal Arts in the already crowded valley between Glory and Riches, they must have appeared at the two upper stage windows above the entrance doorways. This was a show splendid enough to waken any youth to the arts.

In the *haagspel*, the contest of the less ambitious societies, few of the plays had any *figueren*. The play of the Cornblossom Society of Brussels was an interesting exception. To give religious support to their praise of agriculture, they showed three *figueren*, all on the upper stage. The first was God in the Garden of Eden telling Adam and Eve to go out and work the fields, the second showed God and Noah planting a vineyard, and the third, Jesus appearing as a gardener.

Fig. 45.—Two tableaux to illustrate "poetical points," Antwerp, 1561

Quite similar *figueren* were used in plays which were not written for the *landjuweels*. In the theme play of *Charon the Skipper of Hell*, printed at Antwerp in 1551, the show-façade represented in some fashion, perhaps without actual resemblance, the boat of Charon. Charon and Mercurius talk, apparently on the forestage, and point out the famous people in the boat. Perhaps a procession comes out or passes by an opening. At the end of the printed play a list of "nonspeaking characters" includes such people as Milo, Cyrus in armor, Calcas a bishop, Medea, and Helen.

All the *Seven Plays of the Works of Mercy*, played and printed at Amsterdam in 1591, had as a climax the disclosure of a tableau behind a curtain. For six plays that tableau was the silent figure of Christ on the cross. The seventh play ended with a most elaborate dramatization of the Last Judgment. The woodcut shows a full scene on two levels. Christ sits above in the center. Four angels, two on each side, blow trumpets. "Four bolts are shot, and there is a great light. Six good and six damned souls rise. Six angels separate the good from the bad." After the angels speak, Lucifer in hell rattles his chains and calls out his devils. One of the devils grabs a soul and runs in. Christ speaks from above, and there is a dialogue between an angel above and one of the angels below.

Similar development of *figueren* occurred in other places outside the Netherlands. One of the unpublished plays of Virgil Raber, "Der reich Mann und Lazarus," dated 1539, preserved in the city archives of Sterzing, consists of eight *figueren* shown by drawing the curtain from before a tableau while the "Precursor" describes each in rhymed verse.[18]

So far, all the *figueren* described have been of the same types as those we have seen in the *tableaux vivants* of the royal entries. They have all been more or less separated from the main dialogue and no more closely related to the main characters than the personages in the street-shows were related to the prologue-expositor on the

stage in front or to the duke himself in the street. There was also in the drama of the Netherlands another kind of *figuere*, which used the tableau convention to dramatize part of the story of the main characters. This kind of dumb show became more frequent in the seventeenth century. Likewise in England the dumb show, which in the sixteenth century was usually symbolic, was often used by later playwrights to tell a bit of the story in compact, brief form. A few examples had already occurred before the sixteenth century. In the early Dutch play *Esmoreit*, the picturesque scene of a hanging was exhibited as a dumb show between other scenes.[19] Occasionally at the Antwerp festival in 1561 some of the story of Mankind was told pictorially. For instance, in the play of the society from Lierre, Mankind was first disclosed sitting asleep; but after the first action he went in to sit at his books, a globe and other instruments by him. He apparently held that picture during two intermissions, coming out for action after each one. There were several similar uses of picturization in the plays of the Schiedam *landjuweel* in 1603. The subject was the upbringing of a poor orphan. In the Maeslandt play the two orphans, who were main characters in part of the play, were shown once in a *figuere* sitting at their tasks, above them a woman named "Virtuous Instructions," with a rod in her hand named "Fear of the Lord." In the play from Ketel, the Widow, who is a speaking character in part of the play, "exhibits her miserable state sitting in a poor little house with her orphans spinning and weaving." In front of the tableau, Good Instructions points out her plight to Everyman.

Even more like the later English dumb shows were the *figueren* in *Porphyre and Cyprine*, given at Malines in 1620. This play, presented by the Peony Chamber as hosts at the beginning of the *landjuweel*, was one of the earliest tragedies written under the influence of the classics and the French dramatists. Between the acts three incidents which were hard to bring into the regular play were shown by means of tableaux—in one Porphyre encountered a bear, in another he was

---

[18] Evans, "The Staging of the Donaueschingen Passion Play," *Modern Language Review*, XV, 290.

[19] Kalff, *op. cit.*, II, 52.

robbed, and in the third his father's house was burned. At the end of the play there were shown in a *figuere* the dead bodies of the lovers who had killed themselves—an interesting adaptation of the native Flemish show to the purposes of neo-Greek tragedy.

Surprisingly enough, there is little mention of music in connection with the *figueren*. A few songs were sung; a choir sang "Christ Is Risen" for a tableau of the Resurrection given by the Rijnsburgh society at Rotterdam in 1561; the play of the Hague society at Schiedam in 1603 concluded with a scene of spinning and singing; and the Nine Muses made music on a few occasions. Most of the *tableaux vivants* of the street theatres, on the other hand, had incidental music. Trumpets sometimes heralded the arrival of the royal party and played for the opening of the curtain or appearance of the speaker. Still or pantomimed shows were usually accompanied by music during the entire time they were open to view. Likewise, the Elizabethan dumb shows, though they might sometimes have speaking characters standing in front, regularly had musical accompaniment. Apparently in the Flemish plays the spoken, dramatized instruction by means of a teacher who explained the shows to Mankind ruled out music.

As throne-of-honor, as castle, as city, as fountain, as mountain, as heaven, earth, and hell for Judgment Day, or as a framework for all kinds of tableaux, the façade used by the Rederykers followed very closely the traditions of the visual arts as they had been developed in the tableaux of the civic street theatres. With shields, emblems, torches, and a symbol of the Virgin or Lady Rhetoric at the top, it presented the gay atmosphere of a civic festival.

In the use of independent structures on the forestage—the arbor-pavilion and the like—the Rederykers followed the practice of some of the

religious plays. By means of this façade they could present rather realistic effects of the front of a house or a tavern—much more realistic, indeed, than the back curtain of the mountebank stage. Still, the façade was more of a theatrical symbol[20] than an illusionistic picture. It was a show-device which could suggest many kinds of shows, without trying to duplicate any scene in actuality; its principle was convention, not illusion.

FIG. 46.—Stage façade for the *landjuweel* at Haarlem, 1607. Lady Rhetoric and the Seven Liberal Arts on the upper stage. Shields as decoration. British Museum.

Its conventions are clearly quite closely parallel to those of the Elizabethan stage. Both in the way in which it developed from the street theatres and in its use by the dramatist it sheds valuable new light on what Shakespeare meant to the audience. When we cross the Channel from Antwerp to London, we shall find a much more varied use of the façade; but we shall almost think we are seeing just a further development of the Flemish shows.

[20] Cf. the discussion of this principle of symbolism in chap. v, Sec. V.

CHAPTER IV

THE SECOND STAGE FAÇADE

The Elizabethan Stage

I. A SCENIC DEVICE DERIVED FROM ART AND PAGEANTRY

THE second dramatic show-façade—and much the most interesting in all Europe—was developed in the public theatres of England in the latter half of the sixteenth century. It was similar in many ways to the Rederyker façade, for the two stages had derived independently from the same traditions of art and pageantry. Like the Flemish dramatists, the English playwrights used a platform that brought the actor forward into the midst of the audience. But the Elizabethan stage was more than a platform. Like the Flemish stage, it was backed by an elaborate and colorful architectural façade. More than an arrangement of side doors and inner and upper stages, that façade was itself a symbol of castle, throne, triumphal arch, altar, tomb, and several other shows long familiar in art and pageantry. To visualize the English façade as it must have looked to a man of the period is particularly important because it served for a series of plays that have marked one of the highest achievements of dramatic history.

Considering that more has been written about the Elizabethan stage than about any other subject in English literary history, it is amazing that no attention has been paid to its relationship to the conventions of the visual arts. For the Elizabethan stage was not a new invention. Burbage and his builders in 1576 did not look to the Italian perspective stage and say "That will never do for us." They did not, perhaps, look at the engravings of the Flemish stages of the *landjuweels* of 1539 and 1561 or listen to the accounts of the several English people who saw them. The stage they devised (if it had not already been built in innyards) merely carried on the conventions by which they were accustomed to visualize historical and allegorical characters and scenes. In stained-glass windows, in tapestries, in paintings, in wood blocks and engravings, and, above all, in the living pictures of the street theatres erected for royalty or for the annual Lord Mayor's Day procession, the theatre managers and many of the theatre audience had seen portraits, groups of characters, and dramatic scenes presented against an architectural background. The stage façade carried a little further the tendency, which we have already noticed in painting and the street theatres, to combine a number of architectural symbols into one unit of background.

A negative, characterless tiring-house front I am convinced this façade was not. We have failed to look at the traditions behind it, or we should see that it was rich in atmosphere and associations. Our investigators for the last half-century have been so busy stripping the Elizabethan drama of the false clothing acquired in seventeenth-, eighteenth-, and nineteenth-century productions in an illusionistic setting of painted perspective scenery that they have left it too bare. For fear of seeing Shakespeare in the wrong coloring, they have asked us to visualize the background as completely negative—a wall to hide the tiring-room. Only in the rich costumes of the actors and in the many movable properties on the forestage have we been permitted to think of any adornment for the production. It has been known for some time that managers and actors paid large sums for splendid costumes. G. F. Reynolds has led in the effort to show that at least in the use of movable properties—trees, thrones, arbors, walls, tents, shop fronts, moss banks, etc.—the stage preserved some of the conventions and associations of the medieval religious theatres. If we examine other aspects of the period, we realize that not only the properties but the tiring-house façade, as well, preserved rich coloring and associations from other art and theatre forms. With marble columns, with shields and streaming banners, with tapestries and paintings, with clouds and heavenly thrones, it continued not only the outlines but the atmosphere of the street tableaux.

The Elizabethan stage was more closely related to the street theatres than to any other form. There was no continuity either in subject matter or in performance from the medieval religious drama to the public stage.[1] The old religious performances continued for years in provincial towns, but in London the new age was ready for a new theatre form. Nor is the connection between the morality-interlude and the Elizabethan drama too close. But there was a continuity both in purpose and in subject matter from the London street-shows to the public theatre. The living pictures and little dramas of the street platforms were exciting rituals of devotion to rulers, of pride in personal and national feats of glory—rituals which celebrated the memory of England's national heroes and of Christian champions against the infidel or the vision of religious and civic virtues that guide the public life of the nation. They reinforced the glory of a present leader by recalling the glory of similar leaders famed in legend or history, or they celebrated the force of a quality like royal magnanimity, or the horror of civil discord, by presenting well-known examples, likewise gathered from legend or history. This same love of legendary or historical material for its moral pur-

pose was one of the most powerful forces in the drama of Shakespeare and his contemporaries; and the dramatists put on the public stage many of the same stories and heroes that had already been visualized in the street-shows, in tapestries and wall paintings, and even on monuments and tombs and, in the case of allegorical figures, on the engraved frontispieces of books. It should not be surprising, therefore, if the stage effects resembled in many ways the treatment of the same kind of material in art and sculpture and in the living pictures of the street-shows. We have succeeded very well in freeing our minds of concepts of setting, place, and locality, which, developed in later years, could not have existed for the Elizabethans. It is time to examine what concepts did exist for them. In the theatre, more than anywhere else, one sees the object before him in terms of conventions—one finds what one has learned from previous experience to expect. On the Elizabethan stage the audience found much the same kind of background that it had learned from the visual arts and the *tableaux vivants* to expect.

Throughout our discussion of the forms and functions of the sixteenth-century theatres we must remember that a background, except in the case of a few Italian perspective settings, was scarcely ever thought of as a locality that surrounded the action. It regularly kept in the theatres much the same emblematic function it had in the street-shows and for masques and dances—that of a symbolic or decorative device from which the performers entered and into which they disappeared after the performance. We have noticed the mountains, pavilions, and castles from which champions emerged, ready for the tournament, and the castles, rocks, trees, bowers, and other devices from which dancers or speakers stepped in the court masques or the street theatres. That such a concept persisted on the Elizabethan stage is proved partly by the fact that many scenes in plays of the period are first identified by a certain background, then played indefinitely as in front, as within, or anywhere about the place first supposed. It is shown

---

[1] I shall note a number of Elizabethan borrowings from the medieval, especially in those scenes which did not use the façade but brought on portable settings after the pattern of the procession.

most clearly in the wording in Florio's Italian-English dictionary (1611) of the definition of *scena:* "A stage or scaffold in a theater or playhouse. But properly the forepart of a Theater where Players make them ready, being trimmed with hangings, from out which they enter upon the stage. Used also for any place where one doth shew and set forth himself to the world or to view."[2] This is another indication that in the Elizabethan mind the public stage façade was identified with the façade of the street-shows and the royal-audience pavilions and other backgrounds for public displays.

Considering the persistence of this function of setting, we cannot help feeling that Sir Edmund Chambers goes much too far in his theory that all Elizabethan staging was realistic and that every scene was visualized as an actual place in terms of the space relationships of the stage.[3] While many scenes were so visualized and often, as G. F. Reynolds insists,[4] the stage doors were given a realistic meaning which would help make the narrative clear, yet many scenes, I am now convinced, were thought of, not realistically, but in terms of the conventions and effects of the *tableaux vivants.* In sixteenth-century tapestries and paintings the scenes and characters of a story might be compacted into the various doors, arches, or panels of a complex conventionalized architectural structure without the least regard for realistic relationship to background. Often in art and regularly in the living tableaux a throne scene was not presented as an actual scene in a palace: it was a set show built around a throne. The background of the throne might be an arcade or a pavilion of a kind often built in the open for actual kings, or it might be a castle, a mountain, a heraldic emblem, or any other picturesque device (Figs. 4, 6, 11, 13, 14, 17, 20, 31). Before the throne might be placed allegorical

figures (Figs. 36, 37), ancestors of the king, subject or conquered kings, or other famous leaders of ancient story. Sometimes little plays or dances or groups of singers were placed before the throne without any feeling of inconsistency.[5] The throne was a show-device, and from out of it, or out of the larger structure back of it, could issue performers of any kind. The same was true of the other popular devices. The city of Jerusalem, denoted by a castle, would make a picturesque show-background; then before it, or on its walls or towers, or in its galleries, gateways, or windows, might be shown any of the characters, Christian or Saracen, concerned in the siege, often with no question of which would naturally be inside the city and which outside (Fig. 15). Curtius plunged into the gaping Roman street in front of a castle representing Rome.[6] Neptune or a personification of a river would sit, not in the water, but, like a portrait statue, in front of a composite arrangement of waves, reeds, stones, shells, and a water vase. For the Merchant Taylors' pageant on Lord Mayor's Day in London in 1561, four compartments held David, Orpheus, Amphion, and Orion, each placed in front of a painting representing his story.[7] Each was explained by the picture behind him but was not thought of as a part of that picture. The same concept of symbolic background persisted, alongside of more realistic conventions, into the Restoration theatre, where the backdrop showed the outside of a distant city while the actors in front played scenes supposed inside the city.[8] Realistic space relationships the Elizabethan audience did visualize in many scenes, especially scenes of house interiors; but for many of the more picturesque and spectacular effects the stage façade was not considered an actual place

---

[2] Cf. the wording of the 1598 edition of Florio and other evidence presented by Chambers, *The Elizabethan Stage,* II, 539, n. 2.

[3] *Ibid.,* III, 50 ff. and 88 ff.

[4] *The Staging of Elizabethan Plays at the Red Bull Theater,* pp. 111–28.

[5] Cf. the pastoral play performed on a platform with a whole throne scene as background, at the entry of Charles VIII into Rouen in 1485, described above, p. 97.

[6] Brussels, 1578. Reproduced by me in "Renaissance Artists in the Service of the People," *Art Bulletin,* XXV, 58, Fig. 4; cf. also Fig. 40 above.

[7] Clode, *The Early History of the Guild of Merchant Taylors,* II, 267.

[8] Nicoll, *The English Theatre,* pp. 83 f.

but a colorful showpiece or pageant device which, like a setting for a jewel, would display to advantage the characters placed before it or in its openings and galleries.

The transition from the *tableaux vivants* to the English public stage, while not so direct as in the Low Countries, is nevertheless indicated, I believe, in the settings at the Inns of Court. Several variations of a conventionalized façade were used for a series of tragedies produced by the lawyers for the entertainment of Queen Elizabeth. Since almost all these plays were concerned with the political education of the queen—their object being to warn her of the dangers of civil war if the succession were not settled—they were like fully developed street-shows. As would be expected of Renaissance gentlemen with a thorough classical training, the members of the Inns of Court built façades that were simpler and more formal than the backgrounds of the popular *tableaux vivants*.

Their first classical tragedy, *Gorboduc*, produced in 1561, required only two entranceways and a throne (or possibly two thrones) as a setting. One of the five dumb shows makes use of the throne, and there is no material, either in the other dumb shows or in the play itself, that cannot be visualized around and in front of a formal throne, after the pattern of many tapestries and many street-shows. The combination of throne and arcade screen was a commonplace of art from the time of the Hellenistic theatres (Figs. 4, 11, 17, 31).

The next play, *Jocasta*, produced at Gray's Inn in 1566, had the most interesting façade of all, the one most closely related to the patterns of art—a façade in the centuries-old pattern of a center castle gate flanked by two side doors. Here the central castle was the palace doorway of Jocasta, and we cannot doubt that the new Renaissance classical architecture was used. At each side of the central palace was a gateway—one marked "Homoloydes" and the other "Electrae." The following year at the Inner Temple a third variation of the façade was built for the romantic play *Gismond of Salerne*. At the top, in a

pattern we have often seen in the tableaux, was a heaven from which Cupid descended as Prologue to address the queen. The main part of the façade was twofold, one part serving as King Tancred's palace, the other part as Gismond's chamber, with an archway large enough to show her father talking to her at her death scene.

For *The Misfortunes of Arthur*, produced at Gray's Inn in 1587, a complex background even more like the public stage façade was used. Two entranceways, after the medieval convention and the humanistic Terence conventions, served as the houses of Mordred and of Arthur, though they were in actuality supposed to be many miles apart; and a third entrance is spoken of at one moment as the cloister of the nuns. The whole façade, when a messenger arrives from abroad, serves as a pageant symbol of Britain.

These English classical tragedies owed much to the earlier imitations of Seneca in Italy and France. Although the concept of a compact façade was already a commonplace in each country, some historians, such as Rigal, unfamiliar with popular shows and the visual arts, have supposed the French tragedies unplayable in a theatre.[9] But there would have been no difficulty for a painter or a deviser of pageants in sixteenth-century France in staging Garnier's *Antigone*, which compacts several inconsistent places beside and before the gates of the city of Thebes.

One play that has come down to us of the many produced at the English royal court shows us a slightly more primitive façade that was more obviously related to earlier art and pageantry than any used in the plays of the law courts. It is *Horestes* and is presumably the same *Orestes* that was listed in the Revels accounts for 1567–68.[10] The main structure is a castle gate with a battlemented gallery above and serves to symbolize several different cities in succession. Clytemnestra speaks from the walls above; the city is assaulted by an army; Aegisthus is hung

[9] Rigal, "La Mise en scène dans les tragédies du XVIe siècle," *Revue d'histoire littéraire de la France*, XII, 1–50, 203–26; also in his *De Jodelle à Molière*, pp. 31–138.

[10] Chambers, *op. cit.*, III, 44.

from the battlements by means of a ladder; the army of Orestes makes a triumphant entry through the city gates; and then, as a final scene, Orestes is crowned king by Truth and Duty. We have already observed many street-shows in which a castle was a background for a throne scene; and we shall remember this example when examining the many plays on the public stages in which at one moment the façade is considered a castle and the next, a background for a throne.

II. THE APPEARANCE OF THE STAGE FAÇADE

How did the Elizabethan public stage façade look to the spectator and how did it appear to his imaginative fancy? Many modern designers, attempting to reconstruct an Elizabethan stage, have made use of the half-timber tan and brown of Tudor houses. I believe they are quite mistaken. Most of the new buildings erected in England in the latter half of the sixteenth century were of the newer Renaissance architecture, with its classic orders of columns and arches and its marble and gold. What specific information we have indicates a very colorful, rich, and elaborate effect. There are a number of references by contemporaries, both friendly and satirical, to the painted stages and painted theatres. Nashe wrote in *Pierce Pennilesse:* "Our scene is more stately furnished than ever it was in the time of Roscius."[11] The De Witt drawing of the Swan shows two ornate Renaissance columns supporting the heavens. The notes which accompany the drawing say specifically that they were of wood "so painted in imitation of marble that the most critical persons would be deceived."[12] Although the Swan drawing and the seventeenth-century engravings show no columns as part of the façade, I believe we must suppose them in some of the theatres. The Fortune contract called for columns carved with satyrs, not only for the two columns at the front of the stage, but round the "frame" of the house as well.[13] Although the heavens of the Hope Theatre, built in 1613, was to be made

without supporting columns, the contract called for "turned columns upon and over the stage." Except for the free-hanging heavens, the Hope was to be made like the Swan.[14] Many of the *tableaux vivants* had beautiful Renaissance columns and canopies, as notably the Antwerp, Binche, and Brussels shows illustrated here in Figures 29, 30, 31, 32, 34, and 40. For an age of love of display, I cannot believe in the Tudor tan and brown. The beautiful dark oak of the Folger Library stage is designed to please a twentieth-century taste for simple lines and plain materials; it would have been much too dull for the Elizabethans. Heywood compares the Roman stage with that of his day: "In those days from the marble house did wave no sail, no silken flag, or ensign brave: then was the tragic stage not painted red, or any mixed stains on pillars spread."[15] In the same author's play, *The English Traveller*, one character looks about and describes a house in terms that seem very close to what the audience must have seen at the back of the stage: "What a goodly gate .... what brave carved posts .... what goodly fair bay windows .... what a gallery, how costly ceiled, what painting round about .... terraced above, and how below supported."[16] No simple plain background, but a splendid colorful façade, with not only colored marble but flags, ensigns, sails, curtains, and paintings, is indicated by the direct descriptions and references.

In its permanent features this façade must have seemed both to carry out the customary forms of the street theatres and to incorporate the requirements of Vitruvius, who stated: "Tragic scenes are delineated with columns, pediments, statues, and other objects suited to Kings." The later Baroque design of Inigo Jones for the Cockpit Theatre at Whitehall Palace shows similar permanent ornamentation.[17] Although Jones was

[11] *Ibid.*, IV, 239; cf. also *ibid.*, II, 530, n. 2; and Graves, *The Court and the London Theatres*, pp. 69 f.

[12] Chambers, *op. cit.*, II, 362.   [13] *Ibid.*, p. 437.

[14] *Ibid.*, pp. 466 f.   [15] *An Apology for Actors*, p. 22.

[16] Reynolds, *op. cit.*, p. 41.

[17] Reproduced in Chambers, *op. cit.*, Vol. IV, Frontispiece, and in Nicoll, *The Development of the Theatre*, p. 133; cf. also Keith, "A Theatre Project by Inigo Jones," *Burlington Magazine*, XXXI, 61–70, 105–11.

much interested in such Italian examples as the Teatro Olimpico, his design probably bore some resemblance to the Elizabethan façade. It had an upper-stage opening over the large central archway; statues, niches, and garlands above; small compartments with printed names and a motto; and formal side doors.

Let us see now what coloring the stage took on in the imaginative fancy. In other lines of Heywood's *An Apology for Actors* he has Melpomene, lamenting the decline of respect for the theatre, describe the ancient theatre altogether in terms of a glorified Elizabethan stage. She says: "Then did I tread on arras, cloth of tissue hung round the fore-front of my stage: the pillars that did support the roof of my large frame double appareled in pure Ophir gold."[18]

Further, Heywood describes a theatre he supposes Julius Caesar to have built:

> The covering of the stage, which we call the heavens (where upon any occasion their gods descended) were geometrically supported by a giant-like Atlas, whom the poets for his astrology feign to bear heaven on his shoulders; in which an artificial sun and moon, of extraordinary aspect . . . . had their . . . . motions; so had the stars . . . . elements and planets. . . . . In brief, in that little compass were comprehended the perfect model of the firmament. . . . . From the roof grew a loover, or turret, of an exceeding altitude, from which an ensign of silk waved continually, *pendebant vela theatro.*[19]

In several plays written by amateurs outside the public theatres, we find visualized a stage façade which closely resembles the *tableaux vivants* and yet at the same time seems only an imaginative glorification of the public theatre. Hang a few decorations on the Elizabethan tiring-house front, as we know was done on some occasions, and it could fit any of these fanciful accounts. The first description is a speech of a messenger just landed on the shores of England in Hughes's *The Misfortunes of Arthur.* Like an orator in a street-show, the messenger addresses the façade as a symbol of Britain, in these terms: "So here at length the stately type of Troy, and Britain land the promised seat of Brute, decked with so many spoils of conquered kings."[20] We remember at once the stately "types," or ornamental canopies, built to adorn the tops of pulpits, altars, tombs, and religious pageant stages, and the many scenic castles and other devices built in the street-shows for Anne Boleyn, for Edward VI, and in the several royal entries in the 1550's;[21] yet this play was performed at Gray's Inn in 1587—a decade after the patterns of the public stage were well established. In Hughes's mind a façade for a play had the same purpose and the same effect as that for a street tableau.

Similar in many ways are the descriptions of the settings in the plays of William Percy, son of the eighth earl of Northumberland and an amateur playwright. Although his plays contain a number of references to performance at Paul's, there is considerable doubt that the descriptions can be taken to refer to the setting at any theatre, public or private.[22] They are all the more interesting to us, therefore, as they indicate how a person familiar with both public and private playhouses and, of course, with the street theatres as well, would imagine a scene if his fancy were free. Besides the many movable properties, Percy visualized complex façades which are clearly related to the street-shows. For *The Faery Pastoral* he thought of a façade with a "Faery Chapel" below a "canopy, fane, or trophy"—just the words often used to describe the parts of a triumphal arch. Above would be a gallery for musicians, and the whole structure was to be a symbol of Elvida Forest—just as we have seen arched façades in tableaux serving as a symbol of a garden or inclosed orchard. He wanted not only a printed title of the play but a general title for the scene and a particular one for the chapel. He called for "Highest, aloft, and on the top of the music tree the title The Faery Pastoral. Beneath him pinned on post of the tree the scene Elvida Forest. Lowest of all over the canopy, ΝΑΠΑΙΤΒΟΔΑΙΟΝ or Faery Chapel."[23]

---

[18] P. 18.

[19] *Ibid.*, pp. 34 f.   [20] Beginning of Act II.

[21] Cf. the discussion of both the castle and the pavilion in chap. ii, and cf. also the bibliography for chap. ii.

[22] Hillebrand, "William Percy, an Elizabethan Amateur," *Huntington Library Quarterly*, I, 391–416.

[23] Chambers, *op. cit.*, III, 137 f.

As a setting for his *Cuckqueans and Cuckolds Errant*, Percy visualized a complex façade which was a composite of three places, symbolized by three entrances. The entrance of characters from any one doorway located the action, as in the religious drama. Here, although the façade was apparently formal and architectural, signs, images, and removable decorations, besides the titles, gave some visible symbols of place. He called for "Harwich, in middle of the stage Colchester with image of Tarlton, sign and garland under him also. The Rangers Lodge, Maldon, A ladder of ropes trussed up near Harwich. Highest and aloft the title The Cuck-Queanes and Cuckolds Errant. A long form." Tarlton's Ghost gave the Prologue.[24]

There is one more document, even more vivid, which shows that in the mind's eye the Elizabethans visualized the stage in terms of the effects of the street-shows—the passage in the "English Wagner Book" of 1594 describing a stage conjured up by magic. Chambers quotes it as most nearly describing the effect of the public stage, but he does not pursue its implications. The English adapter of the German original adds this sketch of a theatre:

> They might distinctly perceive a goodly stage to be reared (shining to sight like the bright burnished gold) upon many a fair pillar of clearest crystal, whose feet rested upon the arch of the broad rainbow, therein was the high throne wherein the King should sit, and that proudly placed with two and twenty degrees to the top, and round about curious wrought chairs for diverse other Potentates, there might you see the ground-work at the one end of the stage whereout the personated devils should enter in their fiery ornaments, made like the broad wide mouth of a huge dragon . . . . the teeth of this Hell's-mouth far out-stretching. . . . . At the other end in opposition was seen the place wherein the bloodless skirmishes are so often performed on the stage, the walls . . . . of . . . . iron attempered with the most firm steel . . . . environed with high and stately turrets of the like metal and beauty, and hereat many in-gates and out-gates: out of each side lay the bended ordinances, showing at their wide hollows the cruelty of death: out of sundry loops many large banners and streamers were pendant, briefly nothing was there wanting that might make it a fair castle. There might you see to be short the gibbet, the posts, the ladders, the tiring house, there everything which in the like houses either use or necessity makes common. Now above all was there the gay cloud *Usque quaque* adorned with the heavenly

firmament, and often spotted with golden tears which men call stars. There was lively portrayed the whole imperial army of the fair heavenly inhabitants. . . . . This excellent fair theatre erected, immediately after the third sound of the trumpets, there entereth in the Prologue attired in a black vesture, and making his three obeisances, began to show the argument of that Scenical Tragedy, but because it was so far off they could not understand the words, and having thrice bowed himself to the high Throne, presently vanished.[25]

In the action described, devils issue from the hell-mouth and besiege the castle, Faustus defies them from the battlements, and angels descend from heaven to the tower. After the devils assault the castle, the great devil and all the imperial rulers of hell occupy the throne and chairs and dispute with Faustus.

Here is a façade much like the Elizabethan stage, with an elaborate heavens at the top containing clouds, stars, astronomical effects, and a tableau of heavenly persons, from which angels can descend. The main façade serves as a castle of iron and steel with turrets and gates and a gallery above, but it creates the atmosphere of a castle principally by means of banners and streamers—effects which we know were frequent on the show-castle and which, of course, were as easily available to the public theatres. It is difficult to tell whether the author here was supposing three separate mansions—hell, throne, and castle —or one façade that could serve as castle and yet as the background of a throne. As we shall see, the public stage façade could serve the two purposes, just as the show-castles often did. The hell-mouth at one end of the stage may have corresponded to a trapdoor on the public stage—the usual entry for devils—and hence have been in front of, rather than at the side of, the castle. The Henslowe inventory lists among portable properties a hell-mouth. All these descriptions show that the Elizabethan visualized his public stage as closely resembling the little tableau theatres built for king or lord mayor.

III. PAGEANT-SHOWS ON THE ELIZABETHAN STAGE

We are now ready to examine the actual functioning of the Elizabethan façade as a show-

---

[24] *Ibid.*, p. 136.

[25] *Ibid.*, p. 72.

piece. While the façade could be considered realistically as the interior or exterior walls of a house or forgotten completely as some un-localized scene was performed on the apron, yet a number of scenes followed the patterns of the street-shows. For those scenes the background was not negative: it was rich with associations and redolent of that "atmosphere" which most of our historians would deny it. We must look at those scenes in which the façade served as a castle or city, a throne backing, a tomb or altar, a garden, a ship, a seat-of-honor, or a royal pavilion for a tournament. We must watch while its archway and gallery open up to present little tableaux or arranged pictures behind curtains.

The most frequent of the tableau effects on the Elizabethan stage was the castle. We have already observed the widespread use of the castle since the early Middle Ages not only in actual life but in drama and pageantry, in triumphal arches, in fireworks, in heraldry, in furniture, and in illustrative art. We have described many of the show-castles of the street theatres—how they could be hung with tapestries, curtains, and painted cloths; covered with boughs and flowers; or painted red or gold or like marble and decorated with shields, arms, devices, pennons, banners, and torches. We have observed the various conventions and shapes of the castle—now with a heavens above, either of clouds or of a canopy supported by posts or of some astrological symbol (Fig. 34); now with a gallery above for trumpeters, musicians, angels, or armed defenders (Figs. 6, 13, 24, 25, 26, 27). A gallery or throne set high in the castle served for an orator, a king, or a personified virtue to be honored by characters below. Often the large central opening disclosed an inner scene, and side towers or panels contained side doors (Figs. 24, 25). Sometimes the castle served as a backing for a throne, or a portrait figure could be placed in a niche set into the front face. Also the side doors and center and side windows above could be opened up to show other characters. In England in both the fifteenth and the sixteenth centuries the show-castle, to inclose a seated figure, often had built out in front

of it a pavilion or baldacchino supported by two front columns. Sometimes, to include other figures, the platform floor (or apron stage) came forward beyond the throne. In 1520 a poet addressed Henry VIII and Charles V from the apron in front of a castle-throne scene of King Arthur.[26]

The tournament façade I reproduce here (Fig. 33) shows that by the beginning of the sixteenth century the castle façade had already begun to take on Renaissance architectural detail. It did not have to keep the stone walls in order to create the atmosphere of a show-castle. In the Wagner Book vision it had the color of iron and steel and columns of gold and crystal.

How, then, did the Elizabethan stage façade serve as a castle? The most frequent use was in battle scenes in the many historical plays which formed the bulk of the dramatic fare in the last two decades of the century. There was scarcely a play about a historical or legendary hero without a scene of one army appearing before the gates of a city to be defied by the defending leaders on the walls or turret. In Shakespeare's *I Henry VI*, an assaulting army appears successively before the gates of Orleans, the Tower of London, Orleans again, and then before Rouen, Bordeaux, and Angiers. In the scene of Orleans not only does one part of the façade suggest the city, but at the same time another part suggests a tower outside the city from which the English can observe. The English scale the walls, and the French jump down in their nightshirts. Then the English come out of the façade and are supposed to be in the city square—so flexible is the scenic convention. In the third act of *Richard II* the shifting battle forces of Richard and Bolingbroke appear in succession before three different castles.

Most texts are curiously silent about banners and shields used as decorations on the façade. The testimony of the Wagner Book and the example of the street theatres would make us suspect that they were put up more often than they are mentioned. We have always supposed that

[26] Cf. chap. ii (p. 83) and the bibliography for chap. ii, "Entries: England."

the many directions about colors and banners referred to those to be brought on by attendants as part of the moving procession. But it is entirely possible that some directions such as "Drums and Colours. Enter . . . ." refer to banners to be hung, or to be changed, on the façade. Perhaps the detail "out of sundry loops many large banners and streamers were pendant," of the Wagner Book, tells us how such banners could be changed quickly by stagehands out of sight of the audience (Fig. 47). A special effect of changing flags and emblems was dramatized in Heywood's *The Four Prentices of London*, a popular play of the 1590's. The stage directions for a scene of Jerusalem mention the "Standard and Crown" set up above by the Sophy. Two apprentices climb the walls, "beat the Pagans, take away the crowns on their heads, and in the stead hang up the contrary shields, and bring away the ensigns flourishing them, several ways." In a later scene they speak of scaling a tower and putting a cross on the walls.[27]

Let us look at other scenes of banners and emblems. For instance, Act V, scene 5, of *Macbeth*—the scene of the famous "Tomorrow and tomorrow" soliloquy—begins with the entrance of Macbeth and soldiers "with drums and colours." Macbeth says: "Hang out our banners on the outward walls." If we follow the method of Chambers, we shall have to suppose that the scene is some interior room of the castle and that the soldiers leave the stage to hang the banners out of sight. But is this not, rather, another case where the changing or hanging of symbolic decorations on the façade has been dramatized? The façade was not used realistically but as a picturesque background, a tableau of a castle.[28]

More symbolic pageantry is used in the assault scenes in *I Tamburlaine*. On the three days Tamburlaine is before the walls of Damascus, he appears successively with white banners and apparel, offering leniency, then with red, then with black, threatening complete destruction. It is not clear that we are shown the day of white, but we are certainly shown the red and then the black. On the third day the governor leads forth four virgins, who with branches of laurel plead for mercy—a traditional ceremony of submission—at the city gate.

A number of castle scenes follow the pageant-shows even more closely than these scenes of assault. Like the Flemish authors, the English often brought some of the characters onto the stage as spectators of the shows; but the English dramatists were far more adroit in integrating show and spectator than were the authors of the *spelen van sinne*. An ingenious dramatic castle-show takes place in the third act of Munday's *John a Kent and John a Cumber*, in which the two magicians are helping two rival groups of lords pay suit to their ladies. John a Cumber, by means of a musical castle-show, in the very face of their rivals spirits his lords inside to their waiting loves. He opens the gates of the castle (the central opening of the stage façade). Then from the two sides of the stage, from under it, and "forth out of a tree," the four lords enter in turn, each disguised as an "antique," to sing a song warning that love will escape. At the end of each song the singer enters the castle. When all are in, John a Cumber goes in and "makes fast the door." The cheated lords try to break in but are entertained by a pantomime show on the gallery, played to music, in which their successful rivals talk with the ladies.

That all theatres had permanent gates at the center of the façade has been questioned, because such gates would presumably be in the way of elaborate inner-stage tableaux disclosed by the drawing of the curtains. The idea of removable gates is supported by a reference in Middleton's *Family of Love* to seeing in a theatre "Sampson bear the town-gates on his neck from the lower to the upper stage."[29]

The façade as a castle or a city gate was made a very telling showpiece for the opening scenes of

---

[27] Reynolds, *op. cit.*, pp. 102 and 128 f.; cf. the hanging of trophies in other scenes in the same play (*ibid.*, p. 85).

[28] Cf. the placing of horns on the façade in Act IV, scene 1, of *Eastward Ho*. With the horns, it becomes a symbol of a town, "Cuckholds Haven on the Thames." At the end of the scene Slitgut describes each horn as he takes it down.

[29] Reynolds, *op. cit.*, pp. 117 f.; Chambers, *op. cit.*, III, 83.

Shakespeare's *Pericles*. The background was a symbol of a place, but there was no sense of actual location. Gower, as Prologue, locates "this Antioch" and calls attention on the façade to the decapitated heads of those who had come to court the incestuous daughter of Antiochus and, failing to answer the riddle, had been put to death. As though for a *tableaux vivant*, music plays when the daughter enters. Pericles, half-apart from the tableau, reads the riddle, realizes the corruption, and ponders his escape. Is this scene just outside the gates of Antioch or inside the court? It is neither—the whole scene is a pageant-tableau of danger and rottenness at Antioch.

Castle scenes lead us immediately into the many throne scenes; for often the two were closely related. We have already observed how frequently a castle was used as backing for a throne in all forms of art, especially in England. That the drama followed such a pattern is indicated by the last scene of *Horestes*, already mentioned. As a court play of the 1570's, this was produced where the temporary painted settings were presumably more realistic and less conventionalized than on the public stage. The scene throughout the play is a city gate. After Orestes has assaulted the city and hung Aegisthus on the walls, his army marches triumphantly through the gates. Then the final scene shows Orestes' coronation. To anyone familiar with art and pageantry, this combination of throne and castle would seem perfectly appropriate. The fact that throne scenes many times follow castle scenes on the public stage indicates that the dramatists used the same combination of symbols that we have noticed in medieval art. In a number of the chronicle plays the battle scenes are followed by scenes of coronation. Even if there were scenic battlements added in the upper part of the façade to give the appearance of a castle, that would not have seemed inconsistent around a throne. We know that the "town-canopy" consisting of miniature battlements and towers, a commonplace throughout the Middle Ages, persisted sometimes into the Renaissance period as a decoration above beds, pulpits, and royal thrones. We have described the

outdoor pavilion built for Queen Mary to receive the Princess Elizabeth: it was backed by cloth and covered by a canopy of castle battlements. An elaborate throne-show in Heywood's *The Brazen Age* followed and preceded spectacular castle scenes. The Greeks left after a scene before the city gates of Troy and came back on stage before a royal-audience scene at Colchos. Almost immediately was disclosed the tableau of the Fleece guarded by the two fiery bulls and the sleeping dragon. Either in the tableau (which Reynolds suggests was very possibly a painted picture,[30] much like those on the Flemish stages) or in front of the façade, Medea was shown hanging in the air. In the following scene the Greeks were back before Troy and scaled its walls and won.

The transition from castle to banquet scene is just as easy as to throne. We have already noted the medieval painters' convention of showing feasts in front of screen, building, or tower. Many banquet scenes had an important person presiding and hence may easily have used the same seat as that for the throne scenes. In Act II of *Pericles*, Simonides and his daughter play the leading parts in a show suggesting the royal throne-pavilion at a tournament. She describes the shields and devices of the knights as they go by to the fray. After a few offstage shouts to indicate the actual tourney, they re-enter and take their seats at a banquet and dance. In Marlowe's *Dido*, presented at court, one part of the permanent setting is the city gate of Carthage, which is decorated with small pictures of Troy, such as Virgil and scores of medieval painters placed in an open temple. In one scene a banquet is served, placed, if the conventions of the *tableaux vivants* were followed, in front of that colorful decorated city-castle. A number of scenes in *I Tamburlaine* are throne scenes. Act IV, scene 2, is a throne scene; and Act IV, scene 4, begins as before Damascus walls but develops into a banquet scene, as picturesque as any tableau, showing Tamburlaine and Zenocrate enjoying a fine banquet and the captive Bajazet and his wife re-

[30] *Op. cit.*, p. 161.

fusing food. In the same scene Tamburlaine crowns his followers as subsidiary kings. Thus are city-castle, throne, and banquet merged into one colorful tableau.

An interesting variation of the mutation from castle-show to throne- or banquet-show takes place at the end of Heywood's *The Silver Age*. Instead of the coronation or throne scene that ends a number of battle plays, here is a scene of a court trial. The battle has raged at the castle gates of hell, which by the help of Hercules have been overcome. Immediately the gods arrive for a "sessions," appropriately held before the gates of hell, to determine the status of Proserpine. The body of Cerberus, guardian of the gates, is not removed until the end of the sessions. Another scene of a trial, in *Swetnam*, combines an orchard scene with a throne—the fence, an old symbol of a garden, serving here as a barrier around the throne.[31]

Thus there were a considerable number of dual scenes, in which a new kind of scene was brought on, without, apparently, negating the associations and atmosphere of the previous one.

Most of the throne scenes or seated groups on the Elizabethan stage were placed on the main stage, the façade with its hangings being appropriately used as a framing background (see the thrones in Figs. 4, 13, 20, 25). Yet there was another place for giving special honor to a figure or group—a throne or gallery set high above the stage. Following the ancient pattern of the niche-of-honor on the stage façade and the medieval pattern of the heavenly figures at the top of rood screens and altars, many *tableaux vivants* presented a heavenly throne or heavenly niche at the top of a castle or other façade. Often the heavenly throne was converted to a throne-of-honor for a king or for a lady personifying the city or some important civic virtue. Related characters might be placed in niches or on a stage below, as in the arcade-of-honor, already described, which was built for Catherine and Arthur in 1501.[32]

We have seen how the heavenly throne was a determining influence on the form of the Rede-ryker stage. Many of the early Flemish plays and exhibitions were put on in honor of the Virgin, whose image sat above. In others the climax of the play was the disclosure above of a throne-tableau of the Trinity or of the Last Judgment. In later performances the figure of Lady Rhetoric was placed in a throne above, or a living Lady Rhetoric who played the induction was escorted to a throne to watch the contest in her honor (Fig. 44), perhaps to descend later, like an angel, to distribute honors. In still others the main play was brought to a climax by the disclosure of the Seven Liberal Arts or the Muses, arranged in a tableau above (Fig. 46). The singing Arts or Muses, sometimes led by David or Apollo, were popular in Flemish and English street-shows throughout the sixteenth century.

Several plays given at the English court in the 1580's make similar use of the scenic structure for divine or allegorical spectators or supervisors of a show below. Lyly's *The Woman in the Moon* begins with an induction played by Nature and the Seven Planets. They "draw the curtains from before Nature's shop" and go above to a seat to watch the pastoral play. Several times in the course of the play they ascend and descend. Chambers suggests that the gods who play the induction and the denouement of *Rare Triumphs of Love and Fortune* watched the play from battlements, for the Revels accounts mention a city, a battlement, and a cave.[33] These three scenic elements may have been separate structures like those at the Hôtel de Bourgogne, or, in the pattern of many of the street theatres, they may have been compacted into one structure.

On the public stages, about 1589 and 1590, there appeared three plays which made similar use of appropriate divine or symbolic figures who sat above to watch the show. The main characters of Greene's *James IV* demonstrate the vanity of human existence and justify Bohan, the misanthropic Scotsman, in leaving the world. In the induction he meets Oberon, who also

31 *Ibid.*, pp. 45 f.

32 The heavenly throne and the throne-of-honor are discussed in chap. ii, both in the section on the arcade (pp. 86–89) and in that on the façade (p. 95). See also chap. i, p. 29.

33 *Op. cit.*, III, 45 f.

despises the human world. The two go onto the gallery and present shows to each other to prove their points—a contest somewhat like the Flemish dramatic contests. Oberon's characters appear in dumb shows and Bohan's enact a full play. The two contestants in their high position were more than mere spectators watching a play. To many in the Elizabethan audience they must have appeared like figures in the throne-of-honor of a pageant-show.

Peele planned one of the dumb shows of *The Battle of Alcazar* in such a way that it resembled the street theatres even more closely. As in all Elizabethan dumb shows, the actors here came onto the main stage; but above them watched the character they served to illustrate—Nemesis. Similarly, Sly sat on the gallery to watch *The Taming of the Shrew*. In *A Looking Glasse for London and Englande*, a throne-of-honor high on the façade served much the same purpose as the seat for Lady Rhetoric, before whom the Rederyker plays were presented. An angel brings in Oseas the Prophet and seats him in a throne over the stage, from which he views the entire play and at intervals makes moral comments. The throne of blessed souls in heaven, shown by Richard Vennar on the upper stage of the Swan in 1602 in his *England's Joy*, was a tableau very similar to the heavenly throne in the street theatres, in the Flemish plays, and in medieval art.[34]

Since most of the throne scenes in the run of Elizabethan plays were surely on the stage level, we have assumed that all references to a throne were to a portable one set up on the forestage, or possibly on occasion behind the arras. The examples I have given suggest that we should reconsider many of the references. Similar scenes in the street-shows and in the Flemish plays regularly used a heavenly throne. The item in *Henslowe's Diary*, "Paid for carpenter's work and making the throne in the heavens the 4 of June 1595," may as well refer to a throne set high in the façade as to one that could be let down. Similar was the "high throne wherein the King

should sit, and that proudly placed with two and twenty degrees to the top" imagined in the Wagner Book. This may have been supposed set high against the castle façade, as in many of the earlier English shows; from it the king could watch the Prologue and the play enacted below him.

Hence I believe we must conclude that the Elizabethan theatre had a place, high on the façade, for a heavenly throne. Like the King of the Festival in primitive dramatic rites, like the statue of Dionysus on the Greek stage façade or the statue of a Roman emperor on a Roman stage façade, like Christ the Judge in medieval paintings and carvings of the Last Judgment (Figs. 14, 19), like the king or the character Honor in a *tableau vivant* (Fig. 36), like Our Lady or Lady Rhetoric in the Rederyker theatres (Figs. 43, 44, 46)—like all these, a character in an Elizabethan play could sit on a heavenly throne and pass sentence on the action going on below.

Two other scenes in later plays indicate how well the upper galleries of the Elizabethan stage could serve the same function as the upper galleries in the pageants. In the first act of *I Antonio and Mellida*, played by the Children of Paul's at a private playhouse about 1600, Mellida is placed above with two ladies-in-waiting to watch a ceremony below. They comment while her father receives two suitors in turn. When the suitors are gone, Mellida says, "The Triumph's ended." This must have seemed to the audience like a *tableau vivant* of a lady in a gallery-of-honor, with her suitors gathering below. At the end of *II Antonio and Mellida*, Andrugio's ghost is placed above, "betwixt the music houses," to watch the gory deeds that avenge his death. Even a tableau of the Nine Muses—a commonplace of both the pageants and the Flemish plays—was placed on the upper stage in Middleton's *The World Tost at Tennis*, a courtly masque produced in 1620 for the public, probably at the Red Bull.[35]

A similar royal tableau on the upper stage is made quite dramatic in the third act of *Richard III*. When the mayor and aldermen come onto the

---

[34] *Ibid.*, II, 413; and Graves, "A Note on the Swan Theatre," *Modern Philology*, IX, 431.

[35] Reynolds, *op. cit.*, p. 102. Possibly also Jupiter's throne was above in this masque (*ibid.*, p. 54).

main stage, there is revealed on the upper stage a tableau of Richard between two bishops, a book of prayer in his hand. Then Buckingham, in front of the show, makes an oration to Richard, begging him to become king. The similarity to the street-shows, with an orator before the tableau, is here very close.

Discussion of a throne set high brings up again the question of the third story of the façade and the location of the heavens. The wording of stage directions in *I Henry VI* and *The Tempest* suggests to John C. Adams and to others that there was a second gallery, perhaps a music gallery, which could be used occasionally by actors.[36] Prospero, standing "on the top invisible" and watching his enemies mocked by a magic banquet, suggests the throne-of-honor effect.

In art and in the street theatres the heavens was regularly at the top and behind the plane of the façade. The heavenly throne might be in a niche or under a canopy supported by columns; or all the figures might be on the gallery at the top—the regular place for musicians. The association of musicians with heaven was seemingly universal, and extra performers on occasion were placed on the side towers or in windows. One of the symbols of heaven was the almond-shaped Glory of clouds or angels' faces surrounding a heavenly personage. The Glory was used on several occasions in the Elizabethan theatre and persisted to the nineteenth century. Another symbol was a canopy painted underneath with stars, clouds, and sometimes with the signs of the zodiac. In the street-shows such a canopy was supported by columns resting on the top of the scenic structure. The third symbol, often combined with the canopy, was an astrological machine of stars and symbols, often placed in a background of clouds, as in the show at Binche in 1549 which I reproduce here (Fig. 34). When to the Elizabethan façade was added the "shadow," or penthouse roof, borrowed from the throne-canopy, that canopy took on the functions of the various symbols of heaven usually placed within the

façade structure. (Of course throne-canopies and bed-canopies were already treated as a *ciel*, or heavens, and might be decorated with angels and stars and clouds.) Hence the Elizabethan audience might think of either the roof and the bottom of the hut or of the upper part of the façade below that roof as the heavens. The account of the stage of the English actors at Regensburg in 1613 indicates an opening "through which beautiful effects were contrived" underneath the roof, which was supported by six columns.[37] But it is not clear whether the opening was in the top of the façade, after the pattern of the street-shows, permitting astrological and weather effects to be shown, or in the bottom of a canopy-roof covering the main stage. Many of the street-shows had shutters that would open to disclose a heavenly scene—an effect made much of in the perspective settings but evidently not used extensively on the Elizabethan public stage.[38]

Since the Elizabethan theatre borrowed from the *tableaux vivants* both the heavenly canopy supported by columns from the stage floor and a gallery for heavenly figures and musicians, we cannot determine in any particular instance which may have been used. Instead of assuming, however, that all astrological or other celestial effects were shown under the penthouse roof, we should remember the alternate possibility of upper openings and galleries in the façade.

Effects of stars, suns, and moons were far less frequent in the public theatres than in the street-shows; but apparently, like the tableaux, the theatres depended more on symbols, such as the signs of the zodiac, than on the illusionistic imitation of sky. For instance, the marginal directions in the anonymous *Timon of Athens* call for "the sign of the 7 stars." The elaborate astronomical display of five moons in *I Troublesome Raigne of King John* was a machine which made one moon whirl about the others, to symbolize England and her scorn of popish lands.

[36] Adams, "The Staging of *The Tempest* III, iii," *Review of English Studies*, XIV, 413 f.; and *The Globe Playhouse*, chap. ix.

[37] Chambers, *op. cit.*, III, 78.

[38] In *Four Plays in One*, Jupiter in a Glory above is revealed by the drawing-aside of two cloud shutters. The court theatre built in Whitehall in 1665 had oval shutters for the heavens (Boswell, *The Restoration Court Stage*, p. 40).

The similarity of some of the pageant-show façades to the still dramas in stone around tombs and altars we have already noticed. Elizabethan dramatists only occasionally used the theatre façade as a backing for tomb or altar; instead, for most tomb scenes there was a small portable coffin or tomb, or a trapdoor for a grave. However, in the last act of *Romeo and Juliet* the façade becomes the front of the tomb, to which Paris brings flowers and which Romeo opens. This ceremony of bringing flowers, epitaphs, or other tokens to a tomb occurs in a number of plays, and the stage façade seems a fitting background. Claudius, in *Much Ado about Nothing*, hangs an epitaph and has a song sung before the façade, supposed to be the tomb of Hero. A few scenes earlier it had served as an altar for the wedding scene. In *The Atheist's Tragedy*, Act III, scene 1, both epitaphs and coats-of-arms are hung on the pillars. The spectacular death scene of Hercules in *The Brazen Age* is part of a scene of sacrifice at an altar. The thunderbolt from heaven and the hand which descends to bring a star to place in the firmament added a pageantry logical enough to audiences familiar with heavenly figures at the top of the screens of altars and tombs and the images of Gabriel coming down from the top of tombs. In *The Iron Age* King Priam is discovered kneeling at an altar, and characters comment on the priests who prepare the altar—apparently as part of the whole façade. In *The Rape of Lucrece* the façade, before which priests with tapers are kneeling, is supposed to be the oracle of Apollo, and the whole stage, with the canopy above, becomes the temple. Elaborate altar tableaux are arranged in Act V of *Pericles* and Act III of *The Duchess of Malfi*. Pericles in one act goes before the supposed tomb of his daughter, and in the following act before the altar of Diana, to discover that the priestess is his long-lost wife. In *The Duchess of Malfi*, in an elaborate dumb show for which the stage façade is supposed to be the shrine of Our Lady of Loretto, first the cardinal gives up his ecclesiastical robes and is invested with the garments of a soldier, then he banishes the duchess, Antonio, and the children. Two pilgrims comment on the show as spectators. There are not a large number of scenes of altars and tombs involving the façade or the heavens or the inner stage; but when we remember the façades of actual tombs, with curtains carved back of the figure, a canopy with columns, and the heavenly figures carved above and coats-of-arms and banners added for decorations (Figs. 20, 21, 22), we realize that the shift from show-castle to tomb and from a two-story paneled Renaissance façade to altarpiece was a simple one. When we remember how similar in form and decorations were actual altars and tombs, we wonder if it was an accident that in several of these plays altar and tomb scenes came so close together. The Renaissance audience did not have to supply all the atmosphere for these scenes by imagination; there was actually, in their eyes, considerable resemblance.

Even for a garden, the façade was not quite meaningless. The street-shows and stained-glass windows and tapestries all demonstrate that an archway (the gate to the garden) could serve as well for a garden as could a tree or a fountain. A gateway with a single tree or plant set behind or in front of it was perfect; or an arbor, another symbol of a garden, could be decorated like a formal architectural pavilion. We have already noticed the elaborate "Gardyn de Esperans" built for the English court in 1516, which had columns, canopy, rocks, and gold and imitation marble—a tradition which lasted in court functions into the seventeenth century.

An elaborate garden tableau, very similar to the many historical tableaux of the street theatres, was arranged in Shakespeare's *I Henry VI*. The leaders of the houses of Lancaster and York pluck roses of different colors to symbolize their opposition. We need suppose no realistic picture of the Temple garden, even in the imagination of the audience. We must remember the heraldic, conventionalized single plant or family tree set in or before an archway in several of the *tableaux vivants* (Fig. 37). In other garden scenes the background served as the entrance gate or a building looking out over the garden, as Juliet's balcony did. Even fields were sometimes represented by a gate—a scene in *George a Greene* takes place in front of a gate to the wheat close.

In medieval painting another symbol of a garden was a low fence built around the seated or standing character. Such a low railing was used in *tableaux vivants* in Flanders several times in the sixteenth century: for instance, one of the shows at Bruges in 1515 had a fence around a number of plants. In one of the shows at Ghent in 1585 the maiden of Ghent sat on a small throne, a cloth hanging behind her and a canopy above with coats-of-arms; yet, since she was supposed to be in a garden, a small railing surrounded the stage. How similar would the lady have looked sitting on the Elizabethan stage, rushes on the floor, a small railing surrounding the stage, the hangings of the façade behind her, and a colorful canopy above her![39] She would have had all the garden symbols the Renaissance mind needed.

There is some likelihood that English people had seen in a street theatre a ship built into the columns, canopy, and hangings usual as decorations for any device. I have found no English records. Certainly, a number of Englishmen saw such a combination in Paris in 1514, when Mary Tudor, the sister of Henry VIII, arrived to marry Louis XII. The ship, a symbol of the city, was realistic enough, but it was built into a façade of columns supporting a canopy (Fig. 35). Behind the ship was a tapestry, reminding us of the figured backgrounds conventional in medieval painting, and before it was a platform from which an expositor explained the show to the queen. There are references to ship-pageants built for some of the Lord Mayor's Pageants in London.[40] Hence we must suppose that the audience did not face anything completely new when the Elizabethan façade of curtains, columns, canopy, and upper stages was used for scenes on board ship.

[39] Compare the orchard-fence-throne scene in *Swetnam*, mentioned above.

[40] Chambers, *op. cit.*, I, 138.

IV. TABLEAUX AND DUMB SHOWS BEFORE AND WITHIN THE FAÇADE

On the Rederyker stage the most important effects that followed patterns of the *tableaux vivants* were the illustrative scenes—now paintings, now still figures, now pantomime actions—disclosed within the façade by a curtain. The character in front, like the presenter before the street pictures, would describe and explain the inner scene. There were many similar tableaux on the Elizabethan stage which just as clearly were derived from the traditions of the street theatres. Some were lay figures, some were arranged tableaux of actors, and some were parts of the main play, disclosed as tableaux for a startling effect.

The formal dumb shows, however, the most striking pageant effect on the Elizabethan stage, developed in ways quite different from those of the tableaux on the Flemish stages. While Flemish dramatists followed the convention of using a presenter in front of a structure to pull aside the curtain or open the front of the device to reveal a painted or arranged picture inside, the English followed another convention from the street theatres—the procession. This brought the actors onto the forestage, in front of the structure that was used for the main play. A few dumb shows made use of such parts of the structure as doors and throne, but very few were revealed by a curtain. They followed some of the forms of a moving procession and even on occasion used a chariot.

The symbolic purpose of the dumb shows and their connection with the main play relate them very closely to the traditions of art and the *tableaux vivants*. Cunliffe was impressed by their close resemblance to the Italian *intermedii* put on between the acts of serious plays.[41] They have often the same subjects, and the earlier English examples were used to introduce each act. Further, some of the Italian *intermedii* were planned so as to have a symbolic pertinence in theme and mood to the act following. But the

[41] "Italian Prototypes of the Masque and Dumb Show," *PMLA*, XXII, 140–56.

Italian form seems to me an analogous development, motivated by the same interest in allegory and symbolism, from a common storehouse of romantic story and example, rather than a source from which the English shows derived. There is a closer resemblance to the native *tableaux vivants*. From the English pageants the dumb shows derived the characteristic conventions of pantomime action and musical accompaniment—many dumb shows called for appropriate military or infernal or mournful orchestral effects. From them the dumb shows derived a moral and allegorical purpose that was far more serious than the diverting *intermedii* had developed. From them came the great love for the characters of civic allegory: Truth, Discord, Peace, etc., with their appropriate tokens and properties; from them came the selection of ancient examples to reinforce the theme or mood.

The first English classical tragedy given by the lawyers of the Inns of Court inaugurated the English dumb shows. *Gorboduc*, produced in 1561 at Whitehall Palace, set the custom, which became regular in the plays of the law societies and frequent in the public theatres. Possibly because the structure used for the play—one or two thrones and two entrance doors—did not contain an inner stage or curtains that might be drawn to reveal a set tableau, the dramatists chose the processional, front-stage method and thereby set the fashion for later dumb shows. The presenter who usually introduced the *tableaux vivants* and even commented during the pantomime movement was, by these classical-minded authors, equated with the "chorus" and reserved until the end of each act, when he commented on the act and explained the pertinence of the dumb show. In some later plays a Prologue explained the dumb shows, while in others either casual onlookers or regular characters of the play made comments in dramatic dialogue, usually after the show.

The *Gorboduc* shows had much the same mixture of elements from folklore, legend, literature, and allegory that was familiar in the street theatres. The show in the first act used six wild men to demonstrate the old fable of the bound sticks that could be broken only when divided. The one in the second act made use of the throne of the main play to present a royal scene of an imaginary king who refused to drink the draught of Clear Counsel offered him by a grave counselor and drank, instead, the poison presented in a gold cup by a flattering young parasite. That before the fourth act followed the form of the Italian processional triumphs, described so elaborately by Petrarch: each of the three Furies drove before her a king and a queen who had killed their children, to signify the unnatural murders to come. These picturesque groups passed around the stage three times. The third and fifth shows had no story but only symbolized a mood: they consisted of a group of mourners and of a group of soldiers discharging their guns.

Most dumb shows had the purpose of symbolizing by mood or theme the main action. But some later dramatists in England, as well as in the Low Countries,[42] made a different use of the separate pantomimed show—they compacted part of the main story into the briefer form of action without speech, still using the musical accompaniment and striving for a more picturesque arranged effect than was possible in the spoken scenes.

Far more closely related to the street theatres than the dumb shows were the tableaux that were woven into the texture of the plays. They were usually disclosed within the façade by the opening of a curtain, and they had a close dramatic relationship to the characters standing on the outer stage viewing them.

One pattern, developed in the street theatres and used in the masques as well, had a great influence on Elizabethan dramatists: the use of an appropriate character, allegorical or historical, to speak to the audience and disclose and explain the tableau. For example, the legendary founder or hero of the city would stand in front of a device symbolizing the city or an incident in its history and explain the subject to the prince; a doctor in

[42] Cf. chap. iii.

scarlet explained a fleur-de-lis full of Virtues to Louis XII at Paris in 1498; Minerva introduced a tableau of the Five University Faculties to Francis I at Caen in 1532; Ptolemy explained a horoscope to James at Edinburgh in 1579.

The use of a character appropriate to a tableau or even to the entire play became popular in the theatre. While an anonymous "Prologue" to *Tamburlaine* asked the audience to "view but his picture," and a "Chorus" opened the curtains on the tableau of Faustus in his study, Marlowe for *The Jew of Malta* brought Machiavelli to life to present the play and open the curtains on a tableau of Barabas among piles of gold. Sometimes one presenter was used throughout a play, as the Ghost and Revenge of *The Spanish Tragedy*, Gower in Shakespeare's *Pericles*, and Homer in all five of Heywood's plays on the "ages." Sometimes a character in the play would disclose a show he was interested in, like the schoolmaster in Marston's *What You Will*, who drew a curtain to reveal five schoolboys sitting with books in their hands. Similarly, the magician Bacon in *Friar Bacon and Friar Bungay*, whether behind a curtain or on the stage beside him, conjured up a vision of events happening at some distance. And the Duchess of Malfi must see behind a traverse a false tableau of figures of Antonio and her children, as though dead.

Of the Elizabethan scenes which mention a curtain, the majority were arranged tableaux on the inner stage, many of which had the same symbolic or allegorical purpose or the same kind of picturesque detail as the *tableaux vivants*. At the beginning of *The Whore of Babylon*, the Prologue draws a curtain discovering "Truth in sad habiliments, uncrowned: her hair disheveled, and sleeping on a rock: Time (her father) attired likewise in black, and all his properties (as scythe, hourglass, and wings) of the same color, using all means to waken Truth but not being able to do it, he sits by her and mourns." We are reminded of those tableaux in the Rederyker plays in which different characters attempt to wake some sleeping Virtue. An arranged effect was several times used to show the results of violent death, re-

minding us of the Greek *eccyclema*. Thus in *A Looking Glasse for London and Englande*, Act II, scene 1, "He draws the curtains and finds her strucken with thunder, black"; and in the fifth act of *The King of Lombardy*, "He draws the arras, and discovers Albovine, Rhodalinda, Valdaura, dead in chairs." A very dramatic surprise is achieved near the beginning of *II Antonio and Mellida*. Antonio, eagerly awaiting Mellida, sees the curtain stir, then "The curtains drawn, and the body of Feliche, stabbed thick with wounds, appears hung up." Antonio asks: "What villain bloods the window of my love?" The body apparently remained in place during several unrelated scenes until Pandulfo came to claim it and lament over a dead son's fate.

Tableaux of mourning were arranged with the same attention to symbolic cloth and properties that we find in the street-shows.[43] For Lucrece's suicide in Heywood's play there was prepared "a table and a chair covered with black"; and in *The Devil's Law Case*, Act III, scene 3, there was a tableau of "a table set forth with two tapers, a Death's head, a book, Jolenta in mourning, Romelio sits by her."

The principle of prefiguration, so frequent in art and the street tableaux and also in the dumb shows, by which one scene was paired with another of the same theme, was used on a few occasions in the main part of the play itself. Thus in *III Henry VI*, when Henry is alone bewailing the sorrows of civil war, there comes on the stage a son who has just killed his father and then a father who has killed his son. By the help of Friar Bacon's magic glass, in Greene's play, two scholars watch their distant fathers kill each other. Enraged, the two scholars do likewise.

This dramatic effect of using a tableau to illustrate and stimulate the thought of the person seeing it was carried even further in a scene in the second act of *A Woman Killed with Kindness*, which

---

[43] Cf. the miniature of the *tableau vivant* hung in black at Genoa in 1507 which I reproduce in "Renaissance Artists in the Service of the People," *Art Bulletin*, XXV, 59. The black cloth covering the walls and the bed and used for the mourning dress has small splashes of white, as though to suggest ermine with the colors reversed.

approaches modern expressionistic dramatization of inner conflict. While Wendall, alone, is torn between his desire for Mistress Frankford and his respect for her husband, the couple appear together with their son on the balcony, like a vision, to torment and inflame the wavering man.

We might go further and consider the wider and less specific influence of illustrative art and the living tableaux on the Elizabethan drama. We might consider the many scenes which do not advance the drama or develop the conflict but serve to illustrate and symbolize the feelings of the characters about one static situation before the play moves on to another. For instance, in *Promos and Cassandra*, the early play which Shakespeare re-wrote in *Measure for Measure*, are dramatized the erection of tableaux and music stands and the address of welcome for an arriving king; and throughout the play the author presents scenes in the static, symbolic manner popular in tapestries and in the street theatres. To illustrate the effect of the harsh laws of the ruler, a group of prisoners, bound, sing of their woes. Cassandra is shown in many soliloquies or picturesque tableaux, sometimes with song—as begging before Promos, dressed as a page, lamenting her shame, then receiving the supposed head of her brother Andrugio. The two serious scenes in Act V of the first part progress by a color sequence similar to the white, red, and black of Tamburlaine's three-day siege of Damascus. First Polina, the maid that Andrugio loved, appears in a blue gown, as a symbol of her shame; then in the last scene Cassandra in black laments her brother's death and resolves to go to the king. The second part begins with Polina in the shameful blue, now shadowed with black, at the "Temple" praying before Andrugio's tomb; and so on. One could go through a large number of plays pointing out where the choice of material was determined by the habit of picking for illustrative art and street art a static situation that would catch the eye and hold it for a full lyric realization of the emotion. One could list scores of moments: Jane Shore turned out at Aldgate; Titania enamored of an ass; Romeo falling in love

with Juliet, under her balcony, taking leave at the window at dawn, taking leave of her body in the tomb; Helen viewing a stage full of the bodies of her victims; Lady Macbeth looking with horror at her hands; Tamburlaine mounting on a conquered king to his throne—scenes in which dramatic movement stops and the eye is feasted with a picturesque tableau, while beautiful lyric sounds exploit the static emotions of the scene.

The lyric element in the plays, as Miss Welsford has so well pointed out, shows the strong influence of the court masque. But we must remember that the full effect of these tableau scenes did not depend on music and poetry alone; no less important was the visual symbolism derived from the illustrative arts and the living art of the street tableaux.

V. CONVENTIONS OF THE FAÇADE

That some conventions of medieval simultaneous staging persisted in the handling of properties on the Elizabethan stage seems clearly shown by the evidence that Professor Reynolds has amassed.[44] Onto the forestage were brought the portable settings, and there the actors trooped on, played their scenes, and trooped off to make way for the next scene—all with the same kind of processional staging that had been used in the medieval squares. And medieval performers had not hesitated to indicate more than one place at a time. Certainly, characters on the Elizabethan stage were frequently supposed some distance from the properties or scene located and, without leaving the stage, might approach and even enter the place concerned. Professor Reynolds has considerable evidence that properties were left visible on the stage during scenes for which they were not suited, because they were to be used again later, and that in the same scene incongruous properties were employed. Sir Edmund Chambers has admitted that on occasion different doors might be supposed different places farther apart than the distance across the stage; and Professor Reynolds

[44] First presented in two articles in *Modern Philology* in 1905 and summarized with additional evidence in 1940 in *The Staging of Elizabethan Plays at the Red Bull Theater*.

believes that, at the Red Bull at least, more than one curtained place was available for widely separated scenes as distinct as the tents of Richard and Richmond in *Richard III*, Act V. Examining the façade in the light of the façades of art and the street-shows, we can find still further evidence of medieval conventions.

Of course, the convention we have already mentioned of combining the aspects of scenes—castle with throne, and banquet and law court and pastoral scenes before a throne, and garden with triumphal arch—suggests that many of the inconsistencies Professor Reynolds points out were thoroughly acceptable to the audience as part of a show-tableau. In art and pageantry the background might be planned as appropriate for one character or scene, then other characters might be placed in that background as the expediencies of composition, not dramatic verisimilitude, would dictate. But along with the convention that the whole stage might symbolize two or more shows simultaneously, allowing them to overlap in time, there was fully established precedent for the indication of multiple places by different parts of the façade. The principle of compacting several structures into one, apparently never used in the medieval religious plays, was, as we have seen, one of the most important developments in sixteenth-century narrative sculpture, narrative art, and street theatres. Whereas the designers of street-shows usually integrated the decorative details of several scenic devices into one compact form, the designers of tapestries, paintings, and stained-glass windows more often preserved a horizontal arrangement of several different scenes, beside or above one another, united in a single architectural screen.[45]

On the Elizabethan stage there were a number of scenes where certainly the façade suggested different places at the same time. We have already noticed that in *I Henry VI* one part of the façade represented the walls of the city of Orleans and another part—apparently an upper window or gallery—represented a tower from which the English could look into the city. This reminds us of the pattern of the castle flanked by side towers before they were conventionalized into the side panels of the late Renaissance façades. Professor Reynolds points out that in Heywood's *The Rape of Lucrece* one part of the balcony is a hill outside Rome, another part is the walls of the city, while a door below is at the same time thought of as a bridgehead leading to Rome.[46] While in some scenes a shop may have been a free-standing structure on the stage, in others it was clearly discovered as part of the façade. Sometimes several shops were shown at once, or other parts of the façade were used for scenes inconsistent with a shop. The most interesting localizing detail, perhaps, was the grated window, frequently used for a prison window. In painting, it was sometimes part of the same architectural structure that might inclose or stand behind other scenes. For instance, the scene of Herod's banquet was usually in front of a screen or a castle tower representing the palace, and the prison was often a grated window in another tower. But in sixteenth-century paintings the two are sometimes part of one continuous architectural structure. Such was apparently the background for Nicholas Grimald's early Latin tragedy *Archipropheta* of about 1547.[47] The scene was set before Herod's palace, which apparently included the prison. W. J. Lawrence finds some indication that the grated window could be used on both the ground level and the upper stage, and he speculates as to whether it was a removable structure or a permanent feature of the façade.[48]

In all, there is considerable evidence that not

---

[45] Cf. the examples of a composite façade discussed in chap i, especially the "Christ before Pilate" of Mostaert (Friedländer, *Die altniederländische Malerei*, Vol. X, Pl. VII).

[46] *The Staging of Elizabethan Plays at the Red Bull Theater*, pp. 128, 146. Cf. Act IV of *Eastward Ho*, where the whole façade is a symbol of a town, with an emblem of horns visible above; in the same scene, part of the façade is supposed to be a tavern.

[47] Chambers, *op. cit.*, III, 31, n. 3.

[48] *The Elizabethan Playhouse, Second Series*, pp. 40 f., and *The Physical Conditions of the Elizabethan Public Playhouse*, pp. 67 f. Now John C. Adams boldly posits a wicket in one or both of the side doors. He shows how well it conforms with the architecture of the time and how useful it would be in explaining a large number of scenes that present actors at both sides of a door (*The Globe Playhouse*, pp. 153–62).

only the forestage but the façade as well preserved medieval conventions of simultaneous places. Certainly, there was no necessity for supposing that when a place was located by one part of the scene structure—an entrance door or a shop, grated window, or tent inserted as part of the front—all the rest of the façade would have to be the same place. The artists' conventions of simultaneous setting influenced the stage in this case as in others. The theatrical façade was either a symbol of one place or a conventional means of uniting several emblems into a unified design.

Another set of Elizabethan conventions is likewise to be traced to the traditions of art—those having to do with indications of interiors. From the Hellenistic age on, artists, with extremely few exceptions, had thought of themselves as outdoors and had used outdoor forms in their painting.[49] So compelling were the habits of mind established by centuries of art that Renaissance audiences, even where there was a roof over the theatre, supposed themselves outside looking at exterior architectural forms; hence interior scenes had to be indicated by various subterfuges. All the Elizabethan stage methods were those familiar in painting. Thrones, banquets, beds, or writing desks were put in front of arcade screens or castles or any other exterior architectural structure. The medieval convention, derived apparently from the ancient theatre, that such a scene should have a cloth hanging, was carried out on the Elizabethan stage. Of course, the frequent use of painted cloth and tapestries on walls in homes reinforced the association between curtain and interior. The Elizabethan pavilion-canopy over the forestage, with or without its supporting columns, was, as we have seen, a convention of an interior. The inner stage or curtained area likewise followed a pattern taken from painting in opening up the walls of an exterior structure to show the interior. Again, painting furnished the suggestion of bringing onto the clear front area such properties as a bed or characters who would belong properly within the inclosed area. Professor Reynolds has gath-

ered considerable evidence to show that characters coming on stage through the side doors might be considered as outdoors in the first part of a scene, then indoors when the center curtains opened to disclose an interior,[50] in which case the side doors could be considered as part of the same room. Thus it was the center section which established the interior.

VI. THE FORM OF THE FAÇADE

What, then, was this English theatrical façade and how were its various features and conventions derived? It bore only a few relationships to the structure of the pageant wagons, just as its drama was far removed from the Mysteries. Nor did it share anything but its use of a platform and the direct relationship of actor to audience with the stage of the interlude. T. S. Graves tried hard to relate it to the court scenery, by comparing the opposite entrances of the public stage to the two-mansion pattern frequent at court; but that two-mansion arrangement followed the inclosing side-accent form of medieval art. The Elizabethan façade belonged to a different medieval tradition. It was primarily a center-nucleus, center-accent from, which borrowed its side-door extensions from the arcade screen. That combination of center accent and screen was already made in medieval art. Two variant patterns can be seen uniting in both the Rederyker and the Elizabethan stage façades: one is the castle form flanked by two towers, the other a combination of pavilion (for example, over a throne or altar) and arcade screen. The latter is to be seen in the *tableau vivant* of enthroned majesty erected in Brussels in 1594 (Fig. 31). Both can be traced in the Rederyker façade erected in Ghent in 1539 (Fig. 42). The screen of arches cuts through the pavilion and unites the center section of the castle with the side towers.

Much—it now seems too much—has been made of the innyard influence on the English public theatre. While the auditorium closely resembled the innyard, the façade cannot be explained by the custom of playing there. Little

---

[49] Cf. the discussion of conventions of the exterior and interior in chap. i.

[50] *Op. cit.*, pp. 113 ff.

more than the pattern of spectators on an upper balcony viewing the action below can be directly traced to the innyard, and that pattern has many other origins as well. It is highly probable that by the 1540's and 1550's the inns which were important as regular playing places had incorporated the features of the show-façade that had been developed in art and pageantry. Chambers finds reason to believe that structural alterations and rebuilding for the stage were necessary in the London inns,[51] and Graves has pointed out that when away from London the companies preferred to play in halls rather than in innyards.[52] Whether the pattern of the façade was first established in the innyards or only appeared in the first playhouse in 1576, it derived mainly from traditions completely outside the innyards.

From the street theatres and the older traditions of art the Elizabethan façade derived its principal patterns.[53] It was a two- or, more probably, a three-story façade[54] at the back of a platform. At the top was a projecting canopy-roof, which in some theatres was supported by pillars from the stage floor. Above that rose a turret, visible above the rest of the theatre, from which a flag and a trumpeter might announce the performance. Both the upper story and the underside of the canopy-roof derived from monumental sculpture, as well as from the *tableaux vivants*, the power to represent heaven. Either a painted sky-cloth or astrological signs and emblems were visible on occasion, and possibly all the time. The spectacle of a heavenly messenger descending in front of a show-structure—popular in both religious and civic ceremonies—remained popular in the public theatres.

That the upper gallery was the place for musicians had been established in various traditions of art. In painting, singing angels on an upper gallery looked down on such scenes as the Nativity; in the *tableaux vivants*, musicians often played from the top of a castle, an arcade, or a triumphal arch; in the church an organ and the whole choir might be placed on top of the rood screen; and in great halls the minstrels' gallery was held high by an arcade screen. Side doors derived from the archways or niches at the sides of the central pavilion or in the side towers of the castles. They also preserved the pattern of the arcade screen. If they were set at an angle, partly or squarely facing each other, as W. J. Lawrence and a few others would like to believe,[55] they but followed the more complex medieval pattern of adding side wings or houses at the ends of the back screen (Figs. 5, 11, 12). The façades of the street theatres were flat.

For the center section there were several precedents. In the *tableaux vivants* a throne could be set against the flat façade, a tapestry behind it, and a canopy projecting from the top of the façade. Or the throne or a standing statue might be set into a center niche. More often a hanging would cover the surface of the niche, giving it a half-interior quality, though it was not completely inclosed. In most northern art and in many street theatres the center section was the regular place for opening an inner stage to show an arranged interior. Then characters on the front area were considered part of the interior, though the side doors or panels or windows usually retained an exterior quality. This is the regular art pattern of center interior flanked by exterior sides which we have noticed in contrast to the Italian pattern of center exterior. Or triumphal arches and castles, two closely related symbols of a city, had an open arch or city gateway in the center section—often enough with a tableau in a curtained space above the arch and trumpeters on the gallery at the top (Figs. 25, 38).

In color and decoration the showpieces were

---

[51] *Op. cit.*, II, 357, 379 f., and 383.

[52] *The Court and the London Theatres*, pp. 37 ff.

[53] Cf. the center pavilion and conventional façade in painting, discussed in chap. i; the façade in tombs and altars and in *tableaux vivants*, chap. ii; the Flemish Rederyker façade, chap. iii; and the comparison of all theatre façades, chap. v.

[54] Many of the street theatres had three stories.

[55] Lawrence (*The Physical Conditions of the Elizabethan Public Playhouse*, pp. 22–28) bases his argument on the terms "opposite doors" and "opposite sides" and "the one end . . . . the other end," which seem to me not at all conclusive. Adams (*The Globe Playhouse*, pp. 145 f.) supposes doors in oblique side walls because they would fit in better with the octagonal interior he is rebuilding for Burbage. Such assurance is very persuasive but must not be confused with proof.

very live and vivid: imitation marble, gold, silver, and many bright colors sparkled in sun or torchlight; festive tapestries and cloths hung on the front or adorned niche or inner stage; paintings of battles or other appropriate scenes often supplemented the more conventional cloth. We remember that the later Caroline or Commonwealth stage represented in the cut in Kirkman's *Wits* had two paintings of battle scenes on the façade, as well as the functional curtains; and we shall find that formal façades in Italy were decorated with paintings. On cornices, in cartouches and medallions, and on banderoles, the *tableaux vivants* used the printed word to identify places or characters, to give dialogue, or to add mottoes, quotations, or appropriate verse. At least for place names, the Elizabethan stage sometimes continued the custom. Tavern signs added other variations of word and emblem to adorn the stage and identify places. Further, on columns, on the top, anywhere there was space on the structure of a *tableau vivant*, were placed banners, pennons, coats-of-arms, and heraldic and allegorical symbols. They frequently adorned marble tombs as well. We find them on the elaborate Baroque prosceniums, and I strongly suspect they were far more often on the Elizabethan stage than the few accounts would indicate.

Atmosphere the Elizabethan stage did not lack. Even if it had not the footlights of the Baroque perspective scene or the spotlights of the modern plastic stage, it had other means of suggestion and mood. Even if it had no realistic painted settings, it had other ways of persuading the eye that here were scenes of pomp and splendor. Besides the rich costumes and the movable processional properties—the arbors, trees, moss banks, tents, shop fronts, wells, rocks, etc.—shown on the forestage, the façade itself had color and atmosphere and association.

Most of all, the Elizabethan stage had the atmosphere of a festival. The hangings, the painted architectural structure, the processions with banners and music, the special effects of soldiers assaulting castles, of kings holding court, of gods and Virtues descending, of princes being welcomed at city gates—all created the spirit of a festival day when for the inauguration of the lord mayor or the progress of the queen or the return of a triumphant army the streets were decorated and street-shows were erected. The façade had on some occasions the appearance of a triumphal arch; on others, with black curtains hung for tragedies, it suggested a public ceremonial of mourning. It but carried a little further the principle already established in the street-shows that it keep the aspects of several different scenic devices at the same time. On some occasions it was imagined as an actual room or the front of a house or other particular place, but its principal function was to provide the atmosphere and the symbols of a show.

I reproduce a composite drawing (Fig. 47) to show how details from the tableaux would have fitted together in the pattern of an Elizabethan stage. The doors are copied from the Swan drawing and the battle paintings from the scene in Kirkman's *Wits*. Other details are from the English tournament façade of Figure 33, from the Binche pavilion of Figure 34, and from other street-shows. The heavenly throne-of-honor built in London in 1501 must have looked like this heavenly throne with columns supporting the sky. Two- and three-story façades with pavilions and battlements, with heavens, and with upper or lower throne were seen on the streets of London in 1415, 1501, 1522, 1546, and 1554. The pattern of the Elizabethan stage was established in the *tableaux vivants*. Some of the detail, as I have suggested, may have been further conventionalized than this drawing indicates—the battlements may have disappeared in the new architecture, and, as John C. Adams shows,[56] the windows may have been projecting bay windows, screened with lattice casements. But the stage certainly kept the basic conventional patterns and the festive atmosphere of a tableau.

Even in Italy, only a few of the most advanced painters of the Renaissance held the ideal of reproducing an actual place on the stage. They

[56] *The Globe Playhouse*, pp. 256 ff.

used their new techniques to create the illusion of depth and accurate detail, but the architectural structures they represented might be highly conventionalized and quite different from the actual buildings of the time. Columns and by even this much interest in illusion! It was almost as conventional as heraldic devices or carved chessmen, for it dealt primarily in symbols. Clearly not only the *tableaux vivants* of western Europe but the popular theatres of England and

FIG. 47.—Reconstruction of a composite façade with the basic pattern of the Elizabethan stage. Every detail of decoration here is known to have been used on either a theatre or a tableau façade in England or Flanders. In the tableaux the heavenly throne was sometimes in a canopy at the top, as here; sometimes on the upper stage itself.

arches were painted with the illusion of actual depth, but two arches might represent an entire house. The realism of even the most advanced artists was a realism of method which still dealt with highly imaginative content. How much more conventional was the more popular anonymous art of the Renaissance, which was not touched the Low Countries as well must be considered as examples of the visual arts. On the Rederyker and Elizabethan stages came to life the gods, the heroes, the Virtues, the Muses, and the legendary examples of ambition, revenge, or glory or of sloth, civil discord, or tyranny which the people were accustomed to see in paintings, tapestries, and stained glass or in the tableaux of the street theatres. In England those legendary examples spoke to the ear with the words of some of the greatest poets of all time; but they also spoke to the eye with no little richness, excitement, and glory.

Clearly, the Elizabethan stage is close kin to the Rederyker; but, before we make a careful comparison of these two, we must consider several other formal stages of the sixteenth century. Both the arcade façade of the schools and academies and the curtain façade of Germany and Spain can throw further light on the meaning of stage convention in the Renaissance. In the following chapter, after we have examined them, we can make a comparison of all the façade theatres and ask anew what is this principle of architectural symbolism, this principle which distinguishes the northern theatres from the Italian theatres, where we shall find the illusionistic realism of the perspective setting.

CHAPTER V

ARCADE FAÇADE AND CURTAIN FAÇADE

The Curtain Stages of Germany and Spain; the Schools;
the Jesuit Stage; the Teatro Olimpico

WE HAVE examined in detail the Flemish and the Elizabethan stages as parallel examples of the nonillusionistic theatre in the Renaissance. Both were developed from the type of organization which emphasized some feature at the center of the design. But there were two other types of stages in the Renaissance that made use of a formal façade, both nearer the third method of organization which we have traced in medieval art—the flat arcade screen. How did these two types differ from the formal façades in Flanders and England? What did each contribute to the development of the later theatres in Europe?

We have traced this arcade screen as the basis for one of the three types of organization in medieval art.[1] We have watched how it was copied by painters directly from the Greek theatre façade, how it kept the arcade form of arches or panels throughout the centuries when space was neglected, how it could be opened up in the later Middle Ages to show little illusionistic scenes behind. We have watched in the *tableaux vivants*[2] how the arcade screen took on the meaning, now of a throne-of-honor, now of a triumphal arch; how it preserved some of the multiple elements of the medieval processions in the several little inner stages; how it was given a balcony above for musicians or heavenly characters; and how it was ornamented with statues, with paintings, and with curtains. In a later chapter we must trace the influence of the arcade

screen on the proscenium arch, as a formal screen at the front of the stage to frame an illusionistic picture. Here we must examine a whole group of theatres that used the screen as a façade at the back of the main playing area and gave it the function of an architectural symbol. These theatres were primarily nonillusionistic and hence must be related to the Flemish and Elizabethan façades. But into their façades and behind them could be set illusionistic details. Hence we must study them not only for light on the combination of formal and illusionistic in England but also to understand the relation between inner scene and formal frame throughout Europe. In one respect they were more primitive than the Elizabethan theatres—they preserved on the inner stages the medieval convention of multiple places; yet in their careful separation of the formal from the illusionistic they were quite advanced and helped prepare for the conventions of the perspective setting with its formal proscenium arch. They present an important compromise between the theatres of architectural symbolism (organized with an accent at the center) and the theatres of pictorial illusion (organized by wings that inclose the action from the sides).

The study of arcade façades will take us to the Spanish public stage, where a façade structure was concealed behind a solid front of cloth curtains, to the grammar schools all over Europe, to the Jesuit colleges, and to Vicenza, Italy, to the beautiful Teatro Olimpico, which may still be seen in an excellent state of preservation.

[1] Chap. i, pp. 12, 19–23.   [2] Chap. ii, pp. 85–89.

154

I. THE CURTAIN FAÇADE IN GERMANY AND SPAIN

Before the more complex curtain theatre was developed in Spain, a simple form of curtain stage appeared in a number of places and was of special importance in the schools and societies of Germany. Since a curtain was sometimes hung back of the playing area in all the Renaissance theatres in Europe, and especially back of the inner stage, these simple curtain theatres are of considerable interest, not only in connection with the Spanish stage but as a part of the stage history of all Europe.

The archetype of the simple curtain stage may be the cloths hung in churches and later in streets on festival occasions. The "dossal" or "dorsal," hung at the back and sometimes at the sides above the altar, furnished one important pattern of background.[3] Another was the figured or all-over pattern in Gothic miniatures and paintings that was sometimes treated by the artists as a curtain and often imitated in the *tableaux vivants* by curtains or tapestries. Perhaps all these uses of curtains go back to the hangings on the Greek theatre façade. But the immediate origin of the curtain theatres of the Renaissance is to be sought in two kinds of outdoor stages: those of the medieval mountebanks and those for the *tableaux vivants* of the royal entries. When the mountebank could not put his platform against a suitable building, he hung up a cloth as a background. From one or several slits he could make his entrance and even contrive to disclose a person or an arranged scene behind the curtain. The German Fastnachtspiel took over the curtain stage from the mountebanks and in turn passed on its features to the Meistersingers and to a number of school directors. We have already noticed the very frequent use in civic pageantry, especially in the Netherlands, of hangings and painted cloths not only to decorate streets but also on a platform, either as a background for a

tableau or orator or as a curtain in front of a scene which a speaker on the forestage would reveal at the proper time. The tapestries of the richest houses were often borrowed to hang on the street theatres. Especially if the device was a complete structure that inclosed an inner scene, as most of those at Bruges in 1515 were, that inner scene would be hung with tapestry (Figs. 25, 26).

While most German school plays, as we shall see, came under the influence of the Terence woodcuts, yet a number of plays were produced on a curtained stage very similar to those of the mountebanks and of the *tableaux vivants*. We have several woodcuts of the *Spiel von Kinder zucht* by Johann Rosser, played at Ensisheim near Colmar in 1573.[4] They show a stage about fifteen meters long and eight deep, hung on three sides with a figured drapery. When the center curtains are pulled aside, a solid archway is seen, but with only a very shallow inner-stage space behind it. Here is a forestage with a completely neutral background and all space apparently thought of as unified, in a pattern to be used at times by Flemish, Spanish, and English stages alike.

The Meistersingers developed their stage methods in close relation both to these school productions and to the Fastnachtspiel. The society at Nuremberg, especially, interests us because of the plays of Hans Sachs. In the little Marthakirche the Meistersingers erected a platform, hung curtains, and put on their plays. Whether their stage was in the nave, as Köster suggested, or in the transept with its rear stage in the choir, as Herrmann reconstructed it,[5] we are sure that the main stage was surrounded by curtains and that the background curtain could be pulled aside to reveal an inner stage. The scene on the rear stage often bore a real space relationship to the scene on the main stage—such as the interior of the house or temple before which the previous scene had taken place. Here is a kind of

---

[3] Bond, *The Chancel of English Churches*, pp. 59 ff.; Brooks, *The Sepulchre of Christ in Art and Liturgy*, pp. 63 ff. Cf. the platform prepared "in the manner of a stage," hung round with arras and red sarcenet, for the christening of Arthur in Winchester Cathedral in 1486 (Leland, *Collectanea*, IV, 204 f.).

[4] Reproduced by Borcherdt, *Das europäische Theater*, pp. 173 f.; cf. also similar school stages in Cheney, *The Theatre*, p. 357.

[5] The two reconstructions are discussed by Borcherdt, *op. cit.*, pp. 175 f.

simultaneous staging on a front-rear axis, not unknown in the single mansions of the religious plays and still to be important in the French theatres in the seventeenth century.

In most of Europe this curtain back of the playing area took a subordinate place: the architectural forms, if there was money enough to permit any lavishness at all, were much more appealing. Even in the German schools the other type—the Terence façades—soon displaced the simple curtain. In one country only did the curtain stage become of prime importance, and that country was Spain. Whether derived from the schools or the *tableaux vivants* or the mountebanks or from some other source, the curtain stage was established in the public theatres of Spain at just the time the first public theatres were built in England.

In its simplest form the Spanish public stage was a platform like the German school stages, surrounded by neutral curtains. Yet this stage that saw the plays of Lope de Vega was much more than a neutral playing space surrounded on three sides by drapes. Like the Rederyker and the Elizabethan theatres, it could function in two other ways. Onto the forestage could be brought the separate mansions or devices of the medieval processions and religious plays. Or for other occasions the curtains could be drawn aside to disclose one or several of the features of the façade: the center archway, the formal side doors, or the upper gallery. We may say, in fact, that the Spanish stage could function in three quite distinct ways—as curtain theatre, as processional, simultaneous-mansion theatre, or as complex façade theatre. And in Spain, as in most other countries in the Renaissance, there was considerable mixing of methods and conventions. Like the English playwrights, Lope de Vega staged each scene as he came to it, making free use of a very flexible stage.

As neutral curtain theatre, the Spanish stage needs no explanation. Many scenes in Spanish plays, whether interior or exterior, required no localization at all and could be played in front of the curtains or with the help of the curtained inner stage.

As a forestage onto which movable properties could be brought, the Spanish stage functioned in a way very similar to the Elizabethan. In Spain, as in England, tables, chairs, and thrones could be brought in and taken out as needed. Small scenic nuclei, such as trees, wells, and rocks, were brought on for outdoor scenes. Apparently in both countries a property might sometimes remain on stage through other scenes in which it would not be consistent.

The main difference between the Spanish properties and the Elizabethan was that far more elaborate and spectacular devices were brought on in Spain. By means of the elaborate façade at the back, the Elizabethan stage could present mountain scenes, ship scenes, castle tower scenes, without the addition of heavy properties. But in Spain three-dimensional mountains, fountains, ships, walled gardens, forts, and towers were brought onto the forestage, with something of the pattern of a medieval processional play in an English square. When several such properties or mansions were on the stage at the same time, the Spanish scene must have looked much like the simultaneous settings of the Hôtel de Bourgogne in Paris at the time of Mahelot. The main difference was that Mahelot had a painted background of screens, mansions, and sky, which led him more and more to unite the different mansions into one design. On the Spanish stage the mansions were discrete, and the spectators could see the neutral curtains of the background between and above them. As far as we know, there was no more attempt to arrange the stage into a center-focus picture than there had been at Valenciennes in 1547.

While there is no contemporary illustration of a performance on the Spanish stage, we do have a miniature[6] of a *tableau vivant* built at Lille in 1600 for Albert and Isabella, governors of Flanders for the king of Spain, which must have resembled many of the Spanish scenes. It reproduces a show of the death of Finart. A pavilion-canopy sup-

6 Published by Niessen, *Das Bühnenbild*, Pl. 15a, No. 2.

ported by columns holds up curtains to surround the stage on three sides. Before the curtains, in a row, are five separate mansions: a door, a tower, a throne, a hovel, and a tree. While I have come upon no Spanish play which used as many as five different structures in one scene, we are sure that, either by the forestage alone or in combination with elements revealed in the façade, the Spanish public theatres made use of this convention of simultaneous settings derived through the processions and the religious plays from the frieze forms of art.[7]

But not all the Spanish portable mansions were so realistic as those on the Hôtel de Bourgogne stage. Many of them were of the highly conventionalized, emblematic type that we have studied in the processions and in the *tableaux vivants*. They were picturesque show-devices, not imitations of the actual world. Trees, for instance, served as well to symbolize an occasion or to ornament a sudden entrance as to represent an actual place. The tree in *El Robo de Dina* by Lope de Vega turned round by a device to permit an angel to speak.[8] Other trees descended full of birds or opened to present some object. A number of plays used trees as means of portraying a genealogy, after the pattern of the Tree of Jesse in religious art and drama and the tree of royal ancestry painted on many murals and built for many street theatres. Mountains, too, could be spectacular show-devices. At the opening of Lope's *Los Guanches de Tenerife* a mountain on the stage turns round and discloses, built into its back, a half-ship with many standards. As a trumpet sounds, characters in the ship speak to others on the rest of the stage. Then the device is turned back to the first position. While such scenes follow the multiple-scene convention of the religious stages, they clearly derive even more from the

symbols of art and the devices of the street pageants.

It is the façade at the back—the third way of using the Spanish stage—that is most important for us here; for the Spanish theatre, besides its negative functions as curtain theatre and as simultaneous-mansion theatre, was also a façade theatre. Behind the curtains at the back, to be revealed part by part as needed, was the complete outline of a conventional façade, as we have seen it developed in altars, tombs, paintings, street-shows, and the Flemish and Elizabethan theatres. There were formal side doors, a central *nicho*, or inner stage, where an arch was sometimes visible, and an upper gallery. Any one part could be used separately, and, when all were revealed, the background must have been very similar to the façade in Flanders or in England.

The central *nicho*, which was opened up principally for interior scenes, was the same type of inner stage known all over Europe. Only in Italy, where the main setting was regularly exterior, was the little inner stage usually made an exterior. Leone di Somi, who wrote his *Dialogues* in the 1550's or 1560's, more than a decade before the public theatres of Spain were built, had heard of the custom on the Spanish peninsula of showing an interior by removing a curtain from a niche, and he disapproved of it heartily.[9] While most Italian architects preferred to make the inner stage an exterior, authors and managers in the rest of Europe used it regularly for interiors. Even Furttenbach, who followed Italian practice as far as his German conditions would permit, recommended (besides exterior scenes) a tapestried room on the inner stage.

The upper balcony, a feature of practically every Renaissance theatre, was of frequent and varied use in Spain. But in Spain, as in England, one of the most spectacular uses was as a castle-show.[10] Here defenders of the walls of a city or castle defied the enemy, or soldiers climbed to it by ladders for safety or to dislodge the enemy. Up the ladders and onto the gallery they carried

---

[7] Cf. the discussion of the frieze and processional forms in chap. i.

[8] The details of Spanish plays and stage directions which I cite are all printed in Rennert's "The Staging of Lope de Vega's Comedias," *Revue hispanique*, XV, 453–85. Both in this article and in his book, *The Spanish Stage in the Time of Lope de Vega*, Rennert draws conclusions which seem inadequate now. The subject needs a thorough re-examination.

[9] Nicoll, *The Development of the Theatre* (1937), p. 254.

[10] Cf. above, chaps. ii and iv.

banners and standards to make a colorful display. On this gallery were other picturesque castle-shows—for example, in Lope's *El Cerco de Santafe*, two Moorish women enter to a battlement (apparently on the balcony) and tie a Moor to a tree.

H. A. Rennert pictures the balcony as a structural extension of the gallery or *corredor* built around the courtyard for the audience.[11] He cites stage directions which indicate that curtains hanging in front of it could be arranged to permit characters to appear at different places or at different windows. To this balcony Rennert assigns scenes which were supposed to take place on a balcony, a tower, a wall, or a mountain. Yet we know that on some occasions walls and mountains were brought onto the forestage. Portable scenic towers were frequent in other theatres and could have been used for such scenes as the prison tower in Calderón's *La Vida es sueño*. In a theatre in which either movable painted structures could be brought on or a permanent balcony at the back could be used conventionally, we cannot know which method may have been used in any particular instance in which the directions are not explicit. The frequent mention of actual structures gives me an impression of a staging more often like the French than like the English, to which Rennert constantly compares it. A complete re-examination of the Spanish theatre is needed.

The frequent use of the balcony for characters looking down on action below reminds us not only of many medieval paintings and choir screens and street theatres but more particularly of a conventional form in Spanish sculpture of the fifteenth century. Duran i Sanpere publishes pictures of a number of carvings of spectators on a gallery at the top of a conventional screen watching a scene placed in front of the screen. In the church of Santa María of Castellón de Ampurias, the Last Supper is carved as taking place in front of an arcade screen with a rood loft above.[12] Onlookers, safe on a gallery, in a small scene in the high altar of the cathedral at Tarragona, watch St. Thecla and the beasts before a screen that has two side doors.[13] In the Saragossa high altar, similar onlookers watch St. Lawrence's martyrdom from the gallery at the top of the back screen.[14] Thus a number of examples in art and theatre attest the familiarity in Spain with the separate parts of the façade and also with its structural pattern. The curtains hung on it were equally familiar. The Spaniards, in covering the entire structure (as we assume they did), only carried a little further the conventional combination of screen and curtains inherited in all countries from ancient art and theatre.

The most spectacular use of the façade was to reveal arranged tableaux suddenly to the audience. Spanish stage usage was similar to that in England and Flanders and on the Jesuit stages; and, as in England, we cannot be sure which of the disclosed scenes may have been merely behind curtains and which were behind definite parts of the façade structure.[15] The staging of these Spanish tableaux reminds us constantly of the street-shows. Music usually played while the curtains opened; the properties were usually symbolic and the arrangement of people picturesque. Lope de Vega for *Arauco domado* gives this direction: "*Chirimias* sound and a curtain is drawn, behind which is seen an arch of greenery and flowers and on a carpet below it Don Garcia stretched on the ground." "Those doors are opened and there is seen, within, a stage and in the midst Amete tied to a stake" is Lope's direction in *El Amete de Toledo*. Again for *El Duque de Viseo* we read: "They disclose the duke, bleeding, and on one cushion the crown and the scepter and on the other Doña Elvira with her hand on her cheek." For Lope's *El Serafin humano* was prepared an elaborate tableau of a genealogical-allegorical tree, similar to the Tree of Jesse and the many family trees built for French royal entries. The directions read: "There is disclosed with music a tree to whose trunk is fixed St. Francis as if the

---

[11] *The Spanish Stage in the Time of Lope de Vega*, pp. 93 f.

[12] Duran i Sanpere, *Los Retablos de piedra*, Vol. II, Pl. 113.

[13] *Ibid.*, Pl. 49.   [14] *Ibid.*, Pl. 84.

[15] Reynolds (*The Staging of Elizabethan Plays at the Red Bull Theater*, pp. 130 ff.), suggests that many discoveries on the Elizabethan stage may have been behind removable curtains, not in a structural rear stage.

tree came out of his chest: at the sides are its branches and on them are seated those who will be designated; but in the middle of the tree must be St. Clara and then St. Louis, king of France, and the Child on the top. There will be four branches, two on each side and in each two saints."

The formal doors were apparently first disclosed by pulling aside the curtains. Sometimes the directions indicate simply that a door or doors open; other directions call for more complicated transformations of the doors and even some elaborate structures. A gate of rocks and branches fell open to disclose a cave and a body on a cloth in Lope's *Las Batuecas del duque de Alba*. In his *Arauco domado* "a tree is set at the *vestuario* and the trunk opens in two doors, where Lautaro is seen." A chapel with an altar is disclosed in his *Las Pobrezas de Reynaldos*. We are reminded of the picturesque doors which opened for the tableaux at Bruges in 1515 for Charles V (Fig. 26).[16]

On other occasions the back wall approached even more closely the pageant effects of the show-façade. I have described in chapter ii the elaborate architectural façade built in Lisbon in 1619 for the entry of Philip II of Portugal.[17] That structure of columns, arches, statues, and curtains had two formal side doors, one for the Portuguese and one for the Moors. Above was an elaborate Glory, where curtains revealed a symbol of the heavens from which cloud machines descended. For us, the most interesting part of the façade is the middle section, in which there were two "niches" (the same word that is used for the inner stage of the public theatres), each eight palms wide, and between them a pilaster three palms wide. Each niche contained two devices, built and painted as naturalistically as any late medieval pageant. Curtains covered the niches, and apparently a cloth painted to represent rocks opened to reveal further realistic scenes. The niche at the right contained both the throne of Aeolus, god of the winds, and his house, whence the four winds came. In the left-hand niche were

a hell-mouth, which opened and shut, and a black rock full of infernal flames. This combination of realistic devices with formal columns, arches, and curtains was frequent in the street tableaux, as we have seen, throughout the Renaissance.

It is clear that the Spanish public theatre in many scenes followed the same street-theatre pattern, revealing the realistic devices as needed. In Lope's *Amar, servir y esperar*, at different parts of the curtained background characters are revealed in two small boats. Two allegorical characters appear in separate devices disclosed in the façade in *La Vitoria del marques de Santa Cruz*—Religion "in the center above within a half-castle, in another part, Victory on a little galley [*galera*]."

Both painted pictures and lay figures were used for some shows, in much the same way as we found them in the *tableaux vivants*. In *El Casamiento en la muerte* "a rock turns and a painted battle is seen." For *El Bautismo del príncipe de Marruecos* "there is to be a cloth painted blue with some golden rays and no face, and with music is seen in another part Christ *de bulto*." In *El ultimo Godo* we read, "Spain enters and a curtain is opened, within which is seen a cloth with many little pictures of kings." On at least one occasion the whole façade was transformed into a show of colored lights with a character above, placed as in a throne-of-honor. In *La Imperial de Oton*, Lope writes: "They enter and with music is revealed the *lienço* [wall, façade, or cloth] of the *vestuario* with many lights in colored papers and Margarita on top." This must have looked much like the throne-of-honor arcade, already described, that was built in London in 1501 for Catherine of Aragon.[18]

Sometimes the whole background was turned piecemeal into one or more boats by the placing of sails and standards, masts, and prows in various parts of the façade. Rennert points out that boat scenes were often played offstage, but he finds several examples in Lope's plays of this partial visualization on the stage. In *El Arenal de Sevilla* "some prows of barques with green

---

[16] Cf. chap. ii, pp. 64, 79, 105; and chap. vii, pp. 199 f.

[17] *Ibid.*, p. 102.

[18] *Ibid.*, pp. 88 f.

branches are seen, and two or three Araez with oars." But poops and sails were even better than prows. In *El Bautismo del príncipe de Marruecos*, we read, "a poop of a barque with a sail is disclosed"; and in *El Amete de Toledo*, "in one part of the top of the stage is seen a Turkish galley with its sails and crescents and in the poop Moors and Amete and Angelina. . . . . Another curtain is drawn in the other part and a galley of San Juan is seen, full of standards with the white crosses." We have already described a similar show of realistic parts of a ship built into an architectural façade in a French *tableau vivant*, and the use of the stage and gallery of the English public theatres for ship scenes. [19]

The most elaborate directions Rennert has found call for the staging of a tableau of Judgment Day in Lope's *El Cardenal de Belén*. This follows the traditions of medieval art and must have produced an effect rather like the street-show in Lisbon in 1619. It reads: "Let an angel sound a trumpet and above let there be seen a half-arch in the midst of which is a Judge, a hell-mouth at one side with some souls and on the other St. Michael with a scales." Later we read: "Let Marino go out below beating and lashing the lion"; and, at the end of the scene: "Let everything close and the saint be going down." Apparently most of this tableau was on the balcony.

This half-arch is intriguing. Was it a movable arch set in place for this scene or a permanent structure over the center niche? Even if there was no permanent arch of the kind usually to be found in the façades of the street theatres, the Spanish authors on several occasions arranged such an arch at the center. We have already noticed the arch of greenery and flowers prepared for a Corpus Christi procession in *Arauco domado*. In Lope's *El Saber por no saber*, we read: "With the music two doors of a chapel open and an arch of silver with some lamps at the sides is seen."

Thus we see that Spanish playwrights, while they might, like the Meistersingers, use the curtains as a neutral background and, like the

English and Flemish, use the formal side doors, center niche, and gallery conventionally, very often used on the forestage or set into the façade the pictorial scenic devices of the religious plays and civic pageants. The back wall, even if it was completely covered with curtains (and we are not sure that it was completely covered), followed the same pattern of façade we find in all countries and produced another variation of the combination of formal elements with illusionistic details.

The other type of arcade façade—the architectural screen with columns, arches, and architrave—was developed in the schools and academies all over Europe. It served to unite the arcade handed down from the Greek theatre in medieval art with the new humanistic attempts to reconstruct the ancient theatre façade directly.

II. THE "TERENCE STAGES"

The humanistic movement from Rome and Ferrara to Basle, Munich, Strassburg, Paris, Louvain, and Oxford released a flood of school productions of classical plays and of new plays on classical models. A new type of stage, derived both from medieval art and from Vitruvian precept, was developed. From the simplest columns and curtains of a poor northern school to the magnificent Teatro Olimpico, built for a rich club of scholarly connoisseurs, the new stage satisfied both the conscious desire to reproduce the splendors of the ancient theatres and, at the same time, the space concepts and conventions implicit in a new age. Much as scholars and architects interested in the new learning might try to imitate the Roman theatre, they nevertheless used the forms and patterns of their own time. Hence we find that these "Terence stages" owed much to the traditions of art and pageantry in western Europe (which, of course, were adapted originally from the Hellenistic theatre) and resembled in many ways the kindred architectural stages of the Rederykers and the Elizabethans.

The basic form chosen for the new school and academy stages was the arcade screen. Its beginnings and its further development grew out of

[19] *Ibid.*, pp. 76, 99; and chap. iv, p. 144.

a

b

Fig. 48.—Two arcade façades. Illustrations for an edition of Terence (Lyons, 1493). Names above doorways. Glimpses of small inner stages. Center arranged as a pavilion.

a close interrelationship between theatre production and the graphic arts. From fifteenth-century painting the theatre director took over space concepts which called not only for a neutral forestage but also for the opening-up of areas behind the screen where small realistic interiors could be disclosed. The woodcuts in the early editions of Latin plays copied the screen, with its glimpses of interiors, and spread the knowledge of this type of stage all over Europe. When later variations were devised, they likewise were imitated by engravers and in turn became the models for directors to copy.

While some early productions of Latin plays, like those at Ferrara in 1485 and 1491, used castles and other medieval scenic forms, the revivals at Rome started the new arcade tradition. About 1485, under the leadership of Pomponius Laetus, a group of people interested in the classics undertook the production of several plays in what they supposed to be the ancient manner. Their authority was Vitruvius, recently rediscovered. In his pages they found mention of painted scenery with columns, pediments, and statues and a classification of the houses represented in the various kinds of plays. In the middle of his discussion of the theatre they found a description of the kinds of columns and architraves to be used on the stage. But there was no account of how the "houses" were to be organized. While later architects visualized these columns and architraves as part of the realistic houses of perspective street scenes, the early producers did not. They thought of the "houses" as the compartments in an arcade, and the columns and architraves as those they already knew in the arcades of the street theatres. They were perhaps led in this direction by some of the illustrations in the fifteenth-century manuscripts of Terence. In a number of the miniatures in the beautiful "Terence des ducs," now at the Arsenal Library in Paris, two houses are crowded together so that their fronts form one solid façade.[20] A similar arcade effect was

reached for a different reason in a late fifteenth-century French manuscript of Terence, now in the Royal Library in Copenhagen. Following the medieval theory that Terence was read by a poet and acted in pantomime by the performers, one scene shows a poet standing on a platform projecting into the audience.[21] Behind him on three rear stages framed by columns are three different groups of actors. The new students of the classics may have copied such illustrations; but, of course, the arcade was already a commonplace both in art and in the street theatres.

From the texts of the plays they could see that each of the principal characters should have a house. That meant that about five houses should be built together as on an open street. When the architect organized the columns, curtains, and architraves in the style of the new Renaissance architecture, he produced an arcade façade very similar to that of many street theatres. While attempting to re-create the Roman stage, he produced a special adaptation of the traditions of medieval painting.

The first illustrated edition to follow the new scenic convention was printed by Trechsel in Lyons in 1493, and it set the style for woodcut illustrations for the next half-century. This book —a complete edition of Terence—was produced by Godocus Badius, a Fleming who knew Flemish art and had studied in the school of Pomponius Laetus in Rome, where he had learned the new Italian ideals of Terence productions.[22] The woodcuts show a pleasing arcade with curtains, sometimes flat, sometimes shaped forward in the center like a medieval pavilion, and sometimes with open arches at the sides (Fig. 48).[23] A few curtains are pulled aside to show realistic interiors. Here, in full, is the new tradition—an arcade that can serve either as a unified place or as a multiple structure with several separate inner stages revealed by curtains.

[20] Especially those for *Eunuchus*, Act IV, scene 7. Martin, "Le 'Terence des ducs' et la mise en scène au moyen âge," *Bulletin de la Société de l'Histoire du Théâtre*, Vol. I, Pl. 10.

[21] Herrmann, *Forschungen zur deutschen Theatergeschichte*, pp. 277 ff.; Borcherdt, *op. cit.*, p. 72. The miniature is also reproduced in *Theatre Arts Prints*, Ser. IV, Pl. 6.

[22] Herrmann, *op. cit.*, pp. 300 ff.

[23] Other examples reproduced by Nicoll, *op. cit.*, pp. 83 f.

The Venice edition of Terence of 1511 copied the Lyons woodcuts in a flat, less splendid form, and this was followed by many later editions. In the Venice Plautus of 1518 the arcade is even more conventional. There are no curtains, but views of distant landscapes are placed behind the arches. At each side is a side house, bearing no

the back of the stage was a highly decorated arcade screen divided into five sections by columns with gilded bases and capitals, each section framing a doorway covered with curtains of gold cloth. Above was a frieze of beautiful paintings and a gilded cornice. At the two ends of the screen were two great towers with doors, one

FIG. 49.—Formal arcade back of more realistic side wings. Pambosco's *Il Pellegrino* (Venice, 1552)

relation to the back screen—a realistic stage wing with one side drawn in converging perspective lines. This combination of perspective wing and arcade was important, we shall find, for both the perspective setting and the proscenium.

The best description we have of the arcade in actual production tells us of a performance of the *Poenulus* in Rome in 1513 by followers of Laetus. The stage was almost a hundred feet wide, twenty-four feet deep, and about eight feet high—much larger than most groups could afford. At

marked "Via ad forum."[24] These towers, relics of the castle towers so frequent in medieval art, soon disappeared from the Terence tradition but were important in the development of the proscenium. The screen, with its upper story of paintings, shows a very close resemblance to the arcades built in street theatres throughout Europe.

Everywhere that humanistic education penetrated, the Latin plays were studied. Terence was the model for a good Latin style, and the growing

[24] Borcherdt, *op. cit.*, pp. 75 f.

ideal of courtly sophistication approved teaching the youth the worldly ways of the characters of Plautus and Terence so that he might be prepared for the actual world. H. W. Lawton counts 461 editions of Terence which appeared in western Europe between 1470 and 1600 and 59 other editions of one or two plays. He estimates that 50,000 copies appeared in France.[25] Performances in schools and academies were quite frequent. Northern producers followed the tradition of the woodcuts as best they could without such generous patrons as the Italians had. At Leipzig in 1530, Rektor Muschler copied the Lyons woodcuts for his school performances and established the tradition of the arcade for the local students. When Queen Elizabeth was in Cambridge in 1564, her surveyor erected a stage in King's College Chapel for a student presentation of Plautus' *Aulularia*.[26] The stage was built across the breadth of the building, so that the small chapels at the end might serve as separate houses. The traditional architectural screen of arches and curtains was still the type of background for academic productions in 1605 when Inigo Jones devised a scheme (following Vitruvius) of turning sections of it around for scene changes. The production was made in the hall of Christ's Church College, Oxford, for a visit of James I. Jones built

a false wall fair painted and adorned with stately pillars, which pillars would turn about, by reason whereof with the help of other painted cloths, their stage did vary three times in the acting of one tragedy. Behind the foresaid false wall there was reserved 5 or 6 paces of the upper end of the hall, which served them to good use for their houses and receipt of the actors, etc.[27]

III. THE JESUIT FAÇADE

The first complex arcade façade to be derived from the Terence tradition was developed in southern Germany by the Jesuits. In the schools and productions of the Jesuits the arcade was elaborated with curtained inner stages and with a balcony, and occasionally with a medieval device such as a mountain. Soon after the middle of

the sixteenth century the Jesuit colleges of southern Germany had established, in close relation to the Flemish productions, a complex type of setting which combined the formal arcade with several elements of illusion from the medieval stages.

Almost immediately after the order was founded to lead a militant Counter Reformation, the Jesuits had begun to make full use of the drama, not only to teach the students of their fast-growing academies and colleges, but to impress on the public the unfaltering power and glory of the Catholic church. Intent on combating the disruptive individualism of extreme humanism and Protestantism, they used drama, processions, and festivals in their effort to show the unity of all classes of mankind. Whereas in the Middle Ages the court chapels, the churches of the religious orders, and the public churches had often been separate from one another, the new churches, of which the spectacular Michael's Church in Munich was an example, were planned, like the processions and plays, to impress and unify all groups.

The Jesuit drama, while it took over elements from the Netherland moralities, from the popular religious plays of medieval tradition, and from the Italian Plautine school comedies, yet developed a distinct character and outlook of its own.[28] Less concerned with pure allegory than the humanistic moralities and disdaining the polemics of Protestant moralities, it nevertheless had a strong didactic purpose. A Jesuit play was like a dramatized sermon that stated its theme but dwelt mostly on historical examples. The Counter Reformation had turned against the individualism of the Renaissance and found itself united in spirit with the political ideals of the Baroque age —an age of absolute monarchy. No longer appeared the old theme of Everyman facing death alone; rather, the new themes showed the triumph of faithful hosts led to victory by a royal leader— Constantine the Great in triumph over the

---

[25] *Térence en France au XVIe siècle*, pp. 271, 281, and 566.

[26] Nichols, *The Progresses of Queen Elizabeth*, I, 166.

[27] Leland, *op. cit.*, I, Part II, 631.

[28] I base my discussion of the historical and artistic aspects of Jesuit drama on Müller's *Das Jesuitendrama* and of the production methods on Flemming's *Geschichte des Jesuitentheaters*.

heathen, Godfrey of Boulogne and his victory over Islam, Michael and the triumph of the church over all enemies, Tasso's vision of the liberation of Jerusalem.

The closest affiliation of Jesuit drama was with the Netherlands. Not only did many of the early leaders study with Netherland humanists, but the first plays were taken directly from Flanders. In 1548, Levin Brecht, a Franciscan friar in Louvain, wrote and produced the play *Euripus* on a theme related to *Homulus* and *Everyman*. It was printed the following year and found its way to the newly established Jesuit orders throughout the Empire. In four cities it was the first play they produced, inaugurating drama in the Cologne and Vienna orders in 1555 and at Munich and Prague in 1560. Soon new plays were written within the order, but the influence of Netherland humanists remained strong for decades.

From the Flemish allegories (and hence from the street-shows) come the pattern of a Prologue who taught Mankind a lesson by showing tableaux behind a curtain.[29] The Jesuit dramatists kept the little tableaux; but, instead of returning to the lecture of the Prologue, as the Flemish dramatists did, the Jesuits proceeded to add after each silent tableau a spoken play which dramatized the whole story that had been indicated in the tableau. The little pantomimed tableaux were used throughout the history of Jesuit drama, but, like many of the street-shows and of the dumb shows in England, they served principally to demonstrate the text the audience was to keep in mind while seeing the main play. Hence the emphasis was just the reverse of that of the *spelen van sinne*. In the Flemish *spelen* the illustration remained incidental to the sermon on the forestage; here it was the main play, the Prologue serving only to introduce the separate dumb shows and point out their significance to the main play, as the Chorus did in *Gorboduc*.

Because the historical play, the type most frequently given, required a number of inner stages, the Jesuit dramatists could not use directly the Flemish façade in the compact form it had de-

veloped by 1560. Instead, the more primitive arcade of three to five arches, long familiar in art, pageantry, and the Terence school productions, was adopted. To it were added some of the features of the medieval religious stages. The result was a group of inner stages, sometimes set with full properties and eventually with painted background. Flemming describes such an arrangement as a "cubic simultaneous stage."

In 1577, with the production of *Hester* in the market place of Munich, the cubic simultaneous stage first appeared in fully developed form and established a pattern that was dominant in Jesuit drama for a century and influential in such places as the Oberammergau stage up to the present time.

Flemming analyzes this production of *Hester* in some detail[30] and points out its resemblance to the Teatro Olimpico and to the Spanish and English theatres of the time, without suspecting a common heritage in art and pageant traditions. Only the resemblance to the Flemish can he explain as due to direct influence.

At the center of the arcade façade for *Hester* was a large compartment, in which, by the drawing of a curtain, could be revealed a throne for the coronation and for the assembly of God and the heavenly hosts, seats and table for a large banquet, or an altar for the marriage. The crowds for these scenes might fill the large forestage. In this center throne-pavilion flanked by arches, we recognize a much closer relation to the street theatres of the royal entries than to the Rederyker stages.

The arcade extended on both sides of the center pavilion to include at least three interior scenes behind other arches, and apparently a formal door. Several scenes take place at a door: one with a guard and one a scene of leave-taking. Never does anyone seem to go directly from the forestage into the center palace, but always by this formal door, which must, therefore, have been next to the palace compartment. Also at this door, not a separate mansion, was the seat of

---

[29] Flemming, *op. cit.*, pp. 190 f.; cf. also chap. iii above.

[30] *Op. cit.*, pp. 20 ff. and 278 ff., with diagrams in Introd., pp. xv and xvi.

FIG. 50.—The Teatro Olimpico of Vicenza. Back wall and side walls drawn in one elevation; compare the ground plan added below. Drawing found among the drawings made by Palladio himself. Possibly brought to England by Inigo Jones. In the Burlington Collection at the Royal Institute of British Architects, London.

rose to affluence and fame.[39] For its tragedies performed from time to time in various buildings, Andrea Palladio, the famous architect, a charter member of the Academy, built temporary settings. For a while the academicians occupied the palace of the arch-dean, Porto, where Serlio is said to have erected a wooden theatre, but soon they undertook the building of a splendid theatre just for their scholarly performances of ancient plays. Palladio made the plans, and in March, 1580, the building was begun. The architect died the following August, however, leaving his son Scillo Palladio to finish the building in 1584. The perspectives were built by Vincenzo Scamozzi.

At carnival time, March 23, 1585, the new theatre was opened with a magnificent performance of *Oedipus the King*. Present were not only the nobility from Venice but the Empress Maria of Austria and the ambassador of France. We have an ecstatic letter written by one of the spectators, Filippo Pigafetta, to his lord, who could not be present. He wrote:

Palladio wanting to leave behind him a work of art of perfect workmanship, persuaded these academicians of Vicenza, called "Olimpici," who having, because of the noble institution of their academy, recited and produced many times Eclogues, Pastorals, Comedies, and Tragedies, and other such pleasures, in order to rejoice and please the public, to construct a theatre according to the ancient use of the Greeks and Romans.[40]

On the opening night, the audience arrived to find the whole stage hidden behind one large curtain. At one-thirty in the morning, after the guests had spent hours in sociability and in feasting on wine and fruit and on the splendor of one another's dress and the sight of the ladies getting themselves settled in the orchestra, the play began.

The hour of lowering the curtain having arrived, first there was a very sweet odor of perfumes, to give to understand, that in the city of Thebes, which was represented, odors were dispersed, according to ancient history, to soften the disdain of the gods. Then the trumpets and drums were

played, and small fireworks were set off, as well as four pieces of size. Then, in a twinkle of the eye, the taut curtain fell before the stage. Here it would be very difficult to express in words, or even to imagine, the great joy and the immeasurable pleasure which came upon the spectators at the sight. After that beginning, from the interior perspectives came a harmonized music of diverse instruments and voices, telling that in the city hymns were sung and praises rendered, and odors were going up in smoke to obtain from the gods health and alleviation of hunger, and of a long pestilence which oppressed the city.

After describing the splendid architectural façade, Pigafetta proceeded to the perspective inner scenes.

The perspective within is equally admirable, and very well understood and seen by five principal parts, or rather entrances, which present seven streets of the city of Thebes, represented with a show of lovely houses, and palaces and temples, and altars in the antique style, of most fine architecture, and of solid wood so that they may last always. The expense for this came to 1500 ducats.

The use of illusionistic settings on inner stages behind the façade was in no wise due to the Romans. Indeed, Vitruvius said the perspective settings should all tend to the same vanishing-point. Nor was it a new invention of the architect. Already suggested in the illustrations of Barbaro's edition of Vitruvius in 1567, it but carried a little further the tendency developed in the Terence school tradition of placing separate scenes behind the arched openings. It followed a pattern we have noted frequently in painting of opening up the arches of a medieval arcade screen to show small illusionistic scenes. In Italian art those extension scenes are usually exteriors. The edition of Plautus published at Venice in 1518 has exterior landscapes.[41] It is noteworthy that the Teatro Olimpico has only exterior scenes behind the façade. On the other hand, the Jesuit theatres, which were first developed in Germany about the same time as the Teatro Olimpico and which resemble it in many ways, have principally interiors behind the façade.

Yet the façade of the Teatro Olimpico did unite all the little inner scenes into one place. They were all part of one city, and the façade then

---

[39] Hammitzsch, *Der moderne Theaterbau*, pp. 15 f.

[40] A letter once in the Ambrosiana, published in *Raccolta milanese*, a volume of miscellanies, in 1756–57, and republished in a pamphlet *Due lettere . . . .* (copy in Yale-Rockefeller Theatre Collection).

[41] Cf. the scene reproduced without proper identification in Freedley and Reeves, *A History of the Theatre*, Fig. 44, after p. 64.

became itself a symbol of that city. The medieval convention of multiple settings, which persisted in the Terence stages, in the Jesuit stages, and at times on the Spanish stage, was here replaced by a Renaissance convention of unity. While all those others used separate curtains for the separate inner stages, here the whole setting was

to the front of the stage. Yet, for this aristocratic academy, elements of the court stage—the perspective settings—were borrowed and placed behind the formal openings in the façade. They were so cleverly arranged, however, that every seat in the house afforded a vista down one of the long streets in perspective—a most successful de-

Fig. 51.—Arcade screen as a backing for a throne, Louvain, 1594. Street theatre for a play of the "Judgment of Solomon," given at the conclusion of the religious procession.

hidden behind one large curtain and was all disclosed at one time.

It is probably significant that this theatre of a club of equals follows, both in its auditorium and in its stage, a different tradition from that of the court. Here the auditorium is not dominated by the royal box; instead, all seats are of about equal importance. Hence the architect could not build a unified perspective setting but followed the form of the arcade screen—its main axis parallel

vice to make each of the spectators feel as important as a prince. In the court theatres only the royal box had a correct view of the perspective.

The courtly academicians and their more courtly guests felt that they had been transported back to the ancient world—that they had only added modern splendor to an ancient form. The modern historian has taken too literally their own estimate of what they were doing. He has considered the Teatro Olimpico as merely a direct imitation, a reproduction of the ancient Roman façade. We now see that the architects for the Olimpici really created in the patterns of their own day as surely as if they had set out to produce the most up-to-date theatre. The Teatro Olimpico might have been exactly the same if neither Vitruvius nor the ancient theatre had ever been rediscovered. The formal façade, with its beautiful columns and architraves, its statues, its narrative friezes on an upper story, its plaque above the center door for the title of the academy and Palladio's name, its side wings, its three archways—all these were but more splendid examples of what was already familiar to public and architects in paintings, in tapestries, in arcades built as street theatres, and in earlier productions of classic comedies in the schools. The concept of space, the concept of unity, the intermixing of formal and illusionistic features—all were characteristic of the new age, not of the ancient theatre. Follow as they might the writings of Vitruvius and the remains of Roman antiquity, Palladio and Scamozzi thought and created after the patterns of their time.

The Teatro Olimpico was the crowning glory of the tradition of the arcade screen. After it there was nothing left to accomplish. The Jesuit colleges built several splendid permanent façades for plays in the eighteenth century, but they introduced no new elements. The principal importance of the arcade screen in later times was as a formal frame for the perspective setting; and that story must be left for a later chapter, for it is the story of the shaping of the perspective setting. All the arcade screens, as we shall see, were related to that proscenium frame. Absurd as Sheldon Cheney's theory of the origin of the proscenium is in detail, his perception that the frame for the inner stage on the Teatro Olimpico was related to the proscenium arch was correct. There was being worked out in many places in Europe this same combination of formal symbol and illusionistic picture.

But for all their use of illusionistic detail, the curtain façades and arcade façades belong with the other façade theatres. They gained their unity by compacting a number of separate elements into one conventionalized symbol rather than by organizing them into the illusion of reality. Now that we have examined them in detail, we can ask what light they throw on the other façade theatres. What can we learn from them about the basic problems of using an architectural structure as a symbol of reality, so that we may understand the Elizabethan stage more fully? We are ready for a comparison and summary of all the theatres of architectural symbolism.

V. THE PRINCIPLE OF ARCHITECTURAL SYMBOLISM

In contrast to the processional forms of the Middle Ages, the façade theatres did achieve unity: for the portable "properties" or the disparate mansions they substituted one compact structure; in both design and the convention of time and place, the many emblems became one. While movable units might be brought onto the forestage on the principle of the processional and separate elements might be disclosed behind curtains on the principle of the multiple stage, yet the background façade dominated the stage and gave it its characteristic form and convention.

This unity was achieved in exactly the opposite way from the unity of the Italian perspective setting. In Italy the unity was reached by keeping the separate mansions separate, emphasizing the realism of each, and organizing them into one illusionistic picture of a street. In the façade theatres the separate emblems were subordinated, abstracted, superimposed on each other, or so blended that they did not conflict but became part of one architectural whole. Inevitably the neutral elements—curtains, archways, columns, architraves, canopies, and balconies—occupied a large part of what the audience saw and gave a unity of design to the stage. Yet the structures were far from purely negative—they resembled the conventionalized throne-canopies, castles, triumphal arches, and arcades in the street theatres, in the sculptured tombs and altars, and in the backgrounds in painting, and they kept the festival atmosphere and the decorations of a street-show.

They differed from one another in the way that the different emblematic devices were subordinated to the one architectural symbol. At one extreme was the arcade, which preserved the multiple convention of presenting many separate places at one time—on the separate inner stages or in panels set into the façade. That multiple principle was sometimes used in England, but for the most part the opposite tendency was followed there—the tendency to superimpose a number of symbols on one another so that they not only coincided in space but also overlapped in time. Thus the Elizabethan façade was one emblem—superimposing castle, throne, pavilion, tomb, altar, and triumphal arch—rather than a number of emblems held separate but united in a long arcade. Yet, in spite of these differences, our comparison of the formal stages of the Renaissance—the Rederyker, Elizabethan, academic, Meistersinger, and Spanish stages—reveals such a remarkable similarity in all that we are tempted to explain each one in terms of the others. Such a comparison certainly convinces us that no one of them was an isolated local invention. All stemmed from a common background—the traditions of the visual arts as adapted by the designers of the *tableaux vivants*.

The closest kinship was between the Rederyker stage and its Elizabethan cousin of a generation later. Both used a formal architectural façade which could symbolize a castle, a throne-of-honor before which subsidiary figures were grouped, or a town, country, or house from which characters walked. Or occasionally the different parts of the façade could represent at one time several places, by the convention of simultaneous setting used in medieval art and religious drama. Onto the forestage in both England and Flanders could be brought, procession-wise, such elaborate structures as arbors and thrones, or simply the tables, chairs, and beds of interior scenes. Or arranged tableaux could be revealed by drawing a curtain. G. F. Reynolds has suggested that in England sometimes the curtained space was a

temporary structure. We know that in the Low Countries some temporary structures were brought on for curtained scenes, to supplement by a more realistic device the formal curtained openings in the façade. Likewise in the use of a presenter to introduce the tableaux, both English and Flemish dramatists followed common traditions of pageantry.

The Spanish public stage, like the Elizabethan and Flemish, preserved from the medieval stage the processional convention that trees, altars, walls, arbors, thrones, and other such separate properties might be brought onto the open playing area. But, more significantly, the back wall of the Spanish stage, behind the curtains, presented the same pattern of center *nicho*, or inner stage, and upper gallery that we have found in theatre façades throughout Europe.

The Spanish producers, following a convention frequent in the street tableaux, would insert into the different parts of that back wall such illusionistic devices as gates and doors, shop fronts, chapel fronts, tents, clouds, and rocks. We are sure that in England shop fronts, gates, and a grated window could be shown as part of the background. We wonder if still other effects may have been fastened into the façade. In the staging of sea scenes, Spanish dramatists carried the combination of illusionistic details in the formal façade even further by using prows, masts, sails, and poops set into the doorways and galleries. There was no thought of complete illusion, but a few illusionistic details could heighten the effect of a symbolic show. The Elizabethans used very realistic language and business in their sea scenes. While very little is to be found in the records, they may also have added many realistic visual details to the façade.

The Spanish, apparently, more frequently made an independent use of the separate parts of the stage, but it is clear now that on many occasions the Elizabethans also preserved the multiple principle of the Middle Ages.

That multiple principle was even more important in the academy stages and the Jesuit theatres, yet here, too, there was not only the

whereby unity could be gained and the medieval mansions still be kept separate.

The principle by which that unity was achieved set off the Italian perspective scene very definitely from both the flat arcade screen of the academic and the Jesuit stages and the compact façades of the Flemish and Elizabethan. Italian designers, following fifteenth-century Italian painters, chose to organize the picture by means of the third of the painters' principles: the side accent. They made use of the rather realistic side houses, traditional in painting, to inclose the central playing area from the outside.

This use of side accents which inclosed the scene also distinguished the perspective setting from the medieval, for it reversed the relationship between the characters and the setting. In both medieval art and the medieval theatre, as we have noticed, the scenic device served as a nucleus around which the characters or actors could be organized. In the perspective scene the character or actor was put in the center, and the scenic elements were organized into a complex background which seemed to inclose that center. While the scenic nucleus left the space around it indefinite, unbounded, and elastic, the inclosing principle limited the space and defined it with mathematical exactness.

The perspective setting differed from both the medieval religious theatres and the façade theatres by making a new compromise between time and space. The medieval drama moved easily in time and could progress from one scenic nucleus to another as an artist does in drawing a frieze; hence the different nuclei could not be organized in space. The façade theatres, as we have seen, made a considerable concession to time. But the perspective setting achieved its organization in space by attempting—for the first time in history—to rule out time. Only between the acts and scenes was time permitted to pass freely. Hence our modern theatre, ever since the Renaissance, has had the concept that each picture must be complete in space, as it would be seen at one time. We may change the picture many times (in the movies countless times); but, except for a few experiments, we have kept this Renaissance concept that each stage picture—both actors and setting—must be a complete spatial unit, a complete illusionistic image of reality. In spite of the apron stage that persisted into the nineteenth century, we have had the concept that the actor is supposed to be immersed and inclosed in the space of the setting. While the symbolic façades of Flanders and Elizabethan England served only to set off the actor and make him more distinct, the perspective setting taught us to merge actor completely into picture.

CHAPTER VI

THE ITALIAN PERSPECTIVE SCENE

I. PICTORIAL ILLUSION

WHILE the conventional façades were all derived from the showpieces, either of sculptured marble or of the painted wood and cloth of the street-shows, the theatres of pictorial illusion stemmed directly from the new developments in Italian painting of the fifteenth century. In the perspective scene the designer for the first time in Europe undertook to present on the stage a complete illusionistic picture of an actual place. With a combination of houses built in three dimensions and a back shutter painted with more distant details, he reproduced the kind of perspective street scene his predecessors in the fifteenth century had already worked out in painting.

The ideals of those painters determined the type of structure that the architect developed and the type of stage that was to dominate the theatre for more than three hundred years. If the illusionistic pictorial theatre had been devised at any other period, it might have been very different. As it was, it began at the moment when Italian painting was dominated by the desire to present architectural structures and street scenes in very clear relief. The Florentine school had worked out the principles of linear perspective, and painters of the latter part of the fifteenth century gave us the clearest lines and the most sharply drawn effects of three dimensions that we have ever had.[1] They had not yet dissolved that Florentine architecture into the aerial perspective, the soft atmosphere, of Baroque painting. What a different theatre we should have had if there had been no illusionistic theatre until the time of El Greco or Rembrandt!

[1] Cf. chap. i, pp. 49–51.

As it was, the theatre designer took over from the painter a clear-cut architectural structure: a flat painted cloth or shutter at the back and two rows of houses inclosing the playing space from the sides. Although later generations reduced those wings to flat painted forms, the stage kept the structural form of wings and backdrop until the arrival of the spotlights and sculptural forms of the last half-century.

II. THE BEGINNINGS OF PERSPECTIVE SCENERY

Since the perspective street scene of rows of houses going into a deep center had already been developed in fifteenth-century painting, it is surprising that apparently no perspective scenery was built until the first decade of the sixteenth century. Although the new settings were designed and built by men well trained in art and architecture—Bramante, Peruzzi, Giulio Romano, Raphael, Genga, Serlio, Bastiano da San Gallo—who clearly tried to reproduce the effects of painting in three dimensions, there were several decades of experiment before the full perspective scene was achieved. Throughout the century the theatre lagged years behind the newer tendencies in painting.

The painter-architect was confronted with a number of problems when he undertook to build a picture into a stage setting. He wanted to do more than hang up a flat cloth like that of the mountebanks. His chief interest in painting had been in giving the effect of solid, three-dimensional architecture. He knew the castles, pavilions, altars, and arches of the outdoor religious plays and civic pageants, but they were not realistic enough. In his revivals of Plautus and Terence he found that the palace halls and courtyards where he had to work allowed room for only a rather shallow stage. Yet the perspective picture he wanted to build was one of considerable depth. He must compromise between flat forms and solid: he must use both architecture and painting. At the back of his shallow stage he placed a painted cloth, either hung or fastened on a frame or shutter, and thereby set a pattern of painted backdrop or shutter parallel to the stage front that has lasted as long as perspective scenery itself. Between the back shutter and the front he developed his three-dimensional side houses, which came to be called "wings." Earlier architects, as we have seen, had already used for the revivals of Terence a combination of realistic side houses in front of a formal arcade screen. But a real stage picture could not be achieved until the architect substituted for the back screen a back cloth which, painted in perspective, carried on into greater depth the perspective lines of the side houses.[2]

Just when that substitution was made we do not know. At the end of the fifteenth century Bramante and, later, Peruzzi were painting in church niches and on palace walls just such effects of depth. Perhaps for the production of the *Menaechmi* at Rome in 1486 the "painted scenes . . . . the first in our time," which have intrigued all of us, were perspective paintings substituted for the back screen.[3] Perhaps in 1501

when Mantegna was filling the arches around a hall with painted perspective scenes, he also used as a background for the play a painted scene that was partly built out in three dimensions. At any rate, we know that in 1508, for the performance of Ariosto's *Cassaria* at Ferrara, the union of built houses and a painted background was made, and the illusion was created of a large part of a town. An eyewitness described it thus:

> But what has been best in all those festivities and representations has been the scenery in which they have been played, which Master Peregrino, the Duke's painter [Pellegrino da San Daniele] has made. It has been a view in perspective of a town with houses, churches, belfries, and gardens, such that one could never tire of looking at it, because of the different things that are there, all most cleverly designed and executed. I suppose that this will not be destroyed, but that they will preserve it to use on other occasions.[4]

We do not know how much of that scene was built in three dimensions, but Castiglione, describing *La Calandria* in 1513, likewise given before the Duke of Urbino at Ferrara, insisted on the amount of three-dimensional detail. He wrote: "The scene was laid in a very fine city, with streets, palaces, churches, and towers, all in relief, and looking as if they were real, the effect being completed by admirable paintings in scientific perspective."[5] A splendid production was given Ariosto's *Suppositi* at the Vatican in 1519. Raphael designed both the setting, which showed the city of Ferrara in true perspective, and the front curtain, which covered the entire scene.[6]

Vasari gives credit for the development of perspective scenery to Baldassare Peruzzi and has many glowing accounts of the wonderful stage effects that he and many other artists achieved in the first half of the sixteenth century. Vasari's enthusiasm attests the tremendous excitement which artist and layman alike felt over this new court toy—perspective scenery—and the new effects of illusion. His account also attests the close relationship between stage architecture and painting.

---

[2] The back cloth in the early permanent settings could be hung up by cords or fastened to a beam. But when it was designed to be changed, it had to be fastened to one or more frames. Often two frames were placed in a groove to separate in the middle of the scene and be drawn into (i.e., behind) the wings. These frames were the "shutters." The back cloth was mounted on "shutters" until architects in the eighteenth and nineteenth centuries built the stage house high enough to let one down from above. Then it was known as a "backdrop," the term which has come down to our day. From the point of view of the designer, there is no difference between back cloth, back shutter, and backdrop. Only in the later Baroque period did some designers vary the pattern by using a back cloth that was not parallel to the front. A number of the Bibiena designs called for a cloth set at an angle. Obviously, such oblique back cloths could not be mounted on shutters. In Italian, the term *prospettiva* did not change when the method of mounting changed.

[3] These early accounts are quoted and discussed by Campbell, *Scenes and Machines on the English Stage*, pp. 12 ff.

[4] *Ibid.*, p. 49.   [5] *Ibid.*, p. 50.

[6] Borcherdt, *Das europäische Theater*, p. 98; Flechsig, *Die Dekoration der modernen Bühne in Italien*, p. 65.

The type of setting built by these first generations of stage architects is rightly called "stage architecture," for they built out in three dimensions every detail they could. With carved wood, plaster, and painted cloth they erected stage houses that were not to be easily changed. Some of the scenes were used for many years, and those in the Teatro Olimpico are still standing today. The achievement of these early architects is summed up in the writings and engravings of Sebastiano Serlio,[7] a pupil and close friend of Peruzzi. In 1545 Serlio brought out, as part of his whole work on architecture, a book on perspective containing the first scene designs (Figs. 52, 53) and the first account of the perspective stage to be published. Serlio's setting, like most of the others of his time, was a three-dimensional solid structure built on a shallow, sloping rear stage behind the main acting area. Later generations, as we shall see, became absorbed in methods of changing the setting quickly and of drawing and painting details rather than building them out. In the Baroque period, scene painting dominated the stage; but the early Renaissance setting was true architecture.

III. PRINCIPLES OF THE PERSPECTIVE SETTING

While the northern façades were developed by practical workmen who made use of the conventional forms of the time without stopping to speculate why or how, the Italian perspective setting was based on scientific principles which had to be carefully worked out and carefully learned. As the stage settings were the business of the court architect, nearly every book on architecture for more than a century after Serlio contained a section on stage architecture. Several mathematicians wrote at length on the special problems of perspective in three dimensions.

The following three principles, all closely related to the social, philosophical, mathematical, and artistic concepts of the Renaissance, furnished the basis for the perspective setting.

1. An exact relation, unknown before, was established between audience, actor, and setting when the eyepoint from which the stage picture was viewed was fixed at one definite point (the duke's box). The vanishing-point for all lines of depth was fixed opposite that eyepoint, at the center of the picture.

2. All the space of the stage picture was unified by the concept of one picture plane and one frame. Yet there were many difficulties to be overcome before all the space of the stage was pushed back of that plane and a single proscenium established.

3. The concept that space was measured by a succession of planes all parallel to the picture plane was realized on the stage, as in painting, by the duplication of similar or identical forms, one visible behind the other. When this principle of duplication was applied to the picture plane of the whole stage, it produced a series of stages, one behind the other. Not only was there an inner stage behind the main stage, but there was a forestage in front of the main stage, a complex proscenium arch of several planes, and even on a few occasions a second inner stage behind the first. Sometimes there was a tendency to put a formal frame, a proscenium arch or arcade screen, at each successive plane. When this principle of duplication was applied to the side houses and heavens, it gave us the rows of wings and borders so characteristic of the perspective setting for more than three hundred years.

1. EYEPOINT AND VANISHING-POINT

For a painter it was a fairly simple thing to establish a fixed eyepoint. He was encouraged by the new mathematical concepts of space in the fifteenth century to represent exact measurable depth in geometrical relation to one chosen point, just as in analytical geometry we consider all space in the universe as abstract and measurable from any point by a definite system of coordinates. As soon as a painter was interested in

---

[7] I have collaborated on translations of the stage theories of Serlio, Sabbatini, and Furttenbach for the Yale Theatre Collection. The other accounts between 1568 and 1649, by Barbaro, Vignola, Sirigatti, Ubaldus, Aguilonius, Accolti, Dubreuil, and Chiaramonti, I have translated in the Appendix to my dissertation, "Perspective in the Renaissance Theatre" (1937). Typewritten copies are in the Yale University Library.

developing a single picture as a complete narrative unit rather than as part of a sequence, he could forget the time art and shifting viewpoint of the frieze and develop his space around one eyepoint.[8]

For the stage architect the single fixed eyepoint was not so simple. Only when a new aristocratic society brought in a courtly audience in which only a few people counted was perspective possible. The Renaissance architect had to reverse completely the older relationship of scenery to audience. In early medieval drama the scenic element was merely a nucleus. The actors, in a small arc, were placed around this center. The large democratic audience formed a circle outside—a circle that almost surrounded both scenery and actors. When there was more than one unit, the audience moved along to surround the next nucleus, just as the public might view the frieze in art. The form was a time art, the audience democratic.

The space art of perspective, which depended on a single fixed eyepoint, was possible only when duke and cardinal in the Renaissance were rich enough and important enough to create an aristocratic theatre just to please themselves. For the first time, the architect could build a scene for a small ducal party and forget completely such other people as were permitted to look on at the princely entertainment. In the medieval theatre there were many viewpoints on the arc of a circle, with each scenic element as a center. The rich Italian princes, at the beginning of an age of absolutism, made themselves the center of the circle: the scenic elements were on the arc of the circumference. Scenery was no longer a nucleus but began to inclose the actor, as it has continued to do to the present day.

The dependence of the fixed eyepoint on a court society is demonstrated further in the Renaissance academies we have already considered.[9] Organized on a basis of equality of members, they used mostly the formal arcade screen, which looked equally well to all. On the other hand, the Renaissance auditorium, modeled

by scholarly architects on the democratic Roman *cavea* and kept in that form in the academic Teatro Olimpico, was soon dominated in the princely courts by the royal box and later by the tiers of galleries which kept the strata of society separate—in some theatres even to the present day.

Some theorists first located a convenient place for the duke's box before the center of the stage and then marked out the scenery to suit. Sabbatini in 1638 gave a method for determining the exact distance the box should be from the stage. He would sight along a square and move backward and forward until the lines from the edge of the stage formed a right angle.[10]

The vanishing-point, of course, had to be opposite the fixed eyepoint; there and only there would the whole perspective look well. Both points were above the level of the hall. The duke's box was raised, and designers for the theatre followed Renaissance painters in locating the vanishing-point just a little below the center of the picture. In the stage picture this would be a point below the center of the back shutter but above the sloping floor of the stage. As the front of the stage platform was usually a little more than five feet (or the height of a person) above the floor, that meant that the vanishing-point must have been more than ten feet above.

In order to make all constructed planes in depth actually tend toward that vanishing-point, the four sides of the picture were built to slope in toward the center. The floor sloped upward until it met the back shutter (hence the terms "upstage" and "downstage"); the heavens sloped down; and the two rows of houses were balanced more or less symmetrically on floor lines that converged toward the central vanishing-point.

In order that the scene might appear much deeper than the stage, the actual vanishing-point was placed some distance behind the shutter. In the Baroque period the stage was made much deeper and the slope much more gradual, which pushed the actual vanishing-point very far back. Fernando Bibiena in 1711 recommended

[8] Cf. above, chap. i, pp. 45–49.   [9] Cf. above, chap. v.   [10] *Pratica di fabricar scene e machine ne' teatri*, Part I, chap. viii.

that it be placed 67½ *braccia* (about 100 feet) behind the back shutter.[11]

Some general perspective theorists were interested in the question of other locations of the vanishing-point. Aguilonius has a discussion of the *optica*, the way by which we look in a direct line; the *anoptica*, by which the vanishing-point is set high and we look upward as to mountains; and the *catoptica*, by which we look down toward a low vanishing-point, as into a valley.[12] Painters sometimes used a vanishing-point that was high, or at the side, or even outside the picture. The extant scene designs, however, would indicate that, until the end of the seventeenth century, stage architects regularly kept the vanishing-point at the center. The most interesting Renaissance variation was the preservation of the multiple extension scenes, which were sometimes painted on the back shutter and sometimes built out on little inner stages. As we shall see in chapter vii, they might preserve the tradition of a multiple vanishing-point, so frequent in medieval painting.

2. THE PICTURE PLANE

The second important principle of the perspective scene was that all space should be considered as back of one picture plane and that that plane should be defined by a proscenium frame. Painters achieved this concept by the middle of the fifteenth century. But the three-dimensional problem was so complex that not until the middle of the seventeenth century did stage architects succeed in making the proscenium really dominate all the space. As a result of experiments in the sixteenth century, three different kinds of prosceniums were evolved, and three different planes were established, one behind the other, at which a proscenium could be used—forestage, main stage, and inner stage. But that is such a complicated story that we must devote to it a whole separate chapter.

3. THE DUPLICATION OF SIMILAR FORMS

The third principle upon which the perspective scene was based was the mathematical concept of measuring space in successive planes of depth. We have already noticed how that concept, reached by mathematicians and writers on art, was related to the methods of attaining depth used by the early Renaissance painters. By the fourteenth century, painters had learned that they could get a great effect of depth by placing one, two, or many successively smaller arches within an arch at the back of the scene. I have discussed the tendency to treat not only single back arches but whole arcade screens by the same process of duplication.[13] For the structure of perspective settings this principle of duplication was even more important—it gave a definite pattern to floor and heavens; and it was the basis for the wing, the most characteristic feature of the perspective theatre, the one which distinguished it from all previous theatre forms and from the later box sets and plastic stages.

The sloping floor of the stage had to be built solid and unbroken; for, in spite of the steep grades, actors were expected to use at least the first street entrances (the first "streets"), and in some places the entire depth of the setting, in disregard of the discrepancy between full-sized actors and small diminished houses. Yet the stage depth was carefully indicated on the floor, where some elaborate pattern of tiles was painted, with prominent lines which were parallel to the front of the stage but which got closer to each other by exact degrees, according to the law of perspective diminution, as they carried the eye to the back of the stage.

While the heavens could not be painted with any such straight lines, it was actually constructed in a series of overlapping sections, each one lower than the one in front, and the last resting on the back shutter. Besides allowing the separate lighting of each section, this division permitted cloud machines and heavenly messengers to descend between the sections—an illusionistic substitute for the conventional heaven-

---

[11] *L'Architettura civile*, p. 129.   [12] *Opticarum*, pp. 682 f.

[13] Cf. chaps. i and vii. Professor Brieger in his lecture "The Baroque Equation: Illusion and Reality," at the Metropolitan Museum of Art on January 27, 1943, pointed out how double theatres and a succession of courtyards became an absorbing interest with Bernini and other Baroque architects.

pavilion at the top of the façades in northern theatres.

When the principle of duplication was applied to the side house by painters in the middle of the fifteenth century, it produced the two rows of houses down a long street, vanishing toward the center of the picture, which was to be the most typical kind of perspective scene throughout the four centuries of its existence. To actually build out those rows of houses on the stage, the architects devised three different types of wing—the angle (sometimes called "Serlian") wing, the *periaktoi*, and the flat wing. Each brought its own special problems in perspective.

The earliest type was the angle wing, built of two frames—a front and a perspective face. There are two ancestors of this type, one in the theatre and one in painting. The end houses of a medieval platform stage (when there was an inclosing screen) needed only two sides, one toward the audience and one toward the center of the stage. Hell in the Valenciennes miniature is a two-story building with a front and a side face. The end houses of the Terence scenes mentioned above[14] were apparently of the same type; but, although the structure of two frames had already been used on the medieval stage, the shape and arrangement of the Renaissance wing owed much more to the side house of painting. As I pointed out in chapter i, the side house in late medieval and early Renaissance painting was usually composed of two sides—a front parallel to the picture plane and a side with vanishing lines, set at an obtuse angle to the front face. It was frequently a two-story house with a vestige of the open-baldacchino form in a large arched opening on either face in the lower story. In a number of pictures that arch was multiplied, especially on the perspective face, so that, instead of a single arch, a row of arches was seen going into the picture space. Such an open loggia was more realistic than a lower story opened by one large arch, because it resembled a portico or a row of columns very close to the building—architectural features frequently built in Italy at the time.

[14] Chap. v, p. 162.

The Tragic Scene, especially, was ornamented with stately loggias of Renaissance columns. Barbaro listed "the high palaces and beautiful loggias" appropriate to such a scene.[15] Serlio put into his Tragic Scene handsome rows of classic columns leading the eye into the depth (Fig. 52). We can see at stage left two such rows of columns and arches on the perspective faces of the houses, while there is only a single arch in the house on stage right. In his Comic Scene he also used a loggia (Fig. 53), but with Gothic arches, which he spoke of as "an open portico with arches in the style of our times leading to another house."

The long house, receding toward the vanishing-point with many arches and columns, appears in a number of stage designs of the early sixteenth century. The more characteristic form of the later sixteenth century, however, took, not the column and arch of the house as the unit to be multiplied, but the whole house. The result was a long row of small houses on each side of the stage, each house set behind the one before and separated from it by an entrance space called a "street." The two rows of houses or wings exactly balanced each other, for the smaller houses were made more nearly identical than the highly individualized houses of the time of Serlio.

The later writers on perspective theory—Ubaldus, Chiaramonti, and Furttenbach[16]—called for very regular settings with all the perspective faces on each side of the stage on a single floor line in symmetrical rows, and each house balanced by a house at the same depth in the other row. Furttenbach and Dubreuil tell us —what a number of designs indicate—that often trees and parts of landscapes were painted on the same balanced geometric wings which were used for architectural scenes.[17] This exact balance and exact spacing according to diminishing proportion dominated the scene until the time of the Bibienas at the end of the seventeenth

[15] *La Pratica della perspettiva*, p. 130.

[16] Ubaldus, *Perspectivae libri sex*, pp. 296 ff.; Chiaramonti, *Delle scene e teatri*, pp. 71 f.; Furttenbach, *Mannhaffter Kunstspiegel*, p. 120.

[17] Furttenbach, *op. cit.*; Dubreuil, *La Perspective pratique*, Vol. III, Treatise IV, Pratiques xi and xii.

century; and even after that it remained an important principle.

The angle wing, built out in depth with cornices, door thicknesses, panels, and columns, **approached** actuality in its three-dimensional

in spectacle was so great that some architects began to plan a number of scene changes, for which lighter forms were necessary. They tried using a light angle wing of two flat frames, the detail painted on rather than built out in three

FIG. 52.—Serlio's Tragic Scene. 1545

detail; but it was practically impossible to change such a wing during a performance. Architects of the first half of the sixteenth century usually built one setting for the main play, then provided the effects for the musical *intermedii* by bringing on a procession of chariots and movable pageant wagons and portable properties. But the interest

dimensions. Sabbatini gives several methods—all rather complicated—for changing a setting composed of light angle wings. But architects soon began to experiment with other forms which would permit easier, more rapid changes during the play.

The first movable form developed was a three-sided wing built to revolve on a pivot—the ancient *periaktoi*, which had the recommendation of Vitruvius. How early this type was used we do not know. In the street theatres in France a turning, three-dimensional scenic structure had been

stage, and again in *La Pratica della perspettiva* in 1568 he spoke of the ancient custom.[18] The account of perspective in Vignola's *Le due regole della prospettiva pratica* of 1583, first recommended them for the modern theatre and described their

FIG. 53.—Serlio's Comic Scene. 1545

used since the late fifteenth century, if not earlier, to produce a sudden or magic transformation or disclosure. Whether Renaissance architects were conscious of the resemblance between such miniature revolving stages and the neo-Vitruvian painted prism, we do not know. Barbaro in the ground plans of his edition of Vitruvius in 1567, placed *periaktoi* at the side entrances of the classic

use in Florence in 1569. Vignola planned one large triangular *periaktoi* for his back shutter and a smaller one for each side house. Only one face of each would be seen by the audience at a time; and, when each was turned to the next side, a complete change of scene was secured. According to this account, the *periaktoi* might be made of two,

18 P. 130.

three, four, five, or six sides, depending on the number of scenes to be shown.[19] This form, especially the one large prism at the back of the scene, resembles the turning device of the *tableaux vivants.*[20]

But, in order to reproduce by means of *periaktoi* the same effect as the angle wings, it was necessary to show two faces at a time, not just one. Furttenbach describes how this was accomplished by using two narrow, wedge-shaped *periaktoi* for each wing. The two were set to touch each other at the corner of the wing. On one prism was painted a front face, and on the upstage one, a perspective face.[21] When the scene was to be changed, the two were turned in opposite directions until the other long sides, painted as another scene, were turned to the audience. Of course, in the new positions the *periaktoi* did not form an angle wing, but the inside of a corner. If the different wings were placed near enough together and the first wing near enough to the proscenium, the audience could not see beyond them, and an effect of a wall with many corners was produced. Furttenbach found these corners effective in a garden scene.

Of course, in order to turn smoothly the *periaktoi* could not be cut in perspective lines at top and bottom. Architects had to paint the vanishing lines on each face and to paint the corner above to blend with the sky and that below as part of the floor. We see in this treatment of the *periaktoi* a tendency that was becoming stronger in the late Renaissance—the tendency to paint the planes and objects desired without regard to the actual structure of the parts of the scenery.

With the development of the third type, the flat wing, designed to slide in a system of grooves in the floor, the *periaktoi* disappeared from the theatre. The two-dimensional form displaced both the fully three-dimensional angle wing and its substitute, the *periaktoi.*

Some flat wings had already been used in un-

important positions at the back of the scene, probably early in the sixteenth century. They were built in accordance with the principle of perspective that objects at a distance tend to lose their thickness. Leonardo da Vinci stated this principle clearly near the beginning of the sixteenth century,[22] and we see the application in Serlio's account of scenery. Serlio made the perspective face of each upstage house narrower than that of the one farther downstage, and he made the last house on each side a flat wing, with a front face but no perspective face at all. In describing the two frames of a house in the Tragic Scene, he wrote: "If the house is set far back, however, one frame will be sufficient so long as all its parts are skillfully designed and painted." Likewise, he applied the built-out cornices and other solid details only to the downstage houses.

Thus we see that, although the downstage houses were built by real construction in three dimensions, yet farther upstage, from the time of the beginning of perspective scenery, objects were represented by painting on flat surfaces. The construction provided not the actual form of the house but only flat surfaces on which the form could be painted.

It was the development of the mathematical theory of three-dimensional perspective which laid the basis for the painted flat forms. In the early architectural books by Serlio, Barbaro, and Vignola are described empirical devices for drawing the lines on the stage houses and on the back shutter *in situ* or on a model. The most successful device was to erect a cord from the vanishing-point on the back shutter to the eyepoint where the duke was to sit. Then vanishing lines could be drawn on both wings and shutter by sighting over the cord or by casting a shadow from a candle. But soon the problem began to intrigue the mathematicians. In 1600 Guido Ubaldo, Marchese del Monte (known by the Latin form of his name, Ubaldus), published a large volume on the mathematics of perspective, with a whole section devoted to the problem of laying out stage

---

[19] Pp. 91 f.   [20] Cf. chap. ii, p. 107.

[21] *Op. cit.*, pp. 116 ff. Plans reproduced by Hammitzsch, *Der moderne Theaterbau,* p. 30, and Nicoll, *Stuart Masques,* p. 64.

[22] Cf. chap. i.

scenery. He examined the different devices proposed for particular cases and, a generation before Descartes' work on analytical geometry, worked out in detail a general geometric scheme of co-ordinate cords by which could be drawn not only the correct vanishing lines on the perspective faces but any house or object at any angle on any plane surface whatever on the stage.

streets, at any angle, on any face of the scene.[23] Chiaramonti used the method two decades later in drawing the corner in the middle of the front face as though part of it went toward the vanishing-point.[24] Sabbatini in 1637 and 1638 carried the principle still further and planned all kinds of three-dimensional elements to be painted on the two flat surfaces of angle wings. He describes

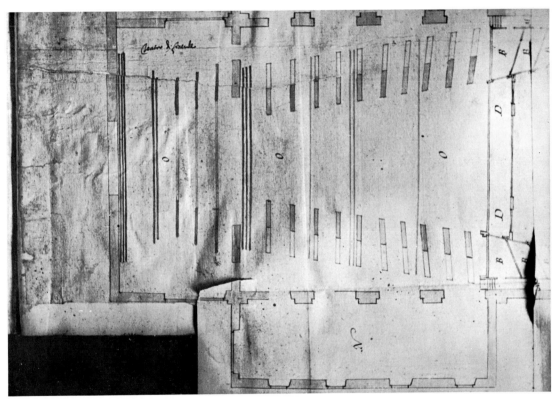

FIG. 54.—Ground plan of a Baroque theatre by Carlo Fontana, 1660. Flat wings. Inner stage. Three positions for the *ferme.* Yale-Rockefeller Theatre Collection.

Ubaldus first tackled the perspective face of the angle wing. He worked out methods not only for drawing on it windows and doors in depth but also for drawing lines that created the illusion that a portion of this perspective face was part of the front face and that the corner came at what was really the middle of the flat face. The section below the new corner could be painted as part of the stage floor and the section above painted as sky or cut off. He pointed out that by the same method one might draw whole

methods for drawing windows, arches, shop fronts, cornices, steps, tavern signs, balconies, and an entire piazza on single flat faces. He planned a most ingenious balcony to look like a straight unit, although it was drawn on two different faces of an angle wing.

When this much could be done by paint, what was the point in building three-dimensional structures? The architectural integrity of the scene was gone. The interest in draftsmanship had

[23] *Op. cit.*, pp. 301 ff.   [24] *Op. cit.*, pp. 88 ff.

overcome the interest in construction. The Baroque scene painter inherited the theatre from the architect.[25]

Flat wings for the entire scene came in near the beginning of the seventeenth century. Early designs of Aleotti, the architect of the Teatro Farnese, show that he planned a whole scene of flat wings early in the century.[26] Designers kept the same system of duplication, with two balanced rows of wings leading to the backdrop; and by the middle of the century they had established everywhere the new system of flat wings which slid in grooves—the dominant system to the end of the nineteenth century. Only in the first house (later called the "tormentor" or "return") did the angle wing survive.

Some designers continued to paint two faces on the flat wing—most of the eighteenth-century flat wings preserved in Stockholm are painted as though they were actually angle wings. Gradually, however, other forms were developed, such as columns, more appropriate to flat wings than houses.

Thus we see that the Baroque scene kept both the classical fondness for symmetry and balance and the Renaissance mathematical concept of space as measurable from any one chosen point in a succession of planes of depth. On the stage that concept led to the division of depth by a series of three or more picture planes, one at the proscenium, one at the first house, and a third at the back shutter. Between the very front of the stage and the shutter, depth was defined by two rows of wings on straight ground lines, set to appear exactly the same distance one from the other as the eye was led by exact mathematical steps into the distance.

The perspective setting was the one Renaissance type of stage which achieved the new ideal of illusion already dominant in painting. While it made some concessions to older forms and conventions, it really achieved a three-dimensional picture. It was the one large theatre which permitted a complete change of setting and hence a variety of spectacular effects; it was the only theatre which had a real principle for organizing a variety of disparate elements into a unit. It is no wonder it drove out all other forms.

Perfectly adapted to the ideals of the court, it was introduced into French and English court productions early in the seventeenth century. Such was the influence of the aristocracy in the Baroque period that with slight adaptations it was established even on the public stage by the middle of the seventeenth century and dominated the public theatre into the twentieth century—long after a more democratic society ought to have developed its own theatre forms.

[25] Kernodle, "Farewell to Scene Architecture," *Quarterly Journal of Speech*, XXV, 649–57.

[26] Rapp, "Ein Theaterbauplan des Giovanni Battista Aleotti," *Schriften der Gesellschaft für Theatergeschichte*, Vol. XLI.

FIG. 55.—A Baroque setting by one of the Galli-Bibiena family. Flat wings in long balanced rows. Extension scene painted on back shutter. Yale-Rockefeller Theatre Collection.

CHAPTER VII

FRAMING THE PERSPECTIVE SCENE

The Inner Stage, the Proscenium, and the Front Curtain

THE proscenium frame was not a new invention of the Renaissance; it was taken over from the frames given to pictures and to the *tableaux vivants* in the fourteenth and fifteenth centuries. But the adaptation was not just a matter of taking a formal frame and putting it in front of a stage picture; the theatre architect had to extricate the framing elements from the details of the picture itself. In the northern *tableaux vivants* that was fairly simple: he kept one of the emblematic symbols as frame—castle, arcade, pavilion, or triumphal arch. The frame itself was an important part of the show. But for the perspective scene the problem was much more complex. The architect had to learn to handle inner stages, forestages, formal side wings, parapets, and valances, as well as a unified proscenium arch. He had to learn to separate the formal from the illusionistic elements.

I. FORMAL AND ILLUSIONISTIC ELEMENTS

The complete achievement of the perspective setting, as we discovered in chapter vi, depended on the establishment of a single picture plane for the whole scene and the development of a formal proscenium arch and front curtain to define that picture plane. Only after the frame had been established did designers separate the illusionistic elements of the setting from the formal elements, for there was little separation of the two in the traditions of painting and the theatre in the fifteenth century. Several complex patterns were established in the new theatre before designers restricted the formal elements to certain parts of the stage and said, "This is the frame,"

and the illusionistic elements to their areas and said, "This is the picture itself."

Not all of the early Italian perspective scene was illusion. Not all the side houses were realistic angle wings carrying a street back to great distance. Not every back shutter continued the open street scene to the horizon. While the side house set the main pattern, it did not easily drive out the many other traditional scenic forms. Arcade screen, triumphal arch, center pavilion, obelisk, castle tower, formal architectural façade, cloth curtain—these and others found a place on the stage along with the side house. They brought with them some of their own meanings and conventions. At first, an effort was made to fit them into the perspective street scene, under the pretense that they were realistic. Finally, they were restricted to the places where they could act as framing devices to mark the picture planes. With that function they were conceded a partial control of the back shutter, where the inner stage might be opened up, and a complete control of the very front of the stage. The formal proscenium and the front curtain evolved as a framing and inclosing element and finally left the main picture between proscenium and back shutter to the perspective ideal of illusion.

Several of the earlier stage settings in court theatres of the sixteenth century were filled with the scenic devices associated with festivity. We must remember that in Italy, no less than in the northern countries, a play was a celebration and that one of the functions of scenery was to give a festive air. The court function in Mantua in 1501 for which Mantegna provided paintings of the "Triumphs of Petrarch" was adorned with all kinds of special decorations. Not only the stage where the play was performed, but apparently the whole room, was decked out with caves, grottoes, arches, niches, heavens, woods, columns, paintings, architectural panels, shields, and coats-of-arms.[1] The very performance of *La Calandria* in 1513, which we have noticed for its scenery in perspective,[2] included a number of devices brought directly from the street theatres. Although the scene represented a street, it was a street taken at the moment when it was transformed into a colorful show. At the center was an eight-sided temple painted with beautiful narrative pictures and decorated with statues and columns of imitation marble and cornices of gold and ultramarine. Several openings were cut out in the shape of shields, filled with glass, and lighted from behind to shine like precious stones.[3] Very like a street decoration! That was not all. At one side stood a splendid triumphal arch on which was painted in imitation of marble the story of the three Horatios. At the sides of the arch were columns and niches with figures of Victory, and above was an armed knight on horseback, his lance piercing a naked man. At the two sides of the knight were altars on which lights burned.

Further, men who wrote about the stage were concerned almost as much with the older show-effects as with the illusion of perspective. Serlio, following Vitruvius, mentions the houses, palaces, etc., of the perspective scene. Then he goes on to add details he was fond of: "triumphal arches, soaring columns, pyramids, obelisks, and a thousand other marvels, all enriched by innumerable lights . . . . like so many sparkling jewels—diamonds, rubies, sapphires, emeralds, and other gems."[4] Leone di Somi, writing also in the middle of the sixteenth century, was likewise as much concerned with the effect of festive decoration as he was with the illusion of actuality. He was as enthusiastic about torches placed on top of the scenery as any street decorator. He wrote:

> Now it has been a custom, both in ancient and modern times, to light bonfires and torches in the streets, on the housetops, and on towers, as a sign of joy: and hence arises this theatrical convention—the imitating of such festive occasions. The lights are put there for no other purpose but to imitate in the very first scene this mood of gaiety.[5]

In spite of the avowed ideals of realism and illusion of the perspective design, these non-illusionistic, conventional showpieces continued to make their appearance within the scene, along with the more realistic side houses.

Gradually the illusionistic structures were separated from the formal architectural pieces by conceding two conventional places for the non-illusionistic: the one, the decorative framing elements at the very front of the stage, and the other, the arcade façade at the back. Let us look first at the formal back screen.

II. BACK SHUTTER AND INNER STAGE

The arcade which we found at the back of the Terence stages persisted long after some architects had substituted a painted shutter. Many a perspective scene in the Renaissance led back, not to an endless street scene, but to a definite arcade façade painted on the back shutter (Fig. 49). Closely related, of course, to the arcade façades of the Teatro Olimpico, the humanistic schools, and the Jesuit academies, it, too, could show one or several separate little scenes within the arches.[6] Sometimes the little scenes were painted on the back shutter, but on other occasions the arches were cut out to permit actual little inner stages to be seen.

The pattern of a formal screen between two realistic side houses is very frequent in art, as we have seen, from the time of the Byzantine painters. It appears in a number of the woodcut illustrations of plays from the end of the fifteenth century; and in woodcuts of the sixteenth century

---

[1] Campbell, *Scenes and Machines on the English Stage*, pp. 45 f.

[2] Cf. chap. vi, p. 177. The description is quoted by Campbell (*op. cit.*, pp. 49 f.).

[3] See Kernodle, "The Magic of Light," *Theatre Arts Monthly*, XXVI, 717–22.

[4] Chambers, *The Elizabethan Stage*, IV, 355. Chambers reprints the passages on the theatre from the 1551 edition of Serlio.

[5] Nicoll, *The Development of the Theatre* (1937), p. 252.

[6] Cf. chaps. i, ii, and v.

we can see the development and clarification of the idea that the back wall could be a formal façade or arcade behind realistic side houses. We have already noticed the importance of the arcade as a background in the several editions of Terence following the influential edition at Lyons in 1493.[7] The large cut of the stage facing the audience in the Venice edition of 1497 shows that the combination of side wings with back screen had been thought of. Most significant are the illustrations of the Venice Plautus of 1518.[8] The single side houses are very realistic, though small in scale; they have windows and doors and a second story and resemble the realistic side houses in perspective painting of the time. Yet at the back there is a purely formal arcade screen of Renaissance detail, through the arches of which are seen glimpses of distant landscapes.

Toward the middle of the sixteenth century the side houses were multiplied, and the screen was pushed farther and farther back. Sometimes it was only a triumphal arch like that in Serlio's Tragic Scene; often, however, it might have any of the arches, columns, niches, statues, paintings, cornices, and architraves that we find on any façade as a separate showpiece. A beautiful example appeared in the Venice edition of Terence of 1545:[9] the front scene was a realistic perspective scene with several wings and a sloping floor leading back to a formal colonnade. Likewise the illustration of Pambosco's *Il Pellegrino*, published in Venice in 1552 (Fig. 49), had a perspective scene of houses in front of a façade of five pilasters with statues framing six panels containing either niches or paintings. Serlio himself, without recognizing the inconsistency, recommended the combination. He wrote: "I recommend painting on the back shutter statues or similar objects supposedly of marble or of other material, as well as scenes of history and legend."[10] The statues and historical paintings were stock-in-trade of the street-shows.

[7] Cf. chap. v.

[8] Freedley and Reeves, *A History of the Theatre*, Fig. 44, after p. 64.

[9] Reproduced by Borcherdt, *Das europäische Theater*, Fig. 69.

[10] Chambers, *op. cit.*, IV, 362.

Into the seventeenth century, in spite of the increasing interest in great depth, the formal façade at the back shutter continued to appear in many scenes. Sometimes it was an arcade of one or two stories through which one could see distant landscapes or several long streets vanishing in perspective; sometimes it was made somewhat more realistic, to resemble the front of a temple, palace, or other imposing building. At any time it might be decorated with the traditional statues and pictures of the street-shows and even be given an upper gallery for spectators or musicians. We shall later examine the façades and temples of this type frequently mixed with regular perspective elements in the settings for the English masques.[11]

The greatest importance of the formal back screen was as a frame for the inner stage, and as such it helped set a pattern for the proscenium at the front of the stage. It has not often been recognized how important the inner stage was in the Italian perspective scene, and how similar it was to the inner stage in Spain, France, Flanders, and England.

The concept of a small space opened up behind the back screen may be traced to the Greek theatre, with its large center doorway, within which a small scene could be shown. The screen in Hellenistic art and again in medieval art could be opened up to allow either exterior or interior to be seen. The pattern, as we have noticed, was frequent in the fourteenth and fifteenth centuries.[12] Artists might show several small street scenes leading either to one vanishing-point or to several and might use the back arcade to separate and frame little scenes that had no space relationship to one another or to the space in front of the screen. Already in painting of the fifteenth century the screen could serve as a proscenium frame for small single or multiple extension scenes.

When perspective scenery was introduced in the sixteenth century, architects took great pleasure in building out in relief all possible detail of their scenes. While sometimes, following

[11] Chap. viii.   [12] Cf. chap. i, pp. 29–31.

art tradition, they painted the screen and the little extension scenes on the flat surface of the back shutter, they soon began actually opening the shutter to show an inner stage. Although it was quite inconsistent with the convention of unity and continuity of space of the perspective scene, they often showed here little interiors or exteriors, even faraway scenes not related to the scene in front. Frequent in medieval art and theatre, this multiple convention was preserved into the new era as an easy way to show spectacular tableaux or some distant scene without a complete change of setting. The French, as we shall see, gave the convention further development by means of a *ferme*, or downstage shutter.

In the Baroque period the inner stage was a regular feature of the perspective scene. The Teatro Farnese, begun in 1618–19, allowed about as much space for the inner stage as for the stage proper. Furttenbach gives us elaborate directions for spectacular effects of seas, ships, whales, and storms, as well as for thrones and interiors, to be disclosed by pulling aside the back shutters. He calls this inner stage the "rear pit," because it was built with a loose floor, to be removed for the complicated sea effects.[13] In the English theatre, as we shall see, the inner stage persisted into the eighteenth century, with small wings and another shutter, duplicating in reduced size the perspective system of the main stage.

The inner stage of multiple scenes persisted in some places. Many seventeenth-century designs show a painted prospect at the back, with the late medieval pattern of an arcade and three separate distant vistas (Fig. 58). Sabbatini gives examples of these, both with a single vanishing-point for all three and with separate vanishing-points. The designs for the Hanover court theatre, opened in 1690, show three little perspective stages going off in three directions behind the back shutters, each with eight or nine sets of wings—an inner stage as deep as the main stage.[14]

Two developments late in the seventeenth century led to the breaking-up of the Baroque symmetrical scene and caused the structural inner stage to disappear. The first was the French *ferme*, to be described in chapter viii. It was a shutter or back cloth that could be used in various places farther downstage than the Italian back shutter. It was so flexible that there was no need to build a permanent inner stage; and, since it was used realistically, it rarely was painted with the conventional arcade. The other development was the oblique backdrop of the Bibienas. For their operatic spectacles at the courts at Vienna and elsewhere they abandoned the deep, narrow setting that led to a vanishing-point at the center and experimented instead with side vanishing-points and with prominent backdrops set at oblique angles rather far downstage. These backdrops they might cut out to show distant vistas, but there was no place for the regular inner stage.[15] Of course, such elaborate effects were possible only at court, and the public repertory theatres in most cities kept into the twentieth century a symmetrical setting and a backdrop parallel to the front. Even when designers were completely devoted to the ideal of illusion, they often preserved the Renaissance convention that the architectural structure painted on the backdrop might be quite separate from the wings— a palace front, for instance, seen back of wood-wings.

III. THE PARTIAL FRAME AND THE FORMAL SIDE HOUSE

Although the complete front proscenium had appeared in some of the *tableaux vivants* in the fourteenth century, it was not applied to the perspective scene at the very beginning. Before it was applied, architects had already begun to develop three separate framing devices—a front parapet below, a valance above, and the first side houses. These partial proscenium elements often persisted alongside the complete proscenium. Hence the convention was established of a rather complex frame, and the vestiges of the separate devices were seen in the grand drapes and formal "tormentors" and "returns" of the

---

[13] *Mannhaffter Kunstspiegel*, pp. 120 ff.

[14] Hammitzsch, *Der moderne Theaterbau*, p. 132.

[15] Gregor, *Wiener szenische Kunst*, pp. 76 ff.

later perspective stages of the eighteenth and nineteenth centuries.

Whereas the painter in oil or water color had his surface and a simple frame to define his picture plane,[16] stage architects found their concept of a picture plane much more complicated. They began in the early sixteenth century by considering each surface of the scenery, and even the floor, as a separate picture plane on which objects were to be painted. These different planes they related to one another by various hit-or-miss rules of three-dimensional perspective. It was the middle of the seventeenth century before they consistently thought of the whole scene as being behind one abstract picture plane, and in some places it was another century and a half before the whole stage was put behind the plane of the proscenium frame.

The treatment of the floor was greatly complicated by the old tradition of the forestage. In most forms of art and theatre before the Renaissance the characters were brought forward in front of most of the scenic background. Until that forestage could be abolished, the proscenium itself had to be regarded as a scenic device, and, accordingly, there could be no clear location of a picture plane for the stage.

The forestage persisted in a number of Renaissance theatres. Some of the perspective stages, as frankly as the mountebank, the Elizabethan, the Rederyker, and the Terence stages, kept a free forestage and set all the scenery back of the main playing area. Serlio, for instance, separated his twelve-foot front platform completely from the area for the scenery. He marked out this front platform in perfect squares and began the application of perspective only on the rear stage, with a sloping floor painted in

diminishing squares. However, he planned that the actors would use the front houses of the perspective scene and the first entrances behind them. As later architects designed a deeper stage and a floor not so sharply sloped, it was possible to act on the sloping floor, which could be brought to the front of the stage if desired.

Even after the floor was integrated with the perspective scene and the stage sloped from the very front, many architects continued to think of the floor as a separate picture plane rather than as one element in a unified picture. Chiaramonti treated the stage floor from the front parapet to the back shutter as one scenic plane and worked out on it, rather than on the side houses, the proportionate diminution of all objects as they receded farther in the distance. It was at the front edge of the floor that he set up the actual dimensions from which all others were computed.[17] In other words, he chose the plane of the front parapet as the plane for computation, though the other framing elements might be placed farther back.

The front parapet, used, doubtless, at the front of most medieval platforms, might be decorated in the Renaissance with a formal design. Into it were built steps by which dancers might descend to the main floor of the hall and windows for workers under the stage (Figs. 52, 53); or these details might be painted on when there was no need for actual steps and windows[18]—such is the hold of convention. While sometimes integrated with the rest of the proscenium, the front parapet in many theatres remained a separate framing element. Sometimes it was moved farther back in the hall, to separate the musicians' pit from the rest of the auditorium (Fig. 55).

Directly above the parapet, at the top of the hall, there might be a framing valance to finish the heavens at the front and to mask lights for the stage. Although the early writers on perspective say nothing about how the heavens should be finished at the front, they probably used a formal valance as soon as they had front cur-

---

[16] Of course, as I pointed out in chapter i, the painter often had difficulty in deciding just which plane he should relate his space to. Down to the early Renaissance, and occasionally after, painters used an architectural screen or some other feature with some space indicated in front of it. They only gradually learned to place that screen at the picture plane. Just as the Greek theatre originally suggested such a forestage in painting, so in the Renaissance the stage may have preserved for the painter older concepts of space. Cf., further, Michalski, *Die Bedeutung der ästhetischen Grenze für die Methode der Kunstgeschichte.*

[17] *Delle scene e teatri*, pp. 47 ff. and 56 ff.

[18] Furttenbach, *op. cit.*, p. 122.

tains and rows of heavens—that is, quite early in the sixteenth century. Serlio mentions no framing feature, but his account of suns, moons, and thunderbolts implies a heavens, and he probably used as definite a finish above as his plates show at the parapet below. The typical device at the top was a valance of cloth, wood, or plaster, ornamented with elaborate festoons, symbolic figures, coats-of-arms, rosettes, and tassels.

A far more important development than either the valance above or the parapet below was the use of the first side house as the framing element—as the plane of the picture. Apparently at the time of Serlio not all architects thought of the first houses as the most important ones, from which all others diminished. Serlio himself placed a small house at each side to lead the eye up to the larger house behind it. Then from the second house his perspective lines converged sharply to the vanishing-point.[19] Even in his day, however, some architects, and later all, made the first house the largest. The Baroque scene was much more regular than Serlio's, with houses that were nearly all alike and roof and cornice lines that continued from the first houses straight back to the vanishing-point.

The first house served most of the theorists on perspective for their picture plane. Whether they placed it at the very front or left a free forestage, they established their actual dimensions on it and from it computed the diminished size of all objects back of it. It is significant that, when the complete formal proscenium arch was achieved, the dimensions of all objects in perspective were computed not from the plane of the arch but from the plane of the first house. Today in our professional theatres the scene begins not with the proscenium frame, which has become a permanent part of the building, but with the movable scenery back of that frame.

In view of this tendency to treat the first house as the picture plane, we are not surprised to find that it was often made more formal than the other houses. Since the earlier type of angle

[19] Chambers, *op. cit.*, IV, 360.

wing could scarcely be changed by backstage workers but had to remain throughout all scene changes, any realistic design would be inconsistent with later scenes. Hence the designer often gave it a formal architectural design with columns, architraves, niches, and sometimes curtains.

A large number of designs from the middle of the sixteenth century through the nineteenth show the formal first house (Fig. 59). In the Renaissance it was often a partial proscenium and might be decorated with niches, statues, allegorical figures, or paintings. After the complete proscenium was established, it was usually less conspicuous. The tormentor and return of the present day are its descendants.

IV. FRAMING DEVICES FROM THE STREET THEATRES CASTLE, ARCADE, PAVILION, AND TRIUMPHAL ARCH

A formal framing element is very old in art. In antiquity the frame was either a strip with a longitudinal pattern, such as the cable or bead-and-reel, or a molding whose elements, such as the acanthus leaf or egg-and-dart, faced uniformly inward toward the area inclosed. The frame was an organic, indivisible unit. But in northern art the organic continuity was disregarded, and the border was made up of odd fragments, some of them geometrical patterns, but some of them the same scenic devices that were used in the pictures themselves. Hence we find in medieval and Renaissance art not only formal framing borders but also the several traditional emblematic scenic devices used as frames. In the *tableaux vivants* the formal border was rare, but four of the scenic devices were very important as framing prosceniums for a picture within; those four were the castle, the arcade, the pavilion, and the triumphal arch.

The earliest street device to be used as a complete proscenium arch was the castle. Between its two side towers and underneath the central gable the front wall could be removed to reveal a complete scene within. Some of the castle-shows in Paris in 1389 had quite large scenes inclosed by the structure.[20] How they must have looked we can judge from the illustrations for the tableaux at Bruges in 1515 (Figs. 25, 26), nearly all of which were boxlike structures, shaped like castles or similar buildings and opened by large swinging doors to disclose the living pictures within. Castle prosceniums were also used for medieval

We have noticed the "prospect of four castles" at Ferrara in 1491.[22] Apparently the actors merely used the castles as a scenic device from which they came out to play. In the sixteenth century, however, the center section of the castle was likely to be opened up so that a street scene might be put in between the two side towers (Fig. 57).

FIG. 56.—Castle-proscenium for a puppet theatre. Miniature from the manuscript of the "Romance of Alexander," *ca.* 1340. Bodleian Library, Oxford.

puppet shows, as is indicated by the well-known miniature of a puppet show in the marginal decoration of the fourteenth-century manuscript of the "Romance of Alexander" in the Bodleian Library (Fig. 56).[21]

In Italy before the end of the fifteenth century, as I have already pointed out, towers and castles served as background for a number of court plays.

The architect imagined the audience outside the gates of a city looking into the street scene within. The result was a proscenium frame of two side towers that must have been much like that of the medieval puppet stage of the Alexander manuscript.

The most interesting example of this castle proscenium was built in 1513 for the performance of *La Calandria* before the Duke of Urbino. Castiglione describes the setting in a letter that

[20] Cf. chap. ii and bibliography.

[21] This and another castle puppet show from the same manuscript are reproduced by Nicoll, *op. cit.*, p. 71.

[22] Chap. ii, pp. 83 f.

has been misunderstood by Lily Bess Campbell and others. It is now clear that the front parapet of the stage was painted as a rampart and that two bridge-steps led out to the audience. At the sides were two tall towers, which, like innumerable earlier towers, served for musicians. The audience was supposed outside the city, in or beyond the moat, looking through the gate and down the city street.

The scene [i.e., the acting area] was an outer street of the town between the city wall and its last houses. The wall with its two towers was represented in the most natural way possible, rising from the floor of the stage to the top of the hall. One tower was occupied by the pipers, the other by the trumpeters, and between the two there was another finely constructed rampart. The hall itself, where the audience sat, occupied the place of the moat and was crossed as it were by two aqueducts. The scene was laid in a very fine city, with streets, palaces, churches, and towers, all in relief, and looking as if they were real, the effect being completed by admirable paintings in scientific perspective.[23]

Here within the proscenium were assembled the houses, temples, arches, and altars which we have already noticed in considering the mixture of pageant and realistic devices.

Not only an open street scene but formal arcade screens, as well, could be flanked by framing towers. The beautiful arcade of columns and curtains of gold which I have described,[24] built in Rome in 1513 for the *Poenulus* of Plautus, was flanked at the two sides by great towers, one of which was marked "Via ad forum." Likewise at Lyons in 1548, at the king's landing place, an elaborate Roman screen of painted niches and statues was framed at the ends by two round medieval towers decorated at the top with emblems of the king.

Towers as framing elements continued in the perspective scene to the end of the seventeenth century. We see several interesting examples in the Turin ballets of the 1660's and 1670's (Fig. 59). Also into the Baroque theatre we can trace another framing element from the castle—the parapet, built either against the front of the stage platform to hide the structure underneath the stage or several feet from the stage to make a pit for a front curtain or an orchestra. While side

columns and overhead arch most frequently were decorated with the latest Renaissance and Baroque details, the parapet below the scene often was painted with the heavy stones of the medieval castle.

I have already told in full the story of the arcade and how it served to inclose small scenes.[25] It remains only to point out that some later prosceniums continued to be built in the multiple-arch form of the arcade. Sometimes the side arches were made into little prosceniums, sometimes into formal proscenium doors, sometimes into niches for statues at the sides of the main proscenium opening.

The pavilion as a framing element is more medieval than Renaissance. In art, sculpture, and the medieval theatre it was very important. With a canopy, four columns, and an occasional curtain hanging on one, three, or four sides, it adorned and framed in three dimensions an object or a group of people.[26] As it was flattened in the Renaissance and combined with a façade to be seen from one side, it furnished an important framing pattern for the theatre. We can visualize the flattened form best in some of the wall tombs which used a half-pavilion and a flat scene of statues facing the front (Figs. 20, 21, and also 29).

In the street theatres the pavilion was adapted very early to the purpose of framing a scene to be looked at from the front. In 1486, Anne of Brittany, entering Paris as the bride of young Charles VIII, found on the first street platform a little scene of France and Brittany at war until Peace brought them together. The scene was framed by a pavilion sustaining a canopy with a figure of Hercules crushing the Hydra. Underneath, as a background, was hung a beautiful cloth of the royal colors, gathered at the top into a crown.[27]

The two side columns and the architrave and pediment of the flat pavilion façade were very effective in framing a small scene set against the façade, as we see from the miniatures of the

---

[23] Campbell, *op. cit.*, pp. 49 f.   [24] Chap. v.

[25] Chaps. i, ii, and v.   [26] Chaps. i, ii, iii, and iv.

[27] Chap. ii, pp. 84 f., and bibliography.

Paris tableaux of 1514 (Figs. 35, 36, 37) and those at Lyons in 1515.[28] Most of the larger framing structures, however, followed other scenic devices. The pavilion, the earliest nonillusionistic form, contributed mainly a pattern of two side columns supporting an elaborate canopy. By the Renaissance many other devices had the same pattern, and we can no longer trace the distinctive features of the pavilion.

FIG. 57.—City gate as proscenium frame. From Pélerin's *De artificiali perspectiva* (1505).

A formal arch which served both as a setting and as a frame for a distant scene was popular in medieval art in both the north and the south. In the Gothic period two newer forms increased the importance of the arch as a frame: the stone window frames for stained glass and the columns and architraves used as marginal decorations around the illustrations, as well as the columns of text, in manuscripts. While northern artists continued to use decorated Gothic arches throughout the fifteenth century, Italian painters early began painting formal Renaissance arches and then

triumphal arches, either behind the characters or near the front, to frame the scene. Roger van der Weyden in Flanders was very fond of a Gothic archway which might frame an interior, a scene of curtains, an open pavilion leading to a landscape, or a landscape directly. After him Quentin Metsys, Memling, and Jan Gossaert carried on the tradition and introduced Renaissance detail.

In all four of the countries we are mainly concerned with, a free-standing arch combined with a curtain had been used as a scenic framing device long before there was any attempt to build perspective scenery on a stage. Some kind of framing device had been used with a front curtain in a banquet hall in Lille in 1453 for three successive scenes of Jason and the Golden Fleece, and at Bruges in 1468 for the twelve labors of Hercules. Among the Bruges street-shows of 1515 not only were there box structures shaped like castles, civic buildings, or altarpieces, each of which had an arch framing an interior, but also a beautiful archway was erected at the Square of the Easterlings just to frame a painting of Atlas holding the world.[29]

In both English and French street-shows the arch as a symbol of a garden could inclose and frame other garden symbols, such as the *lis* in France and the bush of red and white roses in England. At Rouen in 1485 arches were used to frame several of the *tableaux vivants*. In the sixteenth century, especially at Lyons, a number of street-shows used triumphal arches to frame all kinds of shows: grottoes, painted water scenes behind statues of river gods, and whole *tableaux vivants*. In French *ballets de cour*, both with the *décor dispersé* and later, after the scenery was concentrated on a stage, a triumphal arch framing a scene or painted view was popular.

In Italy the triumphal arch achieved its greatest popularity, and consequently it became quite frequent on the stage and in indoor entertainments. How it was used before perspective scenery was devised we learn from an account of an entertainment given in 1492 at Castelcapuano for the King of Naples. At one side of the hall was

[28] Guigue, *L'Entrée de François Premier Roy de France en la cité de Lyon;* reproduced by Mourey, *Le Livre des fêtes françaises*, pp. 23–29; see also bibliography for chap. ii, "Entries: France."

[29] Cf. chap. ii and bibliography.

erected an arch with satin curtains, from which the actors and shows were to appear. The curtains were opened to disclose, one after the other, Pallas, Fame, Apollo, and Memoria, who either walked forward or were drawn in on a pageant wagon.[30] This pattern continued throughout the period of the Renaissance court operas: after a

identified with the formal side doorways of other show-façades.

Show-arches, before the perspective scene was established, had already used patterns of placing an orchestra of musicians in a gallery above the arch or on the ground at the foot of the structure.[31] The musicians' gallery in the English

FIG. 58.—Arcade screen at the back of a perspective scene, about 1640. Three different vanishing-points for painted extensions. Yale-Rockefeller Theatre Collection.

disclosure within the proscenium arch, the singers and dancers might come forward onto the floor of the main hall to perform, surrounded by the audience. Considering the importance of the triumphal arch as an independent show or as a frame for a smaller scene, we are not surprised that the proscenium arch adopted many of its aspects. The side arches either survived in the proscenium as side niches for statues, or they were

theatre of the Restoration was directly above the arch, and it was in a similar position in Munich in 1662 for the opera *Antiopa giustificata*.

V. THE COMPLETE PROSCENIUM FRAME FOR THE PERSPECTIVE SCENE

The complete Renaissance proscenium frame was not a co-ordination of the various partial frames developed separately. It was a complete

[30] Croce, *I Teatri di Napoli*, p. 9.

[31] Cf. chap. ii.

showpiece itself, derived, like the Renaissance façade, from several of the emblematic devices which had been used to inclose tableaux on street stages from the fourteenth century on. Like other Renaissance devices, it was elaborately decorated with columns, pediments, niches, statues, mottoes, heraldic and ornamental em-

front curtain was usually designed as part of the whole device; indeed, on a number of occasions a curtain was hung over the entire proscenium and was suddenly dropped at the beginning of the play, so thoroughly was the proscenium considered one of the spectacular scenes of the play. Most prosceniums had some curtain hangings,

Fig. 59.—Partial proscenium and castle towers as wings. *Il falso amor bandito* (Turin, 1667). Formal façade at back shutter, showing small perspective scene either painted on shutter or built on inner stage. Yale-Rockefeller Theatre Collection.

blems, banners, festoons, and draperies. It took over features from the triumphal arch, from the arcade screen, and even from the complex façade. It often had side doors or niches and even side arches large enough for separate scenes. In this respect it was a cousin, not a descendant, of the Teatro Olimpico. Above could be a musicians' gallery or some emblems of the heavens. In niches and panels were placed single statues, allegorical groups, or paintings, similar to those which adorned other scenic devices. The

either shaped out in plaster or of actual fabrics—silks and brocades in rich red, silver, or gold.

The modern theatre inherited both the complete and the partial proscenium. Alongside the complete proscenium persisted each part. Here we might find a valance hanging from the ceiling to hide lights or a curtain, there a parapet to separate the pit of the musicians—the orchestra—from the audience. In America so many people have wanted to sit in the orchestra pit that the parapet has been gradually pushed back until it now separates the "orchestra" from the standing room and the lobby. Behind the front curtain our stage picture has its own inner frame: tormentors at the sides and a hanging tab to mask the lights above—persistent relics of the elaborate grand drapes of the Victorian theatre and the valance and formal side houses of the Renaissance.

Curiously enough, it is that inner proscenium which has greater importance in the theatre today. The main proscenium has been reduced by modern architects until the stage is little more than a hole in the auditorium wall. But back of the curtain, for many plays, the designer puts an inner proscenium to set a particular style. We have returned to the Renaissance concept—that the frame is part of the show, one of the ephemeral structures to be designed and built specially for each occasion.

To summarize the history of the proscenium frame: It was derived both from a complete frame and from partial framing elements in the traditions of medieval art. The complete frame was often treated as part of the background in painting; and, when the *tableaux vivants* were built on street stages in the fourteenth and fifteenth centuries, the traditional emblematic elements of castle, arcade, pavilion, and triumphal arch were used as frames. Hence, when complete prosceniums were built early in the sixteenth century for the perspective settings, the prosceniums were not neutral but were treated as symbolic settings themselves and were decorated with the ornaments, symbols, and allegorical characters of the tableaux. From this treatment of the proscenium as setting and from the pattern of a framing element for the inner stage was established the apron stage as a playing area inclosed or backed by the proscenium. The forestage was further complicated by the partial proscenium elements developed from the separate medieval mansions. Some sixteenth-century productions used only the partial elements, some only the complete frame, and some both. The Baroque productions in the seventeenth century used both and made the complete frame more neutral and a permanent part of the theatre, at

the same time making the partial elements into the flexible "tormentors" and "returns" that have come down to our day. While the late medieval and early Renaissance producer used his frame as a setting, gradually in the later sixteenth century and more definitely in the seventeenth century the producer separated the formal frame from the illusionistic picture within. Although the shape of the proscenium was determined in the Gothic and the early Renaissance period, the real concept of an illusionistic picture stage behind a formal frame was developed in the Baroque period.

VI. THE FRONT CURTAIN

The complete front curtain to cover the entire scene was first developed in the *tableaux vivants* in the fifteenth century, in close imitation of the coverings for pictures used in churches and houses. That relation is seen in the spectacular show built in Ghent in 1458 to reproduce with living figures the celebrated "Adoration of the Lamb" by the brothers van Eyck.[32] This three-story stage, thirty-eight feet high and fifty feet long, was covered by a white curtain which was drawn aside at the arrival of the duke. As early as 1453, for the famous banquet at Lille, a front curtain over a small stage had been used to disclose in succession three scenes of the story of Jason. For the series of banquets given at Bruges in 1468, tableaux of the labors of Hercules were disclosed behind a front curtain. After each tableau a verse explaining the show was displayed in front of the curtain. Regularly, from 1453 on, the removal of the curtain was accompanied by the playing of musical instruments—an adaptation for theatrical purposes of the church rituals at the unveiling of altars, pictures, and shrines.

These early Flemish curtains were all plain white or green cloth and were drawn to the side. Similar were the ones indicated in the sketches of shows in Brussels in 1496 (Fig. 23). But in Bruges in 1515 appeared two other types, both closely related to the traditions of art. A number of the

[32] See chap. ii, p. 65.

Bruges shows were built in the form of shrines or boxes, with wooden door-shutters that opened on hinges (Fig. 26). Like shrines, both the front and the back of the swinging shutters were painted with characters and mottoes appropriate to the tableau within. The other new type of curtain was a portcullis over the archway of a castle (Fig. 25). Built and painted to resemble an actual castle gate, this was one of the first curtains to be raised at the beginning and lowered at the end of the show—an arrangement that did not become common until the middle of the seventeenth century.

The falling curtain, which was to become the most important in the Renaissance, had classical precedent; for the Romans had used it and Donatus describes it in a treatise that was included in nearly every Renaissance edition of Terence. It also appeared in late medieval entertainments over small separate scenic units before such units were brought together on one stage. Hall records a setting revealed at a court disguising at Greenwich in 1527 "by letting down of a curtain."[33] As W. J. Lawrence has pointed out, this peculiar falling curtain became the regular front curtain for perspective scenery,[34] and a pit was often built to receive it so that it would not be in the way of actors or audience. Both Sabbatini and Furttenbach, in the seventeenth century, describe the handling of one or several such curtains.

Although the purely formal curtain existed from medieval times, yet here, as in the case of the settings, Renaissance architects often mixed formal with illusionistic. Like the door-shutters and portcullis at Bruges in 1515, the curtain might be painted with a scene appropriate to the tableau to be disclosed, or it might be used as a scenic background itself. In the French and English court masques the front curtain might as often be a special scene painted on a cloth as a formal fabric;[35] sometimes it even had practical doorways and other more solid features. Eventually, in the Baroque period, illusionistic wing and backdrop were separated from both proscenium and curtain. But these formal elements, like the formal façade, still kept symbolic associations. Columns, arches, and rich cloth hangings could create the atmosphere of a show from the outside as well as the most handsome perspective settings within.

Throughout the Renaissance, the principal use of the formal front curtain was to permit the sudden disclosure, to the accompaniment of drums, trumpets, and other music, of the stage picture. Only late in the seventeenth century did producers generally use it to mask a change of setting. The early stage architect was expected to produce a wondrous, magic effect when his settings changed before the very eyes of the audience. Even with an illusionistic perspective setting, the function of the scenery was still to surprise and delight. In the *tableaux vivants* the audience had seen withered trees turned to living ones and spheres turned round to reveal boats or thrones full of beautiful ladies. To have used a curtain to hide such a change would have cheated the audience. The front curtain was more often a positive show itself, not merely a cover. It retained that positive function until the recent taste for plain fabrics drove out the painted picture and the "grand drapes" of Victorian days.

[33] Chambers, *op. cit.*, I, 155.

[34] *The Elizabethan Playhouse* [*First Series*], pp. 109–21.

[35] Nicoll, *Stuart Masques*, pp. 39 f., 66 f., 74, 77, 80, 83, and *passim*.

CHAPTER VIII

COMPROMISES IN FRANCE AND ENGLAND

The Baroque Scene

EUROPE was too small to hold so many independent theatres. France, Flanders, England, and Spain kept their native forms thriving throughout the sixteenth century, but all succumbed by the middle of the seventeenth century to the new illusion and the painted perspective scene. We, safe in the twentieth century, may point out the flexibility, the speed, the continuity possible on the more symbolic stages; yet all those stages gave way to perspective. We may blame the change on many things—on the decline of the native drama in Flanders, England, and Spain; on the prestige of Italian writers, painters, and court architects; on the love for spectacular settings that had a new kind of illusion. Whatever the reasons, producers and public alike took to the imported toys and preferred the Italian methods to all others. As perspective was gradually introduced in northern Europe in the first half of the seventeenth century, especially in Paris and London, the new principles came into sharp conflict with the old. There was some confusion, reflected in the bitter controversies over unity of place; and a number of compromises were established which were incorporated into the theatres of the following centuries.

In Italy perspective scenery established itself practically at the beginning of secular drama, with no apparent struggle. The architects responsible for producing court plays and entertainments were the very ones most interested in carrying the ideals of painting to the stage. While many traditions of the medieval and school stages were absorbed into Renaissance stage practice,

yet almost from the beginning of the court theatre in Italy the main conventions of perspective scenery prevailed. The new principle, as we have seen, established two conventions: the illusion of reality and unity of place. It required, in brief, that everything seen on the stage at one time be planned as it would appear from one definite eyepoint.

Under the domination of this concept, perspective scenery in Italy developed as an integrated form, and this form was assumed by the critics, in so far as they thought in terms of the theatre of their times. The new principle is clearly reflected in the writings of Castelvetro, the critic who was most closely related to the actual theatre of his day. He thought of unity of place not in terms of the ancient theatre but exactly in terms of the convention of illusion of the new perspective scenery—that everything must be within the view of one person. In his commentary on Aristotle, published in 1570, he stated that "the place for tragedy is restricted not only to one city or town or landscape [*campagna*] or similar place, but also to that view which can be seen by the eyes of one person."[1]

The new principles were not established so easily in Paris and London. Both cities had thriving popular theatres with their own conventions, derived from earlier traditions of the stage. Only gradually could the new be introduced, and then only after the court theatres had adopted the perspective convention and had created an interest in it.

It was much easier for the court theatres to

[1] *Poetica d'Aristotele vulgarizzata e esposta*, p. 535.

take over the new methods, and in both France and England they made the change some time before the public theatres. In both the French *ballets de cour* and the English masques, architects who knew Italian practice replaced the old system of *décor dispersé* with a stage and perspective scenery in the first quarter of the seventeenth century. These courtly entertainments easily permitted radical change. Each performance was a new production, in which change and novelty would be welcomed; and royal and princely patrons had money for daring experiments. In the public playhouses there was a continuity of tradition and little money for radical changes. It was not until the 1640's in Paris and 1660 in London that the public stage fell into line with the court ideals.

I. PERSPECTIVE IN THE FRENCH COURT PRODUCTIONS

There were a few isolated court productions in France in the sixteenth century which borrowed the new type of scenery directly from Italy. The first appearance of a perspective setting was in Lyons in 1548, as part of a conscious importation from Italy of drama, players, designers, and method. Henry II and his Italian wife, Catherine de Medici, passing through the city, were the guests of Cardinal Hippolyte d'Este, who entertained them with a magnificent performance of *La Calandria*. Italian players presented the Italian play, and an Italian artist, Andrea Nannoccio, built the perspective scene, composed of houses at the sides of the stage and a painted view of the city of Florence at the back.[2] Also, in 1586 another interesting production in the provinces of France used Italian perspective scenes. At Nantes, five-sided *periaktoi* were built for a performance of *L'Arimène* by Nicolas de Montreux.[3]

The flat painted curtain hung at the back of street theatres also helped in introducing the principles of perspective to the stages of western

Europe. At this same reception of Henry II at Lyons in 1548, one of the street theatres had as a background a flat painted cloth, a perspective view of a city square representing Troy.[4]

The medieval mountebank stages and those of the early *commedia dell'arte* seem to have had a flat plain curtain as a background for the action, with entrances from which characters could appear or merely peek. At an early time this curtain was doubtless painted with a perspective scene. Several seventeenth-century illustrations show such a perspective curtain at the back of a platform stage. The drawings of Callot for *I Balli di Sfessani*,[5] probably reflecting *commedia dell'arte* scenes observed on his trip to Italy before 1621, show a simple cloth with a scene drawn in perspective. The well-known print of the stage of a mountebank, Gille le Niais, made in Paris about 1640, illustrates a similar use of a perspective painting as a background for dramatic action.[6] We shall see that the painted perspective curtain back of the playing area was familiar in England both in court and in academic productions and was not unknown in the public theatres.

In Paris three-dimensional perspective scenery made its way first, very gradually, in the *ballets de cour*, those spectacles compounded of dialogue, song, dance, and scenery, for the entertainment of royalty and court society, which were very similar to the English masques. The typical sixteenth-century *ballets* used the *décor dispersé*, with units of scenery scattered about the main floor of the hall as nuclei for dance and action, each unit denoting a separate place. There was no convention of unity and no attempt to use the scenery to form an inclosing picture for the action. Yet a few of the elements of the perspective scene were present. For the *Ballet de la Royne* in 1581, one unit of the scattered scenery was an arbor with a central arch and a curtain; within the arch was a small inner stage with a sloping floor and a painted perspective scene at the back.[7]

---

[2] Solerti, "La Rappresentazione della *Calandria* a Lione nel 1548," *Raccolta di studii . . . ded. ad A. d'Ancona;* and Brouchard, *Les Origines du théâtre de Lyon*, pp. 25 f.

[3] Holsboer, *L'Histoire de la mise en scène*, p. 137.

[4] Cf. chap. ii, p. 107.

[5] Cheney, *The Theatre*, p. 226.

[6] Reproduced by Holsboer, *op. cit.*

[7] Prunières, *Le Ballet de cour en France*, pp. 92 f.

The first *décors successifs* in the *ballets* in 1610 and 1615 used a type of perspective that differed from the Italian. Instead of the open central area with a number of houses at the sides leading the scene to a small back wall or back shutter, this French type of perspective, as indicated in these *ballets* and in some features of the scenery at the Hôtel de Bourgogne, attained depth on a shallow stage by a back cloth that was pierced to allow another back wall to be seen.

The *Ballet d'Alcine* of 1610 was the first to present the whole scene as a unit at one end of the hall, and the *décor successif* was substituted for the older *décor dispersé*. For the first time a forest was shown on a cloth pierced by three openings through which greater depth could be seen. It fell, like the early Renaissance front curtain, to disclose a palace with a pyramid in front of it. This scene also vanished *tout à coup;* hence it must have been on a cloth or frame that could easily be removed.[8] The next important *ballet*, the *Ballet du triomphe de Minerve*, presented in 1615, was designed by an Italian, Francini.[9] But still the perspective seems to have been the French type of a shallow stage with pierced or cut-out painted curtains.

Light is thrown on this type of perspective by the section on scenery in Volume III of Dubreuil's *La Perspective pratique*, published in 1649.[10] Dubreuil presents stage perspective scenes composed of one or two flat painted frames or curtains cut out to give glimpses of a second or third painted frame behind. All could be placed in a shallow stage. The only side houses he describes are single flat wings or four-sided *periaktoi* at each side to inclose a shallow scene in front of a painted back shutter. These are very similar to the settings for the early *ballets* and are closely related to some of the effects we shall find in the Hôtel de Bourgogne.

The first appearance of the Italian type of perspective scenery with angle wings was for the production of the *Ballet de la délivrance de Renaud*

in 1617, again designed by Francini. For the scene changes the rock wings at the sides were drawn off and wood-wings were revealed. At the back, however, the change was accomplished, not by the Italian system of shutters and inner stage, but by the turning device familiar in French street-shows since 1485. A grotto in the first act, the whole back section turned round to show a garden on the other side, while a third scene was a desolate cavern. Still there was no great depth; for only two wings were used on each side, the stage floor was still level, and the turning device at the back was an important part of the whole design.[11]

The fullest development of the French system of perspective came with the performance in 1641 of *Mirame*, written and supervised by Richelieu for the opening of the Théâtre du Palais Cardinal. Here were all the trappings of the perspective scene: proscenium and front curtain and side wings leading to a back shutter. Yet the stage was not nearly so deep as Italian stages of the time, and there were still only two flat wings on each side.

The deep perspective stage with an open central area leading past a number of wings came when Torelli, the "wizard," was imported from Venice and produced *La finta pazza* at the Petit Bourbon in 1645. The first scene showed a view of Paris, apparently with six wings on one side and at least four on the other. The second scene made use of three typical Italian miniature scenes of perspective, painted on the back shutter to give an astounding effect of depth. The whole scene represented a garden, with rows of vases leading back to the center of the stage, where three paths separated and seemed, by the ingenuity of the perspective, to continue more than a thousand steps.[12]

With *La finta pazza* (1645) and *Andromède* (1647), the musical spectacles of the French court were brought into line with the Italian type of deep perspective scenery that has remained the tradition of opera down to the present time. Yet either from the French court

---

[8] *Ibid.*, pp. 147 ff.   [9] *Ibid.*, pp. 149 ff.

[10] Translated in the Appendix of my dissertation, "Perspective in the Renaissance Theatre."

[11] Prunières, *op. cit.*, pp. 151 f.   [12] Holsboer, *op. cit.*, p. 152.

or from the public stages, some elements of the shallow stage which did not exist in Italian Renaissance theatres were taken over by designers of the Baroque and Rococo periods.

II. MEDIEVAL TO MODERN AT THE HÔTEL DE BOURGOGNE

The public stages of Paris, especially the Hôtel de Bourgogne, made use of the one stage form of the Renaissance that was based directly on the religious theatres of the late Middle Ages. It was the one form that tried to organize the disparate mansions on a small area, neither destroying their separate identities, as the façade theatres had done, nor giving them a new principle of unity, as perspective did. It is no wonder that France saw so much confusion and bickering over the principle of unity of place in the 1630's and 1640's, when the old methods were in direct conflict with new ideals. Most historians have surveyed the controversy over the unities without realizing that it grew directly out of the conflicts in theatre conventions of the time.

Fortunately, the Hôtel de Bourgogne in this period of transition is more completely documented than any other theatre of the time. In the *Mémoire*,[13] a collection of notes and sketches by Mahelot for plays produced between 1633 and 1636, we can study the conflict of the two sets of ideals. In the notes of Laurent and other designers for the same theatre we can watch the development of compromise forms until the 1680's, when the conflict was over.

At the Hôtel de Bourgogne there was a continuity of tradition from the religious stages of the late fifteenth and early sixteenth centuries. The medieval method was to place a number of separate mansions on a long shallow stage, with perhaps a screen at the back and ends, as in the Cailleau illustrations for the Valenciennes production of 1547. When the Comédiens du Roi, the company for which Mahelot was the designer, rented the Hôtel de Bourgogne from the Confrérie de la Passion, they took over the scenery of that brotherhood and with it the methods of

staging that had been handed down for generations and adapted to the progressively smaller stages which the brotherhood had used.

The Confrérie had established itself in 1402 in the Hôpital de la Trinité, a room whose dimensions we know—forty meters long by twelve meters wide. A stage at one end that was twelve meters (forty feet) wide must have required a certain amount of crowding of the mansions of the religious dramas; but they were still kept separate, and probably each one had enough space around it so that the actors could move some distance and still not walk on the area definitely associated with the next house.

After a stay in the Hôtel de Flandre, the Confrérie in 1548 had a hall built on the old grounds of the Hôtel de Bourgogne. Instead of a stage forty feet wide, they had one about twenty-two feet wide and sixteen feet deep. Here they preserved the convention of simultaneous staging and jammed five, six, or seven mansions together around the sides and back of the stage. As there were usually two or three houses or "compartments" on each side, balanced symmetrically about a center architectural screen or a wider compartment, there could have been no more than six to nine feet for each compartment.[14] That meant not only putting the houses together and even in front of each other, and probably making them smaller, but overlapping the imagined areas located by different houses. An actor would come out of a certain house, say a palace, and establish the floor in front of the house (by conventions of medieval staging and medieval painting) as belonging to that palace. But the other houses were so close that he must almost touch the forest upstage or the bedroom at the other side or the ship downstage. Then in the next scene actors might come out of the bedroom and speak, but they must stand directly in front of the palace. And so on.

In the earlier medieval simultaneous settings, each house was an independent unit. When the mansions were put on a platform, one house might have a relationship of design with the other

[13] *Le Mémoire de Mahelot, Laurent et d'autres décorateurs.*

Holsboer, *op. cit.*, pp. 108 ff.

houses by being on a line with them or by being of size and proportions that would harmonize with them, but there was no convention that the stage space relation was one of verisimilitude. The floor in front of a house was usually supposed to be the space in that house or next to it; but the next house might be considered to be far away in time and place.

vention that everything seen on the stage must be imagined as within the view of one person.

The Mahelot sketches show that between 1633 and 1636 there was a complete confusion of the two systems. The houses themselves and the architectural screen at the back preserved the forms of the medieval stage with very few changes (Fig. 60). Each house was a miniature repre-

Fig. 60.—Mahelot's sketch of a multiple setting at the Hôtel de Bourgogne in the 1630's

Perspective scenery, however, demanded a new illusion of reality. Two houses were now believed to have the same space relationship that the actual houses on the stage appeared to have. Instead of being divided into many different vague sections, space was unified into one definite, continuous area. The scene might be very inclusive, and the houses, decreasing in perspective, might represent a distance far greater than the actual size of the stage; but they were all organized by one convention of unity—the con-

sentation of a whole scene—a miniature palace, prison, forest, butcher-shop, mountain, ship, tent, or hell. A single house might represent a city. Sometimes a whole house would be little larger than the doorway, and some small houses were scarcely more than the baldacchinos of medieval art with columns supporting a roof. The doorways of many houses were hung with curtains that were pulled aside for entrances or to reveal action within. Sometimes the structure of a whole house would be covered with a painted cloth that could represent one scene but could be removed to show an entirely different scene, the house itself. At the back was the architectural screen, usually a closed arcade with three panels, sometimes pierced by one or three openings. Behind it there was a space of about three feet, and several entries in the *Mémoire* call for another scene behind to give an effect of distance similar to those described by Dubreuil. For woodland

Yet in the sketches of Mahelot we also see the devices of perspective and other evidences of the realistic tendency toward a unified illusionistic design. While the mansions on the medieval stage rarely pretended to look exact or complete, these houses are more realistic. Both designer and playwright were beginning to treat the whole scene as a single complete place. Perspective, with its illusion of a unified reality, was destroying the

Fig. 61.—Mahelot's sketch of a scene with a perspective back cloth at the Hôtel de Bourgogne in the 1630's

scenes the back screen was of the same paneled type, but now the panels were made up as leafy arches or as a flat leafy wall. All these forms and conventions were derived from the medieval religious stage and from painting. At the same time, two engravings by Abraham Bosse of the *commedia dell'arte* characters at the Hôtel de Bourgogne about 1630 show that at least on some occasions the stage manager could put up a formal arcade screen very similar to the Terence façades (Figs. 62, *a*, *b*).[15]

[15] One of these has been widely reproduced (e.g., Cheney, *op. cit.*, p. 311). The other, not so well known, shows a similar formal arcade screen with side houses, and in addition footlights.

conventionality that made simultaneous staging possible.

The details of the perspective scene are frequent in the Mahelot designs. In several instances in his notes Mahelot calls the back screen a per-

It is reproduced by Gregor, *Weltgeschichte des Theaters*, p. 286. Another sketch, apparently from the same time, by François Chauveau, shows a similar formal background: a prominent center archway in an arcade screen, with galleries above the screen and formal angle wings at the sides. Cheney reproduces an inaccurate sketch made from it (*op. cit.*, p. 316), with audience and other characters added. Another illustration of a formal arcade screen at the Hôtel de Bourgogne (1686) is reproduced by Dubech, *Histoire générale illustrée du théâtre*, II, 288.

spective.[16] For a number of plays, notably for *Pandoste*, for *Cintie*, and for *Cornélie*, he displaced the back screen by a cloth painted as a complete perspective scene of an open street vanishing into great distance. The houses painted on the back cloth continue the vanishing lines of the front houses as exactly as in any scene in Italy (Fig. 61).[17] The side houses, as well as the back screen, were influenced by the principles of perspective, even when each represented a different locality. They are set at a regular perspective rake, making the scene narrower at the back than at the front. The tops of the houses are given quite definite slanting lines; and, on the sides, the cornices, windows, and doors have lines that slant toward some vague central vanishing-point. The downstage houses are larger than those upstage, and the lines from one house are often carried on by corresponding lines in the next. When an arcade screen closes the back, it is often smaller than the last side house, to continue the vanishing effect.

It seems to me probable that the floor was sloped, although no direct evidence is known. The sketches are inconclusive but make a sloping stage seem likely. The perspective faces of houses are drawn with sharply vanishing lines at both top and bottom. Lancaster finds that a contemporary stage of Paris of about the same dimensions, the stage of Fontenay le Comte, had a slope.[18] A sloping stage was used for the *ballets* by 1619. The sky, which filled out the picture above, would doubtless have been slanted to match the houses, which were shorter upstage, but not slanted so much as to prevent the use of cloud machines—a chariot and a Glory—directly above the back screen.

The entries in the latter part of Mahelot's notes show more frequently than those at the beginning the tendency to think of the whole stage as a unified scene. While the early notes list the separate houses in order, a number of later ones begin by mentioning the type of the entire scene; for instance, one is mentioned as a perspective

scene, with a frieze, pilasters, and a balustrade, and streets and houses so free that one can enter and leave easily.[19] The new authors as well as the designer were beginning to imagine the whole stage as one scene. The play that was located in a place known to the audience encouraged more realistic, unified scenery. The shops of a well-known fair, the banks of the Seine, the Place Royale, and the fortress of Marcilly[20]—these real places demanded the perspective convention of a unified setting. The early perspective stage of Italy had abounded in real scenes—Florence, Rome, Ferrara, Mantua.

At the same time two new literary types—the pastoral and the neoclassic comedy—made the playwright and the designer think more in terms of the unified scene. The different leafy houses of the pastoral easily blended together to give an effect of unity. In this decade of the 1630's Mairet and his followers were very successful with pastorals, imitated from the Italian, in which the unities were strictly observed. Rotrou's *Les Ménechmes*, a play from Plautus, brought to the French stage the unity of Latin comedy. The entries in Mahelot show that the designer thought of the scenes in this play as unified. The entries for pastorals usually begin, "Il faut que le théâtre soit en pastorale"; and the entry for *Les Ménechmes* begins, "Il faut le théâtre en rues et maisons." All this is but a part of the tendency to greater realism which Lancaster finds in every aspect of literature in the period.[21]

At a time when the court *ballets* were using the new unified perspective scenes, it must have been confusing for theatre patrons on one day to see a completely unified street or pastoral scene and then on the next to be carried back to the convention of five different mansions representing five different places, especially when those mansions were united by the same perspective lines. It is no wonder that people of taste protested, that they condemned the new authors who, like Corneille, wrote under such conditions. It has not usually been recognized that they were fighting

[16] *Le Mémoire de Mahelot*, pp. 90, 100, 102.

[17] *Ibid.*, pp. 72 and 74 f.

[18] *History of French Dramatic Literature in the Seventeenth Century*, Part I, p. 714.

[19] *Le Mémoire de Mahelot*, p. 98.

[20] *Ibid.*, pp. 100, 94, 99, 81.   [21] *Op. cit.*, p. 383.

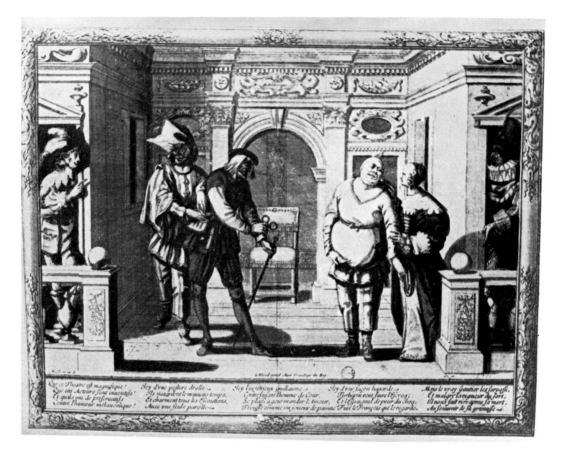

Fig. 62.—Engravings by Abraham Bosse of a formal arcade and side wings at the Hôtel de Bourgogne in the 1630's

not a system of changing settings, such as we have today, but a mixture of medieval staging and perspective that brought only confusion.

III. THE CONTROVERSY OVER UNITY OF PLACE AND THE FRENCH SOLUTIONS

The impatience felt by the classicists at simultaneous staging came out in the stream of critical pamphlets that started with the *Cid* controversy of 1637. Two documents in particular, which are closely related to stage practice of the 1630's, show us how the confused conventions were regarded and what solutions were offered. The well-known strictures of Georges de Scudéry on *Le Cid*, as Holsboer points out, were not directed at the practice of changing the setting so much as at the fact that when all the places were shown at the same time the spectator could not tell where the actor was supposed to be. Scudéry wrote: "The theatre is in this play so badly understood that when there is represented in one place, almost without making any change in the setting, the apartment of the King, that of the Infanta, the house of Chimène, and the street, the spectator most of the time does not know where the actors are."[22] Scudéry objected to the presence of the other mansions in a scene that was supposed to be one particular place, which implies that he might have accepted a solution that involved no such overlapping of different places.

D'Aubignac's *La Pratique du théâtre*, perhaps the most comprehensive and important discussion of dramaturgy and theatre practice of the period, shows us the reasoned attitude of a classicist who was thoroughly familiar with the theatre of his time. This work was published in 1657, but most of the plays the author refers to had appeared between 1630 and 1645, that is, during the years before perspective scenery had driven out the conventions of simultaneous setting.

D'Aubignac was strong in his condemnation of the scenery of the earlier period, when widely separated places could be represented by the actors' walking from one part of the stage to

another or by a slight change of the setting, as by removing a curtain from over a compartment. He wrote: "The corruption and the ignorance of the last century carried disorder in the theatre to such a point that actors appeared in diverse parts of the world, and to pass from France to Denmark you needed only three strokes of a fiddle stick, or to draw a curtain."[23]

But D'Aubignac indicates elsewhere that he would accept the turntable change of scenery that French street theatres had used since the fifteenth century. If the scenes representing France and Denmark were shown in succession so that one would not be seen while the other was used, then there would be no confusion. Of course, some critics went so far as to oppose any change of place, even if there was a complete change of illusionistic scenery.

Strong as was the impulse toward unity, it was not to dominate the theatre completely. The practice of showing a number of places on the stage was of long standing and continued to have great appeal for the audience. Only a few authors were willing to limit a play to a single small scene for a whole performance. The critics were willing to accept compromises, and the notes for the 1670's and 1680's made by Laurent and other successors of Mahelot prove that compromises were often used.

Out of the confusion of simultaneous and perspective forms, four different solutions were offered to permit the representation of more than one restricted place. The first—the least important for the public theatres—was our modern *décor successif*, by which the entire scene is changed and the entire acting area is supposed to be changed with the scenery. Early French street theatres, as we have seen,[24] used such a complete change, sometimes by means of the turning device of which D'Aubignac approved. The method was used in the *intermedii* and musical spectacles of Italy from the early sixteenth century on. It appeared in the *ballet* in 1610 and became regular

[22] Holsboer, *op. cit.*, p. 79.

[23] *La Pratique du théâtre*, p. 99.

[24] Notably at Rouen in the late fifteenth century (cf. chap. ii).

in the big operatic productions of the 1640's and 1650's.[25] The *Mémoire* of Laurent shows that it was used occasionally in the professional play-houses in the last quarter of the century.[26] As in Italy, however, regular comedy and tragedy in France made little use of the method that was to become the most important arrangement in later centuries.

The second solution was the Italian street scene of foreshortened space. By means of the effect of illusionistic perspective lines, a number of houses in a space much larger than the actual size of the stage could be represented without loss of unity. This solution received further impetus from the current interest in the representation of recognizable places. Corneille discovered the advantages of the public square surrounded by many houses in writing *La Place Royale*, performed in 1635. In the *Examen* of the play he defended the convention of having people speak in a public place what they would naturally speak only in private.[27] D'Aubignac recommended this solution and spoke of the unified perspective scene in almost exactly the same terms that the Italians used, saying that the space should be conceived as within the distance at which a man could be recognized.[28] The commentary on Terence written early in the eighteenth century by Gilles Ménage shows that this solution was accepted by the classicists. He would accept places much larger than the size of the stage, even a whole quarter of a city, if it was made to look like one place by perspective lines.[29]

The third solution retained the multiple scenes of the medieval stage but prevented the overlapping of space and confusion of locality by a row of formal frames—that is, by the arcade façade already developed in so many places in Europe. Although La Mesnardière in *La Poëtique*

(1639) recommended this solution of the confusion of conventions in the Paris theatres,[30] there is no indication that it was tried at the time. The notes of Laurent, however, give evidence that in the last quarter of the century some occasional use was made of a double stage, to show at the same time two different rooms.[31] But this multiple stage by the time of Laurent was subservient to the conventions of the *ferme*, and it is that we must consider next.

The fourth method—the device of the *ferme*—represents the major compromise made between the three-dimensional Italian perspective scene and the surviving conventions of the Middle Ages, a compromise which in both France and England permitted a change of scene that was acceptable to the strictest advocates of unity of place. By this device a shutter or drop, painted usually as some exterior, was used rather far downstage. When the scene it located was over, sometimes while the characters were still on the stage, the *ferme* would open and "discover" another scene. By the convention the characters were then in the place represented by the new scene. Hence the space used by the actors in front could not be said to have changed locality when the *ferme* disappeared to expose a different scene and a different floor area behind. This was a modified arrangement of the multiple stage, with one area upstage of the other and completely concealed when the downstage area was used. As the inner scene was usually the interior of the building represented on the *ferme*, the two scenes had a space relationship that approached that of the actuality they represented. Of course, the device was also used for places not so closely related as interior and exterior.

D'Aubignac heartily approved of this change back of the actors, comparing it to the ancient *proscenium* or forestage. Any change at the back would be a

decoration, in which the variety always ravishes the onlookers, even those quite accustomed to it, when it is brought off well. Thus we have seen a view of the façade of a temple

[25] Prunières, *op. cit.*, pp. 147 f.; Holsboer, *op. cit.*, pp. 152 f.

[26] Laurent called for complete changes of scene for *Le Menteure* (p. 110), *Le Conte d'Essex* (pp. 114 f.), *Jodelet* (p. 115), *Miriane* (p. 116), *Crispin musicien* (p. 117), and *Le Festin de piere* (pp. 124 f.).

[27] Holsboer, *op. cit.*, p. 126; Lancaster, *op. cit.*, Part I, p. 539.

[28] *Op. cit.*, pp. 103 and 107.

[29] Holsboer, *op. cit.*, p. 72.

[30] *Ibid.*, p. 71.

[31] *Le Mémoire de Mahelot*, pp. 133 f.

adorned with beautiful architecture, and then when it opens, we have discovered an order of columns in perspective, an altar, etc., so that we cannot say the place changes, but that it undergoes a beautiful decoration.[32]

I describe this use of the *ferme* as a compromise between the modern and the medieval because it was an application to the entire scene of a two-dimensional device which on the medieval stage was used for only a single mansion. Many medieval pictures show curtains over parts of the structures of the houses; and a number of medieval plays call for curtains that will disclose another scene, especially an interior.[33] The Hôtel de Bourgogne, according to the entries of Mahelot, brought this medieval practice down into the seventeenth century. In many plays a compartment was covered with a painted curtain, which in the course of the play was drawn away to show the compartment itself as a different place.[34] Of course, the device persisted into the Renaissance in other theatres of Europe. It gave the form and convention to the "arras" and the "study" in England and to the curtained compartments of the Terence and Jesuit stages. The Italian perspective scene used it in the form of back shutter and inner stage; but, as we have seen, that shutter was small and far back and did not occupy the prominent position downstage that the *ferme* did in France. The French form was more logical because it permitted a change of all, or almost all, the picture within the proscenium frame, while a change at the shutters could not alter or mask the side wings of the main perspective scene. It was the flat compromise form used in the French theatre that passed the device on to the following centuries. The later entries in the *Mémoire* prove that the convention was well established in the last quarter of the seventeenth century. A typical entry reads thus: "The scene is of houses, a room

[made ready] at the back. A *ferme* opens to allow the room to be seen."[35]

Here again we must compare this form and shaping of the stage with the account of Dubreuil. The stage he was concerned with gave prominence to a painted perspective scene at the back of a very narrow stage. Sometimes he placed that scene behind a proscenium with no side houses and sometimes behind a single set of side houses.[36] The wings seem as primitive as those in some of the Italian scenes about 1510. Some of the later entries in the *Mémoire* indicate that a similar arrangement of houses and the *ferme* quite far downstage continued into the 1680's. The entry for *L'Amante amant* reads: "The scene is two houses on the sides close to the *ferme* with their door and window. The *ferme* opens at the fourth act and there appears a room where there is a door."[37] We see that both the practice and the theory of the French theatre gave authority for a flat stage and a very prominent flat perspective cloth or shutter.

Thus in France, in a peculiarly French way, the Baroque scene emphasized flat, two-dimensional forms. We have seen how in Italy, at the time the stage was being made very deep and the back shutter was being pushed farther and farther back, the solid wing was abandoned for the flat wing. Where the Italian scene emphasized long rows of wings, the French stage emphasized the *ferme*. In both countries this interest in painted, rather than structural, effects emphasizes the tendency of the Baroque artist, pointed out by Wölfflin, to substitute soft, insubstantial, painted effects of aerial perspective for the strong three-dimensional effects of linear perspective used in the early Renaissance.

After the *ferme* was established, there was no longer need for a structural inner stage, for the *ferme* permitted discoveries of tableaux at a number of different points. Hence the French *ferme* rather than the Italian shutter was the ancestor

---

[32] *Op. cit.*, pp. 101 f.

[33] Examples from late medieval plays are collected by Stumpfl, "Die Bühnenmöglichkeiten im XVI. Jahrhundert," *Zeitschrift für deutsche Philologie*, LIV, 42–80.

[34] Lancaster, *op. cit.*, Part I, pp. 720 ff.; and Stuart, "Stage Decoration and Unity of Place in France in the Seventeenth Century," *Modern Philology*, X, 395.

[35] Direction for *Le Cocher*, 1684 (*Le Mémoire de Mahelot*, p. 142).

[36] *La Perspective pratique*, Pratiques ii, xi, xii.

[37] *Le Mémoire de Mahelot*, p. 134.

of the system of wing and shutters or wing and drop that dominated the repertory theatres of the eighteenth and nineteenth centuries and persists in opera and vaudeville houses today. The performance was arranged so that a shallow scene could be played "in one" before a drop or shutters (usually an exterior) while the scenes requiring a larger number of properties were being set behind. The shutters in grooves would be opened in succession (or the drops would be lifted) as the acts called for scenes "in two" or "in three," and so on. Thus the modern stage has inherited a device from the individual mansion of the medieval stage—a device which was adapted to the entire stage at a time when perspective demanded that everything shown at one time be designed as a complete unit.

IV. COMPROMISE IN ENGLAND

It is usually supposed that in 1607, for Jonson's *Masque of Blackness*, Inigo Jones at one stroke introduced the principles of Italian perspective and reorganized the scattered medieval elements formerly used in court masques. Then in 1660 (or at least by 1663), we are told, Davenant and Killigrew adapted perspective scenery to the public stages, making some concessions, such as apron and proscenium doors, to the Elizabethan stage. But, as a matter of fact, both in court masques and on the Restoration stages, important concessions were made to native street theatres and to the nonillusionistic devices which differed from the Italian perspective system. Even the main French compromise, the *ferme*, was also included in the final Baroque English scene.

The designers of the English masques did not change over to perspective scenery in one production. In fact, it was a good many years after 1607 before any scene of perspective wings that could be called Italian was built. And through more than half of the period of production, the masques depended on forms as well known in English street theatres as they ever were in Italy. Professor Nicoll in his study of the Stuart masques has made good use of Italian methods to explain

English practice. But in doing so he has obscured the really extensive use of native devices in the early masques; and in several instances he has interpreted descriptions by considering what the Italians would have done, where it seems to me the designers more probably followed what we know was done earlier in England. The English masques used the street-theatre devices more frequently than the Italian perspective stage did; and in several instances light is thrown on the masques by reference to the traditions of the tableaux.

For instance, a number of early masques used a device by which one object was revolved on a turntable and pivot to show an entirely different one on the other side. In Jonson's *Hymenæi* of 1606 a microcosm or globe turned on an axis, and the other side was built to present the masquers in a glittering concave, a mine of metals.[38] Again in Jonson's *Masque of Beauty* of 1608, the throne of Beauty was on a turntable. These elaborate turning effects were not like the Italian *periaktoi*, which were built of flat frames of canvas and painted as houses or landscape; rather, they were built-out devices like the turning effects at the back of the French *ballets de cour* and the revolving tableaux built on the streets at Rouen and Antwerp. At Rouen in 1485 two elaborate turning trees, one with twenty-four musicians sitting on the boughs, entertained Charles VIII. In 1550 Henry II saw there a turning sphere similar to this one in *Hymenæi*. When the sphere turned, it disclosed a scene of Francis I with a family tree growing out of his breast.[39] A similar revolving device in Antwerp in 1600 presented several tiers of beautiful ladies.

Again, the arcade façade, which was the most important element in a number of masques, resembles the arcade-of-honor of the street-shows rather than the compartment arcade of Italy. The "Lararium" or seat of the household gods in Jonson's *Entertainment at Theobald's* of 1607, was an

[38] Details of the English masques are given by Nicoll, *Stuart Masques and the Renaissance Stage*, pp. 54 ff.

[39] Reproduced by Dubech, *op. cit.*, III, 105; cf. chap. ii p. 107, and bibliography.

arcade-of-honor, placing the gods in niches in a façade of columns, cornices, and friezes. An even more elaborate "House of Fame" in the *Masque of Queens* of 1609 was a two-story façade of statues of poets with their heroes. Between the columns were paintings of land battles, sea fights, triumphs, loves, sacrifices, and "all magnificent subjects of honor." At the very top, on a turntable, was a throne-of-honor for the masquers, with the figure of Fame on the opposite side. We are reminded at once of the arcade-of-honor built on the streets of London in 1501 for the entry of Prince Arthur and Catherine of Aragon. This had as a background for a tableau of Virtues a two-story arcade, the first story formed of paintings framed by pillars. Above were three seats—a heavenly throne in which sat the figure of Honor and two empty seats marked for the prince and princess (see Figs. 4, 14, 31).

The sea throne of Tethys in Daniel's *Tethys' Festival*, with four niches of attendant nymphs, even if it made use of the *periaktoi*, as Professor Nicoll supposes, presented a solid arcade tableau derived from native pageant traditions. A similar solid arcade appeared in Campion's *Lord's Masque* of 1613, with paintings of the story of Prometheus. Even to the last masques, the arcade façade remained important. *Luminalia* of 1638 had a half-oval arcade for the throne, and *Salmacida spolia* of 1640 presented its masquers in a heavenly throne above an arcade of statues of ancient heroes.

The castle, long familiar in street tableaux, served not only as a conventionalized central palace with open arches and gallery in *The Temple of Love* and *Britannia triumphans* but also as a partial proscenium of towers for *Tethys' Festival* and *The Masque of Flowers*. Here the towers and gates were similar to the tower prosceniums in Italy at the very beginning of perspective scenery.[40]

The triumphal arch, which, of course, had already been assimilated into the court theatre in Italy, appeared in England both as a proscenium

in *Somerset's Masque* and *Lovers Made Men*, and as a seat at the back of the scene for the masquers in *Prince Charles' Masque at Richmond*.

While, from 1617 on, there were numerous full perspective scenes of houses, groves, and seascapes, yet throughout the period the English masques were a mixture of Italian perspective with native pageant devices—with solid rocks that split open, with bowers and temples hung with trophies, with turning globes, with revolving bats, owls, and stars, with castles, arcade thrones, and sparkling obelisks. Of the perspective effects, the cut-outs of the French type, called "relieves," were almost as important as the Italian wings and back shutters.

The question of perspective scenery in England outside the court masques is complicated by the lack of any very definite information. Much as the English enjoyed building and seeing stage spectacles, they rarely recorded the details beyond the cost sheets. The financial accounts of the Revels office indicate that for the plays at court fairly elaborate painted settings were constructed throughout the sixteenth century. Much the same devices seem to have been used as for the street-shows and for the religious plays. A frequent pattern, which reminds us of the early Dutch romantic plays, placed two structures, as, for instance, a castle or city and a wood, on the platform at the same time. It would seem likely that some elements of the Italian perspective scene were borrowed even in the sixteenth century. Many Italian artists were brought to England and many Englishmen traveled in Italy. Barbaro, who later edited Aristotle and Vitruvius and wrote on stage perspective, had been Venetian ambassador to England in 1548.[41] Yet there is no direct evidence of perspective scenery at the English court of the sixteenth century. From other indications, such as the statement of 1573 that the duties of the Master of the Revels included "insight of perspective and architecture," Miss Campbell is convinced that many scenes were organized by perspective. She cites the frequent mention in the Revels accounts of "cities" and

---

[40] Cf. the discussions of the castle in chaps. i and ii and the castle as proscenium in chap. vii.

[41] Campbell, *Scenes and Machines on the English Stage*, p. 75.

"towns";[42] but some of these were undoubtedly castles symbolizing a whole city. Whether the street scenes were built out entirely in wings, as Miss Campbell believes, or, as seems more likely to me, were built of one or two side houses and a painted back cloth, they would go far to establish the convention that everything on the stage must be imagined within the view of a single person. Yet some plays continued to require on the stage at the same time places not closely related. The strictures of Sir Philip Sidney on the stage practice of his day take on a new meaning when we realize that perspective lines and unified scenes had probably already begun to destroy the convention of simultaneous settings but had not completely displaced them. Sidney wrote:

There is both many days, and many places, inartificially imagined. But if it be so in *Gorboduc*, how much more in all the rest? where you shall have Asia of the one side, and Afric of the other, and so many other under-kingdoms, that the player, when he cometh in, must ever begin with telling where he is, or else the tale will not be conceived.[43]

For the sixteenth-century productions at Black-friars and at Paul's, where the staging was similar to that at the Hôtel de Bourgogne, a number of plays that were influenced by the Italian introduced both the unified scene of a large public square surrounded by houses and the scene of an open forestage with small separate scenes grouped at the back. Lyly's pastoral plays, *Gallathea* and *Love's Metamorphosis*, used a completely unified setting. *Endymion* violated the unity of place, but *Sapho and Phao* used places that were not much farther apart than the perspective convention would have permitted. *Mother Bombie* required an open forestage with seven separate houses at the back. We have seen how both these compromises —the large public square and the multiple scene on the rear stage—were acceptable to seventeenth-century classicists in France.

There is an intriguing possibility that flat painted perspectives may have been used on the Elizabethan public stage. Henslowe's "City of Rome" for *Dr. Faustus* is provocative, and there is a reference to a perspective stage curtain in the

dialogue of *Cynthia's Revels:* "Slid! the boy takes me for a piece of prospective (I hold my life) or some silk curtain, come to hang the stage here: Sir Cracke I am none of your fresh pictures, that use to beautify the decayed arras, in a public theatre."[44] But the public stage was preoccupied with its own conventional symbolism and cannot have made much use of illusionistic curtains.

The Elizabethan stage did already have, of course, a convention similar to the *ferme*, even before we know of its use in France. In a number of Elizabethan plays, the scene was changed from an exterior to an interior, while actors were on the stage, merely by opening the arras of the inner stage. The convention that the apron stage was part of the interior located by the inner stage— a convention inherited from medieval painting and stage—was so well established that the space the actor occupied would suddenly, without his moving, be supposed to have changed from exterior to interior with the opening of the curtain.[45] When there was little or no illusionistic scenery, it was not so difficult to imagine this change.

But in the Restoration theatre, nonillusionistic elements—the large apron and the formal side doors—were brought over from the Elizabethan and combined with illusionistic perspective scenery placed within the proscenium behind the apron. Now the audience was asked to believe that the scene changed completely every time there was a change in the few wings and the small back shutter. The scenery was supposed to create the illusion of a unified realistic place, yet the walls and the doors of the proscenium, which surrounded most of the acting area, were not changed at all. Actors on the apron were suddenly changed from exterior to interior, and beds might be brought out as in Elizabethan times.[46]

[42] *Ibid.*, pp. 104 ff. and 107 ff.
[43] Chambers, *The Elizabethan Stage*, III, 40.

[44] *Ibid.*, p. 133, n. 2.

[45] Reynolds, "Two Conventions of the Elizabethan Stage," *Modern Philology*, XVII, 35–43, and *The Staging of Elizabethan Plays at the Red Bull Theater*, pp. 113 f.; and Bradbrook, *Themes and Conventions of Elizabethan Tragedy*, pp. 8 f.

[46] Lawrence, "Proscenium Doors: An Elizabethan Heritage," *The Elizabethan Playhouse* [First Series], pp. 157–90; and "The Persistence of Elizabethan Conventionalisms," *The Elizabethan Playhouse: Second Series*, pp. 151–88.

Under these conditions we are not surprised to find some protest at the confusion of conventions and a desire to associate the downstage scenes with those "discovered" farther upstage in some space relation that would be nearer the actual relation of the different parts of the stage floor. We see in the comment Dryden gives to Crites, his classicist in *An Essay of Dramatic Poesie*, a protest at an incomplete change of scene and a willingness to accept such an arrangement as the French *ferme*, which by convention could disclose a second place at a finite distance from the first without demanding that the apron space change also. Dryden has Crites admit that

by the variation of painted scenes, the fancy, which in these cases will contribute to its own deceit, may sometimes imagine it [the stage] several places with some appearance of probability; yet it still carries the greater likelihood of truth if those places be supposed so near each other as in the same town or city; which may all be comprehended under the larger denomination of one place.[47]

That the principle of the *ferme* or "discovery" was acceptable to the classicists in England as not violating the principle of unity is shown by the fact that Addison used it in *Cato* in 1712. The back scene opened up in the last act to show the philosopher dying in his chair.[48] But, of course, in England the classicists did not dominate the stage, and other playwrights did not hesitate to use the *décor successif*, that is, as far as a change of the wings and back shutter meant a complete change of the picture. For the apron and proscenium doors persisted into the nineteenth century, and the "return," or formal first house, has persisted to the present day—relics of the mixture of conventions in the Renaissance.

The Restoration stage had still another convention that made a compromise with the principles of illusion of the perspective scene. On some occasions painted scenery still meant to the English only a symbol placed back of the actors rather than an actual place surrounding them. In several plays the actors on the forestage were supposed in a city, while the painted prospect behind them showed a distant view as from outside the city, sometimes outside the city walls.[49] This is just the symbolic use of painting we have found in the *tableaux vivants*. Many of the Flemish tableaux had shown paintings of castles symbolizing Jerusalem or Rome (Figs. 15, 27, 40) as a background for the characters who were supposed to be inside the cities. Indeed, in 1661, for the entry of Charles II in London, several triumphal arches had been erected with just this symbolic relationship of living figure and painting. Behind the living figure of Bacchus was a painting of Silenus and dancing satyrs; behind Ceres was a painting of Harvest in a dragon-drawn chariot; behind Flora, a garden; and behind Pomona, an orchard.[50] The English public stage derived its conventions from the living traditions of art as well as from Italian perspective.

[47] Dryden, "*An Essay of Dramatic Poesie,*" in Clark, *European Theories of the Drama*, p. 178.

[48] Discussed by Lawrence, *The Elizabethan Playhouse: Second Series*, pp. 174 ff.

[49] Nicoll, *The English Theatre*, pp. 83 f.

[50] Withington, *English Pageantry*, I, 246; cf. chap. ii and bibliography.

CONCLUSION

The Pictorial Heritage of the Theatre

AND that is how our modern theatre began! Not as a new invention—its details and principles were already familiar to both architects and audience; not as a revival of the ancient theatre—it drew from the concepts and habits of its own times; not as a development of the medieval religious theatre—it required a more complex and at the same time more unified stage than had existed in the Middle Ages. But, rather, as an entirely logical development in the history of the visual arts—the realization in three dimensions of the forms and conventions of painting, sculpture, and the *tableaux vivants*.

The modern theatre grew out of the desire to see and hear with living actors the historical rulers, romantic stories, and allegorical fancies already portrayed by the painters—out of the desire to enhance the personalities and events of the present by endowing them, through a dramatic re-enactment, with the glamour of history and the approval of allegory. Paintings, tapestries, and statues were brought to life; living actors replaced portraits; and architects tried to build in three dimensions the settings and backgrounds of pictures. Not only were the problems and conventions of painting reproduced, but new problems soon appeared demanding new solutions. Instead of trying to reorganize the forms of the medieval theatre, the artist became a theatre architect and carried on in the theatre the traditions of art.

In western Europe the artist experimented with *tableaux vivants* for nearly two hundred years before there were authors and producers ready to take the next step and turn his living pictures into full plays. In Italy, where the royal entries were more purely processional, he was less interested in the little street theatres. At the beginning of the sixteenth century he found the Italian princes ready to finance the direct translation of perspective paintings into stage settings.

We have traced, as an outgrowth of these different experiments, the development of two opposite principles—illusion and symbolism—in the theatres of Flanders, England, France, Germany, Spain, and Italy. Then we have watched how the two came together in the Baroque period and caused conflict until compromises were worked out. The Baroque perspective scene, with its illusionistic picture back of a formal frame, dominated the stage of all sophisticated cities from the middle of the seventeenth century until the beginning of the twentieth. It is still important in opera and in some repertory theatres to this day.

Although we have changed many of the details in the last fifty years, yet we have kept most of the basic patterns established in the Renaissance. We have streamlined the proscenium arch, but we still have a formal frame for the picture—a heritage of the sixteenth century. We have abandoned the deep street scene of forced perspective, but we still expect to see within the proscenium a complete picture—we still carry on the pictorial heritage. For outdoor scenes we still expect to see the sky slope from the proscenium (or the valance, now called a "teaser") down toward the horizon. We have leveled the sloping floor, but we still plan the design of the setting from one eyepoint where the duke's box used to be. We still expect to see in most of our indoor settings side walls set at an angle, preserving the old floor lines of the perspective street scene, and a back wall parallel to the front. We are still fond of distant painted views seen through openings in the back wall. Experiment as we may with abstract

216

settings, with symbolic settings, with stylized settings, we still expect to see for most of our plays a complete picture—a close imitation of the real world. We are dominated by the same love of illusion that took over the theatre in the sixteenth century and gradually supplanted all other ideals. All our modern experiments have not changed the basic outlines of the Baroque stage or driven out the ideal of illusion developed in the Renaissance.

Most of our very modern experiments in methods of staging, in fact, have but gone back to various experiments which were tried in the sixteenth century. Our curtains and drapes around the stage, for instance, are used much as was the curtain stage of the Renaissance, when, as now, the curtains were pulled aside and doors, windows, and other set pieces put in the openings. In the time of Lope de Vega, complete little hills, trees, shop fronts, and towers were set in front of a neutral curtain, just as we set cut-out scenery now. The need for economy and simplicity doubtless was the reason for the use of curtain stages in the schools of the sixteenth century, as it is for their use in schools today. Our revival of processional staging—bringing on the furniture and small units of scenery before the audience—is the same borrowing from the medieval processions that the Elizabethans and others made in the Renaissance.

Our interest in symbolism as a revolt against modern realism is merely a repetition of one of the strong tendencies of the Renaissance. In England and Flanders, and occasionally in other countries, the Renaissance dramatists made use of the symbols familiar in art and the street-shows. They used the façade as an emblem and arranged in front of it, or in its openings or galleries, a number of scenes—such as throne scenes, castle scenes, seat-of-honor scenes, soliloquy scenes, or disclosed-tableau scenes—which combined the remembered symbolism of the façade with picturesque arrangement of characters and the suggestive atmosphere of banners, shields, tapestries, and other changeable trappings. The conventional shape of the façade and the atmosphere of the *tableaux vivants* gave a strong symbolic character to the Elizabethan and Flemish scenes. The two large stone towers which Robert Edmond Jones provided as a background for the various scenes of *Richard III* achieved much the same kind of symbolism in the twentieth century. Like the Elizabethan façade, these towers permitted small changes for the different scenes and yet gave the play unity by keeping one symbol for the entire play. This approach to the unit setting, so fresh today, was one of the forgotten achievements of the Renaissance.

Another modern approach to the unit setting was also developed in the Renaissance. Lee Simonson for *Marco Millions* and for *Faust* provided a neutral skeleton of columns and arches, visible all the time, to serve as a framework for the smaller inserts and inner scenes that provided the illusion and spectacle. We have seen here how all the façade theatres of the Renaissance used that same combination of formal and illusionistic elements.

We think of stylization as a new toy of the twentieth century. If we omit details in a design and reinforce or exaggerate certain characteristic qualities, we get a "streamlined" effect that especially delights us. Here also we are but retracing one of the tendencies of the sixteenth century. While medieval scenic elements, for all their symbolism, kept a close resemblance to the objects they represented, Renaissance stage architects stylized those symbols until they almost lost that resemblance. The heraldic fleur-de-lis kept the basic outline of a lily. The medieval tree might be the tree in Paradise, the Tree of Jesse, or a royal genealogical tree, but it kept the basic pattern. The ship in French *tableaux vivants*, although it had columns at the sides and a canopy above, yet showed sails, masts, and a complete rigging. But on the Flemish and Elizabethan stages stylization was carried much further. The castle almost disappeared, and only its skeleton of arch, side doors, and upper gallery remained to support the castle decorations of tapestries, banners, and shields.

The modern stylizations of Craig and Appia—

the reduction of the forms of reality to steps, screens, and pylons—correspond very closely to the stylization in all countries in the Renaissance. Architects then were striving to substitute simple sculptural space forms for the fussy detail of reality. Craig and Appia wanted a grandeur that was primitive in its austerity, while Renaissance architects strove for a grandeur that was sophisticated and elegant. Like Craig and Appia, they turned to simple columns and arches and beautiful proportions to escape the pettiness of realism and achieve nobility of soul. Even in their realistic perspective street scenes they often forgot to build actual houses and, instead, designed colonnades, triumphal arches, gables, and architraves in harmonious, noble proportions. In Flanders and England they were able to carry stylization even further and produce façades that were beautiful and simple—far simpler than the earlier symbols of reality.

The modern tendencies since the time of Craig and Appia have followed a direction that closely parallels the development from the architectural solidity of the early Renaissance to the use of much lighter structures and the dependence on scene paint in the Baroque theatres. Like the early Renaissance architects, Craig and Appia (and the early realists as well) thought of their new stage completely in terms of sculptural, heavy, three-dimensional structures. With the development of stage lighting, we are no longer so interested in the heavy pylons, steps, and arches, or the heavy constructions of the realists of forty years ago. We have discovered how to use much lighter, more conventionalized walls, screens, and cut-out pieces.[1] I have shown here how the Baroque designers substituted painted flat wings and drops for the heavy constructions of the early Renaissance—how the painter inherited the stage from the architect. We can see from the Pompeian theatrical paintings and the comments of Vitruvius how, at least once before in history, the heavy architecture of the stage had been melted into airy fancies by later painters. Apparently in

every age the new forms of the theatre are first worked out in three dimensions by stage architects, then later reinterpreted in much lighter forms. In the Baroque age the new interest which led to that change was scene painting; in the twentieth century the new medium is light. But the problem of adapting an architectural structure to new needs is much the same today as it was in the sixteenth century. While our needs, we are sure, differ considerably from those of the Renaissance, yet we want to know why that age gave the theatre the form which has come down to us.

The perspective, illusionistic setting, when given a splendid formal frame, delighted the artistic taste of the Renaissance because it reproduced a spectacular and complex unified painting. It satisfied the deep, half-conscious longings of the age by creating, with very real, mathematically spaced side wings, an illusion of infinite distance. It flattered the social aspirations of the age by focusing the whole stage design on the duke's box in the center of the auditorium and setting opposite that box the throne scenes of all the glorious kings of history and chariot scenes of the kings of the sky. The new setting designed by this ideal of realism did not limit the dramatist to one place, for it could be quickly changed and a second, third, or tenth complete scene shown in its place. Both the Renaissance and the Baroque age found in the perspective wings very gorgeous tangible palaces, which yet led by undeviating mathematical progression to the infinite. Sometimes better even than such a palace as Versailles, the perspective setting could achieve a combination of sensual actuality, kingly glory, and divine magnitude.

We may be helped in our modern problem of increasing the symbolic—the atmospheric—power of our emblems of reality, if we understand that this perspective setting, which in the nineteenth century was a worn-out convention of illusion, had in its inception many of the elements of symbolism. Throughout the Renaissance, throne scenes were almost as frequent on the perspective stage as in Elizabethan drama and

[1] See my article "Farewell to Scene Architecture," *Quarterly Journal of Speech*, XXV, 649–57.

were frankly arranged as shows right in the middle of an outdoor setting. Castle towers remained popular as wings and were only occasionally made realistic as part of actual fortifications. Most striking of all mixtures of symbols, the city scene was often represented on the perspective stage as symbolically as in the *tableaux vivants* or on the Elizabethan stage. Even late in the seventeenth century the setting might show a city in the distance, or the outside walls, yet serve as a background for characters supposed to be in that city. Even in the perspective theatre the ideal of illusion had to share the scene with the ideal of symbolism.

In front of and behind the perspective stage the different framing elements had both the structural patterns of the symbolic stages and some of the meaning and atmosphere. At the back of a number of perspective settings was a formal façade very similar to those built in Flanders and England. The center opening might frame a throne or an inner stage. Above might be a gallery for onlookers or musicians, or a complete upper-stage scene directly over the inner stage. At the sides were often formal archways with glimpses of distant exteriors. On this façade might be statues, columns, painted pictures, cloth hangings, and even a projecting pavilion. The Italian stage, as some designers arranged it, had much in common with the Elizabethan.

At the front of the perspective setting, the proscenium followed the same patterns as the architectural façades. Like them, it was decorated with cloth hangings, banners, shields, statues, allegorical figures, and cartouches for printed names and mottoes.

Clearly, Renaissance architects did not invent theatre forms and theatre conventions to suit themselves or the poets. They played variations on a few basic patterns that had already been worked out in medieval and early Renaissance painting and sculpture. In Italy they arranged the characters and the side wings according to the pictorial patterns that Florentine painters had developed. In the school theatres they thought they were reviving the forms of ancient Greece and Rome, but unconsciously they followed the concepts of space of their own day. In Flanders and England they adapted the conventionalized façades of the *tableaux vivants* and used the symbolism and conventions of the street theatres. In all cases the pictorial traditions were so strong that, much as the dramatists might try to visualize their events as actual life or history, yet in scene after scene they fell into the patterns already familiar in the visual arts. We can learn much about the meaning of their drama, and much about the beginnings of the modern stage, by tracing the influence of the other pictorial arts on the Renaissance theatres.

The Renaissance stage architect faced much the same problem that the designer faces today. He had to take the traditional visual patterns of his age and shape them into stages that would serve at the same time both as a symbol of reality and as an invocation to a world of glamour, nobility, and allegorical significance. He found his patterns in painting, sculpture, and the *tableaux vivants*, and out of those patterns he established the complex forms and conventions of the modern stage.

BIBLIOGRAPHY*

CHAPTER I. THE BEGINNINGS OF SCENIC BACKGROUND

Part I is a full bibliography of all works that have come to my attention which deal with the interrelationship of the theatre and painting or sculpture before 1600. Fischel is almost the only one to deal with the Renaissance. Most are concerned with the influence of the theatre on painters. Mâle has received the widest attention. Van Puyvelde makes important corrections to Mâle, and two recent studies, by Miss Galante-Garrone and Miss Shull, have traced the influence of art traditions on the medieval religious theatres in Italy and in England.

See Part II for the works consulted for the art backgrounds for chapter i.

I. Art and Theatre

Aurigemma, S. "Mosaico con scene d'anfiteatro in una villa romana a Zliten in Tripolitania," *Dedalo*, IV (1923–24), 333–61 and 397–414; V (1924), 197–217.

Bergmans, P. "Note sur la représentation du retable de l'agneau mystique des van Eyck en tableau vivant à Gand en 1458," *Annales de la Fédération Archéologique et Historique de Belgique*, XX (1907), 530.

Bonnell, John K. "The Easter *Sepulchrum* in Its Relation to the Architecture of the High Altar," *Publications of the Modern Language Association*, XXXI (1916), 664–712.

Borcherdt, Hans Heinrich. *Das europäische Theater im Mittelalter und in der Renaissance*. Leipzig, 1935.

———. "Theater und bildende Kunst im Wandel der Zeiten," *Euphorion*, XXXII, 184.

Bréhier, Louis. *L'Art chrétien: son développement iconographique des origines à nos jours*. Paris, 1928.

———. "Les Miniatures des homélies du Moine Jacques et le théâtre religieux à Byzance," in Académie des Inscriptions et Belles-Lettres (Fondation Piot), *Monuments et mémoires*, XXIV (1920), 101.

Brieger, Peter. "The Baroque Equation: Illusion and Reality." Lecture given at the Metropolitan Museum of Art, January 27, 1943, for a symposium on drama and the other arts.

Brooks, Neil C. *The Sepulchre of Christ in Art and Liturgy, with Special Reference to the Liturgical Drama*. ("University of Illinois Studies in Language and Literature," Vol. VII, No. 2.) Urbana, 1921.

Bulle, Heinrich. *Untersuchungen an griechischen Theatern*. ("Abhandlungen der Bayerischen Akademie der Wissenschaften, philosophisch-, philologisch-, und historische Klasse," Vol. XXXIII.) Munich, 1928.

Clément, F. "Liturgie, musique et drame du moyen âge," *Annales archéologiques* (ed. Didron), VII (Paris, 1847), 303 f.; VIII (1848), 77 f., 304 f.

* Arranged by chapters and special subjects.

Cohen, Gustave. *Histoire de la mise en scène dans le théâtre religieux français du moyen âge*. Brussels, 1906; rev. ed., Paris, 1926.

———. "The Influence of the Theater on Mediaeval Art." Lecture given at the Metropolitan Museum of Art, January 26, 1943, for a symposium on drama and the other arts.

Cube, G. von. *Die römische 'Scenae frons' in den pompejanischen Wandbildern 4. Stils*. ("Beiträge zur Bauwissenschaft," No. 6.) Berlin, 1906.

Durand, Julien. "Monuments figurés du moyen âge exécutés d'après des textes liturgiques," *Bulletin monumental*, 1888, pp. 521 ff.

Escher, K. "Die Engel am französischen Grabmal des Mittelalters und ihre Beziehungen zur Liturgie," *Repertorium für Kunstwissenschaft*, XXXV (1912), 97–119.

Fischel, Oskar. "Art and the Theatre," *Burlington Magazine*, LXVI (1935), 4–14, 54–67.

Franck, K. "Über geistliche Schauspiele als Quellen kirchlicher Kunst," *Christliches Kunstblatt*, 1899.

Friend, A. M., Jr. "The Portraits of the Evangelists in Greek and Latin Manuscripts," *Art Studies*, V (1927), 115–47; VII (1929), 3–32.

Galante-Garrone, Virginia. *L'Apparato scenico del dramma sacro in Italia*. Turin, 1935.

Guthmann, J. *Die Landschaftsmalerei der toskanischen und umbrischen Kunst von Giotto bis Raphael*. Leipzig, 1902.

Hewitt, Barnard Wolcott. "The Theatre and the Graphic Arts." Dissertation, Cornell University, 1934.

Holl, Karl. "Die Entstehung der Bilderwand in der griechischen Kirche," *Archiv für Religionswissenschaft*, IX (1906), 365–84.

Köster, Albert. "Das Bild an der Wand: Eine Untersuchung über das Wechselverhältnis zwischen Bühne und Drama," *Abhandlungen der königlichen Akademie der Wissenschaft, philosophisch-historische Abteilung*, XXVII, 267–302.

Kraus, Franz X. *Geschichte der christlichen Kunst*. Freiburg im Breisgau, 1896–1908.

Krueger, F. M. *Über das Verhältnis von Bühne und bildender Kunst*. 1911.

Künstle, Karl. *Ikonographie der christlichen Kunst*, Vol. I. Freiburg, 1928.

La Piana, George. "The Byzantine Theatre," *Speculum*, XI (1936), 171–211.

Little, A. M. G. "Scaenographia: The Ancient Stage and Painting," *Art Bulletin*, XVIII (September, 1936), 407–18.

Lynch, William F., S.J. "Ecclesiastical Art and the Early Liturgical Theater—Kinship with the Greek." Lecture given at the Metropolitan Museum of Art, January 26, 1943, for a symposium on drama and the other arts.

M. "Mysterien Bühne und bildende Kunst," *Kunstchronik*, Vol. XV, No. 4 (new ser., 1903).

MAETERLINCK, LOUIS. "L'Art et les mystères en Flandre, à propos de deux peintures du Musée de Gand," *Revue de l'art ancien et moderne*, XIX (April, 1906), 308–18.

———. "L'Art et les rhétoriciens flamands," *Bulletin du bibliophile et du bibliothécaire*, April, 1906.

———. *Le Genre satirique, fantastique, et licencieux dans la sculpture flamande et wallonne*. Paris, 1910.

———. *Le Genre satirique dans la peinture flamande*. ("Mémoires couronnés et autres mémoires publiés par l'Académie Royale de Belgique.") Brussels, 1903.

———. "Nos peintres rhétoriciens au XVe et XVIe siècle," *L'Art moderne*, August 5 and 26, 1906.

———. "A propos d'une œuvre de Bosch au Musée de Gand," *Revue de l'art ancien et moderne*, XX (October, 1906), 299–307.

MÂLE, ÉMILE. *L'Art religieux du XIIIe siècle en France*. Paris, 1902.

———. *L'Art religieux de la fin du moyen âge en France: étude sur l'iconographie du moyen âge et sur ses sources d'inspiration*. Paris, 1908.

———. "La Cène et les 'mystères,'" *Gazette des beaux-arts*, 1906, pp. 290 f.

———. "Le Drame liturgique et l'iconographie de la Résurrection," *Revue de l'art ancien et moderne*, XXXIX (1921), 213–22.

———. "Les Influences du drame liturgique sur la sculpture romane," *ibid.*, XXII (August, 1907), 81–92.

———. "Une Influence des 'mystères' sur l'art italien du XVe siècle," *Gazette des beaux-arts*, 1906, pp. 89 f.

———. "Le Renouvellement de l'art par les 'mystères' à la fin du moyen âge," *ibid.*, XXXI (1904), 89–106, 215–30, 283–301, 379–94.

———. "Les Rois mages et le drame liturgique," *ibid.*, 1910, pp. 261 f.

MESNIL, JACQUES. "De Mysteriespelen en de plastike Kunsten," *Onze Kunst*, Vols. IX and X. Republished in his *L'Art au nord et au sud des Alpes à l'époque de la renaissance*. Brussels and Paris, 1911.

MEYER, KARL. "Geistliches Schauspiel und kirchliche Kunst," *Geigers Vierteljahrsschrift für Kultur und Literatur der Renaissance*, I (Leipzig, 1886), 162, 356, 409.

MONE, F. J. *Schauspiele des Mittelalters*. 2 vols. Karlsruhe, 1846.

MOREY, C. R. *Roman and Christian Sculpture*, Part I: *The Sarcophagus of Claudia Antonia Sabina and the Asiatic Sarcophagi*. ("Sardis Publications," Vol. V, Part I.) Princeton, 1924.

PANTZER, F. "Dichtung und bildende Kunst des deutschen Mittelalters in ihren Wechselbeziehungen," *Neue Jahrbücher für das klassische Altertum*, VII (1904), 2.

PUYVELDE, LEO VAN. *Schilderkunst en Tooneelvertooningen op het Einde van de Middeleeuwen: Een Bijdrage tot de Kunstgeschiedenis vooral van de Nederlanden*. Ghent: Koninklijke Vlaamsche Academie voor Taal- en Letterkunde, 1912.

RÉAU, LOUIS. *L'Art du moyen âge*. Paris, 1935.

ROHDE, ALFRED. "Das geistliche Schauspiel des Mittelalters und das gemalte Bild bei Meister Bertram von Minden," *Monatshefte für Kunstwissenschaft*, XV (1922), 173 ff.

———. *Passionsbild und Passionsbühne: Wechselbeziehungen zwischen Malerei und Dichtung im ausgehenden deutschen Mittelalter*. Berlin, [1926].

ROTHES, WALTHER. *Christus des Heilands Leben, Leiden, Sterben und Verherrlichung in der bildenden Kunst aller Jahrhunderte*. Cologne, 1910.

SCHUBRING, PAUL. *Cassoni: Truhen und Truhenbilder der italienischen Frührenaissance* (Leipzig, 1923), I, 46 ff.

SÉCHAN, LOUIS. *Etudes sur la tragédie grecque dans ses rapports avec la céramique*. Paris, 1926.

SEPET, MARIUS. *Les Prophètes du Christ*. Paris: Bibliothèque de l'Ecole des Chartes, 1867, 1868, 1877.

SHULL, VIRGINIA MOORE. "The Stagecraft of the Mediaeval English Drama." Dissertation, Yale University, 1941.

SIMONSON, LEE. *The Stage Is Set*. New York, 1932.

STRZYGOWSKI, JOSEF. "A Sarcophagus of the Sidamara Type in the Collection of Sir Frederick Cook, Bart., and the Influence of the Stage Architecture upon the Art of Antioch," *Journal of Hellenic Studies*, XXVII (London, 1907), 99–122.

TEGENGREN, HELMER. "Bildkonst och Drama: En Wecksellstudie," *Acta Academiae Aboensis, Humaniora*, Vol. XII, No. 2 (Abo, 1939).

TINTELNOT, HANS. *Barocktheater und barocke Kunst: Die Entwicklungsgeschichte der Fest- und Theaterdekoration in ihrem Verhältnis zur barocken Kunst*. Berlin, 1939.

TSCHEUSCHNER, K. "Die deutsche Passionsbühne und die deutsche Malerei des XV. und XVI. Jahrhunderts in ihren Wechselbeziehungen," *Repertorium für Kunstwissenschaft*, XXVII, 289–307, 430–49, 491–510; XXVIII, 35–58.

WEBER, PAUL. *Geistliches Schauspiel und kirchliche Kunst in ihrem Verhältnis erläutert an einer Ikonographie der Kirche und Synagoge*. Stuttgart, 1894.

WEIGELT, CURT H. *Sienese Painting of the Trecento*. New York, n.d.

II. OTHER WORKS CONSULTED FOR CHAPTER I

ADAMA VAN SCHELTEMA, FREDERIK. *Die altnordische Kunst: Grundprobleme vorhistorischer Kunstentwicklung*. Berlin, 1923.

ALBERTI, LEONE BATTISTA. *Della pittura libri tre*. Trans. and ed. HUBERT JANITSCHEK: *Leone Battista Alberti's kleinere kunsttheoretische Schriften*. ("Quellenschriften für Kunstgeschichte und Kunsttechnik des Mittelalters und der Renaissance," No. 11.) Vienna, 1877.

AMES, A., JR. "Depth in Pictorial Art," *Art Bulletin*, VIII (1925), 5–24.

ANCONA, ALESSANDRO D'. *Origini del teatro italiano*. 2 vols. 2d ed. Turin, 1891.

BARNES, ALBERT C., and MAZIA, VIOLETTE DE. *The French Primitives and Their Forms*. Merion, Pa., 1931.

BERENSON, BERNHARD. *Essays in the Study of Sienese Painting*. New York, 1918.

———. *Studies in Medieval Painting*. New Haven, 1930.

BERLIN, STAATLICHE MUSEEN. *Altertümer von Pergamon*. 1885———.

BERSTL, HANS. *Das Raumproblem in der altchristlichen Malerei*. ("Forschungen zur Formgeschichte der Kunst aller Zeiten und Völker: Forschungen zur Kunstgeschichte Westeuropas," Vol. IV.) Bonn, 1920.

BIEBER, MARGARETE. *Die Denkmäler zum Theaterwesen im Al-tertum.* Berlin and Leipzig, 1920.

———. *The History of the Greek and Roman Theater.* Princeton, 1939.

BOINET, AMÉDÉE. *La Miniature carolingienne.* Paris, 1913.

BORENIUS, TANCRED, and TRISTRAM, E. W. *English Medieval Painting.* Florence and Paris, 1927.

BUNIM, MIRIAM SCHILD. *Space in Medieval Painting and the Forerunners of Perspective.* New York, 1940.

CLARK, KENNETH. "Architectural Backgrounds in Renaissance Pictures," *Journal of the Royal Institute of British Architects,* XLI (1934), 325 ff.

COHEN, GUSTAVE. *Le Théâtre en France au moyen âge,* Vol. I: *Le Théâtre religieux.* Paris, 1928.

COLONNA, FRANCESCO. *Hypnerotomachia Poliphili.* Venice, 1499.

———. *Hypnerotomachie, ou discours du songe de Poliphile.* Paris, 1546.

CROWE, JOSEPH ARCHER, and CAVALCASELLE, G. B. *The Early Flemish Painters.* London, 1857; 2d ed., 1872.

CURTIUS, LUDWIG. *Die Wandmalerei Pompejis.* Leipzig, 1929.

DEIMLING, HERMANN, and MATTHEWS (eds.). *The Chester Plays.* 2 vols. London: Early English Text Society, 1893–1916.

DELBRÜCK, RICHARD. *Beiträge zur Kenntnis der Linienperspek-tive in der griechischen Kunst.* Dissertation. Bonn, 1899.

DESTRÉE, JULES. *Roger de la Pasture van der Weyden.* 2 vols. Paris and Brussels, 1930.

DOEHLEMANN, KARL. "Die Entwicklung der Perspektive in der altniederländischen Kunst," *Repertorium für Kunst-wissenschaft,* XXXIV (1911), 392–422; 500–535.

———. "Nochmals die Perspektive bei den Brüdern van Eyck," *ibid.,* XXXV (1912), 262–67.

———. "Die Perspektive der Brüder van Eyck," *Zeitschrift für Mathematik und Physik,* Vol. LII, No. 4 (1905).

———. "Die Verwertung der Linearperspektive zur Datie-rung von Bildern," *Die graphischen Künste,* XXIX, No. 4 (Vienna, 1906), [Suppl.]: *Mitteilungen der Gesellschaft für vervielfältigende Kunst,* pp. 10–13.

DOUGLAS, ROBERT LANGTON. *Fra Angelico.* 2d ed. London, 1902.

DURRIEU, COMTE PAUL. *La Miniature flamande au temps de la cour de Bourgogne (1415–1530).* Brussels and Paris, 1921.

DVORAK, MAX. *Kunstgeschichte als Geistesgeschichte.* Munich, 1924.

EBERSOLT, JEAN. *La Miniature byzantine.* Paris and Brussels, 1926.

EDGELL, GEORGE HAROLD. "The Development of the Archi-tectural Background in the Painting of the Umbrian Renaissance." Dissertation, Harvard University, 1913.

Evangiles avec peintures byzantines du XIe siècle. MS grec 74, Bibliothèque Nationale. Paris, n.d.

EVANS, JOAN. *Pattern: A Study of Ornament in Western Europe, 1180–1900.* 2 vols. Oxford, 1931.

EVEN, EDWARD VAN. *L'Omgang de Louvain.* Louvain and Brussels, 1863.

FASOLO, VINCENZO. "L'Architettura nelle pitture del rinas-cimento," *L'Architettura,* VIII (1928–29), 193 ff. and 241 ff.

FERRARI, GIULIO. *La Tomba nell'arte italiana dal periodo pre-romano all'odierno.* Milan, 1919.

FLICKINGER, R. S. *The Greek Theater and Its Drama.* Chicago, 1926.

FOCILLON, HENRI. *L'Art des sculteurs romans: recherches sur l'histoire des formes.* Paris, 1931.

FRANCESCA, PIERO DELLA. *De prospectiva pingendi.* Strassburg, 1899. From MS in the Biblioteca Palatina, Parma.

FREY, DAGOBERT. *Gotik und Renaissance als Grundlagen der modernen Weltanschauung.* Augsburg, 1929.

FRIEDLÄNDER, MAX J. *Die altniederländische Malerei.* 14 vols. Berlin, 1924–37.

FURTTENBACH, JOSEPH. *Mannhaffter Kunstspiegel.* Augsburg, 1663.

GOLDSCHMIDT, ADOLPH. *Die Elfenbeinskulpturen aus der roman-ischen Zeit, XI.–XIII. Jahrhundert.* 2 vols. Berlin, 1926.

———. *Die Elfenbeinskulpturen aus der Zeit der karolingischen und sächsischen Kaiser, VIII.–XI. Jahrhundert.* 2 vols. Berlin, 1914 and 1918.

———. *German Illumination.* 2 vols. Florence, Paris, and New York, 1928.

GREGOR, JOSEPH. *Weltgeschichte des Theaters.* Zürich, 1933.

GRISEBACH, A. "Architekturen auf niederländischen und französischen Gemälden des XV. Jahrhunderts: Ein Bei-trag zur Entwicklung der Formensprache der nordischen Renaissance," *Monatshefte für Kunstwissenschaft,* V (1912), 207–15, 254–72.

GRÜNEISEN, W. D. "La Perspective: esquisse de son évolu-tion des origines (1. la perspective dans l'art archaïque oriental et dans l'art du moyen âge)," *Mélanges de l'Ecole de Rome,* 1911.

HABICHT, VICTOR CURT. *Niedersächsische Kunst in England.* Hanover, 1930.

HAIGH, A. E. *The Attic Theatre.* 3d ed. Oxford, 1907.

HARTEL, WILHELM RITTER VON, and WICKHOFF, FRANZ. *Die Wiener Genesis.* Vienna, 1895.

HAUCK, GUIDO. "Die malerische Perspektive," *Wochenblatt für Architekten und Ingenieure,* Vol. IV (1882).

———. *Die subjektive Perspektive und die horizontalen Curvaturen des dorischen Styls.* Stuttgart, 1879.

HINKS, ROGER. *Carolingian Art: A Study of Early Medieval Painting and Sculpture in Western Europe.* London, 1935.

HORB, FELIX. *Das Innenraumbild des späten Mittelalters.* Zürich, 1938.

HORST, CARL. *Die Architektur der Renaissance in den Niederlanden und ihre Ausstrahlungen,* Part I: *Architektur in der Malerei und Innenarchitektur.* The Hague, 1930.

HÜGEL, J. *Entwicklung und Ausbildung der Perspektive in der klassischen Malerei.* Dissertation. Würzburg, 1881.

IMAGE, SELWYN. "Architecture in Painting," *Architectural Association Journal,* XXVI (London, 1911), 112–21.

IVINS, WILLIAM M. *On the Rationalization of Sight, with an Examination of Three Renaissance Texts on Perspective.* ("Metropolitan Museum of Art Papers," No. 8.) New York, 1938.

JAENSCH, E. R. "Über die Wahrnehmung des Raumes," *Zeitschrift für Psychologie,* Suppl. Vol. VI (1911).

JANTZEN, HANS. *Das niederländische Architekturbild.* Leipzig, 1910.

JONES, LESLIE WEBBER, and MOREY, C. R. *The Miniatures*

of the Manuscripts of Terence Prior to the Thirteenth Century.
2 vols. Princeton, 1930–31.

JONG, J. DE. *Architektur bij de Nederlandsche Schilders voor de Hervorming.* Amsterdam and Malines, 1934.

KERN, G. JOSEPH. "Die Anfänge der zentralperspektivischen Konstruktion in der italienischen Malerei des 14. Jahrhunderts," *Mitteilungen des Kunsthistorischen Instituts in Florenz,* II (Berlin, 1913), 39–65.

——. *Die Grundzüge der linear-perspektivischen Darstellung in der Kunst der Gebrüder van Eyck und ihrer Schule.* Leipzig, 1904.

——. "Perspektive und Bildarchitektur bei Jan van Eyck," *Repertorium für Kunstwissenschaft,* XXXV (1912), 27–64.

KERNODLE, GEORGE R. "The Medieval Pageant Wagons of Louvain," *Theatre Annual,* 1943, pp. 58–76.

——. "The Outdoor Setting," *Theatre Arts Monthly,* XXI (July, 1937), 558–61.

KERNODLE, GEORGE R. and PORTIA. "Dramatic Aspects of the Medieval Tournament," *Speech Monographs,* IX (1942), 161–72.

KNOWLES, JOHN A. "Disputes between English and Foreign Glass-Painters in the 16th Century," *Antiquaries' Journal,* V (1925), 148–57; also in *Annales bruxelloises,* XXXII (1926), 207–13.

KÖMSTEDT, RUDOLF. *Vormittelalterliche Malerei.* Augsburg, 1929.

KÖRTE, WERNER. *Die Wiederaufnahme romanischer Bauformen in der niederländischen und deutschen Malerei des XV. und XVI. Jahrhunderts.* Dissertation, Leipzig. Wolfenbüttel, 1930.

KÖVES, TIBOR. *Les Problèmes de la peinture chrétienne du IVe au IXe siècle (l'espace, la composition, la conception de la plastique).* Paris, 1927.

KRISTELLER, PAUL. *Biblia pauperum: Unicum der Heidelberger Universitäts-Bibliothek.* Berlin, 1906.

KRÖNIG, WOLFGANG. *Der italienische Einfluss in der flämischen Malerei im ersten Drittel des XVI. Jahrhunderts: Beiträge zum Beginn der Renaissance in der Malerei der Niederlande.* Würzburg, 1936.

LABORDE, A. DE. *Les Miracles de Nostre Dame.* Paris: Société Française de Reproduction de Manuscrits à Peinture, 1929.

LEONARDO DA VINCI. *Notebooks.* Trans. EDWARD MCCURDY. New York, 1923.

LETTENHOVE, BARON KERVYN DE, and OTHERS. *Les Chefs-d'œuvre d'art ancien à l'Exposition de la Toison d'Or à Bruges en 1907.* Brussels, 1908.

LOOMIS, LAURA HIBBARD. "The Table of the Last Supper in Religious and Secular Iconography," *Art Studies,* V (1927), 71–88.

MARIANI, V. "La Prospettiva come elemento d'illusione nell'architettura del rinascimento," *Cultura,* 1924, pp. 355 f.

MARLE, RAIMOND VAN. *The Development of the Italian Schools of Painting.* 19 vols. The Hague, 1923–38.

——. *Iconographie de l'art profane au moyen âge et à la renaissance.* 2 vols. The Hague, 1931–32.

MARTIN, HENRY, and LAUER, PHILIPPE. *Les principaux manuscrits à peinture de la Bibliothèque de l'Arsenal à Paris.* Paris, 1929.

MERTON, ADOLPH. *Die Buchmalerei in St. Gallen vom neunten bis zum elften Jahrhundert.* Leipzig, 1912.

MICHALSKI, ERNST. *Die Bedeutung der ästhetischen Grenze für die Methode der Kunstgeschichte.* ("Kunstwissenschaftliche Studien," Vol. XI.) Berlin, 1932.

MORRISON, JANE. "The Central Building in Italian Painting." Dissertation, University of Chicago, 1937.

MORTIMER, RAYMOND. "Architecture in Italian Pictures," *Architectural Review,* LXVII (1930), 60–68.

MÜLLER, R. *Über die Anfänge und über das Wesen der malerischen Perspektive.* Dissertation. Darmstadt, 1913.

NELSON, PHILIP. *Ancient Painted Glass in England, 1170–1500.* London and New York, [1913].

NICOLL, ALLARDYCE. *Stuart Masques and the Renaissance Stage.* New York, 1938.

OFFNER, RICHARD. *Italian Primitives at Yale University.* New Haven, 1927.

OMONT, HENRI AUGUSTE. *Miniatures des plus anciens manuscrits grecs de la Bibliothèque Nationale du VIe au XIVe siècle.* 2d ed. Paris, 1929.

PACIOLI, FRA LUCA. *De divina proportione.* Published with a German translation by CONSTANTIN WINTERBERG: *Quellenschriften für Kunstgeschichte und Kunsttechnik des Mittelalters und der Neuzeit,* Vol. II (new ser.; Vienna, 1896).

PANOFSKY, ERWIN. "Once More 'The Friedsam Annunciation and the Problem of the Ghent Altarpiece,'" *Art Bulletin,* XX (1938), 419–42.

——. "Die Perspektive als 'symbolische Form,'" *Vorträge der Bibliothek Warburg, 1924–25* (Hamburg, 1927), pp. 258–330.

PÉLERIN, JEAN (VIATOR). *De artificiali perspectiva.* Toul, 1505, 1509, 1521, and 1635.

PETER, RUDOLF. *Studien über die Struktur des Sehraums.* Dissertation, Hamburg, 1921.

POLLUX, JULIUS. *Vocabularium [Onomasticon].* Venice, 1502. Section on the theatre translated by EDITH HAMILTON. Typewritten copy in Department of Drama Library, Yale University.

POST, CHANDLER RATHFON. *History of Spanish Painting.* 8 vols. Cambridge, Mass., 1930–41.

POUDRA, NOËL GERMINAL. *Histoire de la perspective ancienne et moderne.* Paris, 1864.

PRIOR, EDWARD S. and GARDNER, ARTHUR. *An Account of Medieval Figure-Sculpture in England.* Cambridge, 1912.

RAPKE, KARL. *Die Perspektive und Architektur auf den Dürer'schen Handzeichnungen, Holzschnitten, Kupferstichen, und Gemälden.* ("Studien zur deutschen Kunstgeschichte," No. 39.) Strassburg, 1902.

READ, HERBERT EDWARD. *English Stained Glass.* London and New York, 1926.

REYMOND, M. "L'Architecture des peintres aux premières années de la renaissance," *Revue de l'art ancien et moderne,* XVII (1905), 41 ff.

RICE, B. TALBOT. *Byzantine Art.* Oxford, 1935.

RICHARDSON, E. P. "De Witte and the Imaginative Nature of Dutch Art," *Art Quarterly,* I (1938), 4–17.

RICHTER, GISELA M. A. "Perspective, Ancient, Medieval, and Renaissance," in *Scritti in onore di Bartolomeo Nogara* (Rome, 1937), pp. 381–88.

RIZZO, G. E. *La Pittura ellenistico-romana.* Milan, 1929.

Roblot-Deloudre, L. "Les Sujets antiques dans la tapis-serie," *Revue archéologique,* 1917, pp. 296–309; 1918, pp. 131–50.

Rodenwaldt, Gerhardt. "Cortinae: Ein Beitrag zur Datierung der antiken Vorlage der mittelalterlichen Terenz-illustrationen," *Nachrichten der Gesellschaft der Wissenschaften zu Göttingen, philologisch-historische Klasse,* 1925, pp. 33–49.

Rosenthal, M. *Die Architekturen in Raffaels Gemälden.* 1909.

Rushforth, Gordon McNeil. *Medieval Christian Imagery as Illustrated by the Painted Windows of Great Malvern Priory Church.* Oxford, 1936.

Schuritz, Hans. *Die Perspektive in der Kunst Albrecht Dürers: Ein Beitrag zur Geschichte der Perspektive.* Frankfort, 1919.

Smith, E. Baldwin. *Early Christian Iconography and a School of Ivory Carvers in Provence.* Princeton, 1928.

————. *Egyptian Architecture as Cultural Expression.* New York and London, 1938.

Spengler, Oswald. *The Decline of the West.* 2 vols. New York, 1926.

Springer, Anton. *Frühchristliche Kunst und Mittelalter.* 12th ed. Leipzig, 1924.

————. *Die Kunst der Renaissance in Italien.* 12th ed. Leipzig, 1924

Strong, Mrs. Arthur. *Roman Sculpture from Augustus to Constantine.* London and New York, 1907.

Strowski, Fortunat. "Le Décor simultané," *Art sacré,* May, 1936, pp. 138 f.

Swindler, Mary Hamilton. *Ancient Painting.* New Haven, 1929.

Toesca, P. "Prospettiva," *Enciclopedia italiana,* XXVIII (Rome, 1935), 357–60.

Vasari, Giorgio. *The Lives of the Painters, Sculptors, and Architects.* Trans. A. B. Hinds. ("Everyman" Ed.) New York, [1927].

Vavalà, Evelyn Sandberg. *La Croce dipinta italiana e l'iconografia della passione.* Verona, 1929.

Venturi, A. *Storia dell'arte italiana.* 11 vols. Milan, 1901–38.

————. "Les Triomphes de Pétrarque dans l'art représentatif," *Revue de l'art ancien et moderne,* XX (1906), 81–93, 209–21.

[Vitruvius]. *Vitruvius: The Ten Books on Architecture.* Trans. Morris Hicky Morgan. Cambridge, Mass., 1914.

Vitzthum von Eckstädt, Graf Georg. *Die pariser Miniaturmalerei von der Zeit des Heiligen Ludwig bis zu Philipp von Valois.* Leipzig, 1907.

Volkmann, Johannes. *Die Bildarchitekturen, vornehmlich in der italienischen Kunst.* Berlin, 1900.

Wallerstein, Victor. *Die Raumbehandlung in der oberdeutschen und niederländischen Tafelmalerei der ersten Hälfte des XV. Jahrhunderts.* ("Studien zur deutschen Kunstgeschichte," No. 118.) Strassburg, 1909.

Weale, V. H. James. *Hubert and John van Eyck.* London and New York, 1908.

Weisbach, Werner. "Petrarca und die bildende Kunst," *Repertorium für Kunstwissenschaft,* XXVI (1903), 265–87.

Werner, Karl [Ernst]. *Die Linearperspektive auf den Gemälden Hans Holbeins des Älteren.* Göttingen, 1912.

Westlake, Nathaniel Hubert John. *A History of Design in Painted Glass.* 4 vols. London, 1881–94.

Winkler, Friedrich. *Die altniederländische Malerei: Die Malerei in Belgien und Holland von 1400–1600.* Berlin, 1924.

————. *Die flämische Buchmalerei des XV. und XVI. Jahrhunderts: Künstler und Werke von den Brüdern van Eyck bis zu Simon Bening.* Leipzig, 1925.

Wölfflin, Heinrich. *Principles of Art History: The Problem of the Development of Style in Later Art.* Trans. M. D. Hotlinger. London, 1932.

Wolff, Georg. *Mathematik und Malerei.* Leipzig and Berlin, 1916; 2d ed. rev., Leipzig, 1925.

————. "Zu Leon Battista Albertis Perspektivlehre," *Zeitschrift für Kunstgeschichte,* V (1936), 47–54.

Wulff, Oskar. *Altchristliche und byzantinische Kunst.* 2 vols. Berlin, 1914.

————. "Die umgekehrte Perspektive und die Niedersicht: Eine Raumanschauungsform der altbyzantinischen Kunst und ihre Fortbildung in der Renaissance," in *Kunstwissenschaftliche Beiträge August Schmarsow gewidmet.* Leipzig, 1907.

Zemp, J. *Die schweizerischen Bilderchroniken und ihre Architekturdarstellungen.* Zürich, 1897.

Zucker, Paul. *Raumdarstellung und Bildarchitekturen im florentiner Quattrocento.* Leipzig, 1913.

CHAPTER II. SHOW-PICTURE AND SHOW-ARCHITECTURE: THE *TABLEAUX VIVANTS*

I. General Works Consulted*

Bapst, Germain. *Essai sur l'histoire du théâtre.* Paris, 1893.

Baskervill, Charles Read. "Dramatic Aspects of Medieval Folk Festivals in England," *Studies in Philology,* XVII (January, 1920), 19–87.

Bishop, Edmund. *On the History of the Christian Altar, with a Bibliographical List.* Stratton-on-the-Fosse, 1906. Reprint from *Downside Review,* No. 71, 1905.

Block, K. S. (ed.). *Ludus Coventriae; or The Plaie Called Corpus Christi.* ("Early English Text Society Series," Extra ser., No. CXX.) London, 1922.

Bond, Francis. *The Chancel of English Churches.* London, 1916.

Bonnell, John K. "The Easter *Sepulchrum* in Its Relation to the Architecture of the High Altar," *Publications of the Modern Language Association,* XXXI (1916), 664–712.

Borcherdt, Hans Heinrich. *Das europäische Theater im Mittelalter und in der Renaissance.* Leipzig, 1935.

Borenius, Tancred, and Tristram, E. W. *English Medieval Painting.* Florence and Paris, 1927.

Brooks, Neil C. *The Sepulchre of Christ in Art and Liturgy, with Special Reference to the Liturgical Drama.* ("University of Illinois Studies in Language and Literature," Vol. VII, No. 2.) Urbana, 1921.

* For the "Royal Entries" see Part II.

BROTANEK, RUDOLPH. *Die englischen Maskenspiele*. Vienna, 1902.

CANESTRARI, GIUSEPPE. *Il Castello d'amore: una festa del medio evo*. Vicenza, n.d.

CHAMBERS, EDMUND K. *The Mediaeval Stage*. 2 vols. Oxford, 1903.

CLEPHAN, R. COLTMAN. *The Tournament: Its Periods and Phases*. London, 1919.

COHEN, GUSTAVE. *Histoire de la mise en scène dans le théâtre religieux français du moyen âge*. Brussels, 1906; rev. ed., Paris, 1926.

————. *Le Théâtre en France au moyen âge*, Vol. I: *Le Théâtre religieux*. Paris, 1928.

COLLIER, J. P. *The History of English Dramatic Poetry to the Time of Shakespeare*. 3 vols. London, 1831.

COULTON, C. G. *Life in the Middle Ages*. Cambridge, 1930.

CREIZENACH, WILHELM. *Geschichte des neueren Dramas*. 5 vols. Halle, 1893–1909.

CRIPPS-DAY, FRANCIS HENRY. *The History of the Tournament in England and in France*. London, 1918.

CROSSLEY, F. H. *English Church Monuments, A.D. 1150–1550*. London, 1921.

DAVIES, GERALD STANLEY. *Renascence: The Sculptured Tombs of the Fifteenth Century in Rome, with Chapters on the Previous Centuries from 1100*. London, 1910.

DEARMER, REV. P. *Fifty Pictures of Gothic Altars*. ("Alcuin Club Collections," Vol. X.) London, 1910.

DESTRÉE, J. *Les Sculpteurs bruxellois au 15e et 16e siècle*. Brussels, 1888.

DIDRON, ADOLPHE NAPOLÉON. *Christian Iconography, or the History of Christian Art in the Middle Ages*. ("Bohn's Illustrated Library.") 2 vols. London, 1907. See esp. Vol. II, Appendix, which contains the Byzantine *Guide to Painting* of probably the twelfth century.

DILLON, VISCOUNT, and HOPE, W. H. ST. JOHN (eds.). *Pageant of the Birth, Life, and Death of Richard Beauchamp Earl of Warwick K.G. 1389–1439*. Photoengraved from MS Cotton Julius E. iv, British Museum. London, 1914.

DUBECH, LUCIEN. *Histoire générale illustrée du théâtre*. 5 vols. Paris, 1931–34.

DURAN I SANPERE, AGUSTÍ. *Los Retablos de piedra*. ("Monumenta Cataloniae," Vols. I and II.) Barcelona, 1932–34.

EVEN, EDWARD VAN. *L'Omgang de Louvain*. Louvain and Brussels, 1863.

FERRARI, GIULIO. *Bellezze architettoniche per le feste della Chinea in Roma nei secoli XVII e XVIII*. Turin, n.d.

FISCHEL, OSKAR. "Art and the Theatre," *Burlington Magazine*, LXVI (1935), 4–14, 54–67.

GALANTE-GARRONE, VIRGINIA. *L'Apparato scenico del dramma sacro in Italia*. Turin, 1935.

GREGOR, JOSEPH, and OTHERS. *Monumenta scenica: Denkmäler des Theaters*. Vienna and Munich, 1925–30.

HASSETT, MAURICE M. "History of the Christian Altar," *Catholic Encyclopedia* (New York, 1907), I, 362–67.

HERRMANN, MAX. *Forschungen zur deutschen Theatergeschichte des Mittelalters und der Renaissance*. Berlin, 1914.

HIGGINS, ALFRED. "On the Work of Florentine Sculptors in England in the Early Part of the Sixteenth Century, with Special Reference to the Tombs of Cardinal Wolsey and King Henry VIII," *Archaeological Journal*, LI (1894), 129–220, 367–70.

HOFFMANN, RICHARD. *Bayerische Altarbaukunst*. Munich, 1923.

HOLL, KARL. "Die Entstehung der Bilderwand in der griechischen Kirche," *Archiv für Religionswissenschaft*, IX (1906), 365–84.

HORST, CARL. *Die Architektur der Renaissance in den Niederlanden und ihre Ausstrahlungen*, Part I: *Architektur in der Malerei und Innenarchitektur*. The Hague, 1930.

KALFF, GERRIT. *Geschiedenis der Nederlandsche Letterkunde*. 7 vols. Groningen, 1906–12.

KERNODLE, GEORGE R. "The Magic of Light," *Theatre Arts Monthly*, XXVI (November, 1942), 717–22.

————. "The Medieval Pageant Wagons of Louvain," *Theatre Annual*, 1943, pp. 58–76.

————. "Renaissance Artists in the Service of the People," *Art Bulletin*, XXV (March, 1943), 59–64.

KERNODLE, GEORGE R. and PORTIA. "Dramatic Aspects of the Medieval Tournament," *Speech Monographs*, IX (1942), 161–72.

KNOWLES, JOHN A. "Disputes between English and Foreign Glass-Painters in the Sixteenth Century," *Antiquaries' Journal*, V (1925), 148–57.

KÖRTE, WERNER. *Die Wiederaufnahme romanischer Bauformen in der niederländischen und deutschen Malerei des XV. und XVI. Jahrhunderts*. Dissertation, Leipzig. Wolfenbüttel, 1930.

LABORDE, LÉON EMMANUEL SIMON JOSEPH, MARQUIS DE. *Les Ducs de Bourgogne: études sur les lettres, les arts et l'industrie pendant le XVe siècle*. 3 vols. Paris, 1849–52.

[LA MARCHE]. *Mémoires d'Olivier de la Marche*. 4 vols. Paris: Société de l'Histoire de France, 1883–88.

LEMAIRE, R. "L'Eglise des 'Sept Sacrements' de van der Weyden," in *Mélanges Moeller* (Louvain, 1914), I, 640.

MAETERLINCK, LOUIS. *Le Genre satirique, fantastique et licencieux dans la sculpture flamande et wallonne*. Paris, 1910.

————. *Le Genre satirique dans la peinture flamande*. Brussels, 1903.

————. *R. van der Weyden et les "Ymaigiers" de Tournay*. Brussels, 1901.

[MAHELOT]. *Le Mémoire de Mahelot, Laurent et d'autres décorateurs de l'Hôtel de Bourgogne et de la Comédie-Française au XVIIe siècle*. Ed. H. C. LANCASTER. Paris, 1920.

MANDER, KAREL VAN. *Het Leven der doorluchtighe Nederlandtsche en Hooghduytsche Schilders*. Amsterdam, 1604, 1617.

MANN, MGR. HORACE KINDER. *Tombs and Portraits of the Popes of the Middle Ages*. London, 1929.

MORICE, ÉMILE. *Histoire de la mise en scène depuis les mystères jusqu'au Cid*. Paris, 1836.

NIESSEN, CARL. *Das Bühnenbild: Ein kulturgeschichtlicher Atlas*. Leipzig, 1924–27.

PARFAICT, LES FRÈRES. *Histoire du théâtre françois depuis son origine jusqu'à présent*. 15 vols. Paris, 1745–49.

PARK, THOMAS. *Nugae antiquae*. London, 1804.

PRIOR, EDWARD S., and GARDNER, ARTHUR. *An Account of Medieval Figure-Sculpture in England*. Cambridge, 1912.

PUYVELDE, LEO VAN. *Schilderkunst en Tooneelvertonningen op het Einde van de Middeleeuwen*. Ghent: Koninklijke Vlaamsche Academie voor Taal- en Letterkunde, 1912.

REYNOLDS, GEORGE F. "Some Principles of Elizabethan Staging," *Modern Philology*, II (April, 1905), 581–614; III (June, 1905), 69–97.

ROY, M. "Collaboration de Philibert Delorme aux préparatifs de l'entrée de Henry II à Paris et du sacre de Catherine de Médicis en 1549," *Revue du XVIᵉ siècle*, 1919.

RUSHFORTH, GORDON MCNEIL. *Medieval Christian Imagery as Illustrated by the Painted Windows of Great Malvern Priory Church*. Oxford, 1936.

SCHNEIDER, RENÉ. "Le Thème du triomphe dans les entrées solennelles en France à la renaissance," *Gazette des beaux-arts*, I (February, 1913), 85–106.

SCHUBRING, PAUL. *Das italienische Grabmal der Frührenaissance*. Berlin, 1904.

SHULL, VIRGINIA MOORE. "The Stagecraft of the Mediaeval English Drama." Dissertation, Yale University, 1941.

STUMPFL, ROBERT. "Die Bühnenmöglichkeiten im XVI. Jahrhundert," *Zeitschrift für deutsche Philologie*, LIV, No. 1 (May, 1929), 42–80; LV, No. 1 (March, 1930), 49–78.

VASARI, GIORGIO. *The Lives of the Painters, Sculptors, and Architects*. ("Everyman" Ed.) New York, [1927].

VENTURI, A. "Les Triomphes de Pétrarque dans l'art représentatif," *Revue de l'art ancien et moderne*, XX (1906), 81–93, 209–21.

WARD, ADOLPHUS WILLIAM. *A History of English Dramatic Literature to the Death of Queen Anne*. London and New York, 1899.

WEBB, GEOFFREY. *The Liturgical Altar*. London, 1933.

WEBER, PAUL. *Geistliches Schauspiel und kirchliche Kunst in ihrem Verhältnis erläutert an einer Ikonographie der Kirche und Synagoge*. Stuttgart, 1894.

WEISBACH, WERNER. "Petrarca und die bildende Kunst," *Repertorium für Kunstwissenschaft*, XXVI (1903), 265–87.

WELSFORD, ENID. *The Court Masque*. Cambridge, 1927; New York, 1928.

WILLIAMS, RONALD BOAL. *The Staging of Plays in the Spanish Peninsula Prior to 1555*. ("University of Iowa Studies in Spanish Language and Literature," No. 5.) Iowa City, 1935.

WORP, JACOB ADOLF. *Geschiedenis van het Drama en van het Tooneel in Nederland*. 2 vols. Groningen, 1904–8.

II. THE ROYAL ENTRIES

As there is no general bibliography of the accounts of entries in all countries of Europe, I give here extensive supplements to the bibliographies of separate countries. Lünig, Modius, and Godefroy published compendious collections but missed hundreds of accounts. Alenda y Mira has the most widely useful bibliography, since it not only covers Spain well but includes all entries in other countries in which any of the Hapsburgs was concerned. Withington furnishes a full index to the English entries; I include here references to his summaries, to his principal sources, and to a few accounts which he missed. I have attempted a full listing of all French entries, including those in Godefroy and many which he missed, and of all Low Country entries. Hence my list plus Alenda y Mira's plus additional sources mentioned in Withington would give a comprehensive bibliography of the entries in western Europe. I list only those Italian entries which I have found to include street theatres:

many Italian entries were purely processional. I list only a few entries in Germany. The real development of the street theatres took place in an area bounded by Lyons, Antwerp, and London. As their germinal importance for the theatre was in the sixteenth century, I list only a few entries after 1600.

Following a list of works concerning entries in more than one country, references are arranged by countries: Italy, France, the Low Countries, England, and others. Under each country, after general collections and chronicles, the individual entries are arranged by date.

A. ENTRIES: WORKS INCLUDING MORE THAN ONE COUNTRY

ALENDA Y MIRA, JENARO. *Relaciones de solemnidades y fiestas públicas de España*. Madrid, 1903.

[BÉVY, C. J. DE]. *Histoire des inaugurations des rois, empereurs et autres souverains de l'univers depuis leur origine jusqu'à présent*. Paris, 1776.

[LIPPERHEIDE]. *Katalog der Freiherrlich von Lipperheide'schen Kostümbibliothek* (Berlin, 1896–1905), Vol. II, Nos. 2468–2849.

LÜNIG, JOHANN CHRISTIAN. *Theatrum ceremoniale historico-politicum oder historisch- und politischer Schau-Platz aller Ceremonien welche bey Papst und Kayser auch königlichen Wahlen und Croningen. . . . .* 2 vols. Leipzig, 1719–20.

MODIUS, FRANCISCUS. *Pandectae triumphales*. Frankfort, 1586.

[RUGGIERI]. *Catalogue des livres rares et précieux composant la bibliothèque de M. E. F. D. Ruggieri*. Paris, 1873.

VINET, ERNEST. *Bibliographie méthodique et raisonnée des beaux-arts, L'Art officiel*, Nos. 468–820 (Paris, 1874).

There are a number of engravings reproduced by Gregor in *Monumenta scenica* and by Niessen in *Das Bühnenbild;* a few by Dubech in *Histoire générale illustrée du théâtre*, Vols. II and III.

B. ENTRIES: ITALY

General Works

ALENDA Y MIRA, JENARO. *Relaciones de solemnidades y fiestas públicas de España*. Madrid, 1903.

BURCKHARDT, JACOB. *The Civilisation of the Renaissance in Italy*. London, 1928.

CALVETE DE ESTRELLA, JUAN CHRISTOVAL. *El felicissimo viaje d'el ... Principe D. Phelippe ... desde España à sus tierras de la baxa Alemaña*. Antwerp, 1552.

CROCE, BENEDETTO. *I Teatri di Napoli dal rinascimento alla fine del secolo decimottavo*. Bari, 1916.

GACHARD, LOUIS PROSPER. *Collection des voyages des souverains des Pays-Bas*. 4 vols. Brussels, 1874–82.

GERSTFELD, O. VON. *Hochzeitsfeste der Renaissance in Italien*. Esslingen, 1906.

GHINZONI, PIETRO. "Trionfi e rappresentazioni in Milano," *Archivio storico lombardo*, XIV (1887), 820–31.

MANZI, GUGLIELMO. *Discorso di G. M. sopra gli spettacoli, le feste, ed il lusso degli Italiani nel secolo XIV. con note ed illustrazioni*. Rome, 1818.

MICHIEL, G. R. *Origine delle feste veneziane*. Milan, 1829.

SAVIOTTI, A. "Feste e spettacoli nel seicento," *Giornale storico della letteratura italiana*, XLI [1903], 55.

TODERINI, TEODORO. *Cerimoniali e feste in occasione di avvenimenti e passaggi nelli stati della Republica Veneta di duchi, archiduchi ed imperatori della casa d'Austria dall'anno 1361 al 1767*.... Venice, 1857.

Tutti i trionfi, carri, mascherate o canti carnascialeschi andati per Firenze dal tempo del Magnifico Lorenzo de' Medici, fino all' anno 1559. 2 vols. Florence, 1750.

WEISBACH, W. *Trionfi*. Berlin, 1919.

Particular Accounts

1443. Alfonso at Naples. CROCE, *I Teatri di Napoli*, pp. 5 f.

1473. Eleanor of Aragon at Rome. C. CORVISIERI, "Il Trionfo romano di Eleonora d'Aragona nel giugno del 1473," *Archivio della Società Romana di Storia Patria*, I (1878), 475–91; X (1887), 629–87.

1473. Eleanor of Aragon at Ferrara. L. OLIVI, *Delle nozze d'Ercole d'Este con Eleonora d'Aragona*. Modena, 1887.

1482. Celebration of Corpus Christi by Pope Pius II at Viterbo. BURCKHARDT, *Civilisation of the Renaissance*, pp. 414 f.

1490. Isabella d'Este at Mantua. ALESSANDRO LUZIO and RODOLFO RENIER, "Il Lusso d'Isabella d'Este, marchesa di Mantova," *Nuova antologia di scienze, lettere, ed arti*, LXVIII (4th ser.; June, 1896), 441–48.

1494. Charles VIII at Naples. *S'ensuyt l'entree et couronnement du Roy nostre sire en sa ville de Napples faite le XXII. jour de fevrier mil CCCC IIIIXX et XIIII.* 1494. Collected in MS Fontaneu, Vol. CXLIX, Nouv. acq. fr. 7644, Bibliothèque Nationale, Paris.

1494. Charles VIII at Florence. *La noble et excellente entree Du Roy Nostre Sire en la ville de Florence qui fut le XVI. jour de novembre mil CCCC IIIIXX et XIII.* N.p., n.d. [1494]. Collected in MS Fontaneu, Vol. CXLIX.

1495. Charles VIII at Naples, Rome, Siena, and Pisa. THÉODORE GODEFROY, *Le Ceremonial françois* (Paris, 1649), I, 682. Hereafter cited as "Godefroy, *Cf.*"

About 1502–3. Louis XII at Rome. *L'Entree du Roy nostre sire a Romme.* N.p., n.d. Collected in MS Fontaneu, Vol. CXLIX.

1507. Louis XII at Genoa. JEHAN DESMARESTZ (dit MAROT), *La Magnanime victoire du roy tres Crestien Loys XII. par luy obtenue en l'an mil cinq cens et sept au moys de may Contre les Genevoys ses rebelles.* MS fr. 5091, Bibliothèque Nationale, Paris.
La conqueste de Gennes ... . Genoa, 1507.
GODEFROY, *Cf*, I, 696, 700, 702, 712, 715.

1507. Louis XII at Milan. GODEFROY, *Cf*, I, 518.

1509(?). Louis XII at Milan. *Œuvre nouvellement translatee de rime italiene ... Louis XII ... a Milan.* Lyons, 1509.

1515. Francis at Milan. *L'Ordonnance faicte a l entree du trescrestien roy de france Francoys de Valoys ... Dedans la ville de Millan. 1515.* N.p., 1515.
GODEFROY, *Cf*, I, 751.

1535. Charles V at Naples. GACHARD, *Voyages*, II, 573–81, Appen. XIII.

1536. Charles V at Messina. *Ibid.*, pp. 567–72, Appen. XII.

1548. Philip of Spain at Milan. *La triomphale entrata del.... Prence di Spagna nell'inclitta città di Melano.* N.p., [1548].
CALVETE DE ESTRELLA, *El felicissimo viaje* ... .
WILLIAM SEGAR, *Honor Military, and Civill, contained in foure Bookes* (London, 1602), pp. 157 f.

1548. Philip at Mantua. *Descritione delli archi et dechiaratione delle statone et apparati publici....* Mantua, 1549.

1551. Charles V at Milan. *Trattato del intrar in Milano di Carlo V.* Milan, 1551. With plates.

1559. Duke of Sessa, governor-general, at Milan. *I grandi apparati e feste fatte in Melano....* Milan, 1559.

1565. Marriage of Francesco de Medici and Johanna of Austria at Florence. G. VASARI, "Descrizione dell' apparato fatto in Firenze per le nozze dell'ill. ed ecc. Don Francesco de' Medici.... e della ser. Regina Giovanna d'Austria," in *Le Opere di G. Vasari* (Florence, 1882), VIII, 517–622.
PIERO GINORI-CONTI. *L'Apparato per le nozze di Francesco de' Medici e di Giovanna d'Austria, nelle narrazioni del tempo e da lettere inedite di Vincenzio Borghini e di Giorgio Vasari. Illustrato con disegni originale.* Florence, 1936.

1571. Lucrezia d'Este at Pesaro. "Solenne entrata in Pesaro di Lucrezia d'Este, sposa a Francesco Maria della Rovere. 1571, " in *Raccolte ferrarese*, No. 1 (Ferrara, 1869).

1576(?). Henry III of France at Mantua. *La Somptueuse et magnifique Entree du tres chrestien roy Henry III de ce nom ... en la cite de Mantove ... .* Paris, 1576.

1581. Maria of Austria at Vicenza. FILIPPO PIGAFETTA, *Due lettere descrittive l'uno dell'ingresso a Vicenza della Imperatrice Maria d'Austria nell'anno MDLXXXI....* Padua, 1830.

1591. Cardinal Morosini at Brescia. *Il sontuoso apparato fatto dalla Magnifica Città di Brescia nel Felice Ritorno dell' Illus. & Reverendiss. Vescovo suo Il Cardinale Morosini....* N.p., n.d.

1598. Margarita of Austria and Albert and Isabella at Ferrara. *De gheluckighe Incomste des . . . . Coninghinne van Spaengien Vrou Margarita van Oostenrijck, in . . . . Ferrare . . . . Beschreven door den Ridder Reale . . . . Overgheset uyt het Italiaens in Nederduytsch.* 1598.

C. ENTRIES: FRANCE

The most important collection of descriptions is Godefroy's. The principal bibliography is by Le Vager, who lists the printed documents and manuscript accounts in the Bibliothèque Nationale and a few elsewhere. His list includes 12 manuscript accounts and 142 printed accounts before 1600 in Paris but does not include several published by Godefroy.

General Works

BABEAU, ALBERT. *Les Rois de France à Troyes au XVIe siècle*. Troyes, 1880.

BAPST, GERMAIN. *Essai sur l'histoire du théâtre*. Paris, 1893.

CHARTROU, JOSÈPHE. *Les Entrées solennelles et triomphales à la renaissance (1484–1551)*. Paris, 1928.

[CHASTELLAIN]. *Œuvres de Georges Chastellain*. Ed. BARON KERVYN DE LETTENHOVE. 8 vols. Brussels, 1863–66.

[FROISSART]. *The Chronicle of Froissart*. Trans. LORD BERNERS. 6 vols. London, 1901–2.

GODEFROY, THÉODORE. *Le Ceremonial françois*. 2 vols. Paris. 1649. Hereafter cited as "Godefroy, *Cf.*"

———. *Entreveues de Charles IV Empereur, de son fils Vvenceslaus Roy des Romans, & de Charles V Roy de France, à Paris l'an*

*1378 et De Louys XII Roy de France, & de Ferdinand Roy
d'Arragon, à Savonne l'an 1507.* Paris, 1612.

[LA MARCHE]. *Mémoires d'Olivier de la Marche.* 4 vols. Paris:
Société de l'Histoire de France, 1883–88.

MATHIEU, JOSEPH. *Les grandes processions à Marseille depuis le
moyen âge jusqu'à nos jours.* Marseilles, 1864.

[MONSTRELET]. *The Chronicles of Enguerrand de Monstrelet.*
Trans. THOMAS JOHNES. 2 vols. London, 1840.

MOUREY, GABRIEL. *Le Livre des fêtes françaises.* Paris, 1930.

*Relation des entrées solennelles dans la ville de Lyon, de nos rois,
reines, princes, princesses, etc.* Lyons, 1752.

Trésor des harangues faites aux entrées des Rois, Reines, etc. 2 vols.
Paris, 1680.

TUETEY, ALEXANDRE (ed.). *Journal d'un bourgeois de Paris
(1405–49).* Paris: Société de l'Histoire de Paris, 1881.

VAGER, PAUL LE. *Les Entrées solennelles à Paris des rois et reines
de France ... conservées à la Bibliothèque Nationale: bibliographie sommaire.* Paris, 1896.

Particular Accounts

1313. Edward II of England and his queen, Isabel, entertained at Paris. LOUIS PETIT DE JULLEVILLE, *Histoire
du théâtre en France,* Part I: *Les Mystères* (Paris, 1880),
II, 186 f. Description by Godefroi de Paris.

1321. Charles the Fair at Rheims. GODEFROY, *Cf,* I, 147.

1328. Philip at Rheims. *Ibid.,* p. 148.

1350. John II at Rheims. *Ibid.,* p. 149.

1364. Charles V at Rheims. *Ibid.,* p. 151.

1380. Charles VI at Rheims. *Ibid.,* p. 154.

1389. Charles VI at Lyons. *Relation des entrées solennelles dans
la ville de Lyon,* pp. 1–4.

1389. Isabel at Paris. FROISSART, *Chronicle,* V, 275 ff.

1390. Charles VI at Dijon. ERNEST PETIT DE VAUSSE, *Entrée
de Charles VI à Dijon en février 1390.* Dijon, 1885.

1420. Henry V and Charles VI at Paris. CHASTELLAIN,
Œuvres, I, 187 f.
MONSTRELET, *Chronicles,* I, 450 f.
GODEFROY, *Cf,* I, 652.

1422. Henry V at Paris. Petit de Julleville, *Les Mystères,*
II, 10.

1424. John, Duke of Bedford, at Paris. "Journal d'un bour-
geois de Paris," in MICHAUD and POUJOULAT (eds.),
*Nouvelle collection des mémoires pour servir à l'histoire de
France* (Paris, 1837), III, 243 f.

1429. Charles VII at Poitiers and Rheims. GODEFROY, *Cf,* I,
163.

1431. Henry VI of England at Paris. *Extrait des comptes de la
ville de Paris.* MSS fr., nouv. acq. 3243, Bibliothèque
Nationale, Paris.
TUETEY (ed.), *Journal d'un bourgeois de Paris,* pp. 274 f.
ROBERT WITHINGTON, *English Pageantry* (Cambridge,
Mass., 1918), I, 138–41.
GODEFROY, *Cf,* I, 169.

1437. Charles VII at Paris. GODEFROY, *Cf,* I, 653–58.

1442. Frederick, Archduke of Austria, at Besançon. LA
MARCHE, *Mémoires,* I, 270 ff.

1442. Isabel of Portugal at Besançon. *Ibid.,* p. 280.

1450. Charles VII at Caen. L. PUISEUX, *Entrée triomphale de
Charles VII à Caen en 1450.* Caen, 1868.

1451. Duke of Savoy and his daughter at Bourg. M. BROS-
SARD, "Entrée du duc de Savoie et de sa fille à Bourg
en 1451," *Annales de la Société d'Emulation de l'Ain*
(1881), pp. 216–28.

1461. Philip the Good and Louis at Rheims for Louis's
coronation. LOUIS PROSPER GACHARD, *Collection de
documents inédits* (Brussels, 1835), II, 162–75.
GODEFROY, *Cf,* I, 172.

1461. Louis XI at Paris. *Journal de Jean de Roye.* Ed. BER-
NARD DE MANDROT (Paris: Société de l'Histoire de
France, 1894–96), I, 27–29.
MOUREY, *Le Livre des fêtes françaises,* pp. 7 f.
CHASTELLAIN, *Œuvres,* IV, 73 ff.
GODEFROY, *Cf,* I, 179.

1474. Charles the Bold at Dijon. *Entrée de Charles le Téméraire
et les funérailles de Philippe le Bon à Dijon, 1474.* Introd.
by HENRI CHABEUF. Dijon, 1903.

1483. Dauphine (Marguerite of Flanders) at Paris. MON-
STRELET, *Chronicles,* II, 453.

1484. Charles VIII at Rheims. GODEFROY, *Cf,* I, 184.

1484. Charles VIII at Paris. *L'Entree du roy nostre sire en la
ville et cite de Paris.* Ed. L. LUCAS. Rheims: Société des
Bibliophiles de Reims, 1842.
GODEFROY, *Cf,* I, 208.

1485. Charles VIII at Rouen. *Prologue de l'entree du roy ....*
N.p., n.d. The same, edited by CHARLES DE BEAU-
REPAIRE with title *L'Entrée et séjour du roi Charles
VIII à Rouen en 1485.* Caen, 1854. The same, facsimile
reproduction. Rouen: Société des Bibliophiles Nor-
mands, 1902.

1486. Charles VIII at Troyes. GODEFROY, *Cf,* I, 675 ff.

1486. Anne of Brittany at Paris. *Sensuit le sacre de la tres
chrestienne Royne de France.* N.p., 1486. Reprinted in
GODEFROY, *Cf,* I, 681 ff.

1493. Charles VIII at Grenoble, etc. MONSTRELET, *Chronicles,* II, 463 ff.

1495. Charles VIII at Lyons. *Ibid.,* p. 481.
GODEFROY, *Cf,* I, 685.

1498. Louis XII at Rheims. *Le Sacre du Roy très crestien Loys
douziesme de ce nom fait à Reims l'an mil CCCC 1111XX et
XVIII le XXVII jour de may.* N.p., n.d.
GODEFROY, *Cf,* I, 231.

1498 Louis XII at Paris. *L'Entree du roy de France tres cr. Loys
douziesme de ce nom a sa b. ville de Paris ... mil CCCC.
1111XX et XVIII ... .* N.p., n.d.
GODEFROY, *Cf,* I, 233, 238, 686.
BAPST, *Essai sur l'histoire du théâtre,* pp. 129–31. Expense accounts.

1501. Anne of Brittany at Paris. GODEFROY, *Cf.* I 686.

1502(?). Archduke Philip of Austria at Paris. *L'Entree faicte
A Paris par trespuissant prince et seigneur L'archeduc de
Austriche, conte de Flandres ... .* N.p., n.d.
GODEFROY, *Cf,* II, 713, 735.

1503. Archduke Philip at Lyons. GACHARD, *Voyages,* I, 281 f.

1503. Archduke Philip at Montpellier. CHARLES D'AIGRE-
FEUILLE, *Histoire de la ville de Montpellier depuis son
origine jusqu'à notre temps* (Montpellier, 1737), I, 233 ff.

1504. Anne of Brittany at Paris. GODEFROY, *Cf,* I, 690.

1506. François de Rohan, archbishop of Lyons, at Lyons.

L'Abbé Reure, *L'Entrée à Lyon de François de Rohan, archevêque de Lyon ... , le 14 août, 1506.* Lyons, 1900.
Georges Guigue, *Entrée à Lyon de l'archevêque François de Rohan ... 14 août 1506.* (Extrait de *La Bibliothèque de l'Ecole des Chartes,* Vol. LXIII.) Paris, 1902.

1507. Louis XII at Lyons. *L'Entree du Roy a son retour de Gennes ... .* Archives de la ville de Lyon, BB. 25, fols. 162–66. The same, edited by Georges Guigue, *Entrée de Louis XII à Lyon, le 15 juillet 1507.* Lyons, 1885.
Relation des entrées solennelles dans la ville de Lyon, pp. 6 f.

1508. Louis XII at Rouen. *L'Entree royale et magnifique de tres chrestien roi de France Louis XII ... en ... Rouen ... mil cinc centz et huict.* N.p., n.d. Reprinted with another more confused account of the same in P. le Verdier, *L'Entrée du Roi Louis XII et de la Reine à Rouen (1508).* Rouen: Société des Bibliophiles Normands, 1900.

1509. Louis XII at Paris. Godefroy, *Cf,* I, 730.

1510. Louis XII at Troyes. Babeau, *Les Rois de France à Troyes,* pp. 14 ff.
Godefroy, *Cf,* I, 730.

1514. Mary Tudor at Abbeville. *L'Entree de la Royne ... a Abeville.* N.p., n.d.
Sensuit l'ordre qui a esté tenu a l'entrée de la Royne à Abbeville, in H. Cocheris, *Entrées de Marie d'Angleterre, femme de Louis XII, à Abbeville et à Paris.* Paris, 1859.

1514. Mary Tudor at Paris. *L'Entree de tres excellente Princesse Madame Marie d'Angleterre ... Paris ... VI jour de novembre ... mil cinc cens et quatorze.* N.p., 1514. The same, in H. Cocheris, *Entrées de Marie d'Angleterre, femme de Louis XII, à Abbeville et à Paris.* Paris, 1859.
L'Ordre des joustes faictes a Paris a l'entree de la Royne. Le pas des armes de l'arc triumphal ... . Redige et mis par escript par Montioye roy d'armes. N.p., 1514.
Charles Read Baskervill, *Pierre Gringore's Pageants for the Entry of Mary Tudor into Paris: An Unpublished Manuscript.* Chicago, 1934.
Monstrelet, *Chronicles,* II, 513.
Godefroy, *Cf,* I, 731–51.

1515. Francis I at Paris and elsewhere. Monstrelet, *Chronicles,* II, 515 ff.

1514/15. Francis I at Paris. *L'Ordre du sacre et couronnement du Roy ... . 1515.*
Godefroy, *Cf,* I, 266, 275.

1514/15. Francis I at Rheims. Godefroy, *Cf,* I, 245, 253, 264.

1515. Francis I at Lyons. Georges Guigue, *L'Entrée de François Premier Roy de France en la cité de Lyon le 12 Juillet 1515.* From the manuscript in the Bibliothèque Ducale de Wolfenbüttel. Lyons: Société des Bibliophiles Lyonnais, 1899.
Relation des entrées solennelles dans la ville de Lyon, pp. 8 f.

1516. Charles V at Douai. *See below,* bibliography of entries in the Low Countries.

1517. Cardinal de Luxembourg, papal legate, at Paris. *Journal d'un bourgeois de Paris.* Ed. L. Lalanne. Paris: Société de l'Histoire de France, 1854.

1517. Queen Claude at Paris. *L'Entree de la royne de France a Paris ... .* N.p., 1517.

Sesuit le sacre de la tres crestienne Royne de France lequel fut fait a Sait Denis en france avecques le couronement dicelle ... . N.p., n.d.
Godefroy, *Cf,* I, 472 ff., 753, 759.

1517. Francis I at Rouen. *L'Entree du tres chretien et tres victorieux Roy de France Francoys ... .* Rouen, 1517. The same, edited by Charles de Beaurepaire, with title *L'Entrée de François I dans la ville de Rouen au mois d'août 1517.* Rouen, 1867.

1519. Francis I at Poitiers. Henri Clouzot, *L'ancien théâtre en Poitou* (Niort, 1901), pp. 29 ff.

1520. Francis I and Henry VIII of England at Guînes and Ardres. Godefroy, *Cf,* II, 736.

1521. Charles V at Valenciennes. *See below,* bibliography of entries in the Low Countries.

1521. Francis I at Troyes. Babeau, *Les Rois de France à Troyes,* pp. 27 ff.

1526. Francis I at Paris. Godefroy, *Cf,* I, 762, 764.

1530. Queen Eleanor at Lyons, Bayonne, and Paris. *Nouvelles venues a Lyon ... : la grande triumphante entree ... Bayonne ... .* N.p., n.d.

1530. Queen Eleanor at Bayonne. *La Venue de Mme elionor Royne de France ... en la ville de Bayonne.* Rouen, 1530. *La grand triumphe et entree des enfans de France et de Madame Alienor en la ville de Bayonne ... .* Paris, 1530.
Godefroy, *Cf,* I, 765, 769.

1530. Queen Eleanor at Bordeaux. *L'Entree de la Reyne et de Ms. les enfans de Frans m. le Daulphin et le Duc d orleans en la ville et cite de Bourdeaux.* N.p., 1530.
Godefroy, *Cf,* I, 773.

1530. Queen Eleanor at Paris. *L'Entree de la Royne en sa ville et cite de Paris ... . 1531.*
L'Entree triumphante et sumptueuse ... . 1531.
Godefroy, *Cf,* I, 487, 494, 506, 777, 780.
Bapst, *Essai sur l'histoire du théâtre,* p. 132.

1531. Queen Eleanor and the Dauphin in Normandy. *Les Entrées de la reyne et de M. daulphin ... en ce pays de Normandie ... . 1531.* The same, edited by A. Pottier. Rouen: Société des Bibliophiles Normands, 1866.

1531. Queen Eleanor and the Dauphin at Dieppe. *L'Entree de la royne et de M. le Daulphin ... Dieppe. 1531.* Facsimile of the same. Rouen, 1899. The same, edited by E. de la Germonière, *Miscellanées de la Société des Bibliophiles Normands, Mélanges* (Rouen, 1913), Vol. LX.

1532. Francis I at Caen. "Entrée de François I à Caen en 1532, d'après de Bras," in *Cavalcade historique de Caen.* Caen, 1863.

1533. Francis I at Le Puy. Account in *Chroniques de Estienne Médicis,* ed. Augustin Chassaing. Le Puy, 1869. Also in *Mémoires de Jean Burel,* ed. Augustin Chassaing (Le Puy, 1875), p. 5.

1533(?). Francis I at Béziers. *Entrée de François Ier dans la ville de Béziers (Bas Languedoc).* Ed. Louis Domairon. Paris, 1866.

1533. Queen Eleanor at Lyons. *L'Entree de la Royne faicte en ... Lyon.* Lyons, 1533.
Godefroy, *Cf,* I, 804.

1533. Dauphin at Lyons. *L'Entree de Monseigneur le Daulphin ... Lyon ... 1533.* N.p., n.d.

1533. Francis I at Montferrand. "L'Entrée de François Ier à Montferrand en 1533," *Bulletin historique et scientifique de l'Auvergne*, Nos. 1–4, 1888, pp. 22–57.

1533. Pope Clement VII and Francis I at Marseilles. GODEFROY, *Cf*, I, 816, 820.

1533. Queen Eleanor at Troyes. BABEAU, *Les Rois de France à Troyes*, pp. 40 ff.

1539. Francis I and Charles V at Poitiers. *Triumphes D honneur faitz par le commandement ... Poictiers ...* . Paris, 1539.
GODEFROY, *Cf*, II, 750.

1539. Francis I and Charles V at Poitiers and Orleans. *Sensuivent les triumphantes et honorables entrees ... Roy Francoys ... et de la S. M. I. Charles V ... Poictiers et Orleans. 1539.* Lille, n.d.

1539. Charles V at Orleans. *La triumphante et excellente entree de L empereur ... D orleans ...* . Paris, n.d.
C. F. VERGNAUD-ROMAGNESI, *Entrée de Charles-Quint à Orléans en 1539* (Extrait de *La Revue orléanaise*). Paris and Orleans, 1846.
GODEFROY, *Cf*, II, 757.

1539. Charles V at Paris. *L'Ordre tenu et garde a l'entree de treshault et trespuissant prince Charles Empereur ... Paris ... 1539.* N.p., n.d.
La magnifique et triumphante entree ... Empereur ... Paris. Lyons, n.d.
Entrada de Carlos V en Paris el año 1540. N.p., n.d.
El grande y muy sumptuoso recibimento ... en Paris ... Emperador. N.p., n.d.
La sontuosa intrata di Carlo V sempre augusto; in la gran citta di Parigi.... Paris, 1540.
Brevis descriptio eorum quae in adventum . . . . Caroli V. . . . . N.p., 1540.

1540. Charles V at Valenciennes. *See below*, bibliography of entries in the Low Countries.

1547. Henry II at Rheims. GODEFROY, *Cf*, I, 279, 303, 309.

1548. Henry II and Catherine de Medici at Lyons. *Le grand triumphe faict a l'entree ... Henry ... Lyon.* Paris, 1548. More complete edition of the same, with engravings: *La Magnificence de la superbe et triumphante entree de la noble & antique Cité de Lyon faicte au Trescrestien Roy de France Henry deuxiesme de ce nom, et à la Royne Catherine son Espouse le XXIII. de Septembre. M.D. XLVIII.* Lyons, 1549. The same, edited by GEORGES GUIGUE. Lyons, 1928 [for 1927].
Relation des entrées solennelles dans la ville de Lyon, pp. 9–58.
MODIUS, *Pandectae triumphales*, p. 80.
GODEFROY, *Cf*, I, 823–58.

1548. Henry II at Troyes. BABEAU, *Les Rois de France à Troyes*, pp. 44 ff.

1549. Henry II at Paris. *C'est l'ordre qui a este tenu a la nouvelle et joyeuse entree ... Henry II ... Paris.* Paris, 1549.
GODEFROY, *Cf*, I, 858, 879, 885, 887.

1549. Catherine de Medici at Paris. GODEFROY, *Cf*, I, 870.

1550. Duc d'Aumale, governor of Burgundy, at Dijon. "Relation de l'entrée de Mgr. le duc d'Aumale, gouverneur de la Bourgogne, à Dijon 31 Décembre 1550," in *Entrées et rejouissances dans la ville de Dijon.* Dijon, 1885.

1550. Henry II and Catherine at Rouen. *C'est la deduction du somptueux ordre plaisantz spectacles et magnifiques theatres dresses, et exhibes par les citoiens de Rouenville ... a ... Henry second ... et maDame Katharine de Medicis ... premier & second iours d'Octobre, mil cinq cens cinquante ...* . Rouen, 1551. The same, edited by A. BLAUCOUSIN, *L'Entrée à Rouen ...* . Rouen: Société des Bibliophiles Normands, 1882.
LOUIS DE MERVAL, *L'Entrée de Henri II, roi de France, à Rouen ... 1550.* Reproduced with miniatures from manuscript account in Bibliothèque Publique de Rouen. Rouen: Société des Bibliophiles Normands, 1868.
GODEFROY, *Cf*, I, 893.

1551. Henry II at Orleans. *La magnificque et triumphante entree de la noble ville et cité d'Orléans ... Henry II.* Paris and Orleans, 1551.

1551. Henry II at Tours. *L'Entree ... Henry ... Tours.* Tours, 1551.

1559. Francis II at Rheims. GODEFROY, *Cf*, I, 311.

1559/60. Francis II and Catherine de Medici at Chenonceaux. *Les Triomphes fait a l'entree du Roi a Chenonceaux le dimanche dernier jour de Mars. 1559.* The same, reprinted, Paris, 1857.

1561. Charles IX at Rheims. GODEFROY, *Cf*, I, 312, 317, 320.

1563. Charles IX and Catherine de Medici at Sens. "Entrée du roy Charles IX et de la reine Catherine de Médicis à Sens le 15 mars 1563," *Archives municipales de la ville de Sens, 1562–1563* (Auxerre, 1882), pp. 17–30.

1564. Charles IX at Troyes. BABEAU, *Les Rois de France à Troyes*, pp. 51 ff.
GODEFROY, *Cf*, I, 894.

1564. Charles IX at Dijon. GODEFROY, *Cf*, I, 897.

1564. Charles IX at Lyons. *Relation des entrées solennelles dans la ville de Lyon*, pp. 78–90.
GODEFROY, *Cf*, I, 898.

1564/65. Charles IX at Bordeaux. P. TAMIZEY DE LARROQUE, *Entrée de Charles IX à Bordeaux avec un avertissement et des notes* (Extrait de *La Revue des bibliophiles*). Bordeaux, 1882.
GODEFROY, *Cf*, I, 907, 910, 917.

1565. Charles IX, Catherine de Medici, and Elizabeth of Spain at Bayonne. *Recueils des choses notables faites a Bayonne a l'entrevue de Charles IX avec la Royne Catholique, sa sœur.* Paris, 1566.
GODEFROY, *Cf*, II, 763.

1566. Charles IX at Angers. GODEFROY, *Cf*, I, 929.

1571/72. Charles IX at Paris. SIMON BOUQUET, *Bref et sommaire recueil ... entree ... du roy Charles IX ... en sa bonne ville de Paris. avec le couronnement ... Elizabet d'Austriche son espouse.* Paris, 1572.
GODEFROY, *Cf*, I, 519.

1573. Henry (later Henry III) at Orleans. GODEFROY, *Cf*, I, 918.

1574. Henry III at Paris. *Ibid.*, pp. 329 ff., 922.

1575. Henry III at Rheims. *Ibid.*, pp. 321, 331.

1575. Elizabeth, queen-mother, at Orleans. *Ibid.*, p. 927.

1594. Henry IV at Paris. *Entree de Henry IV a Paris en 1594.* 3 engravings.

1595. Henry IV at Lyons. *La Entrata in Lione delle christianissimo Henrico IV re di Francia et di Navarra.* Venice, 1595. *Les Deux Plus Grandes ... Resiouissances de la Ville de Lyon: La Premiere, Pour l'entree de ... Henry 1111. La Seconde, pour l'heureuse publication de la Paix.* Lyons, 1598.
Relation des entrées solennelles dans la ville de Lyon, pp. 110–15.
GODEFROY, *Cf,* I, 930.

1596. Henry IV at Rouen to be made Knight of the Garter. JOHN NICHOLS, *The Progresses and Public Processions of Queen Elizabeth* (London, 1823), III, 398 ff.
GODEFROY, *Cf,* I, 945.

1599. Henry IV at Rouen. *Discours de la Joyeuse Entree de ... Prince Henry 1111 ... en sa ville de Rouen.* Rouen, 1599.

1600. Marie de Medici at Lyons. PIERRE MATHIEU, *L'Entree de tres grande ... Princesse Marie de Médicis ... en la ville de Lyon.* Lyons, 1600.

1600. Marie de Medici at Avignon. *Labyrinthe royal de Hercule Gaulois triomphant ... de ... Henry 1111 Roy de France ... . Represente a l'Entrée triomphante de la Royne en la cité d'Avignon. Le 19 novembre l'an MDC.* Avignon, [1601].

1600. Marie de Medici at Marseilles. GODEFROY, *Cf,* I, 953, 955.

1600. Albert and Isabella at Lille. *See below,* bibliography of entries in the Low Countries.

1601. Marie de Medici at Paris. GODEFROY, *Cf,* I, 959.

1603. Henry IV at Caen. *Discours de l'entree faicte par treshaut et trespuissant Prince Henry 1111, Roi de France et de Navarre, et Tresillustre princesse Marie de Médicis, La Royne son epouse, en leur ville de Caen, au mois de septembre 1603.* Caen, 1842.

1610. The King at Metz. ABR. FABERT, *Voyage du roy a Metz, L'occasion d'iceluy: Ensemble Les signes de rejiouyssance faits par ses Habitans, pour honorer l'entree de sa Majesté.* [Metz], 1610.

1610. Marie de Medici at Paris. *Les Ceremonies et ordre tenu au Sacre et couronnement de la Royne Marie de Medicis Royne de France et de Navarre dans l'eglise de Sainct Denis le 13 May 1610 ... .* Lyons, 1612.
GODEFROY, *Cf,* I, 556 ff., 960.

1610. Louis XIII at Rheims. GODEFROY, *Cf,* I, 404 ff.

1610. Louis XIII at Paris. *Ibid.,* p. 907.

1617. Duchess of Montmorency at Montpellier. *L'Entrée à Montpelier le 18 Juin 1617 de la Duchesse de Montmorency.* Reproduction of first edition, with Introd. by COMTE DE SAINT-MAUR. Montpellier, 1873.

1622. Louis XIII at Lyons. *L'Entree du Roy et de la Royne dans sa ville de Lyon ... 1622.* Lyons, 1624.
Relation des entrées solennelles dans la ville de Lyon, pp. 160–66.

1629. Louis XIII at Paris. JEAN BAPTISTE DE MACHAULT, *Etages et discours ... reception du roy ... Paris.* Paris, 1629.

1632. Henry de Bourbon, Prince de Condé, at Dijon. *Entree de tres Haut et tres Puissant Prince Henry de Bourbon, Prince de Conde ... en la ville de Dijon, le trentiesme du mois de Septembre mil six cens trente deux.* Dijon, 1632.

D. ENTRIES: THE LOW COUNTRIES

As there has been no bibliography of Low Country entries, except the Hapsburg entries listed by Alenda y Mira, I give here a full list of all I have been able to find.

General Works

ALENDA Y MIRA, JENARO. *Relaciones de solemnidades y fiestas públicas de España.* Madrid, 1903.

BLOMMAERT, P., and SERRURE, C. P. (eds.). *Kronyk van Vlaenderen van 580 tot 1467.* ("Maetschappy der Vlaemsche Bibliophilen," No. 3, Part II.) Ghent, 1839–40.

CALVETE DE ESTRELLA, JUAN CHRISTOVAL. *El felicissimo viaje d'el ... Principe D. Phelippe ... desde España à sus tierras de la baxa Alemaña; con la descripcion de todos los Estados de Brabante y Flandes.* Antwerp, 1552.

Chronijke van Vlaenderen. Bruges: Andreas Wydts, 1736.

DESHAISNES, C. *Fêtes et marches historiques en Belgique et dans le nord de la France.* ("Mémoires de la Société des Sciences, de l'Agriculture, et des Arts de Lille," Ser. V, Fasc. 1.) Lille, 1895.

GACHARD, LOUIS PROSPER. *Collection de documents inédits concernant l'histoire de la Belgique.* 3 vols. Brussels, 1833–35.

————. *Collection des voyages des souverains des Pays-Bas.* 4 vols. Brussels, 1874–82.

GRANGE, A. DE LA. "Les Entrées des souverains à Tournai," *Mémoires de la Société Historique et Archéologique de Tournai,* XIX (1885), 5–420. Cf. esp. Bibliography, pp. 417–20.

KALFF, GERRIT. *Geschiedenis der Nederlandsche Letterkunde.* 7 vols. Groningen, 1906–12.

LABORDE, LÉON EMMANUEL SIMON JOSEPH, MARQUIS DE. *Les Ducs de Bourgogne: études sur les lettres, les arts et l'industrie pendant le XVe siècle.* 3 vols. Paris, 1849–52.

MANDER, KAREL VAN. *Het Leven der doorluchtighe Nederlandtsche en Hoogduytsche Schilders.* Amsterdam, 1604; 1617.

Particular Accounts

1301. Philip the Fair at Ghent. P. BLOMMAERT, "Beknopte Geschiedenis der Kamers van Rhetorica te Gent," *Belgisch Museum voor de Nederduitsche Tael- en Letterkunde,* I, 418 f.
Chronijke van Vlaenderen, I, 413 f.

1329. Countess Marguerite at Ghent. *Chronijke van Vlaenderen,* I, 507.

1428. Isabel of Portugal at Bruges. J. A. CROWE and G. B. CAVALCASELLE, *The Early Flemish Painters* (2d ed.; London, 1872), p. 87, citing *Marchant Flandria descripta* (Antwerp, 1596), p. 284; and SANDERUS, *Flandria illust.,* pp. 76 f.

1440. Dukes of Burgundy and Orleans at Bruges. *Chronijke van Vlaenderen,* II, 105–11.

1440. Philip of Burgundy at Bruges. *Ibid.,* p. 272.
BLOMMAERT and SERRURE, *Kronyk van Vlaenderen van 580 tot 1467,* II, 107 ff., 212 ff., 233.

1453. Lille banquet. *Chroniques de Mathieu de Coussy [d'Escouchy],* in BUCHON (ed.), *Choix de chroniques et mémoires sur l'histoire de France ...* (Paris, 1836), chap. lxxxvii, pp. 145 ff. Most complete account.
LA MARCHE, *Mémoires,* II, 348 ff.
LABORDE, *Les Ducs de Bourgogne,* I, 413 ff. Expense accounts.

1455(?). Philip of Burgundy and the Dauphin at Bruges. CHASTELLAIN, *Œuvres*, III, 301 ff.

1458. Philip of Burgundy at Ghent. *Chronijke van Vlaenderen*, II, 212 ff.

BLOMMAERT and SERRURE, *Kronyk van Vlaenderen van 580 tot 1467*, II, 233 f.

P. BERGMANS, "Note sur la représentation du retable de l'agneau mystique des van Eyck en tableau vivant à Gand en 1458," *Annales de la Fédération Archéologique et Historique de Belgique*, XX (1907), 530.

1467. Charles the Bold at Ghent. GACHARD, *Documents inédits*, I, 210.

LABORDE, *Les Ducs de Bourgogne*, II, 703, Appen.

1468. Charles the Bold at Rijssel. *Chronijke van Vlaenderen*, II, 393.

1468. Margaret of York at Bruges. Add. MS 6113, British Museum.

LA MARCHE, *Mémoires*, IV, 95–144.

LABORDE, *Les Ducs de Bourgogne*, II, 293 ff. Expense accounts with directions for preparation of the banquets.

FRANCIS HENRY TAYLOR, "A Piece of Arras of the Judgment," *Worcester Art Museum Annual*, I (1935–36), 1–15.

1496. Joanna of Castile at Brussels. MS in Kupferstich-kabinet, Berlin.

MAX HERRMANN, *Forschungen zur deutschen Theater-geschichte des Mittelalters und der Renaissance*. Berlin, 1914. Publishes the miniatures and a summary of the account.

1497. Philip the Fair at Bruges. *Belgisch Museum voor de Nederduitsche Tael- en Letterkunde*, IX, 155 ff.

1497. Philip the Fair at Amsterdam. *De Intocht van Philip den Schoone binnen Amsterdam 27. Juni 1497: Geschiedkundige Aanteekeningen tot Opheldering van de Maskerade te houden . . . . op 22. Juni. 1880*. Leyden, 1880.

1508. Maximilian I at Ghent. P. KERVYN DE VOLKAERS-BEKE, "Joyeuse entrée de l'Empereur Maximilien à Gand," *Messager des sciences historiques et archives des arts de Belgique*, Vol. XVIII, No. 1 (1850).

1515. Charles V at Ghent. GACHARD, *Voyages*, II, 524–30, Appen. IV. Account in Latin.

1515. Charles V at Middelburg. N. C. LAMBRECHTSEN VAN RITTHEM, "Beknopte Geschiedenis van de Middel-burgsche Rhetorijkkamer het Bloemken Jesse," *Verhandelingen van de Maatschappij der Nederlandsche Letterkunde te Leyden*, III, No. 1 (1819), 145 ff.

1515. Charles V at Bruges. *La tryumphante et solemnelle entree faicte sur le joyeux advenement de ... Charles ... .* MS Codex 2591, National Library, Vienna. JOSEPH GREGOR reproduces part of this, showing costume, in *Monumenta scenica*, Portfolio V, Pls. II and III.

REMY DU PUYS, *La Tryumphante et solemnelle entree faicte sur le nouvel et joyeux advenement de ... Charles ... en sa ville de Bruges l an mil d cent XV. le XVIIIᵉ jour d avril ...* [Paris, 1515]. Same account as the manuscript. The same, reprinted in *Recueil de chroniques, chartres et d'autres documents*. 3d ser. Bruges: Société d'Emulation de Bruges, 1850.

GACHARD, *Voyages*, II, 531–42, Appen. V. Expense accounts.

1515. Charles V at Mons. Gachard, *Voyages*, II, 543–53, Appen. VI. Expense account in French.

1515. Charles V at Louvain. *Ibid.*, pp. 519–23, Appen. III. Expense account in Dutch.

1515. Charles V at Namur. *Ibid.*, pp. 553–56, Appen. VII.

1516. Charles V at Douai. Archives Communales de Douai, Ser. CC, 238, fols. 90, 91, 93, 96, 98, 108, 110, 112, 114. Expense accounts.

EUGÈNE F. J. TAILLIAR, *Chroniques de Douai* (Douai, 1875–77), II, 94 ff.

GACHARD, *Voyages*, II, 556–58, Appen. VIII.

DESHAISNES, *Fêtes et marches historiques*, pp. 20–23.

1520. Charles V at Aix-la-Chapelle. *Die Triumphe van dat Cronemente van den Keyser Ende ope Triumphelijcke incomste van Aken*. Also editions in French and Spanish.

1520. Charles V at Antwerp. PETRUS AEGIDIUS CORNELIUS GRAPHEUS, *Hipoteses, sive argumenta spectaculorum. . . . .* [Antwerp, 1520].

1521. Charles V at Valenciennes. GACHARD, *Voyages*, II, 559–61, Appen. IX.

1531. Charles V at Namur. *Ibid.*, pp. 562 f., Appen. X.

1531. Charles V at Tournai. *Ibid.*, pp. 564–67, Appen. XI.

1540. Charles V at Valenciennes. *Ibid.*, pp. 581–92, Appen. XIV.

1540. Charles V at Tournai. *Ibid.*, pp. 593–95, Appen. XV.

1544(?). Charles V and Francis I at Brussels. *Trionphi del Imperador in la citta de Bruselles. Le lettere de li honorati et superbi Trionphi tra la Maesta Cesarea e el Re di Franza.... fatto in la citta de Bruseles*. Venice, 1544.

1549. Philip at Brussels. *Die blyde Incomste den Hertochdomme van Brabant, in voortijden by haren landtsheeren verleent, ende van Keyser Carolo den V . . . . anno 1549*. Brussels, 1549. Reprinted, Cologne, 1565, 1566, 1612, 1644, 1660; Delft, 1574; Brussels, 1623.

Einzug der Römischen Keyseerlichen maiestat soems des Printzen in Hispanen . . . . zu Brussel im Brabandt den Ersten tag Aprilis. M.D. XLIX. Erffurt, 1549.

CALVETE DE ESTRELLA, *El felicissimo viaje*, pp. 64 ff.

1549. Philip at Louvain. *Ibid.*, pp. 81 ff.

1549. Philip at Ghent. *Ibid.*, pp. 97 ff.

1549. Philip at Bruges. *Ibid.*, pp. 112 ff.

1549. Philip at Ypres. *Ibid.*, pp. 124 ff.

1549. Philip at Béthune. *Ibid.*, pp. 131 ff.

1549. Philip at Lille. *Ibid.*, pp. 134 ff.

1549. Philip at Tournai. *Ibid.*, pp. 148 ff.

1549. Philip at Binche. *Ibid.*, pp. 182 ff.

ALBERT VAN DE PUT, "Two Drawings of the Fêtes at Binche for Charles V and Philip (II), 1549," *Journal of the Warburg and Courtauld Institutes*, III, Nos. 1 and 2 (October, 1939—January, 1940), 49–55.

1549. Philip at Antwerp. CORNELIUS GRAPHEUS, *Spectaculorum in susceptione Philippi Hisp. prin. divi Caroli V caesar. F. an. M.D. XLIX. Antwerpiae aeditorum, mirificus apparatus*. Antwerp, 1550. The same in Dutch. CORNELIUS GRAPHEUS, *De seer wonderlycke, schoone, Triumphelijcke Incompst van den hooghmagenden Prince Philips, Prince van Spaignen, Caroli des vijfden Keyserssone, in de stadt van Antwerpen, anno MCCCCC XLIX.* Antwerp, 1550. The same in French. CORNILLE GRAPHEUS, *La tres admirable, tres magnifique, & triumphante entree ... Prince d'Espaigne ... Anvers. anno 1549.* Antwerp, 1550. CALVETE DE ESTRELLA, *El felicissimo viaje,* pp. 220 ff.

1549. Philip at Dordrecht, Rotterdam, and Amsterdam. *Ibid.,* pp. 276 ff.

1558. Philip at Ghent. *Tractaet der triomphe of blyde inkomst van Philippus van Oostenryck, prins van Spangnien, binnen der stad Ghent den 13 dach in wedemaent. 1558.* Ghent.

1577. Don John at Louvain. JOHN MOTLEY, *The Rise of the Dutch Republic* ("Everyman" Ed.), III, 97 f.

1577. Don John at Brussels. *Ibid.,* p. 103.

1577. William of Orange at Brussels. JAN BAPTISTA HOUWAERT, *De triumphante Inkomste des prince van Oranje 23 Sept. 1577.* Antwerp, 1578.
MOTLEY, *Rise of the Dutch Republic,* III, 175.

1577. William of Orange at Ghent. *De beschryvinghe van het ghene dat vertoocht wierdt ter incomste van den Prince van Orangien binnen der stede van Ghendt den 29 decembris 1577. . . . .* Ghent, 1577.
LUCAS DE HEERE, *Beschryvinghe van het ghene dat vertoocht wierdt ter Incomste van d'excellentie, des Princen van Oraengien binnen der Stad van Ghendt.* Ghent, 1578. The same, ed. P. BLOMMAERT. ("Maetschappy der Vlaemsche Bibliophilen," 2d ser., No. IV.) Ghent, 1852.
MOTLEY, *Rise of the Dutch Republic,* III, 295.

1578. Archduke Matthias at Brussels. JAN BAPTISTA HOUWAERT, *Sommare Beschrijvinghe van de triumphelijcke Incomst van den . . . . Aerts-hertoge Matthias binnen die Princelijcke Stadt van Brussele . . . . 1578.* Antwerp, 1579. Reprinted, Utrecht, 1881.

1580. William of Orange at Amsterdam. *Incomste van den doorluchtighen Vorst ende Heere mijn Heere den Prince van Orangien binnen der vermaerde coopstadt van Amsterdam den xvij en Martii 1580.* Antwerp, n.d.

1582. Francis at Antwerp. *La joyeuse & magnifique entrée de Monseign. Francoys, Fils de France ... en sa tres renommée ville d'Anvers.* Antwerp, 1582.
De blijde ende heerlijcke Incomste van Mijn Heer Franssois van Vranckrijck . . . . in . . . . Antwerpen. Antwerp, 1582.

1582. Francis at Ghent. *L'Entree magnifique de Monseigneur Francoys Filz de France ... faicte en sa metropolitaine et fameuse ville de Gand le XXme d'aoust anno 1582.* Ghent, 1582. Reprinted at Ghent, 1841, with Epilogue by AUGUSTE VOISIN.
De eerlicke incomste van onzen ghenadighen ende gheduchten heere Francoys van Vranckerycke; in syne vermaerde Hoofstad van Ghendt, den 20 augusti 1582. Ghent, [1582].

1582. Francis at Bruges. *De heerlicke incomste van onzen ghenadighen Land-Vorst, myn Heere Francoys van Franckrijk . . . . in zyn vermaerde stadt van Brugge, den xxvii dach july anno M. D. LXXXII.* Bruges. Republished in *Annales de la Société d'Emulation de Flandre Occidentale,* II (2d ser.; June, 1844), 77–93.

1585. Earl of Leicester at The Hague. *Delineatio Pompae Triumphalis qua Robertus Dudlaeus Comes Leicestrensis Hague Comitis Fuit Exceptus Palatium Comitum Hollandiae.* 12 engravings by C. DANKERTS.

1585. Alexander Farnese, Prince of Parma, at Ghent. MS and sketches by LIEVIN VAN DE SCHELDE in *Atlas Goedgebuer,* Archives Communales, Ghent.

1594. Prince Ernest at Antwerp. *Descriptio Publicae Gratulationis, Spectaculorum et Ludorum, in adventu serenissimi principis Ernesti Archiducis Austriae, Ducis Burgundiae . . . . 1594.* Antwerp, 1595.

1594. Prince Ernest at Brussels. *Descriptio et Explicatio Pegmatum, Arcuum, et Spectaculorum, quae Bruxellae Brabant . . . . sub ingressum . . . . Ernesti . . . . archiducis Austriae. . . . .* Brussels, 1594.

1594. Prince Maurice at Amsterdam. J. A. WORP, *Geschiedenis van het Drama en van het Tooneel in Nederland* (Groningen, 1904–8), I, 43.

1596. Archduke Albert at Brussels. Composite engraving in Bibliothèque de l'Arsenal, Paris. Reproduced by DUBECH, *Histoire générale illustrée du théâtre,* II, 168.

1600–1601. Albert and Isabella at Ghent, Courtrai, Lille, Douai, Tournai, Arras, and Cambrai. *Descriptio Pompae et Gratulationis Publicae Ser. Pot. Principibus Alberto . . . . et Isabellae . . . . a Senatu Populoq. Gandavensi . . . . Maximo Aemgliano Vrientio . . . . a secretis auctore.* Antwerp, 1602.

1600. Albert and Isabella at Lille. *Entree solennelle de leurs altesses Serenissimes Albert et Isabel Clara Eugenia Princes et Souverains Seigneurs de ces Pays-bas. Faite dans la ville de Lille le cinq de fevrier 1600.* MS No. 678 (formerly No. 636), Bibliothèque Communale de Lille. 23 miniatures of theatres and arches. Text edited by J. HOUDOY, *Joyeuse entrée d'Albert et d'Isabelle: Lille au XVIe siècle d'après des documents inédits.* Lille, 1873. Several scenes published by A. L. MILLIN in *Antiquités nationales,* V, Part LXI (Paris, Year VII), 5, 20, 27. One scene published by CARL NIESSEN, *Das Bühnenbild* (Leipzig, 1924–27), Pl. 15a, No. 2.

1600. Albert and Isabella at Valenciennes. HENRICO D'OULTREMANNO, *Descriptio Triumphi et Spectaculorum Ser. Pr. Alberto et Isabellae . . . . ac civitatem Valentionis.* Antwerp, 1602.

1600. Albert and Isabella at Brussels, Louvain, and Malines. *Historica Narratio Profectionis et Inaugurationis ser. Belgii Principum Alberti et Isabellae Austriae Archiducum . . . . in Belgium adventus. . . . .* Antwerp, 1602.

1600. Albert and Isabella at Antwerp. JAN BOCK, *Pompae Triumphalis et Spectaculorum in adventu et inauguratione Ser. Princ. Alberti et Isabellae . . . . Antwerpia. . . . .* Antwerp, 1602.

1609. French and English ambassadors in the Netherlands. *Triumphante ende blyde incomste vande ambassadeurs, van Wegen de Coninghen van Vranckryck ende Enghelant, Opt stuck vande Vrede-handel opte lanckduerick bestant tusschen hare Hoocheden, ende de E. Heeren Staten Generael der vereenichde Nederlanden.* Antwerp, 1609.

1635. Ferdinand at Antwerp. JOANNES CASPERIUS GEVARTIUS, *Pompa Introitus honori Ser. Principis Ferdinandi Austriaci . . . . Antwerp . . . . 1635.* Antwerp, 1641. Designed by Rubens.

1636. Ferdinand at Ghent. GUILIELMO BECANO, *Serenissimi Principis Ferdinandi Hispaniarum Infantis S. R. E. Car-*

dinalis Triumphalis Introitus in Flandriae Metropolim Gandauum. Antwerp, 1636.

1639. Marie de Medici at Amsterdam. KASPAR VAN BAERLE, *Blyde Inkomst der . . . . Koninginne Maria de Medicis t' Amsterdam.* Amsterdam, 1639.

1642. Charles I of England at Amsterdam. *Beschrivinge van de blyde inkoomste, rechten van Zeege-bogen en ander toestel . . . . van H. M. van Groot-Britanien . . . . Amsterdam.* Amsterdam, 1642.

1666. Charles II of Spain in Flanders. F. VANDERHAEGHEN, *Inauguration de Charles II en Flandre (2 mai 1666).* Ghent, 1867.

1691. William III of England at The Hague. *De Konincklycke Triumphe vertoonende alle de Eerpoorten, met desselfs besondere Sinne-beelden, in hare beschryvinge, ten getale van in de 60, opgerecht in 's Gravenhage 1691 ter Eere van Willem de III Koningh van Groot Brittanjen.* The Hague, 1691.

E. ENTRIES: ENGLAND

General Works

BREWER, J. S., and GAIRDNER, J. *Letters and Papers, Foreign and Domestic, of the Reign of Henry VIII.* 21 vols. London, 1862–1910.

CLODE, CHARLES MATTHEW. *The Early History of the Guild of Merchant Taylors.* 2 vols. London, 1888.

Documents Relative to the Reception at Edinburgh of the Kings and Queens of Scotland. Edinburgh: Bannatyne Club, 1822.

FAIRHOLT, FREDERICK W. *The Civic Garland: A Collection of Songs from London Pageants.* London: Percy Society, 1845.

———. *Lord Mayors' Pageants; Being Collections towards a History of These Annual Celebrations,* Vol. I: *History of Lord Mayors' Pageants;* Vol. II: *Reprints of Lord Mayors' Pageants.* 2 vols. London: Percy Society, 1843–44.

FEUILLERAT, ALBERT. *Le Bureau des menus-plaisirs (Office of the Revels) et la mise-en-scène à la cour d'Elizabeth.* Louvain, 1910.

———. *Documents Relating to the Office of the Revels in the Time of Queen Elizabeth.* Louvain, 1908.

———. *Documents Relating to the Revels at Court in the Time of King Edward VI and Queen Mary.* Louvain, 1914.

GREEN, MARY ANNE E. WOOD. *Elizabeth: Electress Palatine and Queen of Bohemia.* London, 1855. Rev. by S. C. LOMAS. 1909.

GROSE, F., and ASTLE, T. *Antiquarian Repertory.* 4 vols. London, 1807–9.

[HALL, EDWARD]. *Hall's Chronicle.* London, 1809.

———. *Henry VIII.* Introd. by CHARLES WHIBLEY. 2 vols. London, 1904.

HARRIS, MARY D. (ed.). *Coventry Leet Book.* 3 vols. London, 1907–9.

HERBERT, WILLIAM, *The History of the Twelve Great Livery Companies of London.* 2 vols. London, 1837.

HONE, WILLIAM. *Ancient Mysteries Described.* London, 1823.

JACKSON, JOHN. *The History of the Scottish Stage.* Edinburgh, 1793.

KELLY, WILLIAM. *Notices Illustrative of the Drama and Other Amusements in Leicester, Chiefly in the Sixteenth and Seventeenth Centuries.* London, 1865.

———. *Royal Progresses and Visits to Leicester.* Leicester, 1884.

KINGSFORD, CHARLES L. *Chronicles of London.* Oxford, 1905.

LELAND, JOHN. *Antiquarii de rebus Britannicis collectanea.* Notes by THOMAS HEARN. 6 vols. London, 1770.

NAUNTON, SIR R. *Fragmenta regalia: Memoirs of Elizabeth, Her Court and Favorites.* 1641 and 1653; reprinted, London, 1870.

NICHOLS, JOHN. *The Progresses and Public Processions of Queen Elizabeth.* New ed. 3 vols. London, 1823.

———. *The Progresses, Processions, and Magnificent Festivities of King James the First.* 4 vols. London, 1828.

NICHOLS, JOHN GOUGH. *The Diary of Henry Machyn Citizen and Merchant-Taylor of London, 1550–1563.* London: Camden Society, 1848.

———. *Literary Remains of King Edward the Sixth.* 2 vols. London, 1857.

———. *London Pageants.* London, 1837.

PAUL, SIR J. B. "Processions," *Scottish Review,* XXX (1897), 217–35.

SEGAR, WILLIAM. *Honor Military, and Civill, contained in foure Bookes.* London, 1602.

STOW, JOHN. *Annales, or A Generall Chronicle of England.* London, 1631.

WITHINGTON, ROBERT. "The Early 'Royal-Entry,' " *Publications of the Modern Language Association,* XXXII (1917), 616–23.

———. *English Pageantry.* 2 vols. Cambridge, Mass., 1920. Hereafter cited as "*EP.*"

Particular Accounts

Withington, in *English Pageantry,* gives an exhaustive list of the sources on the royal entries in England and the entries of the Lord Mayors of London. I refer here to his summaries, to his principal sources, and to a few accounts which he missed.

1189. Richard I at London for coronation. MATTHEW PARIS, *Chronica minora* (London, 1866), II, 6 f.
PARIS, *Chronica majora* (London, 1880), II, 348.
JOSEPH STRUTT, *Horda Angel-cynnan, or a Compleat View of the Manners, Customs, &c., of the English People* (London, 1774–76), II, 59.
WITHINGTON, *EP,* I, 124.

1236. Eleanor of Provence at London. PARIS, *Chronica majora,* III, 336.
WITHINGTON, "The Early 'Royal-Entry,' " pp. 616 ff.

1243. Henry III at London. PARIS, *Chronica majora,* IV, 255.

1247. Henry III at London. *Ibid.,* p. 644.

1252. Alexander III of Scotland married to daughter of Henry III at York. *Ibid.,* V, 266 f.

1274. Edward I at London for coronation. "Annales Londonienses" in *Chronicles of Edward I and Edward II,* ed. WILLIAM STUBBS (London, 1882–83), I, 84.
NICHOLS, *London Pageants,* p. 10.
WITHINGTON, "The Early 'Royal-Entry,' " p. 621, n. 12.

1298. Edward I at London after victory over the Scots. "The Chronicle of Dunmow" in Harl. MS 530, fols. 2–13.
WITHINGTON, "The Early 'Royal-Entry,' " pp. 621 f.

1300. Edward I and Margaret of France at London. STOW, *Annales,* p. 208.
WITHINGTON, *EP,* I, 125.

1308. Edward II at London for coronation. "Annales Londoniensis," I, 152.
WITHINGTON, *EP*, I, 125.

1327. Queen Isabella at London. "Annales Paulini" in *Chronicles of Edward I and Edward II*, I, 338 f.
STOW, *Annales*, p. 224.
WITHINGTON, *EP*, I, 126 f.

1327. Philippa of Hainault at London. "Annales Paulini," I, 338 f.

1377. Richard II at London for coronation. T. WALSINGHAM, *Historia Anglicana*, ed. H. T. RILEY (London, 1863), I, 231.
WITHINGTON, *EP*, I, 128.

1382. Anne of Bohemia at London. HERBERT, *History of the Livery Companies*, II, 217 ff.
WITHINGTON, *EP*, I, 129.

1390. Richard II and court in processions at London for tournaments at Smithfield. *The Chronicle of Froissart*, trans. LORD BERNERS (London, 1901–2), V, 419–27.

1392. Richard II at London. *A History of Britain from Brutus to Henry V*. Bodl. MS Ashm. 793, fols. 128b and 129. MAIDSTONE, "De concordia inter regem Ric. II et civitatem London," in *Political Poems and Songs*, ed. T. WRIGHT (1859–61), I, 282 ff.
WITHINGTON, *EP*, I, 129–31.

1399. Henry IV at London for coronation. WITHINGTON, *EP*, I, 132.

1415. Henry V at London after Agincourt. Harl. MS 53, fol. 157b (STRUTT, *Manners and Customs*, II, 50 f.).
Harl. MS 565, fol. IIIb (SIR NICHOLAS HARRIS NICOLAS, *History of the Battle of Agincourt* [2d ed.; London, 1832], pp. 325 ff.).
Cotton MS Julius E. iv, fol. 113 (B. WILLIAMS, *Gesta Henrici Quinti* [London, 1850], pp. 61 ff.).
WITHINGTON, *EP*, I, 132–37.

1421. Henry V and Catherine of France at London. WITHINGTON, *EP*, I, 137.

1432. Henry VI at London. J. O. HALLIWELL-PHILLIPPS, *John Lydgate's Minor Poems* (London, 1840), II, 2 ff.
KINGSFORD, *Chronicles of London*, pp. 97 ff.
H. N. MACCRACKEN, "King Henry's Triumphal Entry into London; Lydgate's Poem and Carpenter's Letter," in Herrig's *Archiv für das Studium der neueren Sprachen*, CXXVI (Braunschweig, 1911), 75 f.
ROBERT FABYAN, *The New Chronicles of England and France* (London, 1811), pp. 603–7.
WITHINGTON, *EP*, I, 141–47.

1445. Margaret of Anjou at London. Lydgate's verses, Harl. MS 3869, reprinted by CARLETON F. BROWN, *Modern Language Review*, VII, 225–34.
WITHINGTON, *EP*, I, 148.

1456. Queen Margaret at Coventry. *Coventry Leet Book*, II, 285 ff.
WITHINGTON, *EP*, I, 149 f.

1461. Edward IV at London and Coventry. WITHINGTON, *EP*, I, 150 f.

1461. Edward IV at Bristol. F. J. FURNIVALL, *Political, Religious, and Love Poems* (London, 1903), p. 5.
WITHINGTON, *EP*, I, 151 f.

1469. Queen Elizabeth at Norwich. HENRY HARROD, "Queen Elizabeth Woodville's Visit to Norwich in 1469," *Norfolk Archaeology*, V (1859), 32 ff.
WITHINGTON, *EP*, I, 152 f.

1474. Prince Edward at Coventry. *Coventry Leet Book*, II, 390 ff.
WITHINGTON, *EP*, I, 153 f.

1483. Richard III at York. WITHINGTON, *EP*, I, 155 f.

1486. Henry VII's provincial tour. LELAND, *Collectanea*, IV, 185 ff.
WITHINGTON, *EP*, I, 157–60.

1487. Queen Elizabeth at London for coronation. GROSE and ASTLE, *Antiquarian Repertory*, I, 296 ff.
WITHINGTON, *EP*, I, 160 f.

1498. Prince Arthur at Coventry. *Coventry Leet Book*, III, 589 ff.
WITHINGTON, *EP*, I, 164 f

1501. Prince Arthur and Catherine of Aragon at London. GROSE and ASTLE, *Antiquarian Repertory*, II, 248 ff.
KINGSFORD, *Chronicles of London*, pp. 234 ff.
WITHINGTON, *EP*, I, 166–68.

1509. Henry VIII and Catherine of Aragon at London. HALL, *Henry VIII*, pp. 507 ff.
WITHINGTON, *EP*, I, 169 f.

1511. Henry VIII and Catherine of Aragon at Coventry. WITHINGTON, *EP*, I, 170.

1520. Charles V at London. LELAND, *Collectanea*, VI, 33.
WITHINGTON, *EP*, I, 174.

1522. Charles V at London. *The descrycpion of the pageantes made in the Cyte of London att the recevyng of the most excellent pryncys Charlys the fyfte Emperour and Henry the viij Kyng off englonde*. MS 298, No. 8 (Library of Corpus Christi, Cambridge), pp. 132 ff.
CHARLES R. BASKERVILL, "William Lily's Verse for the Entry of Charles V into London," *Huntington Library Bulletin*, No. 9 (April, 1936), pp. 1–14.
STOW, *Annales*, p. 516.
WITHINGTON, *EP*, I, 174–79.

1533. Anne Boleyn at London for coronation. Harl. MS 41. Egerton MS 2623, fol. 5.
HALL, *Chronicle*, pp. 798 ff.
WITHINGTON, *EP*, I, 180–84.

1546/47. Edward VI at London. LELAND, *Collectanea*, IV, 310 ff.
WITHINGTON, *EP*, I, 185–87.

1553. Queen Mary at London for coronation. STOW, *Annales*, p. 616.
HOLINSHED, *Chronicles* (London, 1808), IV, 8.
WITHINGTON, *EP*, I, 188 f.

1553. Lord Mayor at London. MACHYN, *Diary*, pp. 47 f.
WITHINGTON, *EP*, II, 13 f.

1554. Philip and Mary at London. JOHN ELDER, *The Copie of a Letter sent in to Scotlande, of the ariuall and landynge, and most noble Maryage of the moste Illustre Prynce Philippe, Prynce of Spaine, to the most excellente Princes Marye, Quene of England*. London, 1555.
La solemne et felice intrata delli Ser. Re. Philippo et Regina Maria d Inghleterra nella Regal citta di Londra alli xviij d' agosto M. D. L. 1111.... N.p., n.d. [Rome, 1554].

JOHN FOXE, *Acts and Monuments*, ed. S. R. CATLEY (London, 1838), VI, 557 ff.
WITHINGTON, *EP*, I, 189–94.

1554. Lord Mayor at London. MACHYN, *Diary*, pp. 72 f.
WITHINGTON, *EP*, II, 15.

1555. Lord Mayor at London. MACHYN, *Diary*, p. 96.
WITHINGTON, *EP*, II, 15.

1556. Lord Mayor at London. MACHYN, *Diary*, pp. 117 f.
CLODE, *History of the Guild of Merchant Taylors*, II, 262 f.
WITHINGTON, *EP*, II, 15 f.

1556. Mayor at Norwich. WITHINGTON, *EP*, II, 16 f.

1558/59. Elizabeth at London for coronation. *The Royall Passage of her Maiesty from the Tower of London, to her Palice of White-hall, with all the Speaches and Deuices, both of the Pageants and otherwise, together with her Maiesties Seueral Answers and most pleasing Speaches to them all.* London, 1558; 1558/59; 1604.
The Passage of our most drad soveraigne lady Quene Elyzabeth through the citie of London. . . . . London, 1558. Reprinted in *Progresses of Queen Elizabeth*, I, 38 ff., and in EDWARD ARBER, *An English Garner* (Westminster, 1877–96), IV, 217 ff.
WITHINGTON, *EP*, I, 199–202.

1561. Lord Mayor at London. CLODE, *History of the Guild of Merchant Taylors*, II, 263 f.
WITHINGTON, *EP*, II, 18 f.

1565. Elizabeth at Coventry. *Progresses of Queen Elizabeth*, I, 192 ff. Hereafter cited as "*Prog. Q. Eliz.*"

1566. Elizabeth at Oxford. *Ibid.*, p. 212.

1566. Lord Mayor at London. JAMES P. MALCOLM, *Londinium redivivum* (London, 1803–7), II, 42 f.
FAIRHOLT, *Lord Mayors' Pageants*, II, 14.
WITHINGTON, *EP*, II, 20 f.

1568. Lord Mayor at London. HERBERT, *History of the Livery Companies*, I, 200.
WITHINGTON, *EP*, II, 21.

1569. Lord Mayor at London. JOHN NICHOLL, *Some Account of the Worshipful Company of Ironmongers* (London, 1866), p. 98.
WITHINGTON, *EP*, II, 21 f.

1572. Elizabeth at Warwick. *Prog. Q. Eliz.*, I, 309 ff.
WILLIAM KEMP, *The Black Book of Warwick* (Warwick, [1898]), p. 96.

1573. Elizabeth at Sandwich. *Prog. Q. Eliz.*, I, 337 f.

1574. Elizabeth at Bristol. *Ibid.*, pp. 392 ff.

1575. Elizabeth at Kenilworth. GEORGE GASCOIGNE, *The Princelye Pleasures at the Courte at Kenelwoorth.* Reprinted in *Prog. Q. Eliz.*, I, 485 ff.
Prog. Q. Eliz., I, 426 ff., 430 ff., 515 ff.

1575. Elizabeth at Worcester. *Ibid.*, pp. 533 f.

1575. Lord Mayor at London. In WILLIAM SMYTHE, "A breffe description of the Royall Citie of London, capitall citie of this realme of England." MS printed in J. HASLEWOOD and SIR E. BRYDGES, *British Bibliographer* (London, 1810), I, 539 f.
FAIRHOLT, *Lord Mayors' Pageants*, I, 20 f. and 24 n.
WITHINGTON, *EP*, II, 22.

1578. Elizabeth at Norwich. *Prog. Q. Eliz.*, II, 136 ff.

1585. Lord Mayor at London. Pamphlet by GEORGE PEELE in the Bodleian. Reprinted in *Prog. Q. Eliz.*, II, 446.
WITHINGTON, *EP*, II, 23 f.

1588. Lord Mayor at London. WITHINGTON, *EP*, II, 24 f.

1590. Lord Mayor at London. [THOMAS NELSON], *The Device of the Pageant: Set forth by the Worshipfull Companie of the Fishmongers, for the right honorable Iohn Allot.* . . . . London, 1590. Copy of pamphlet in British Museum.
ROBERT WITHINGTON, "The Lord Mayor's Show for 1590," *Modern Language Notes*, XXXIII (1918), 8–13.
WITHINGTON, *EP*, II, 25.

1591. Elizabeth at Cowdray and Elvetham. *The Honorable Entertainment given to the Quenes Maiestie in Progresse, at Elvetham in Hampshire by* . . . . *the Earle of Hertford, 1591.* London, 1591. Reprinted in *Prog. Q. Eliz.*, III, 101 ff.

1591. Lord Mayor at London. Pamphlet by GEORGE PEELE, *Descensus astraeae*, in the Guildhall. Reprinted in FAIRHOLT, *Lord Mayors' Pageants*, I, 27.
WITHINGTON, *EP*, II, 25–27.

1602. Lord Mayor at London. CLODE, *History of the Guild of Merchant Taylors*, I, 187.
WITHINGTON, *EP*, II, 27 f.

1603/4. James I at London, *The Archs of Triumph erected in honor of the High and Mighty Prince James, the First of the name King of England, and the Sixt of Scotland, at his Majestie's Entrance & Passage through his honourable City and Chamber of London, upon the 15th day of March, 1603. Invented and published by Stephen Harrison, Joyner & Architect and graven by William Kip.* [London, 1604].
THOMAS DEKKER, *The Magnificent Entertainment given to King James, Queen Anne his wife, and Henry Frederick the Prince, upon the day of his Maiesties Tryumphant Passage* . . . . *through his Honourable Citie* . . . . *of London* . . . . .
London, 1604. 2d ed., entitled *The Whole Magnifycent Entertainment.* . . . . Reprinted by J. SOMERS, *A Collection of Scarce and Valuable Tracts* (1751), *Third Collection*, I, 116; also in *Progresses of James*, I, 337 ff.
GILBERT DUGDALE, *The Time Triumphant.* London, 1604. Reprinted by ARBER, *An English Garner*, V, 648 ff.; also in *Progresses of James*, I, 408 ff.
B. JON[SON]: *His Part of King James his Royall and Magnificent Entertainement.* . . . . London, 1604.
Beschryvinghe vande Herlycke arcus Triumphal opte eere Poorte vande Nederlantsche Natie opghereckt in Londen ter eeren den . . . . *Jacobo Coninck van Enghelant* . . . . *15 Merte 1603.* Middelburg, 1604.
JOHN SAVILE, *King James, his Entertainment at Theobalds: with his welcome to London.* 1603. Reprinted by ARBER, *An English Garner.*
T. M., *The True Narration of the Entertainment of his Royall Majestie.* . . . . Reprinted by ARBER, *An English Garner*, VIII, 485 f.; also in *Progresses of James*, I, 53–120.
J. F. [JOHN FENTON], *King James his welcome to London.* 1603.
Englands welcome to James. . . . . Reprinted in *Fugitive Tracts.* 2d ser. London, 1875.
WITHINGTON, *EP*, I, 222–26.

1605. Lord Mayor at London. ANTHONY MUNDAY, *The Triumphs of Reunited Britannia*. Copies in British Museum and Bodleian. Reprinted in *Progresses of James*, I, 564.
WITHINGTON, *EP*, II, 28 f.

1606. Christian IV of Denmark at London. *The King of Denmarkes welcome: containing his arriual, abode, and entertainement, both in the Citie and other places*. London, 1606.
H.R., *The Most royall and Honourable entertainement, of the famous and renowmed King, Christiern the fourth, King of Denmarke. . . . .* London, 1606. Reprinted in *Progresses of James*, II, 54–69.

1609. Lord Mayor at London. *Camp-bell; or the Ironmongers Faire Field*. Pamphlet in British Museum attributed to Munday.
NICHOLL, *Company of Ironmongers*, p. 143.
WITHINGTON, *EP*, II, 29 f.

1610. Prince Henry at London. ANTHONY MUNDAY, *London Love, to the Royal Prince Henrie*. London, 1610.
WITHINGTON, *EP*, I, 230–33.

1611. Lord Mayor at London. ANTHONY MUNDAY, *Chryso-Thriambos, the Triumphes of Golde*.
WITHINGTON, *EP*, II, 31.

1612. Lord Mayor at London. THOMAS DEKKER, *Troia Nova Triumphans*.
CLODE, *History of the Guild of Merchant Taylors*, pp. 335 ff.
WITHINGTON, *EP*, II, 31 f.

1613. Lord Mayor at London. THOMAS MIDDLETON, *Triumphs of Truth*. Copies in British Museum, Bodleian, and Guildhall. Reprinted in *Progresses of James*, II, 679.
WITHINGTON, *EP*, II, 33–35.

1614. Lord Mayor at London. ANTHONY MUNDAY, *Himatia-Poleos*. Pamphlet in British Museum.
WITHINGTON, *EP*, II, 36.

1616. Lord Mayor at London. *The Fishmongers Pageant on Lord Mayor's Day 1616. Chrysanaleia; or, the Golden Fishing, devised by Anthony Munday. . . . .* Ed. JOHN GOUGH NICHOLS. London, 1859.
FAIRHOLT, *Lord Mayors' Pageants*, I, 40.
NICHOLL, *Company of Ironmongers*, pp. 177 and 180 f.
WITHINGTON, *EP*, II, 37.

1639. Marie de Medici at London. R. DE LA SERRE, *Histoire de l'Entrée de la Reine Mère dans la Grande Bretagne*. London, 1639. The same, ed. RICHARD GOUGH, 1775.

1660. Charles II at London. *A True Relation of the Reception of his Majestie and Conducting him through the City of London . . . . on Tuesday the 29 of this instant May, being the Day of his Majesties Birth*. London, 1660.
London's Glory, Represented by Time, Truth and Fame: at the Magnificent Triumphs and Entertainment of His most Sacred Majesty Charles the II. . . . . London, 1660. Reprinted in *The Dramatic Works of John Tatham*, ed. J. MAIMENT and W. H. LOGAN (Edinburgh, 1879), pp. 293–304.
JOHN EVELYN, *Diary*, ed. W. BRAY (London, 1879), II, 112.
WITHINGTON, *EP*, I, 241–43.

1661. Charles II at London. JOHN OGILBY, *The Relation of His Majestie's Entertainment, Passing through the city of London to his Coronation: with a description of the Triumphal Arches, and Solemnity*. London, 1661.
The Cities Loyalty Display'd: or the Four Famous and Renowned Fabricks in the City of London Exactly described in their several Representations. . . . . London, 1661.
WITHINGTON, *EP*, I, 243–47.

Entries: Scotland

1503. Margaret of England at Edinburgh for marriage to James IV of Scotland. LELAND, *Collectanea*, IV, 258 ff.
WITHINGTON, *EP*, I, 168 f.

1511. Queen Margaret at Aberdeen. Verses of WILLIAM DUNBAR, "The Queine's Reception at Aberdeen," *Poems*, ed. LAING (1834), I, 153 f.

1561. Mary, Queen of Scots, at Edinburgh. DANIEL WILSON, *Memorials of Edinburgh in the Olden Time* (Edinburgh, 1848), I, 71.

1579. Prince James at Edinburgh. *Documents Relative to the Reception at Edinburgh*, p. 30.
WILLIAM MAITLAND, *The History of Edinburgh* (Edinburgh, 1753), p. 37.

1633. Charles I at Edinburgh for coronation. *Documents Relative to the Reception at Edinburgh*, pp. 115 f.
WITHINGTON, *EP*, I, 236 f.

F. ENTRIES: GERMANY, SPAIN, AND PORTUGAL

ALENDA Y MIRA, JENARO. *Relaciones de solemnidades y fiestas públicas de España*. Madrid, 1903.

1478. Matthias, King of Hungary, and Ladislaus, King of Bohemia, at Olmütz. FRANCISCUS MODIUS, *Pandectae triumphales* (Frankfort, 1586), pp. 48 f.

1490. Charles VIII at Vienna. *Sensuit le devis des histoires faittes en la citte de Vienne le premier jour de decembre lan MCCCC 1111XXX*. The same, ed. J. J. A. PILOT, *Entrée et séjour de Charles VIII à Vienne en 1490 ... avec les histoires jouées en cette ville à l'occasion de l'arrivée de ce prince*. (Extrait du *Bulletin de la Société de Statistique de Grenoble*, April, 1851.)

1497. Margaret of Austria in Spain. A poem reprinted in *Belgisch Museum voor de Nederduitsche Tael- en Letterkunde*, IX, 149 ff.

1541. Charles V at Nuremberg. *Vonn Römischer Kayserlicher Mayestat Caroli V . . . . Nürnberg 1541*. Würzburg, n.d. Hans Sachs wrote verses describing the triumphal arches. *See* MAX HERRMANN, *Forschungen zur deutschen Theatergeschichte des Mittelalters und der Renaissance* (Berlin, 1914), pp. 63 f.

1613. Princess Elizabeth at Frankenthal. M. A. E. WOOD GREEN, *Elizabeth: Electress Palatine and Queen of Bohemia* (rev. ed.; London, 1909), pp. 77 f.

1613. Princess Elizabeth at Heidelberg. *Ibid.*, pp. 79–85.

1616. John Frederick, Duke of Württemberg, at Stuttgart. JOHANN AUGUSTIN ASSUM, *Warheffter Relation . . . . Johann Friderichen, Hertzogen zu Wurttemberg . . . . Stuttgardt*. [Stuttgart], 1616.

1619. Frederick and Elizabeth at Prague. *Blyde incomste . . . . Prince Fredericus . . . . Princess Elizabeth . . . . Praghe 4 ende 7 Nov. 1619*. Middelburg, 1619.

1619. Philip II at Lisbon. "Entrada del Católico Rey Don Felipe Segundo ... y breve compendio del imperial recibimiento que le hizo la insigne Ciudad de Lisboa a los 29. de Junio del año de 1619," in JUAN SARDINA

MIMOSO, *Relacion de la Real Tragicomedia con que los Padres de la Compañia de Jesus en su Colegio de S. Anton de Lisboa recibieron a la Magestad Católica de Felipe II de Portugal ... .* Lisbon, 1620.

CHAPTER III.   THE REDERYKER STAGE IN THE NETHERLANDS

I. TEXTS OF THE PLAYS OF THE *landjuweels*

1539. Ghent. *Spelen van zinne by den XIX gheconfirmeirden Cameren van Rhetorijcken, Binnen der Stede van Ghendt comparerende, vertooght . . . . op de questye, welc den mensche stervende meesten troost es . . . . den XII. Junii int Jaer 1539.* Ghent, 1539. Other editions in Antwerp, 1539, and Wesel, 1543 and 1564.
Refereynen int wijse op de vraghe Wat dier ter werelt meest fortse verwint. Item int sotte, op de vrage Wat volc ter werelt meest sotheyt toocht. Item int Amoureuse op den stock Och mocht icse spreken ic waer gepaeyt. Vertoocht binnen Ghendt by de XIX. Cameren van Retorijcke aldaer comparerende den XX. in April M. CCCCC. neghen en dertich. Antwerp, 1581. Another edition, Rotterdam, 1613.

1539. Middelburg. *Veel schoone christelijcke ende schriftuerlijcke Refereynen ghemaicht Wten Ouden ende Nieuwen Testamente . . . . een speel van sinnen opt derde, vierde en vijfste Capittel van twerck der apostelen. . . . . Den boom der schriftueren . . . . gespeelt tot middelburch, in Zeelant . . . . 1539.* Dordrecht, 1592.

1561. Rotterdam. *Spelen van Sinne vol schoone allegatien, loflijcke leeringhen ende schriftuerlijcke ondervvysinghen. Op de vraghe: Wie den meesten troost oyt quam te baten Die schenen te sijn van Godt verlaten. Ghespeelt . . . . Rotterdam, bijde neghen Cameren van Rhetorijcken . . . . XX dach in Julio anno 1561.* Antwerp, 1563. Another edition, Rotterdam, 1614.

1561. Antwerp. *Spelen van sinne vol scoone moralisacien uutleggingen ende bediedenissen op alle loeflijcke consten waer inne men claerlijck ghelijck in eenen spieghel, Figuerlijck, Poetelijck ende Retorijckelijck mach aanschouwen hoe nootsakelijck ende dienstelijck die selve consten allen menschen zijn. Ghespeelt binnen der stadt van Andtwerpen op dLant-Juweel by die veerthien Cameren van Rhetorijcken . . . . den derden dach Augusti . . . . M. D. LXI. Op die Questie: Wat den mensch aldermeest tot conste verwect . . . . met diversse schoonen Figueren.* Antwerp, 1562.
Het landjuweel van 1561. MS II. 13368C, Bibliothèque Royale, Brussels. A collection of manuscripts, music, poems, engravings, and insignia concerned with the Antwerp *landjuweel.*

1596. Leyden. *Den Lust-hof van Rhetorica, waer inne verhaelgedaen werdt vande beschrijvinghen ende t'samen-comsten der Hollantscher Cameren vande Reden-rijckers, binnen Leyden gheschiedt den 26 Mey des jaers 1596.* Leyden, 1596.

1598. Rotterdam. *Der redenrijke constliefhebbers stichtelicke recreatie.* Leyden, 1599.

1603. Schiedam. *Der Reden-ryckers stichtighe tsammenkomste op t'ontsluyt der Vraghe: wat tnoodichst' is om d'arme weesen t'onderhouwen? Ghehouden binnen Schiedam Ao 1603 opten VIen July ende de navolghende dagen: Vervatende zeven Spelen op de Voursz Vraghe ghewrocht . . . . Roode Roosen tot Schiedam.* Schiedam, 1603.

1607. Haarlem. *Const-thoonende Ivweel, by de loflijcke Stadt Haerlem, ten versoecke van Trou moet blijcken in 't licht gebracht . . . . by Zacharias Heyns, Drucker des Landschapes van Over-ijssel.* 1607.

1617. Vlaardingen. *Vlaerdings Redenrijck-bergh met middelen beplant Die Noodigh sijn't Gemeen, en voorderlijck het Landt.* Amsterdam, 1617.

1620. Malines. *De Schadt-Kiste der Philosophen ende Poeten waer inne te vinden syn veel schoone leerlycke Blasoenen, Refereynen ende Liederkens. Gebracht ende gesanden op de Peoene-Camere binnen Mechelen . . . . den 3 mey . . . . 1620.* Malines, 1621.
JAN THIEULLIER, *Porphyre en Cyprine: Treurspel verthoont by de Redenrycke Gulde die Peoen binnen Mechelen, op hen lieder, Blasoenfeest, den derden May anno 1620.* Malines, 1621.

1624. Amsterdam. *Levenders Reden-Feest, oft Amsteldams Helicon op-ghestelt by de Brabantsche Reden-Rijcke vergaderingh uyt Levender Jonst.* Amsterdam, 1624.

1641. Flushing. *Vlissings Redens-Lust-Hof, Beplant met seer schoone en bequame Oeffeningen . . . . 1 Julij 1641 . . . . Vlissinge, De Blaeu Acoleye. . . . . Flushing, 1642.*

II. OTHER PLAYS OF THE REDERYKERS AND CRITICAL WORKS CONSULTED

BLOMMAERT, P. "Beknopte Geschiedenis der Kamers van Rhetorica te Gent," *Belgisch Museum voor de Nederduitsche Tael- en Letterkunde,* I, 417–44.

BRANDS, GERRIT ALBERTUS (ed.). *Tspel van de Christenkercke.* Utrecht, 1921.

BRUSSELS, BIBLIOTHÈQUE ROYALE DE BELGIQUE. *De Nederlandsche Taal en Letterkunde in Belgie.* Brussels, 1936. Catalogue of an exhibition of Flemish manuscripts and books.

BURBURE DE WESEMBEEK, LEO DE. *De Antwerpsche Ommegangen in de XIVe en XVe Eeuw, naar gelijktijdige Handschriften uitgegeven door Ridder Leo de Burbure.* ("Uitgaven der Antwerpsche Bibliophilen," No. 2.) Antwerp, 1878.

BURGON, JOHN WILLIAM. *Life and Times of Sir Thomas Gresham.* 2 vols. London, 1839.

BUSSCHER, E. DE. *Recherches sur les peintres gantois des XIV. et XV. siècles.* Ghent, 1859.

CLAEYS, PROSPER. *L'Histoire du théâtre à Gand.* 3 vols. Ghent, 1892.

CREIZENACH, WILHELM. *Geschichte des neueren Dramas.* 5 vols. Halle, 1893–1909.

DIS, L. M. VAN. *Reformatorische Rederykersspelen uit de eerste Helft van de zestiende Eeuw.* Haarlem, 1937.

DUYSE, PRUDENS VAN. *De Rederijkkamers in Nederland hun Invloed op Letterkundig, Politiek, en zedelijk Gebied.* 2 vols. Ghent: Koninklijke Vlaamsche Academie voor Taal- en Letterkunde, 1900.

ELLERBROEK-FORTUYN, ELSE. *Amsterdamse Rederijkersspelen in de 16de Eeuw.* Groningen, 1937.

ENDEPOLS, H. J. E. *Het Decoratief en de Opvoering van het middelnederlandsche Drama: volgens de middelnederlandsche Tooneelstukken.* Amsterdam, 1903.

EVANS, M. B. "The Staging of the Donaueschingen Passion Play," *Modern Language Review*, XV (1920), 65–76; 279–97.

EVEN, EDWARD VAN. *Het Landjuweel te Antwerpen in 1561.* Louvain, 1861. 35 pls. after Franz Floris and others.

————. *L'Omgang de Louvain.* Louvain and Brussels, 1863. With 36 pls. from the original designs of 1594.

[EVERAERT, CORNELIS]. *Spelen van Cornelis Everaert.* Ed. J. W. MULLER and L. SCHARPE. Leyden, 1898–1900.

GRONDIJS, D. F. *Een Spel van Sinnen van den sieche Stadt.* Borculo, 1917.

HAECHT, WILLEM VAN. *Apostelspelen.* MS 21664, Bibliothèque Royale, Brussels. Part printed in "De vooys Apostelspelen in de Rederijkerstijd," *Mededeelingen des Koninklijke Akademie van Wetenschap en Letterkunde*, Vol. LXV, Ser. A, No. 5.

HELLWALD, FERDINAND HELLER VON. *Geschichte des hollandischen Theaters.* Rotterdam, 1874.

HEPPNER, A. "Jan Steen and the Rederijkers," *Journal of the Warburg and Courtauld Institutes*, III (1939–40), 22 ff.

KALFF, GERRIT. "Bijdrage tot de Geschiedenis van het Amsterdamsche Tooneel in de 17e Eeuw," *Oud Holland*, XIII (1895), 26 ff.

————. *Geschiedenis der Nederlandsche Letterkunde.* 7 vols. Groningen, 1906–12.

————. *Trou moet Blycken: Tooneelstukken uit de zestiende Eeuw.* Groningen, 1889.

KERNODLE, GEORGE R. "The Medieval Pageant Wagons of Louvain," *Theatre Annual*, 1943, pp. 58–76.

LOOSJES, J. *De Invloed der Rederijkers op de Hervorming.* Utrecht, 1909.

MAETERLINCK, LOUIS. *Le Genre satirique, fantastique, et licencieux dans la sculpture flamande et wallonne.* Paris, 1910.

————. *Le Genre satirique dans la peinture flamande.* Brussels, 1903.

MEERSCH, D. J. VAN DER. "Kronyk der Rederykkamers van Audenaerde," *Belgisch Museum voor de Nederduitsche Tael- en Letterkunde*, VI, 373–408.

MOL, JACOB DE. "Van Aeneas ende Dido," in *Den Handel der Amoureusheyt inhoudende vier poetische Spelen.* Rotterdam, 1621. Usually attributed to JAN BAPTISTA HOUWAERT.

RITTHEM, N. C. LAMBRECHTSEN VAN. "Beknopte Geschiedenis van de Middelburgsche Rhetorijkkamer het Bloemken Jesse," *Verhandelingen van de Maatschappij der Nederlandsche Letterkunde te Leyden*, III (1819), 145 ff.

Schiedams Rood Roosjens Spel van David ende Goliath. Rotterdam, 1619.

SIMONS, L. *Het Drama en het Tooneel in hun Ontwikkeling.* 5 vols. Amsterdam, 1921–32.

Een Spel van sinnen opt derde vierde ende twijfste Capittel van Twerck der apostolen. Embden, 1557.

STERCK, J. F. M. *Van Rederijkerskamer tot Muyderkring.* Amsterdam, 1928.

STRAETEN, EDMOND VAN DER. *Le Théâtre villageois en Flandre.* 2 vols. Brussels, 1874.

VISSCHERS, P. "Een Woord over de oude Rhetorykkamers in het Algemeen, en over die van Antwerpen in het Byzonder," *Belgisch Museum voor de Nederduitsche Tael- en Letterkunde*, I, 137–71.

VREESE, W. L. DE (ed.). *Een Spel van Sinne van Charon de Helsche Schippere (1551).* Antwerp, 1895.

WINKEL, JAN TE. *De Ontwikkelingsgang der Nederlandsche Letterkunde.* 6 vols. Haarlem, 1908–21.

WORP, JACOB ADOLF. *Geschiedenis van het Drama en van het Tooneel in Nederland.* 2 vols. Groningen, 1904–8.

Zeven Spelen van die Wercken der Bermherticheyd. Amsterdam, 1591.

CHAPTER IV. THE ELIZABETHAN STAGE

ADAMS, JOHN CRANFORD. *The Globe Playhouse: Its Design and Equipment.* Cambridge, Mass., 1942.

————. "The Staging of *The Tempest*, III, iii," *Review of English Studies*, XIV (1938), 404–19.

ALBRIGHT, VICTOR. *The Shaksperian Stage.* New York, 1909.

ARCHER, WILLIAM. "The Elizabethan Stage," *Quarterly Review*, CCVIII (April, 1908), 442–71.

————. "Elizabethan Stage and Restoration Drama," *ibid.*, CCXLI (1924), 399–418.

BAKER, GEORGE PIERCE. *The Development of Shakespeare as a Dramatist.* New York, 1907.

BOSWELL, ELEANORE. *The Restoration Court Stage (1660–1702), with a Particular Account of the Production of 'Calisto.'* Cambridge, Mass., 1932.

BRADBROOK, M. C. *Elizabethan Stage Conditions.* Cambridge, 1932.

————. *Themes and Conventions of Elizabethan Tragedy.* Cambridge, 1935.

BRANDL, A. *Quellen des weltlichen Dramas in England vor Shakespeare: Ein Ergänzungsband zu Dodsley's Old English Plays.* ("Quellen und Forschungen zur Sprach- und Culturgeschichte der germanischen Völker," Vol. LXXX.) Strassburg, 1898.

CAMPBELL, LILY BESS. *Scenes and Machines on the English Stage during the Renaissance.* Cambridge and New York, 1923.

CHAMBERS, EDMUND K. *The Elizabethan Stage.* 4 vols. Oxford, 1923.

CLODE, CHARLES MATTHEW. *The Early History of the Guild of Merchant Taylors.* 2 vols. London, 1888.

CREIZENACH, WILHELM. *The English Drama in the Age of Shakespeare.* Translated and revised from Vol. IV of *Geschichte des neueren Dramas.* London, 1916.

————. *Geschichte des neueren Dramas.* 5 vols. Halle, 1893–1909.

CUNLIFFE, JOHN W. (ed.). *Early English Classical Tragedies.* Oxford, 1912.

————. "Italian Prototypes of the Masque and Dumb Show," *Publications of the Modern Language Association*, XXII (1907), 140–56.

DEKKER, THOMAS. *Dramatic Works.* Pearson Ed. London, 1878.

DURAND, W. G. "*Palamon and Arcyte, Progne, Marcus Geminus,* and the Theatre in Which They Were Acted as Described by John Bereblock (1566)," *Publications of the Modern Language Association*, XX (1905), 502–28.

FEUILLERAT, ALBERT. *Documents Relating to the Office of the Revels in the Time of Queen Elizabeth*. Louvain, 1908.

———. *Documents Relating to the Revels at Court in the Time of King Edward VI and Queen Mary*. Louvain, 1914.

FLEMMING, WILLI. *Geschichte des Jesuitentheaters in den Landen deutscher Zunge*. ("Schriften der Gesellschaft für Theatergeschichte," Vol. XXXII.) Berlin, 1923.

FOSTER, F. A. "Dumb Show in Elizabethan Drama before 1620," *Englische Studien*, XLIV (1911), 8.

GRAVES, THORNTON SHIRLEY. *The Court and the London Theatres during the Reign of Elizabeth*. Dissertation, University of Chicago. Menasha, Wis., 1913.

———. "A Note on the Swan Theatre," *Modern Philology*, IX (April, 1912), 431–34.

GREEN, A. W. *The Inns of Court and Early English Drama*. New Haven, 1931.

HAZLITT, W. C. *Shakespeare's Library*. 6 vols. London, 1875.

[HENSLOWE]. *Henslowe's Diary*. Ed. WALTER W. GREG. 2 vols. London, 1904.

HEYWOOD, THOMAS. *An Apology for Actors*. London, 1612.

———. *Dramatic Works*. Pearson Ed. 6 vols. London, 1874.

HILLEBRAND, HAROLD N. "William Percy, an Elizabethan Amateur," *Huntington Library Quarterly*, I (July, 1938), 391–416.

KEITH, WILLIAM GRANT. "A Theatre Project by Inigo Jones," *Burlington Magazine*, XXXI (1917), 61–70, 105–11.

KERNODLE, GEORGE R. "Renaissance Artists in the Service of the People," *Art Bulletin*, XXV (March, 1943), 59–64.

LAWRENCE, W. J. *The Elizabethan Playhouse and Other Studies [First Series]*. Stratford, 1912. *Second Series*, 1913.

———. "The Evolution and Influence of the Elizabethan Playhouse," *Shakespeare Jahrbuch*, LXXIV (1911), 18–41.

———. *The Physical Conditions of the Elizabethan Public Playhouse*. Cambridge, Mass., 1927.

LODGE, THOMAS, and GREENE, ROBERT. *A Looking Glasse for London and Englande*. London, 1598. Reproduced in facsimile by JOHN S. FARMER. Amersham, England, 1914.

LYLY, JOHN. *Complete Works*. Ed R. WARWICK BOND. 3 vols. Oxford, 1902.

MALONE, EDMOND. "An Historical Account of the English Stage," in his *The Plays and Poems of William Shakespeare* (London, 1790), Vol. I, Part 2.

MANLY, JOHN MATTHEWS (ed.). *Specimens of the Pre-Shaksperean Drama*. 2 vols. New York, 1897.

MARSTON, JOHN. *Works*. Ed. A. H. BULLEN. 3 vols. London, 1887.

MIDDLETON, THOMAS. *Works*. Ed. A. H. BULLEN. London, 1885.

MUNDAY, ANTHONY. *John a Kent and John a Cumber*. ("Malone Society Reprints.") Oxford, 1923.

NICOLL, ALLARDYCE. *The Development of the Theatre*. Rev. ed. New York, 1937.

———. *The English Theatre*. New York, 1936.

REYNOLDS, GEORGE F. "Some Principles of Elizabethan Staging," *Modern Philology*, II (April, 1905), 581–614; III (June, 1905), 69–97.

———. *The Staging of Elizabethan Plays at the Red Bull Theater, 1605–25*. New York, 1940.

RIGAL, EUGÈNE PIERRE MARIE. "La Mise en scène dans les tragédies du XVIe siècle," *Revue d'histoire littéraire de la France*, XII (1905), 1–50, 203–26. Also in his *De Jodelle à Molière* (Paris, 1911), pp. 31–138.

SCHELLING, FELIX E. *Elizabethan Drama, 1558–1642*. 2 vols. Boston and New York, 1908.

WELSFORD, ENID. *The Court Masque: A Study in the Relationship between Poetry and the Revels*. Cambridge, 1927; New York, 1928.

WRIGHT, LOUIS. "Elizabethan Sea Drama and Its Staging," *Anglia*, LI (1927), 104–8.

CHAPTER V. ARCADE FAÇADE AND CURTAIN FAÇADE: THE CURTAIN STAGES OF GERMANY AND SPAIN; THE SCHOOLS; THE JESUIT STAGE; AND THE TEATRO OLIMPICO

BASORE, J. "The Scenic Value of the Miniatures in the Manuscripts of Terence," in *Studies in Honor of Basil Gildersleeve* (Baltimore, 1902), pp. 273–85.

BERTOTTI-SCAMOZZI, OTTAVIO. *L'Origine dell' Accademia Olimpica*. Vicenza, 1822.

BOND, FRANCIS. *The Chancel of English Churches*. London, 1916.

BORCHERDT, HANS HEINRICH. *Das europäische Theater im Mittelalter und in der Renaissance*. Leipzig, 1935.

BOYSSE, ERNEST. *Le Théâtre des Jesuites*. Paris, 1880.

BROOKS, NEIL C. *The Sepulchre of Christ in Art and Liturgy*. ("University of Illinois Studies in Language and Literature," Vol. VII, No. 2.) Urbana, 1921.

CHASSANG, ALEXIS. *Des Essais dramatiques imités de l'antiquité au XIVe et au XVe siècle*. Paris, 1852.

CHENEY, SHELDON. "Story of the Stage," *Theatre Arts*, VII (January, 1923), 50–57.

———. *The Theatre: Three Thousand Years of Drama, Acting, and Stagecraft*. New York, 1929.

CLARETIE, JULES. *Le Théâtre au collège*. Paris, 1907.

CREIZENACH, WILHELM. *Geschichte des neueren Dramas*. 5 vols. Halle, 1893–1909.

DURAN I SANPERE, AGUSTÍ. *Los Retablos de piedra*. ("Monumenta Cataloniae," Vols. I and II.) Barcelona, 1932–34.

FLEMMING, WILLI. *Geschichte des Jesuitentheaters in den Landen deutscher Zunge*. ("Schriften der Gesellschaft für Theatergeschichte," Vol. XXXII.) Berlin, 1923.

FREEDLEY, GEORGE, and REEVES, JOHN A. *A History of the Theatre*. New York, 1941.

FURTTENBACH, JOSEPH. *Mannhaffter Kunstspiegel*. Augsburg, 1663.

HAMMITZSCH, MARTIN. *Der moderne Theaterbau*. ("Beiträge zur Bauwissenschaft," No. 8.) Berlin, 1906.

HERRMANN, MAX. *Forschungen zur deutschen Theatergeschichte des Mittelalters und der Renaissance*. Berlin, 1914.

HOLL, KARL. *Geschichte des deutschen Lustspiels*. Leipzig, 1923.

JACK, WILLIAM SHAFFER. *The Early Entremés in Spain: The*

Rise of a Dramatic Form. Dissertation, University of Pennsylvania. Philadelphia, 1923.

KEITH, WILLIAM GRANT. "A Theatre Project by Inigo Jones," *Burlington Magazine,* XXXI (1917), 61–70, 105–11.

LAWTON, HAROLD WALTER. *Térence en France au XVIe siècle.* Dissertation. Paris, 1926.

LELAND, JOHN. *Antiquarii de rebus Britannicis collectanea.* Notes by THOMAS HEARN. 6 vols. London, 1770.

[MAHELOT]. *Le Mémoire de Mahelot, Laurent et d'autres décorateurs de l'Hôtel de Bourgogne et de la Comédie-Française au XVIIe siècle.* Ed. H. C. LANCASTER. Paris, 1920.

MARTIN, HENRI. "Le 'Terence des ducs' et la mise en scène au moyen âge," *Bulletin de la Société de l'Histoire du Théâtre,* I (1902), 15–42.

MÜLLER, JOHANNES. *Das Jesuitendrama in den Ländern deutscher Zunge vom Anfang (1555) bis zum Hochbarock (1665).* 2 vols. Augsburg, 1930.

NICHOLS, JOHN. *The Progresses and Public Processions of Queen Elizabeth.* 3 vols. London, 1823.

NICOLL, ALLARDYCE. *The Development of the Theatre.* Rev. ed. New York, 1937.

NIESSEN, CARL. *Das Bühnenbild: Ein kulturgeschichtlicher Atlas.* Leipzig, 1924–27.

PARMIZIANO, PAOLO DONATI. *Descrizione del gran Teatro Farnesiano di Parma e notizie storiche sul medesimo.* Parma, 1817.

PIGAFETTA, FILIPPO (VICENTINO). *Due lettere descrittive l'uno dell'ingresso a Vicenza della Imperatrice Maria d'Austria nell'anno MDLXXXI l'altra della recita nel Teatro Olimpico dell'Edippo di Sofocle nel MDLXXXV.* Padua, 1830.

RENNERT, HUGO ALBERT. *The Spanish Stage in the Time of Lope de Vega.* New York, 1909.

————. "The Staging of Lope de Vega's Comedias," *Revue hispanique,* XV (1906), 453–85.

REYNOLDS, GEORGE F. *The Staging of Elizabethan Plays at the Red Bull Theater, 1605–1625.* New York, 1940.

SCHMIDT, ERICH. *Die Darstellung des spanischen Dramas vor Lope de Rueda.* Dissertation. Berlin, 1933.

SCHMIDT, EXPEDITUS. *El Autó sacramental y su importancia en el arte escénico de la época.* ("Centro de Intercambio Intelectual Germano-Español, Madrid, Conferencias," No. 25.) Madrid, 1930.

————. *Die Bühnenverhältnisse des deutschen Schuldramas und seiner volkstümlichen Ableger im sechzehnten Jahrhundert.* ("Forschungen zur neueren Literaturgeschichte," Vol. XXIV.) Berlin, 1903.

SCHNITZLER, HENRY. "The School Theatre of the Jesuits," *Theatre Annual,* 1943, pp. 46–58.

SHOEMAKER, W. H. *The Multiple Stage in Spain during the Fifteenth and Sixteenth Centuries.* Dissertation. Princeton, 1935.

[SOMI, LEONE DI]. "Dialoghi dell'Ebreo Leone de Somi in materia di rappresentazioni sceniche." Trans. ALLARDYCE NICOLL in *The Development of the Theatre* (rev. ed., 1937), Appen. B, pp. 231–56.

[VITRUVIUS]. *Vitruvius: The Ten Books on Architecture.* Trans. MORRIS HICKY MORGAN. Cambridge, Mass., 1914.

WILLIAMS, RONALD BOAL. *The Staging of Plays in the Spanish Peninsula Prior to 1555.* ("University of Iowa Studies in Spanish Language and Literature," No. 5.) Iowa City, 1935.

CHAPTER VI.   THE ITALIAN PERSPECTIVE SCENE

Translations of the passages on theatre practice by Serlio, Sabbatini, and Furttenbach have been prepared by Kernodle, McDowell, and Rapp for the Yale Theatre Collection. Translations of the passages from Barbaro, Vignola, Sirigatti, Ubaldus, Aguilonius, Chiaramonti, and Accolti are included in the Appendix of my dissertation, "Perspective in the Renaissance Theatre."

ACCOLTI, PIETRO. *Lo Inganno de gl'occhi: prospettiva pratica.* Florence, 1625.

AGUILONIUS, FRANCISCUS. *Opticarum libri sex philosophis juxta ac mathematicis utiles.* Antwerp, 1613.

ANCONA, ALESSANDRO D'. *Sacre rappresentazioni dei secoli XIV, XV, e XVI, raccolte e illustrate.* 3 vols. Florence, 1872.

BARBARO, DANIELE. *La Pratica della perspettiva.* Venice, 1568.

BIBIENA, FERNANDO [GALLI-BIBIENA]. *L'Architettura civile.* Parma, 1711.

BORCHERDT, HANS HEINRICH. *Das europäische Theater im Mittelalter und in der Renaissance.* Leipzig, 1935.

BRIEGER, PETER. "The Baroque Equation: Illusion and Reality." Lecture given at the Metropolitan Museum of Art on January 27, 1943, for a symposium on drama and the other arts.

BULOS, M. *La Perspective à l'usage des gens du monde.* Paris, 1827.

BUZZI, TOMASO. "Il 'Teatro all'antica' di Vincenzo Scamozzi in Sabbioneta," *Dedalo,* II (1927–28), 488–523.

CAMPBELL, LILY BESS. *Scenes and Machines on the English Stage during the Renaissance.* Cambridge and New York, 1923.

CARTWRIGHT, JULIA. *Beatrice d'Este: A Study of the Renaissance.* London, 1899.

CHIARAMONTI, SCIPIONE. *Delle scene e teatri: opera postuma.* Cesena, 1675.

[DUBREUIL, JEAN]. *La Perspective pratique.* 3 vols. Paris, 1642–49.

FLECHSIG, EDUARD. *Die Dekoration der modernen Bühne in Italien von den Anfängen bis zum Schluss des 16. Jahrhunderts.* Dissertation. Dresden, 1894.

FURTTENBACH, JOSEPH. *Architectura civilis.* Ulm, 1628.

————. *Architectura recreationis.* Augsburg, 1640.

————. *Mannhaffter Kunstspiegel.* Augsburg, 1663.

————. *Neues itinerarium Italiae.* Ulm, 1627.

GINORI-CONTI, PIERO. *L'Apparato per le nozze di Francesco de' Medici e di Giovanna d'Austria.* Florence, 1936.

GREGOR, JOSEPH. *Wiener szenische Kunst: Die Theaterdekoration.* Vienna, 1924.

HAMILTON, F. *Stereography, or a Compleat Body of Perspective, in All Its Branches* (London, 1738), II, 370–80.

HAMMITZSCH, MARTIN. *Der moderne Theaterbau.* ("Beiträge zur Bauwissenschaft," No. 8.) Berlin, 1906.

KERNODLE, GEORGE R. "Farewell to Scene Architecture," *Quarterly Journal of Speech,* XXV (December, 1939), 649–57.

KERNODLE, GEORGE R. "Perspective in the Renaissance Theatre." Dissertation, Yale University, 1937.

LEVY, G. R. "The Greek Discovery of Perspective: Its Influence on Renaissance and Modern Art," *Journal of the Royal Institute of British Architects*, L (January, 1943), 51–57.

MARIANI, V. "Il Concetto architettonico nella scenografia del sei e settecento," *Rivista d'architettura e d'arti decorative*, 1923.

MONTAIGLON, ANATOLE DE. *Notice historique et bibliographique sur Jean Pélerin, chanoine de Toul et sur son livre 'De artificiali perspectiva.'* Paris: Société Impériale des Antiquaires de France, 1861.

NICOLL, ALLARDYCE. *Stuart Masques and the Renaissance Stage.* New York, 1938.

PÉLERIN, JEAN (VIATOR). *De artificiali perspectiva.* Toul, 1505, 1509, 1521, 1635.

POZZO, ANDREA. *Perspectiva pictorum et architectorum.... Prospettiva de' pittori e architetti....* 2 vols. Rome, 1693–1700.

RAPP, FRANZ. "Ein Theaterbauplan des Giovanni Battista Aleotti," *Schriften der Gesellschaft für Theatergeschichte*, Vol. XLI (Berlin, 1930).

SABBATINI, NICOLA. *Pratica di fabricar scene e machine ne' teatri.* Ravenna, 1638.

SCHÖNE, GÜNTER. *Die Entwicklung der Perspektivbühne von Serlio bis Galli-Bibiena nach den Perspektivbüchern.* ("Theatergeschichtliche Forschungen," Vol. XLIII.) Leipzig, 1933.

SERLIO, SEBASTIANO. *Il primo [secondo] libro d'architettura.* Paris, 1545.

SIRIGATTI, LORENZO. *La Pratica di prospettiva.* Venice, 1596.

SPINLAMBERTO, GIULIO TROILI DA (DETTO PARADOSSI). *Paradossi per praticare la prospettiva senza saperla.* Bologna, 1683. Translated in *The Mask*, XIII (1927), 59–63.

UBALDUS, GUIDO. *Perspectivae libri sex.* Pesaro, 1600.

VASARI, GIORGIO. *The Lives of the Painters, Sculptors, and Architects.* ("Everyman" Ed.) New York, [1927].

VIGNOLA, GIACOMO BAROZZI DA. *Le due regole della prospettiva pratica, con i commentarii del R. P. M. Egnatio Danti.* Rome, 1583.

CHAPTER VII.   FRAMING THE PERSPECTIVE SCENE

BORCHERDT, HANS HEINRICH. *Das europäische Theater im Mittelalter und in der Renaissance.* Leipzig, 1935.

CAMPBELL, LILY BESS. *Scenes and Machines on the English Stage during the Renaissance.* Cambridge and New York, 1923.

CHAMBERS, EDMUND K. *The Elizabethan Stage.* 4 vols. Oxford, 1923.

CHENEY, SHELDON. "Story of the Stage," *Theatre Arts*, VII (January, 1923), 50–57.

CHIARAMONTI, SCIPIONE. *Delle scene e teatri: opera postuma.* Cesena, 1675.

CROCE, BENEDETTO. *I Teatri di Napoli dal rinascimento alla fine del secolo decimottavo.* Bari, 1916.

FREEDLEY, GEORGE, and REEVES, JOHN A. *A History of the Theatre.* New York, 1941.

FURTTENBACH, JOSEPH. *Mannhaffter Kunstspiegel.* Augsburg, 1663.

GREGOR, JOSEPH. *Wiener szenische Kunst: Die Theaterdekoration.* Vienna, 1924.

HAMMITZSCH, MARTIN. *Der moderne Theaterbau.* ("Beiträge zur Bauwissenschaft," No. 8.) Berlin, 1906.

JORDAN, GILBERT J. "The Curtain on the German Stage: Its Introduction and Early Use," *Publications of the Modern Language Association*, LIII (September, 1938), 702–23.

KERNODLE, GEORGE R. "The Magic of Light," *Theatre Arts Monthly*, XXVI (November, 1942), 717–22.

LAWRENCE, W. J. "The Story of a Peculiar Stage Curtain," in his *The Elizabethan Playhouse and Other Studies [First Series]* (Stratford, 1912), pp. 109–21.

MICHALSKI, ERNST. *Die Bedeutung der ästhetischen Grenze für die Methode der Kunstgeschichte.* ("Kunstwissenschaftliche Studien," Vol. XI.) Berlin, 1932.

NICOLL, ALLARDYCE. *The Development of the Theatre.* Rev. ed. New York, 1937.

———. *Stuart Masques and the Renaissance Stage.* New York, 1938.

SABBATINI, NICOLA. *Pratica di fabricar scene e machine ne' teatri.* Ravenna, 1638.

SERLIO, SEBASTIANO. *Il primo [secondo] libro d'architettura.* Paris, 1545.

[SOMI, LEONE DI]. "Dialoghi dell'Ebreo Leone de Somi in materia di rappresentazioni sceniche." Trans. ALLARDYCE NICOLL in *The Development of the Theatre* (rev. ed., 1937), Appen. B, pp. 231–56.

STUMPFL, ROBERT. "Die Bühnenmöglichkeiten im XVI. Jahrhundert," *Zeitschrift für deutsche Philologie*, LIV, No. 1 (May, 1929), 42–80; LV, No. 1 (March, 1930), 49–78.

WITKOWSKI, G. "Vorhang und Aktschluss," *Bühne und Welt*, VIII, 18–22, 73–76, 104–8.

CHAPTER VIII.   COMPROMISES IN FRANCE AND ENGLAND

AUBIGNAC, FRANÇOIS HÉDELIN, ABBÉ D'. *La Pratique du théâtre.* Additions and notes by PIERRE MARTINO. Algiers and Paris, 1927.

BRADBROOK, M. C. *Themes and Conventions of Elizabethan Tragedy.* Cambridge, 1935.

BROUCHARD, C. *Les Origines du théâtre de Lyon.* Lyons, 1865.

CAMPBELL, LILY BESS. *Scenes and Machines on the English Stage during the Renaissance.* Cambridge and New York, 1923.

CASTELVETRO, LODOVICO. *Poetica d'Aristotele vulgarizzata e esposta.* Vienna, 1570.

CHAMBERS, EDMUND K. *The Elizabethan Stage.* 4 vols. Oxford, 1923.

CHARLTON, H. B. *Castelvetro's Theory of Poetry.* Manchester, 1913.

CHENEY, SHELDON. *The Theatre: Three Thousand Years of Drama, Acting, and Stagecraft.* New York, 1929.

CLARK, BARRETT H. *European Theories of the Drama*. New York, 1930.

CLARK, WILLIAM S. "Corpses, Concealments, and Curtains on the Restoration Stage," *Review of English Studies*, XIII (1937), 438–48.

DUBECH, LUCIEN. *Histoire générale illustrée du théâtre.* 5 vols. Paris, 1931–34.

[DUBREUIL, JEAN]. *La Perspective pratique.* 3 vols. Paris, 1642–49.

GREGOR, JOSEPH. *Weltgeschichte des Theaters.* Zürich, 1933.

HAMMITZSCH, MARTIN. *Der moderne Theaterbau.* ("Beiträge zur Bauwissenschaft," No. 8.) Berlin, 1906.

HOLSBOER, S. WILMA. *L'Histoire de la mise en scène dans le théâtre français de 1600 à 1657.* Paris, 1933.

KERNODLE, GEORGE R. "Perspective in the Renaissance Theatre." Dissertation, Yale University, 1937.

LACROIX, PAUL. *Recueil de ballets et mascarades de cour.* 6 vols. Geneva, 1868.

LANCASTER, HENRY CARRINGTON. "Le Décor de *L'Arimène* de Montreux," *Revue du seizième siècle*, XVI (1929), 335.
———. *History of French Dramatic Literature in the Seventeenth Century.* 4 vols. Baltimore and Paris, 1929–32.

LAWRENCE, W. J. *The Elizabethan Playhouse and Other Studies* [*First Series*]. Stratford, 1912. *Second Series*, 1913.

LYLY, JOHN. *Complete Works.* Ed. R. WARWICK BOND. 3 vols. Oxford, 1902.

[MAHELOT]. *Le Mémoire de Mahelot, Laurent et d'autres décorateurs de l'Hôtel de Bourgogne et de la Comédie-Française au XVIIe siècle.* Ed. H. C. LANCASTER. Paris, 1920.

MALECOT, GASTON LOUIS. "A propos d'une estampe d'Abraham Bosse et de l'Hôtel de Bourgogne," *Modern Language Notes*, XLVIII (1933), 279–83.

[MÉNAGE]. "Le Discours de Ménage sur la troisième comédie de Térence," in ABBÉ D'AUBIGNAC, *La Pratique du théâtre* (Amsterdam, 1715), II, 117 ff.

MIGNON, MAURICE. *Etudes sur le théâtre français et italien de la renaissance.* Paris, 1923.

NICOLL, ALLARDYCE. *The English Theatre.* New York, 1936.
———. *Stuart Masques and the Renaissance Stage.* New York, 1938.

PRUNIÈRES, HENRI. *Le Ballet de cour en France avant Benserade et Lully.* Paris, 1914.

REESE, HELEN. *La Mesnardière's Poëtique (1639): Sources and Dramatic Theories.* ("Johns Hopkins Studies in Romance Literatures.") Baltimore, 1937.

REYNOLDS, GEORGE F. *The Staging of Elizabethan Plays at the Red Bull Theater, 1605–1625.* New York, 1940.
———. "Two Conventions of the Elizabethan Stage," *Modern Philology*, XVII (1919), 35–43.

RIGAL, EUGÈNE PIERRE MARIE. *Le Théâtre français avant la période classique.* Paris, 1901.

SIMSON, OTTO GEORG VON. *Zur Genealogie der weltlichen Apotheose im Barock.* Strassburg, 1936.

SOLERTI, ANGELO. "La Rappresentazione della *Calandria* a Lione nel 1548," in *Raccolta di studii critici dedicata ad Alessandro d'Ancona,* Florence, 1901.

STEVENS, DAVID H. (ed.). *Types of English Drama 1660–1780.* Boston and New York, 1923.

STUART, D. C. "Stage Decoration and Unity of Place in France in the Seventeenth Century," *Modern Philology*, X (1912–13), 393–406.

STUMPFL, ROBERT. "Die Bühnenmöglichkeiten im XVI. Jahrhundert," *Zeitschrift für deutsche Philologie*, LIV, No. 1 (May, 1929), 42–80; LV, No. 1 (March, 1930), 49–78.

TUPPER, J. W. (ed.). "*Love and Honour*" and "*The Siege of Rhodes,*" *by Sir William Davenant.* Boston and London, 1909.

WÖLFFLIN, HEINRICH. *Principles of Art History: The Problem of the Development of Style in Later Art.* Trans. M. D. HOTTINGER. London, 1932.

INDEX

[Reference to the main discussion of a topic is indicated by page numbers in italics. References to entries are arranged chronologically under the names of the cities.]